# Building with Wood

UNIVERSITY OF TORONTO PRESS / Toronto Buffalo London

John I. Rempel

# BUILDING WITH WOOD

and other aspects of nineteenth-century building in central Canada

Revised edition

Revised edition
© University of Toronto Press 1980
Toronto Buffalo London
Printed in Canada
ISBN 0-8020-6428-0

First edition
© University of Toronto Press 1967
Reprinted 1972, 1976
Published on the occasion of the
Centennial of Canadian Confederation
and subsidized by the Centennial Commission /
Ouvrage publié à l'occasion du
Centenaire de la Confédération Canadienne, grâce à une subvention de la
Commission du Centenaire

---

**Canadian Cataloguing in Publication Data**

Rempel, John I., 1905–
   Building with wood and other aspects of
nineteenth-century building in central Canada
   Bibliography: p.
   Includes index.
   ISBN 0-8020-6428-0
   1. Building, Wooden – Ontario.   2. Architecture –
Ontario – History.   I. Title.
NA744.R4 1980   720'.9713   c80-094087-3

To Shawn and Tammy and Geoffrey and Leslie-Anne and Christopher John, because they are the future

# Contents

Preface to the revised edition / ix

Preface to the first edition / xi

1 Introduction / 3
2 Log construction / 25
3 Timber framing / 91
4 Plank construction / 173
5 Barns / 189
6 Church, mill, and bridge / 229
7 Non-wood construction / 261
8 Polygonal buildings / 289
9 Exterior decorative woodwork / 341
10 Woodworking tools / 359
11 Preservation and restoration / 389

Notes / 431

Bibliography / 435

Picture credits / 441

Index / 443

# Preface to the revised edition

Several reasons prompted me to attempt an enlarged edition of *Building with Wood*. In the first place, when the book was originally published I was aware that it was altogether too sketchy in certain areas because of lack of information; it was necessary to call a halt at some point, however, or the work would never have seen print. As well, I became involved by chance in a research project that demanded a thorough knowledge of French timber-building technology on this continent; the findings of these two years of research are set down here in a condensed form. Other areas also, touched on briefly in the previous book, have been expanded by the inclusion of new material uncovered by subsequent research.

For many years now I have also felt the need to provide more information on the preservation of architectural landmarks, particularly for the use of those laymen who are concerned about the survival of our architectural heritage but lack the technical know-how to achieve the desired results. The new section on preservation techniques, I hope, will draw their attention to the problems that may arise and some of the solutions.

As in the previous book, my work here is concerned above all with timber framing, for masonry construction simply did not undergo the same historic mutations as timber construction. Hence the emphasis on building with wood. This is quite aside from the facts that timber framing presents a multitude of structural aspects that do not exist in other forms of construction, that the technological development of timber framing can be fairly easily demonstrated, and that timber may be considered the indigenous building material in North America.

Among the many persons who gave advice the first to be mentioned are Mr A.J. Richardson of the Department of Indian Affairs and Northern Development (Technical Services Branch) and M. Jacques Dalibard, now Executive Director of Heritage Canada; their combined, almost inexhaustible, knowledge of architectural history and building technology in Canada was dispensed most liberally. Generous assistance was also provided by Professors R. Anderson of Laval University and John Bland of McGill University. I also owe much to the encouragement and assistance of Professor Charles Peterson of Columbia University. A special mention to Gerry Hallowell, whose meticulous editing prevented me from committing a number of editorial sins, and to Antje Lingner for her superb design. Last, but not least, is Claire, who always came to the rescue whenever my high school French failed me.

Preparation of this edition was assisted by a grant from the Ontario Arts Council. This book has been published with the help of a grant from the Canadian Federation for the Humanities, using funds provided by the Social Sciences and Humanities Research Council of Canada, and with the assistance of the Canada Council and the Ontario Arts Council through block grants.

Leaside 1980

# Preface to the first edition

My initial research in the subject of this book was prompted by my experiences in teaching and it was maintained largely through sheer stubbornness. I had not been teaching courses in the history of architecture and in building construction to senior high school students for many years before I realized that, although the course covered the usual tourist-attracting buildings of the world and although a student could identify the Parthenon or the Hagia Sophia, he might well not know that Osgoode Hall existed or be able to name a single Canadian architect. To remedy this situation, I began searching the libraries for information on Ontario architecture. But in vain. My determination to find it grew in inverse relation to the absence of it and, being of a practical rather than an artistic inclination, I naturally chose to begin with a study of the structural aspects of Ontario's architecture. Little did I realize that it would take the number of years that it has to collect the information now contained in these pages.

The dearth of literature on the subject has, of course, been repaired in recent years by such books as *The Ancestral Roof* by Miss Marion McRae and Professor T. Adamson, *Toronto: No Mean City* by Professor Eric Arthur, and *The Old Stones of Kingston* by Mrs Margaret Angus. These books, however, are concerned with architecture, whereas this one focuses on the practical aspects of construction and with the types of building. It does not deal with aesthetically significant or historically memorable buildings of the nineteenth century, but rather with the technical methods used in the erection of average, usually unpretentious structures. It is a book about building as such.

It should be recognized at the outset that the study of these methods is somewhat in the nature of archaeology. Construction details of old buildings can only be measured, observed, sketched, and photographed when a building is being demolished. A trained eye is required to detect the significant, and the relative lack of skilled and interested observers combined with the speed with which local authorities and others like to see a building levelled once demolition has begun or been approved make the gathering of information a haphazard and slow process, very much at the mercy of the 'happy accident.' The archaeologist may have months to examine a site; the student of buildings just a century or so old may have only a few days. He does, of course, have many more sites to study, but with the meagre resources at his disposal, primarily of time, he cannot hope to see them all. This work then cannot claim to be a systematically complete treatment of its subject – that would be impossible – but I hope that it forms a sound and accurate groundwork. I can only echo the sentiment of Isham and Brown who wrote in *Early Connecticut Houses* in 1900 that they hoped their 'work may be the means of enlivening and assisting the already awakened interest in these monuments of our colonial history, so that we may have uniform and accurate records of all of them, for we are sadly aware that many must have escaped our notice.'

The measurements given on the drawings, for example, are correct, being taken on the spot from the original structure. I suppose that I am influenced here by the late Dr C.W. Jefferys, under whom I had the good fortune of studying drawing and the history of art. I used to sit in his studio, just watching him draw or paint; he worked with a deliberate precision and a strict insistence on scientific accuracy down to the smallest detail. I have therefore made no effort to avoid complex or technical points as they arise; to have done so would have detracted greatly from the usefulness of the book. Restoring a building, for example, is a matter of correct, practical solutions, not simply sentimental or historical considerations, and it is my hope that this work will provide some of the precise information required for such purposes.

Other sections of the book are, of course, much less concerned with the problems and solutions of the old craft of joinery and could be seen rather as contributions to local history. Some of this material has appeared in the pages of *Ontario History* and the *York Pioneer*, but it has been revised, updated, or expanded for publication here. Of more general interest too perhaps will be the many photographs, selected for the most part from my collection of several thousand; drawings are also mine.

This study is concerned almost entirely with one building material – wood. It is the most widespread, the most easily obtainable, and the 'cleanest'; it is the easiest to work with and the most responsive to the artisan's touch. On the other hand it responds to changes in temperature and humidity to a degree that has been frequently found to be unsettling. It was, of course, not the only – if even indeed the most used – building material of nineteenth-century Ontario, but timber construction methods evolved considerably during that period, whereas masonry (stone and brick) construction, despite its widespread use, changed little. Indeed, its techniques have remained substantially the same for hundreds of years and so do not offer the same interest to the student of history, if not of building.

# Preface to the first edition

One of the advantages of being an amateur historian is that one is free to wander and browse in any field that looks interesting or promising. One area that attracted me was the mid-nineteenth-century fad for polygonal buildings. I used to stop and photograph these oddities as I travelled around the province; they were 'curios' and worth, so I felt, little further thought. Then one day, by pure chance, I came across a copy of the biography of Orson Fowler and realized that there was a story behind these houses. I acquired later a copy of his *The Octagonal Mode of Building*, which opened up a fascinating by-way in the story of building in Ontario.

The forms and expressions of architecture are derived from the contemporary social, economic, and political life of a people and from the climate and natural resources of a place. From these interacting factors there grows a style of building, so native to a time and place that it seems the 'natural' response to that environment. An 'unnatural' solution to the problems of building is one unrelated to the surrounding culture; it becomes, in a few years, either ridiculous or a sham. To be properly understood and appreciated, buildings should thus be studied in the context of their environment. This I have tried to do in these pages.

Credit for encouraging me to edit and organize my notes in their present form and to search for a publisher must go to Dr T. Howarth of the School of Architecture, University of Toronto. Others have assisted by editing portions of the manuscript, by making important suggestions, or by giving valuable assistance. The foremost of these are Dr P.G. Cornell, Department of History, University of Waterloo; Dr John Moir, Scarborough College; and Dr A.G. Reynolds, Registrar and Associate Professor of Church History, Emmanuel College, Victoria University, Toronto. Much assistance has also been received from Mr A. Murdoch and Mr V. Blake of the Department of Public Records and Archives, Queen's Park, Toronto, as well as from Mr Walter Kenyon of the Royal Ontario Museum.

The York Pioneer and Historical Society merits special mention for providing congenial company and unstinting generosity from its collective and apparently inexhaustible store of historical knowledge. Mention should be made of another group of persons whose co-operation permitted me to gather much vital information. These include Brigadier J. McGinnis, Director of the Toronto Historical Board; Mr Ronald Way, former Director of Fort Henry and Upper Canada Village; Mr R. Hough, Superintendent of Upper Canada Village; the Niagara Parks Board; and particularly Mr A. Pryer of Fort George, and the administrative staff of Pioneer Village, Metropolitan Toronto Conservation Authority.

And then there are those many people who, after reading some of my articles, took the trouble to send pictures, newspaper clippings, personal information, or valuable leads, without which much of this book could never have been written. An apology is offered to many not named in the following list: Mr C.L.R. Wanamaker, Belleville; Mr Frank Harding, Meaford; Mrs Marion Lewis, Oshawa; Mrs James Turcotte, Grimsby; Mrs Leona Stackhouse, Picton; Professor F.H. Armstrong, University of Western Ontario; Mr Frederick C. Curry, Brockville; Mr T.B. Higginson, Burks Falls; Mrs R. Surrey, Little Current; Mrs M. Comes, Free Public Library, Jersey City, USA; Mr and Mrs A.D. McFall, Toronto; Mrs J.F. Swayze, King City; Mrs C. Lewis, Denfield; Mr R. Porter, Peterborough Public Library; Mrs P.M. Lamb, Leaside; the staff of the Public Library and Art Museum, London; Mr A. Douglas, Curator, Hiram Walker Museum, Windsor; Mr R.W. Bell, Governor, Goderich Gaol; Mr H. Bell, Aurora; Mr W.B. Epworth, Newmarket; Dr H.H. MacKay, Richmond Hill; Dr and Mrs W.A. McKay, Pickering; Mrs D. Turner, Ottawa; Dr Frank Walker, Toronto; Mr W.R. Wadsworth, QC, Toronto; Mrs Douglas Tanner, Ottawa.

The assistance received from the Research Department of the Education Centre, Toronto Board of Education, as well as from the staff in the Reference Department, Toronto Central Library, is also gratefully acknowledged.

A Senior Fellowship from the Canada Council in 1960 did much to facilitate research, and a grant from the Centennial Commission, formally acknowledged on page iv, assisted with the publication of the book.

A special tribute goes to my good wife who faithfully allowed herself to be driven over countless dusty country roads and who, at the end of the trip, cheerfully brushed dust and cobwebs from my best suit after I had been prowling around unused attics and climbing about abandoned mill frames. She provided me with a translation of Vitruvius' description of log construction, and patiently retyped the whole manuscript in order to bring some organization into the mound of accumulated notes.

J.I.R.

# Building with Wood

# 1
# INTRODUCTION

4  Building with Wood

The first prerequisite for the correct restoration of old buildings is a thorough knowledge of the historical development of building technology as well as of the engineering principles involved in early construction. Since history is always a matter of cause and effect, we must first understand the cause, after which the effect frequently becomes a corollary or a logical conclusion. For this reason, the development of building technology in Ontario and Quebec in the eighteenth and nineteenth centuries will be briefly traced, thus establishing a frame of reference to serve as background to this study.

With the settlement of North America by Europeans, three distinct cultures, each with its own architectural and technological heritage, were superimposed upon, and largely replaced, the native traditions. In general geographical terms, the French may be thought of as settling, initially, the northeastern coastline, with the English in the middle, and the Spanish in the south. This study will concern itself only with the architecture and building skills of the French and the English since, so far as Canada is concerned, the Spanish do not enter the picture at all.

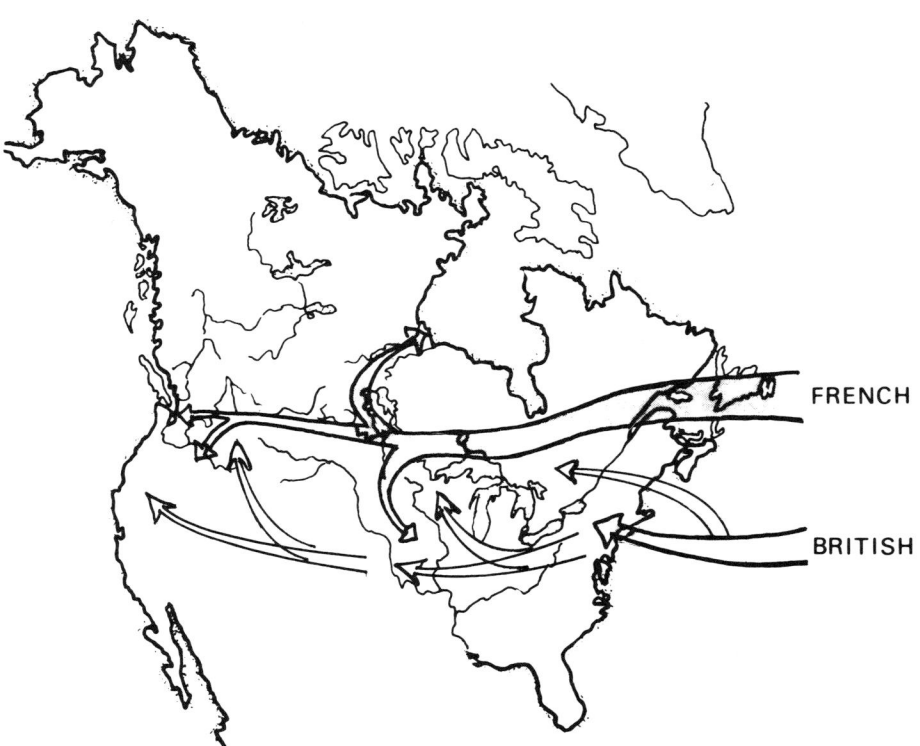

The spread of building technologies in North America

The early settlers of British origin brought their building methods first to the New England colonies; this technology can be called 'Early American' to distinguish it from the later 'Modified American.' The old country technology, however, did not fare well in the new land, mainly because the geography and climate were very different from that of Britain. For example, settlers were quite unprepared for the effect upon a structural frame of an increased temperature range of forty to fifty degrees, or for the effect of intense winter cold upon shallow footings. The need to find proper solutions to the problems of weather and geography led to steeper roofs, porches, weather-boarding, and deeper foundations. A further requirement was greater speed in erection and concomitant simplification of design. European framing methods had attained high sophistication, demanding great skill and a thorough and rigid apprenticeship; joints had become very complicated, requiring great accuracy in the workman with a consequent slowdown in production. In the new land speed was of the utmost importance, since the settler had to provide himself with shelter at once, and then clear large areas of forest for his first ploughing and seeding. The answers to these problems had to be found by trial and error and the search for them led to the 'Modified American' technology.

It is reasonable to assume that an emigrant tradesman might have experienced lack of opportunity in his European home. Tradition or social restrictions might have prevented him from using all his skills and resourcefulness, so that he would have welcomed the challenges of a new land. At any rate, builders began very early to modify home traditions, to simplify, to eliminate effort without sacrificing quality, and to increase the speed of production.

By the time Upper Canada, or Ontario, was founded, this modified technology had become solidly established. It was a strong technology because it had found the answers to existing problems. It was part of the social response to the New World, and thus was a characteristic phenomenon of the time, expressing the nature of a people now unhampered by tradition and capable of an uninhibited approach to new difficulties.

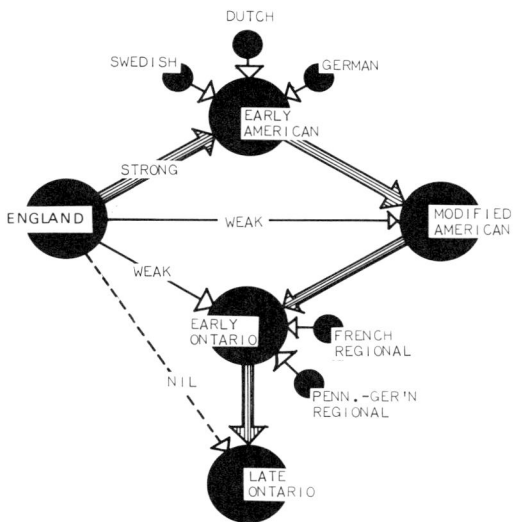

Graphic representation of the various historical influences on early Ontario building technology

From a technological point of view, the Ontario pioneer enjoyed a unique advantage over his American counterpart. The American pioneer came to a land completely unknown to him. The early settlers in Ontario, who were generally United Empire Loyalists, on the other hand, came to a country that was new in name only. The countryside was similar to the one left behind in the American colonies; the west side of the Niagara River, after all, is much the same as the east side, and the north shore of Lake Ontario is not so different from the south shore. Since most of our pioneers had to leave most or all of their material possessions behind, they had to begin on the same level as the first New England settlers. However, they were not far enough removed from the pioneering stage to have forgotten all the lessons, and were thus infinitely better prepared to cope with their environment. They knew beforehand what the end result of their efforts would be, and, no doubt, this knowledge sustained their hopes during the first few years of extreme hardship and deprivation. They were familiar with the methods of pioneering and the rigorous climate. They were spared the 'climate shock' suffered by the Pilgrim Fathers and were able to bring, without any adaptation, American techniques, processes, machines, and tools to their new home. In this similar environment, sawmills, lathing mills, nail and tool factories were identical to those south of the border. The building technology of Upper Canada was thus a direct outgrowth of 'Modified American' technology.

Europe, at the time, was the indisputable technological centre of the world, as exemplified by the export during the eighteenth century of a large number of books dealing with building construction. Because of these books, the best and latest technical knowledge was more widely and more quickly spread to the fringes of the European world. The settlement of Upper Canada accordingly benefited from this improvement in communications as well as from the adaptations that had evolved in response to the North American environment.

The books on building that found their way either through booksellers or in the baggage of immigrants across the Atlantic to the British colonies dealt with every conceivable aspect of architecture; they ranged from weighty and scholarly tomes to small pocket-sized, leatherbound handbooks such as *The Builder's Jewel: or, the Youth's Instructor and Workman's Remembrancer*. There were at least eighty-seven different titles available for sale in North America by 1775. For example, William Halfpenny's *Perspective*, published in England in 1731, appeared on this continent in 1761; and his *Rural Architecture*, published in 1752, was first noted in America in 1760. The timelags in publication were considerable, judged by present-day standards, but more important is the fact that so many of these books were circulating in the colonies. Until the second half of the eighteenth century, there seems to have been a common tradition in frame building methods on both sides of the Atlantic. Isham and Brown have proved, for example, that construction details in early Connecticut houses show all the intricate and involved jointing common in Britain and Europe and described in the standard reference works of those times.[1]

But as this spate of literature on carpentry from England reached its heights, techniques in America began to change. They became simpler and more economical, not only in building construction but in other crafts as well. In these developments one may detect that practical wit and ingenuity which would become known as 'Yankee know-how,' and an emphasis on the benefits of speed and mass production familiar to everyone today. John McGregor, in describing Canada in the 1830s, wrote that 'farmers and labourers born and brought up in America possess, in an eminent degree, a quickness of expedients where any thing is required that can be supplied by the use of edge-tools; and as carpenters and joiners they are not only expert but ingenious workmen.'[2] This 'quickness' of invention was brought across the border by the Loyalists towards the end of the eighteenth century.

This house consists of two standard log houses put together to form a T – something in the manner of the second Langton house but without any artificiality or polite deception.

Lieutenant David Brass of Butler's Rangers gained some renown in the Kingston area as an experienced mechanic particularly adept at installing machinery in saw and grist mills. He advised on the location and construction of the first King's Mill on the Cataraqui in 1783.[3] The settlers of Upper Canada were, on average, probably poorer than their kinsmen to the south, and their natural environment was, if anything, harder and less varied in its resources. Necessity – the proverbial mother of invention – forced our ancestors to prove their ingenuity by finding more and different uses for the materials and equipment available to them.

Although the Loyalists were dominant in the embryonic society of Upper Canada, they were not the only influence. Immigrants came in increasing numbers from across the Atlantic, some of whom arrived unprepared in both mind and equipment for the hardships of the New World. Others, however, through numerous books or letters or even previous visits were acquainted with conditions and came knowing the challenges that a pioneering life would offer. They were largely of the same stock as those who had come from New England and New York, but they did not bring with them the same technical capital. Their training was not wholly relevant to the harsher environment, and the direct British and European influence on construction in Upper Canada was consequently of relatively minor importance.

Indeed, the instances of persisting British techniques are relatively few and far between. There was, for example, the Denis house, one of the small mud houses in York Mills that had to have several feet sliced off its front for the widening of Yonge Street. The house had a hip-roof, fairly rare among early houses, with a wide overhang on all sides produced by means of a 'dragon' beam type of frame; this is, as far as I know, unique in Ontario, though it was very common in England. Unique also is the pair of 'har-hung' barn doors on a farm near Balderson in Lanark County. Such doors have a squared, rather heavy hanging style, called a 'har-tree,' with rounded tapered ends shaped like pins which fit into corresponding holes in the sill and lintel; the door swings on the pins, thus eliminating the need for heavy metal hinges, which may perhaps have been unobtainable when the barn was built. Another example of a European tradition is the roof framing in the Philip Eckhardt house built just north of Unionville in 1794. The gables were recessed several feet in from the end walls, and a typical Continental pent roof was then used to cover the recessed portion of the plan as well as to form an overhang at the gable ends.

There were two other contributions to the building techniques of Upper Canada, attributable to differences in cultural background, namely the French and the Pennsylvania Germans. French methods prevailed in the areas near, or part of, the original French settlements, such as in the Windsor region, where their log construction differed considerably from that of the British Americans. The greatest German contribution was probably the bank barn – a contribution to a type, rather than a method, of building.

Introduction  9

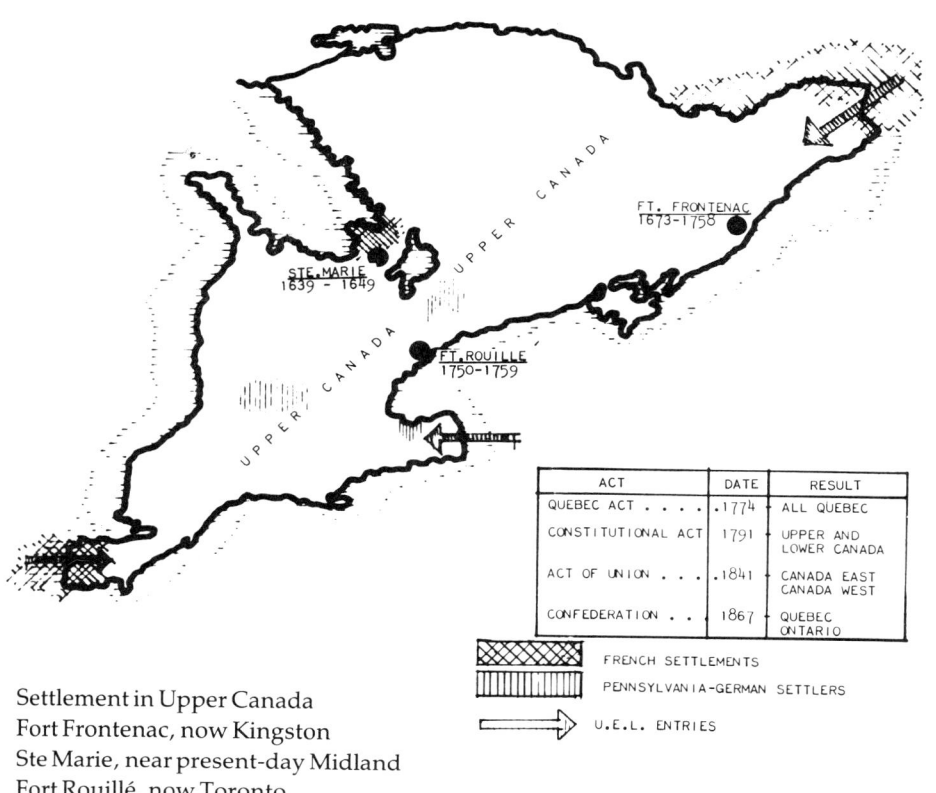

Settlement in Upper Canada
Fort Frontenac, now Kingston
Ste Marie, near present-day Midland
Fort Rouillé, now Toronto

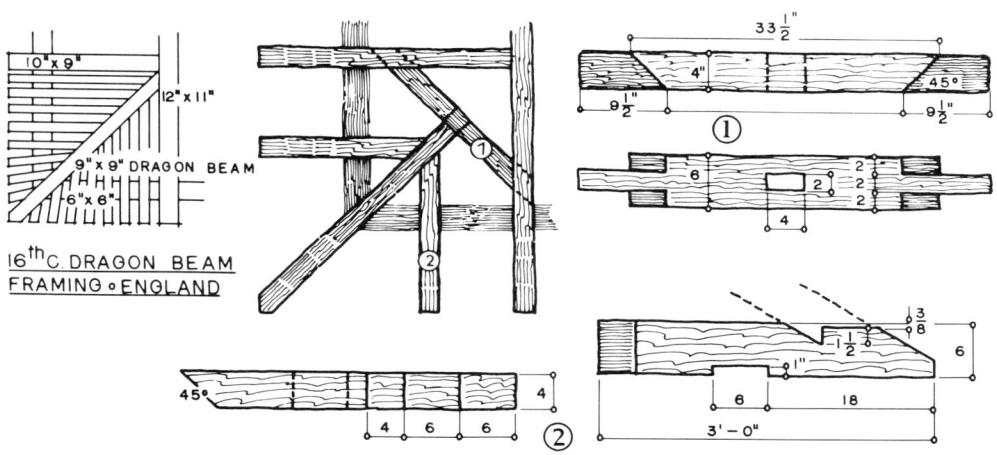

E. DENIS  COTTAGE ∘ CEILING FRAMING ∘ YORK MILLS

Rare in frame construction is the through-tusk tenon, shown here framing the trimmer into the header of a stairwell in Dr John Scott's summer home at Bond Head, near Bradford.

As well as these pockets of regional variation, and the occasional throwback to home tradition by tradesmen who had not yet fully absorbed the prevailing methods, the influence of individual builders can be detected. But instances of structural variation by individuals or groups must always be distinguished from the characteristics of a region as a whole. The need to recognize this distinction is reason enough for a thorough understanding of building practices in order to avoid baseless generalizations, especially where historical preservation is involved.

Although we are concerned here with a frontier society, it is a mistake to assume that the workmanship of those days was generally crude or clumsy, or that building was entirely an unregulated affair of 'chacun à son gout.' In some instances skilled labour was not available, and sometimes, then as now, a man who was short of money would 'do it himself.' But apart from such situations, which may have been common enough in the first years of settlement in remoter areas, the general standard of craftsmanship was high. Tradesmen usually brought their tool chests with them and could thus exercise their skill in America as fully as in Europe. The quality of the early building in Upper Canada is well spoken of by James Brown in his *View of Canada and the Colonists*: 'Another prevalent mistake is, that inferior descriptions of tradesmen suit and find employment almost as well as the best in Canada – the colony, as individuals reason, being young, and therefore in a comparatively rude state, good workmanship is not in request. This may apply to small villages and country settlements; but the case in regard to the towns is for the most part quite the reverse. In the principal towns of

Canada, labour being usually well remunerated, the workmanship required is not inferior to that in the best towns of Britain. Inferior hands experience difficulty in getting employment, while superior tradesmen in most branches are highly prized.' Good carpenters, joiners, and cabinetmakers, Brown reported, commanded the highest wages of all trades – 6/3 per day, or 5/- with board.

Of all building materials, wood has the greatest tendency for movement: it shrinks, expands, and warps in response to changes in temperature or moisture content to a greater degree than any other material used in construction. In these days of plywood, lamination, and other forms of treated or processed wood, this is no longer, of course, wholly true, but in the period covered by this book all builders had to take the movement of natural wood into consideration. For immigrants from Britain, where it was not the practice to season lumber, there must have been some dismaying moments when they discovered how severely the North American climate could affect wood. There are innumerable examples still in existence of log houses in which the timbers were not properly squared and dovetailed at the corners and which now are decidedly out of plumb both vertically and horizontally. Since wood moves more across the grain than with it, the vertical expansion and contraction of horizontal logs can be considerable. In the Banwell house, discussed later, allowance is made for movement in the log fill by the provision of an expansion joint which prevents the fill from straining the frame. And in the present by-laws of the National Building Code for log construction in Whitehorse, it is prescribed that 'The rough buck and jamb shall be of such a length as to have an opening between the header and the lintel log of not less than one-half inch in width for every foot of height of the jamb.' It is to the credit of early carpenters and joiners that many of their frame buildings still in existence are perfectly plumb and true.

The distinction between a carpenter and joiner was not what one might expect – that a joiner was the craftsman skilled in making joints – but rather that the joiner knew all that a carpenter did, including making joints, and could also do the interior finishing woodwork. He was the more skilled of the two, and this lighter and more decorative aspect of his work brought him close to the cabinetmaker. Learning about joints was an important part of the education of the apprentice carpenter in Europe. Builders were fully aware that the strength and rigidity of a frame building depended first on the proper size or 'scantling' of the individual structural components and secondly on the tight and proper joining of the components in such a way that the stress was transferred from one to the other. It was important for such 'joints in compression' that the planes of contact between the timbers be as close as possible to the normal of the line of stress. The techniques of stress transfer had produced, by the end of the eighteenth century in Europe, exceedingly intricate framing. But tables of scantlings, as well as such handbooks as *The Builders' and Workman's Director*, were available as 'ready reckoners' to determine the size of timber required for a given strength or load and the kind of joint most suitable for the purpose. Carpenters were required not only to know the problems of stresses and strains but also to possess great accuracy of workmanship. The skill and precision displayed in wood framing and the work of the stonemasons in buildings of the Gothic period are the two aspects of early construction that command the greatest admiration even today.

But the complex and impressive joints that were characteristic of the early eighteenth century had fallen out of use in North America by the time Ontario was founded. American builders had begun their search for the simplest and quickest, and so cheapest, methods some time about 1750. Only the most basic and essential joint, the mortise and tenon, survived, but it is a joint that is capable of many variations. It has to be remembered, too, that most of the early buildings in Ontario were of relatively small size and so did not demand very intricate framing in any case.

Even from the earliest days in Upper Canada, regulations were imposed on such matters as building methods, materials, size of dwellings, and so on. Such codes have, of course, formed part of the fabric of civilized society at least since the edict of Hammurabi about 1750 BC that a builder be put to death if he built so poorly that the house collapsed and killed the owner. (Perhaps this penalty has its points!) The early settlers of Ontario all came from areas where building by-laws were in force, and one of the first concerns of Governor Simcoe in founding the infant town of York (Toronto) in 1793 was to enact zoning by-laws for the protection of property values. Richard Cartwright, who did not always see eye to eye with Simcoe, wrote to Isaac Todd: '... you will smile when I tell you that even at York, a town lot is to be granted in the front street only on condition that you shall build a house of not less than forty-seven feet frontage, two stories high, and of a certain order of architecture. In the second street, they may be somewhat less in front, but the two stories and the mode of architecture are indispensable; and it is only on the back streets and alleys that the tinkers and taylors will be allowed to consult their taste and circumstances in the structure of their habitation, upon lots of one-tenth of an acre.'[4] Along the Longwood (near London) and Talbot roads, shingles were mandatory for a roof. Along the Dundas Road, a by-law in effect from 1820 to 1840 required 'a reasonably well-constructed log house ... with the minimum dimension of 16'0" by 20'0".'

Prevalent in the early days, as indeed it is yet in the sale of crown land, was the stipulation that if a buyer did not build within a certain time, title to the land would revert to the original owner. Simcoe allowed three years at York for a building to be erected. And at Oakville, on 24 June 1833, the following announcement appeared:

> Town Lots in Oakville
> for Sale at Public Auction
> on Tuesday the 10th. July next at 12 O'clock
> at the Oakville House

The Town Plot of this thriving Village and Shipping Port being now regularly laid out in Streets, Town Lots and Water Lots, the Public are notified that Fifty of these Lots will be disposed of, at the time and place above stated, without reserve, to the Highest Bidder.

The Terms upon which these Lots will be sold are, One-half the Purchase Money to be paid at the time of Sale, and the other Half in Twelve Months – subject to condition of Building a Stone, Brick or Frame House, not less than 24 feet by 18 to be completed within eighteen Months from the day of Sale.[5]

Note that no log houses were contemplated.

Like all by-laws, however, these early ones were not always observed to the letter and were frequently stretched to the limit. Authorities might legislate standards but they had to be rather lenient in enforcing them. On Saturday, 6 September 1800, the lieutenant-governor's office, faced with the fact that on some newly bought lots in York people had not even cleared the land, far less built a house, within the time limit, ordered that 'whereas, the health and convenience of His Majesty's subjects resident in the said Town demand that the ground parts of the same should be cleared as soon as possible: Notice is hereby given to all such persons that they are required within three months from this date to cut and burn all the brush and underwood on their lots; and within six months from the date thereof to fell all trees that are standing thereon, on pain of their lots being forfeited.'[6]

Fire was, of course, an ever present hazard, and the above order from the government at York was also intended as a fire precaution. The regulations 'Made and Ordained in Adjourned Quarter Sessions, May 14th, 1817 – Revised and amended in Adjourned General Sessions, June 21st, 1823' and signed by S. Heward, 'Clk Peace, Home District,' required every home in the town of York to provide a readily available ladder of sufficient length to reach the eaves as well as another one supplied with iron hooks to be hooked over the ridge, in order to reach the chimney top. All chimneys or flues were to be swept once between the first day of November to the first day of the following April if used daily as in kitchens or 'manufactories,' and every four weeks if used intermittently. Several 'leathern' buckets of three gallons capacity were to be placed in a convenient place near the front entrance of each building. Six 'discreet and active' persons were appointed fire wardens and as a badge of authority during a fire they were to wear a white handkerchief tied to the left arm below the elbow.[7] And even in the neighbourhood of Fenelon Falls in 1840 John Langton had to build his workshop at least 66 feet away from his house because of fire hazard.

It is important to remember that well before any building was done in Ontario the French fur traders based in New France had already spread their influence from Acadia on the east coast to British Columbia in the west, and south along the Mississippi. This enormous range is explained by the attempt to seal off the English along the eastern seaboard so as to prevent their penetration inland in search of the same furs. Naturally enough, French craftsmanship followed the routes dictated by commercial and political competition.

The fact that the major fur-trading companies (except, of course, the Hudson's Bay Company) all operated out of Montreal, since there were no other shipping ports readily available, also helps explain the spread of French building skills. The labour supply had to be recruited almost exclusively from the valley of the St Lawrence River. That French tradesmen did spread their construction methods over this immense territory is a fact for which so much evidence still exists as to place it beyond dispute. Up to the middle of the nineteenth century, at least, French methods were used in the construction of most forts and practically all trading posts, and their influence can be seen also in houses and churches scattered across the continent.

The French exported skilled artisans along with their colonists. Each shipload from France brought its own technicians under contract, and thus the early building in the colony is of excellent quality. From the outset these craftsmen, using the building methods of the old country increasingly adapted to conditions in New France, were employed by the wealthy trading companies, the government, and the powerful church orders.

One type of frame construction used was known as 'colombage pierroté.' In this method the spaces in the framed exterior walls were filled with masonry, as in the manner of English half-timber, and then the walls were frequently covered with boards. The English used masonry of stone or brick set in mortar or clay; since the timbers were generally 'green' when used, they shrank away from the fill as they dried and draughty walls were the result. The fill in the French buildings was almost universally of stone in mortar. This form of construction required more skill than the average settler possessed, and so the British colonists tended very soon to abandon it in favour of 'Swedish' log construction, with walls built of horizontal logs, left round, notched and overlapped at the corners.

Another type of fill often used in Europe, particularly in northern France, consisted of planks inserted horizontally into grooved posts that were spaced at convenient intervals. When introduced into Quebec, builders began to use logs with a tenon at each end. Since the winter temperatures were so much more severe in Quebec, and wood was so plentiful, the use of logs instead of planks was a natural development in the New World.

The French colonists were also introduced to the common log construction described above, which they often referred to as 'pièce sur pièce.' With the exception of those found in the crudest huts, logs were generally well shaped and the keying was mainly dovetailed ('les angles des murs se terminent en queue d'aronde ou en « tête-de-chien »'[8]) – a method superior to any other since it was self-draining and therefore less subject to rot at the corners.

In spite of the fact that the grooved post method required greater skill, the design was carried by traders across the whole of Canada and became the accepted method of building trading posts. Examples of the style, used both in large and small buildings, are to be found all the way from Labrador, westward across Ontario and Manitoba, through to Vancouver Island in British Columbia. Indeed, the method occurs in so many localities across the continent that it has come to bear different names: 'Manitoba Frame' or 'Red River Frame' in the mid-west, 'Hudson's Bay Frame' near the west coast, and in some cases west of the Rockies it is referred to simply as 'Canadian.'

The French grooved post and fill method of construction ranged from the northeast, Fort Chimo, Ungava Bay, 'Labrador, 1896' ...

... through Manitoba, McDermot's store near Fort Garry ...

... also in Manitoba, Heartman's trading store, near Fort Garry ... Note the two types of construction: grooved post in the building on the left and common log in the building on the right. The props against the wall on the left were perhaps required because of insufficient tie-beams in the roof. Note also the thatched roof with the hold-downs and the boarded chimneys, just to one side of the ridge pole thus leaving the latter uninterrupted.

... to British Columbia, Fort McLeod ...

... Fort Langley, near Vancouver ... from a sketch by E. Mallandaine, 1848

... and to Vancouver Island, Fort Rupert.

It was used for small buildings, Fort Nascopie in Labrador...

... and it was used for large ones, Fort St James. Notice the hipped roof covered with wooden shingles. The saw-tooth ornament of the eaves, obtained by cutting the bottom row of shingles to arrow-like points, was typical of the buildings of the Hudson's Bay Company.

The reasons for this variety of nomenclature are obscure. The drawing of a Red River settlement, supposedly done by Lord Selkirk in 1817, shows typical buildings of the 'Red River Frame' style. As might be expected, the buildings are essentially one-storey structures, but the gable windows and doors indicate clearly that the spaces within the steep roofs were put to good use (note the ladder giving access to the loft in one building). There can be no doubt about the structural system used in these buildings; it is the Quebec system, which existed long before a Red River settlement was even thought of.

This sketch of a Red River settlement is believed to have been made by Lord Selkirk in 1817.

This little cottage stood on the Red River Road near Winnipeg well into the 1920s; it corresponds perfectly with Lord Selkirk's sketch above.

20  Building with Wood

The fact that the style actually became known as 'Hudson's Bay Frame' is evidence that the men in charge of establishing trading posts for the Hudson's Bay Company realized the advantages of the French system. During an enquiry conducted at Vancouver in the mid-nineteenth century, one witness, having been asked to compare the advantages of the 'American' balloon frame construction with those of the 'Hudson's Bay' or 'Canadian' style, said the latter was much stronger and better adapted to carrying the heavy load of furs stored in company warehouses. Certainly, such large, two-storey warehouses as the one at Fort St James in British Columbia were common enough in the major Canadian fur trade posts. One reason for its acceptance, even in some British military forts such as Fort Pelly in Saskatchewan, may be that this method permitted the erection of much larger structures than would be possible by the more traditional log construction.

French log construction at Fort Pelly, Saskatchewan, built 1824, rebuilt 1842–43, and moved 1856–57

So widely accepted was the Quebec method that it was used even in small building where English log construction would have been quicker. One builder complained that he could have finished his work much sooner had he been allowed to use regular log construction, but he was overruled by the officials in charge. The grooved post method was also on occasion used for non-commercial structures. The first Church of England on the Red River, on the site of the present Winnipeg cathedral, was built according to this method, as was the oldest Anglican church at Fort Simpson on the Mackenzie River in the Northwest Territories. The latter shows the grooved post method being pressed to conform to the 'Ecclesiastical-Gothick' so dear to the hearts of its Anglican builders; the shingled roof has the typical Hudson's Bay Company saw-tooth ornament along the bottom edge.

Another proof of the universal employment of this method is the fact that

The first Church of England on the Red River, Winnipeg

as early as the beginning of the nineteenth century French names for structural members became accepted terminology even among the English. In 1800 Alexander Henry, a Hudson's Bay Company factor, listed the timber required to build the Park River post:

| Henry's spelling | French spelling | English equivalent |
| --- | --- | --- |
| rembrits | rambris | gable lining |
| pinions | pignons | gables |
| cloisons | cloisons | partitions |
| sableries | sablières | wall plates |
| aiguilles | aiguilles | king posts |
| faîtes | faîtes | ridge poles |

A difficulty encountered in unravelling the mysteries of Henry's construction methods was that such terms were frequently misspelled or anglicized and then spelt phonetically. To add to the confusion, Henry, without a doubt, named some pieces wrongly, and even placed several numbers in the wrong column. In spite of these slips, however, it was possible to reconstruct theoretically one of his buildings without much difficulty, once names and figures were sorted out. Proceeding on the assumption that the usual French method of construction was employed, the number of pieces listed coincided perfectly with the theoretical requirements. This seems proof enough to conclude that he used the grooved post method, even though his journal contains no further information on the subject.

The old Anglican church at Fort Simpson, date unknown

## Wood used in our establishment at Park River, autumn of 1800

| | | |
|---|---|---:|
| Stockades, 15 ft. long, oak | | 564 |
| do | 8 ft. oak, for rembrits | 564 |
| do | 6 ft. for 3d lining to bastion | 100 |
| do | 5 ft. over the two gates | 34 |
| do | 7 to 15 ft., oak, for laths | 34 |
| do | 8 ft. for plank for gates | 14 |
| do | 7 ft. for plank for bastions | 20 |
| Pegs, 1½ ft. for stockades, etc. | | 770 |
| | Total | 2,100 |

*For dwelling-house*

| | | | |
|---|---|---|---:|
| Oak logs of | | 10 ft. for the square | 72 |
| do | of | 18 ft. for pinions | 18 |
| do | of | 15 ft. for cloisons | 45 |
| do | of | 9 ft. for the covering | 230 |
| do | contg. | 100 ft. for the sableries | 6 |
| do | contg. | 100 ft. for the covering | 6 |
| do | of | 11 ft. for the aiguilles | 5 |
| do | of | 20 ft. for the faîtes | 3 |
| Squared posts, 8 ft. for doors and covers | | | 14 |
| Posts, 4 ft. for windows | | | 11 |
| Planks, 8 ft. for flooring | | | 105 |
| Boards, 6 ft. for doors, beds, etc. | | | 115 |
| | | Total | 630 |

*For storehouse*

| | | |
|---|---|---:|
| Oak logs of 24 ft. for square | | 12 |
| Pine logs of 13 ft. for pinions | | 20 |
| Oak logs of 9 ft. for covering | | 120 |
| do | of 24 ft. for faîtes | 1 |
| do | of 22 ft. for covering | 2 |
| do | of 11 ft. for aiguilles | 3 |
| Oak posts of 5 ft. for doors | | 2 |
| do | planks of 5 ft. for doors | 3 |
| do | logs of 12 ft. for flooring | 50 |
| | Total | 213 |

*For shop*

| | | |
|---|---|---:|
| Oak logs of 15 ft. for the square | | 15 |
| do | of 13 ft. for the pinions | 20 |
| do | of 9 ft. for the covering | 73 |
| do | of 15 ft. for the faîtes | 3 |
| do | of 11 ft. for the aiguilles | 2 |
| Oak posts of 5 ft. for the doors | | 2 |
| do | planks 8 ft. for flooring | 55 |
| | Total | 170 |

| | |
|---|---:|
| Pieces of timber and wood | 3,113 |
| Oak stick of 55 ft. for a flag-staff | 1 |
| Total | 3,114 |

The technical, if not the historical, development of building with wood may be said to begin with the log house or shanty, move on to some forms of plank construction – which may be considered an intermediate and experimental stage – then on to timber framing, which evolved into balloon framing. (This account omits western framing entirely since it is a development of the twentieth century.) Frame buildings can be classified as three distinct types: residences; barns and mills; and such structures as churches and halls where a relatively large space has to be enclosed without too much interior construction. Of these three, surviving barns and mills are the easiest for today's observer to analyse because of their naked framing; houses, churches, and halls generally have the construction covered except in the attic. Churches and halls are naturally much fewer in number than houses, and this makes an overall view of the methods used in their building more difficult to attain.

# 2
# LOG CONSTRUCTION

Log construction is one of the 'natural' solutions to structural problems; it is consequently very old and has been found in many parts of the world. About 30 BC, for example, in his *De architectura*, Vitruvius described a method used by the Colchians on the south shore of the Black Sea: 'They lay timbers flat on the ground, one trunk to the left and one to the right, spaced one trunk length apart. Other trunks are then laid crosswise on top of them at the ends ... The spaces left because of the thickness of the material are filled with wood chips and mud. By shortening each pair of cross-timbers, they build a pyramid-shaped roof which they cover with leaves and mud.'

This was horizontal timbering. In Anglo-Saxon England, on the other hand, vertical timbering seems to have been prevalent. The walls of the church at Greenstead, Essex, dating back to 1015, are built of vertical oak timbers set into a horizontal oak sill; this church is called a 'stockenchurch' (*stocc* being Anglo-Saxon for trunk or log). In their early frame or half-timber construction, the English often used whole tree trunks for posts, setting the trunks upside down, with the root end up, since the flare at the root provided a larger bearing surface. This use of trunks was especially common for corner posts, and it certainly was a simple method of cornering. The problem of spanning an opening was solved by raising the openings right up to the underside of the plate (the horizontal member linking the corners and supporting the rafters). In this respect, horizontal timbering has an advantage in that each log acts as its own lintel.

Presumably because it was no longer practised in Europe by the age of colonization, vertical log construction did not 'catch on' in North America. References to it are rare. The first settlement at the mouth of the Kennebec River in Maine, established in August 1607 by the Plymouth Company but abandoned the following spring, contained houses built of horizontal logs slotted into vertical posts: the log walls were divided into several bays marked by vertical posts. And in 1701 Fort Pontchartrain, near Detroit, was built – stockade, houses, and church – by driving timbers vertically into the ground side by side. This settlement, the 200 foot square Ville d'Etroit, was founded, however, by the French from Montreal and so cannot be said to be part of the English and New England tradition that dominated Ontario construction.

From vertical timbering it is, in terms of method, but one step to the old British and pre-Saxon form of cruck construction. Crucks were oaks, suitably twisted by nature, which were stripped of branches and split in half the long way. The halves were then set upright with the bends opposed so as to form an arch. Several such arches were set side by side some distance apart, joined with purlins (horizontal members supporting the rafters), roofed over, and walled in. In the better house or barn, the spaces between the timbers and crucks were filled with brickwork in a manner similar to the later half-timber work; in others the fill would probably be wattle and daub: branches and sticks interwoven and covered with clay.

Cruck construction died out in England and Wales by the fifteenth century and so was never attempted in either America or Canada. However, two buildings – a cottage and the 'Glass House,' the earliest glass factory in the British colonies – have been 'reconstructed' in this manner at Jamestown, Virginia, largely on the strength of the method's supposedly being described in Captain John Smith's writings: 'This was our Church, till wee built a homely thing like a barne, set upon Cratchets' ('cratchets' supposedly being a corruption of 'cruck').

The next logical step after cruck building was timber framing – the English 'half-timber' – in which the spaces between the timbers were filled in with brickwork and plaster. The French 'colombage' method was basically similar, except that it was generally also covered with some protective sheathing. Often the spaces between the uprights were filled with stone work; this style was known as 'colombage pierroté.'[1] In Canada, French colonists frequently notched the uprights and slid short logs horizontally in between them, making thereby a kind of combination of log and colombage construction. With one notable exception – Castle Frank – this construction was not accepted by the English in Ontario, again for reasons that can only be conjectural – unfamiliarity, lack of tools, lack of skill were all no doubt factors.

Western – ca 1850. Tenoned logs about 10'-0" long. Probably French influence.

"Castle Frank" was built in this manner. Also used in New England.

The earliest forms of construction used by English settlers in America were frame and half-timber. Harold R. Shurtleff has shown that, although log construction was introduced into the future United States as early as the first half of the seventeenth century and although it was speedier and required fewer tools and less skill, the English did not adopt this form until the eighteenth century, and even then it was generally considered only a stop-gap until they could afford a better building of stone, brick, or wooden frame.[2] This conservatism of the English settlers is reflected in another aspect of their New World structures – their dimensions. It has been suggested that the frequently found internal dimensions of 16 feet by 15 feet in the English cottage are based on the space required for one yoke of oxen.[3] Though this suggestion is disputed,[4] what is not disputed is that these same dimensions do recur in North America, and even to some extent in English-built log cabins in nineteenth-century Ontario, frequently enough to be of some significance.

In all these forms of building originating in England and France, the load is carried by vertical timbers; the stress is with the grain. In log construction, where the logs are horizontal, the stress runs across the grain. The latter, a reversal of the usual structural technique, is found only in the traditional methods of Scandinavia, Germany, Switzerland, and Russia, and is perhaps the result of the plentiful supply of straight-growing trees in those areas – a condition paralleled, of course, in many parts of North America.

Historians generally agree that it was the Swedes who introduced log construction to North America. New Sweden was founded by the Swedish West India Company on Delaware Bay in 1638 and flourished until 1655 when it was surrendered to the Dutch. The workmanship of the Swedish carpenters was first-class. There is a house in Prospect Park, Delaware County, Pennsylvania, built in 1654 with an addition in 1698 (and later owned by John Morton, one of the signers of the Declaration of Independence) which is so well built that there appears to have been no necessity for chinking or daubing. Travellers' accounts in 1679 assert the superiority of the Swedish log house over the English form of house, the Swedish one being much warmer and less draughty. (This coincides with John Langton's ideas on the subject, as we shall see below.)

Swedish log construction has the ends of the logs projecting at the corners; later such corners were sometimes cut off flush with an axe rather than a saw. Logs could be either squared or round; if they were squared and less than about 6 inches thick, the method was called plank construction and the houses plank houses, though there is no definite line of demarcation between plank and squared log construction.

A typical Swedish house plan in America contained one, two, or three rooms, and the fireplace was almost invariably in a corner; even when there was more than one fireplace they were probably never built back-to-back. Doors were low and wide, and the roofs were gabled – both characteristics, however, not being peculiar to the Swedish plan. There are no examples of this type of fireplace in Ontario except in later houses.

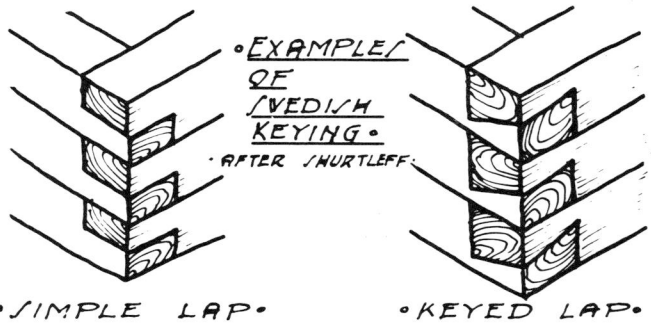

Examples of Swedish keying. After Shurtleff. Simple lap. Keyed lap.

About 1710, Germans from Bavaria, Saxony, and Switzerland began to settle in Pennsylvania, bringing with them their native method of log building. Logs were either round or squared, as in the Swedish method, but at the corners they were keyed or dovetailed to permit a flush corner. The interstices were wide enough to require chinking with wedges of wood[5] as well as clay or lime mortar. There is a well-preserved squared log house at Potter's Bank, Center County, Pennsylvania, in which the logs are keyed with a type of wedge-shaped saddle-notch and the chinking consists of lime mortar with small wedges of wood as fill. Identical keying appears in a schoolhouse built in Waterloo County, Ontario, and a perfect example of this method of chinking may be seen in the old D. Stong house, built near Edgeley in 1832 and now the 'Settler's second home' at Pioneer Village, Toronto. Waterloo County was settled by Pennsylvania 'Dutch' (Deutsch); the Stongs were Holland Dutch.

A typical example of Pennsylvania keying in conjunction with squared logs.
Waterloo schoolhouse, 1820

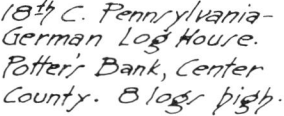

Waterloo County School. 1820. First school in Waterloo. Note similarity in methods of chinking & keying. 7-8 logs high.

18th C. Pennsylvania-German Log House. Potter's Bank, Center County. 8 logs high.

The building that became the 'Settler's second home' (1832) in the Pioneer Village near Toronto before and after restoration. It is the best example in existence of a Pennsylvania-German centre-chimney floor plan. The logs are large, carefully selected, and worked and chinked with wooden wedges, a rare form of chinking in Ontario.

Kathy — here is a copy 2
for the duplicate shelf.

By the middle of the eighteenth century, Pennsylvania was populated not only by Germans but also by the Swedes, Finns, Dutch, Welsh, and Scotch-Irish, as well as by English Quakers. The colony was, as a result, somewhat of an architectural melting pot, especially around Philadelphia. Here the German-speaking colonists were the strongest group but in contact with Swedish and English architecture. It was this mingling of German, Swedish, and English forms that gradually led to the so-called 'Pennsylvania-Dutch' style.

A typical Pennsylvania-Dutch plan had one room occupying the full width of the front half of the house. This room, a combined hall and kitchen, had a fireplace centrally located on the inside wall. The stairway was in either the left or the right front corner. Behind the kitchen were one or two rooms, a living room and/or a bedroom. If the house had two fireplaces, they were generally placed back to back. But in some houses, representative of the merging traditions before the typical synthesis was reached, one may find such arrangements as this Dutch plan with a Swedish corner fireplace on one wall and an English one placed centrally on another. Pennsylvania houses contained one and a half or two storeys, and were built of either logs, brick, or stone. These houses were invariably of excellent and solid workmanship, rather larger than the average house in the colonies.

These developments in Pennsylvania have been treated in some detail, partly because they had an influence in some parts of Ontario and partly because they illustrate the kind of architectural mixing that was going on in the colonies to the south before the Revolution. Along the Hudson and Delaware rivers, (Holland) Dutch and Swedish traditions were well developed before the English arrived, causing resultant modifications in the English colonial style.

References to log houses in the records of the seventeenth and early eighteenth centuries are relatively few – and references to frame houses relatively frequent. One of the few records of log construction can be found in the minutes of the town of Londonderry in New Hampshire which voted in 1724 to build a school 'sixtine foot long and twelve foot Brenth ... to be a logg house seven foot side wall' (that is, seven logs high). The evidence all suggests that log houses were the exception rather than the rule for at least the first hundred years of settlement south of the St Lawrence, and that the English-speaking colonists saw no particular advantage or virtue in them.

At the time of the Revolution there was no trace in American thinking of the 'log cabin myth.' But by the end of the eighteenth century the log cabin was well on its way to becoming a national symbol, expressing and summing up the expansion of the United States across the Alleghenies into the basin of the Mississippi. It represented the frontier, symbolizing not only the political dynamic of the new nation but also its romantic dream – now all but shattered – of mankind returning to nature. A log cabin was the home of the nineteenth-century Adam repossessing the Garden of Eden and, in the symbol's greatest days, thus the preferred birthplace of all politicians. It attained the metaphorical heights of being declared 'the cradle of the American home.'

The people who took the log cabin westward and gave it its place in the American imagination were a people with no strong architectural tradition of their own – the Irish, or rather the so-called Scotch-Irish. These were the Presbyterian Scots 'planted' in Ulster in the early part of the seventeenth century to farm the lands of the expelled Catholic Irish. With their experience of rehabilitating farms in a hostile country, they were ideally suited to pioneering in North America. Their impetus to migrate came from the expiry of their tenant leases after 1717; during the 1720s thousands of them – as many as six thousand in one year – sailed for America and, being of an independent spirit, pushed past the settled parts of Pennsylvania, Virginia, and the Carolinas and settled in the wilderness. They adopted the log house, presumably because it was the quickest, cheapest, and easiest form of construction.

There is, of course, a certain similarity in proportion and fenestration between the log house and the English Georgian or New England 'colonial' type of house. The similarity in the window shapes and design reflects the fact that the glass panes were imported from England and that the frames and sashes would be manufactured in a mill employing carpenters who accepted and indeed would try to reproduce old-country methods. The log house combines a European structural method with these traditional proportions and details from Britain, and is thus a peculiarly American, if not all-American, structure.

It seems to have been fairly common for the chimneys in the American – but not the Ontario – log house or cabin to be built entirely outside the end wall. This was true, for instance, of the very small 'slave cabins' of the southern states; such cabins might have a stone fireplace with a brick top, common in Maryland, or with a catted clay chimney, occurring in Virginia. Lincoln's cabin, now settled at Hodgenville, Kentucky, also has an outside chimney, built of logs and clay. Other examples of log and clay chimneys are common enough to permit one to trace this method back to England. In London, as far back as 1419, they were considered a fire hazard and prohibited, though they continued in use for centuries after, particularly in rural areas;[6] as late as 1719 people were still being fined for using clay chimneys.

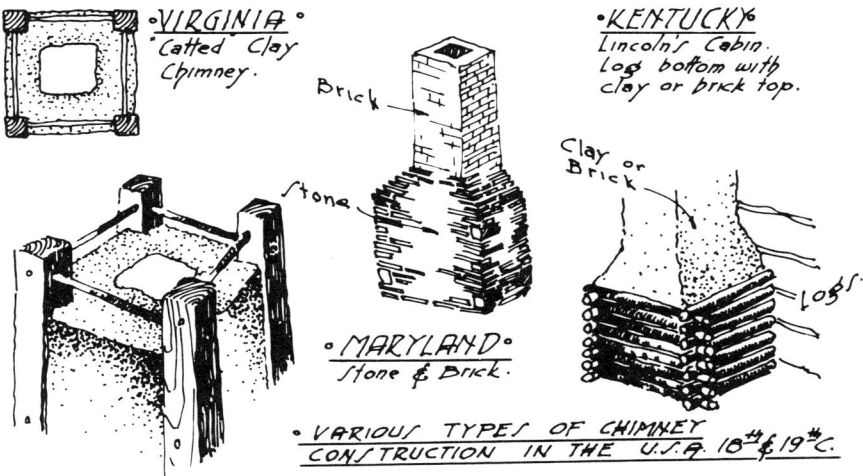

Various types of chimney construction in the U.S.A. 18th & 19th C.

The Smith home in Toronto was built about 1809 and is located on Jane Street near Steeles Avenue. It has a typical centre-hall plan. Unfortunately it has undergone some alterations: the window sashes have obviously been replaced and the porch somehat shortened. The location and the small size of the windows suggest the proportions and fenestration of an early New England garrison house. The pair of quarter-round gable windows add a touch of refinement.

This distinction between a log 'cabin' and a log 'house' seems to have been rather uncertain, but in 1808 it was claimed by Thaddeus M. Harris: 'If the logs be hewed, if the interstices be stopped with stone and neatly plastered, and if the roof is composed of shingles nicely laid on, it is called a log house. A log house has glass windows and a chimney; a cabin has generally no windows and only a hole in the roof for the smoke to escape.'[7] It is convenient to follow the distinction here, for Harris' cabin corresponds to the Canadian 'shanty.' Log houses could be fairly large. In 1770 the court of Botetourt County in the piedmont of Virginia (settled by the Scotch-Irish) ordered 'a log cabbin twenty four feet long and twenty wide for a Court House with a clapboard roof with two sheds, one at each end for jury rooms.' (Clapboarding here could mean either some sort of wood shingles or clapboarding as we understand it today.) This is the same plan, incidentally, that was followed in John Galt's log cabin and office built near Guelph, Ontario, about 1827.

The log house has always been associated with the early settlers in Ontario – somewhat incongruously perhaps since many of them were of English origin and the English in America had been the last to adopt it as a building form, so strong was their tradition of timber framing (or so conservative was their thinking!). But by the time the Loyalists left for Upper Canada, building with horizontal logs had become accepted by all as the natural method for those pioneering a wooded country. It still is to some extent, for the building by-laws adopted in 1960 by Whitehorse in the Yukon embody regulations covering log construction.

Log houses are, in a way, the Cinderella of architectural history; unhelped by fairy godmother or prince charming, they have not inspired much serious interest or study from either architect or historian, probably because they were unpretentiously functional and were usually built with the intention of eventually being abandoned.

The civil and military establishments sent out by Britain to govern Upper Canada brought with them 'expert hewers and dovetailers of logs' and even in some instances pre-cut timbers in order that their authority should be housed in suitable splendour. This practice of importing at least the main structural timbers in prefabricated form was much commoner in early Canadian history than is generally supposed. Perhaps the first buildings to be shipped were dismantled houses from Ste Croix to Port Royal in 1605.[8] When the New England troops arrived at Grand Pré to fight the French in 1710–11, they brought with them 'materials for two blockhouses' (which, incidentally, were not erected since the commander of the expedition, Colonel Arthur Noble, thought that winter and distance would prevent a French attack – an error of judgement that cost him his life and the surrender of his men);[9] and when New Englanders later arrived to settle in pre-Loyalist Nova Scotia, they brought with them not only tools and cherished pieces of furniture but also pre-cut and hewn timbers to build their new homes.

The average settler in Upper Canada, however, came in relative poverty to 'rough it in the bush.' There is ample evidence that his first shelter, if not simply a summer hut of boughs and branches, was typically built of logs and of so unpretentious a nature that it could hardly be called a house at all. Two openings – one for a door and one to permit the smoke to escape – characterized the shanty, as they did the 'cabins' to the south. The average shanty seems to have been about 12 feet wide by 20 feet long, with a wall height of 8 feet or eight logs; it was roofed with 'wooden troughs': halved cedar logs hollowed out and laid alternately with one trough up and the next inverted. Two men, handy with an axe, could put up a shanty in two days. In his *Travels in North America, 1827–1828*, Basil Hall wrote that he contracted with two men to have his house built. It was to be thirteen logs or the equivalent in feet high, 20 feet wide, and 28 feet long. The roof was to be shingled and the gable ends boarded up; there was to be one door in the middle of one wall; and about an acre was to be cleared to make the house safe from falling trees. This sounds like a shanty – no windows are mentioned – but it was

Evan McIlraith house near Hopetown, Lanark County, north of Brockville, 1820–40. Of all the log houses inspected, this one has the greatest charm and the most 'atmosphere' of them all. The chimney is original, well-laid stone with a projecting course at the top to form a cap. A typical New England feature is the projecting stone course just above the roof junction; it acted as the equivalent of modern flashing to keep the rain away from the joint below. Its efficiency is doubtful, but it is a construction detail rarely found in Ontario.

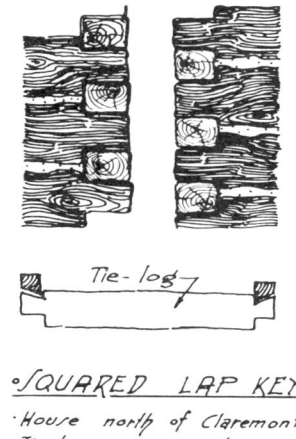

○ SQUARED LAP KEY ○
·House north of Claremont·
Tie-log across ends.

rather larger than usual. The walls of a shanty were commonly chinked with 'slats and moss,' which means that the logs were probably round (the log house at Shanty Bay illustrates this method). Squared logs require less chinking.

A shanty was, of course, considered as only a temporary building, every settler no doubt hoping to build within two or three years a more permanent log house or a frame, brick, or stone house. Many log houses were also expected to have a relatively short life. Mrs Traill describes how the log house of one family in her neighbourhood had so deteriorated after twenty years that they decided to build a frame one, holding the usual bee for the purpose. Young Strickland's log house, built by his own efforts near Peterborough in 1832, was later struck by lightning and he replaced it with a frame house on a stone foundation; his mentioning the foundation suggests that his first house rested on the bare ground. Sometimes, however, if the log house were still in good condition, a settler would not rebuild but would cover it with a brick veneer as a sign of his increasing wealth. This was particularly true for some reason during the Crimean War when farmers had several prosperous years.

The amount of care expended on building a log house largely determined its life span. Some are still in use after 150 years, but Anne Langton considered John's cabin to be in great need of repair after only eight years; it was becoming, as she said, 'crazy and cold.' On 22 November 1793, Governor Simcoe wrote to the Duke of Richmond: 'the season having been so favourable, the Troops are hutting themselves at the Post [Fort York] with great expedition: from the selection of material, I have reason to believe that they will build comfortable Barracks of log work, which will last, it is presumed, for 7 years ...'[10] (Log barracks are not to be confused with blockhouses.) It is uncertain whether he meant that seven years was the length of time the barracks would be needed or that he expected them to be structurally unsound by the end of that time. He probably meant the latter, but he was greatly mistaken in this instance, for some of these log barracks were in existence as late as 1859, when they were covered with clapboard to give them a 'semi-respectable' appearance.

For many years I was amazed at the absolute similarity in size as well as proportions between the smaller brick farm house of the 1850s and earlier log houses. The resemblance was altogether too startling. A house near Rosemont on Highway 89 provides the explanation.

Log construction 37

There were other log houses, however, which were built with the hope of their being as permanent as any other form of house. Among the many examples are Captain Steele's residence of 1833, John Langton's second house of 1837, the Smith house near Edgeley built about 1809, and the Samuel Frazer house near Midland, built about 1855. The story of this last house has a special interest. Samuel de Burgh Frazer, a nephew of the Michael Macdonnell who was private secretary to Lord Selkirk, fell in love with an eighteen-year-old girl, Amelia Jeffery, daughter of a Midland family. Samuel intended to build the best and most modern house in the district for his bride. He did most of the work himself, using the best materials and workmanship. No expense was spared: it was 42 feet long and had two storeys; eight hundred panes of glass were bought for the windows. It was ready by the appointed wedding day, and Samuel drove to the bride's home to take her to the Anglican church. However, he had forgotten one thing: Amelia was a staunch Presbyterian and insisted she be married by a minister of that persuasion; and Samuel for his part retorted that in that case he

The Samuel Frazer home near Midland, an excellent example of later sophisticated log houses. The design is very well handled indeed, the log work is first-rate, and the side lights in the first-floor windows were a sign of opulence and modernity in its day.

38  Building with Wood

would not consider himself married at all. No compromise was possible. Samuel got back into his buggy and drove off. Nobody lived in the house for years; it was later rented, but it was not kept in good repair and was finally abandoned. A bank manager bought the house about 1950 and spent a considerable sum of money renovating it.[11] Now, standing on the brow of a hill at the approach to Midland, it is one of the best-preserved log houses of its type in the province.

In the same general area, near Penetanguishene, Lafontaine, and Lefaives Corners, there are a good number of log houses which were built in the latter half of the nineteenth century – a time when there were ample building materials available other than logs. All these houses are of excellent workmanship, well proportioned, and carefully planned. They too were built to last.

'The Woods,' near Shanty Bay, was one of the larger log houses of Upper Canada; erected in 1832, the house was destroyed by fire in 1925. The floor plan, made by Edward O'Brien, is from a letter written by his wife Mary.

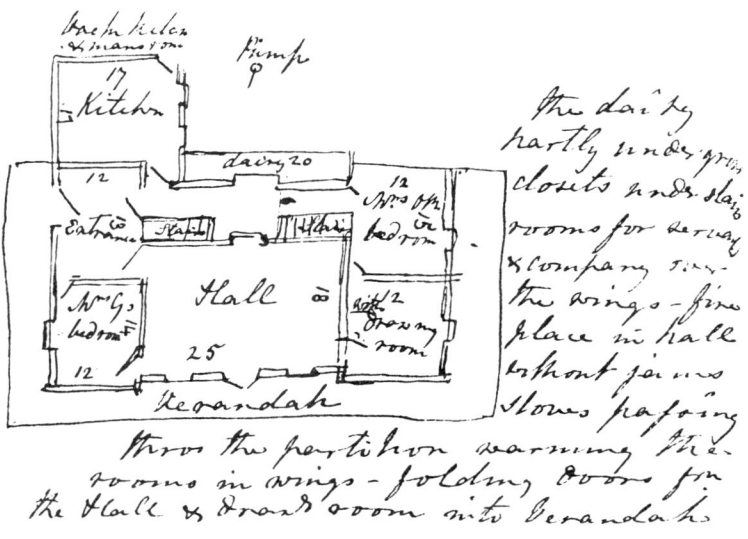

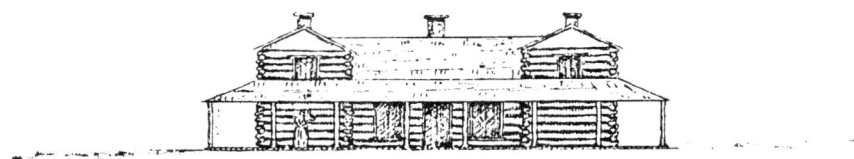

A house in Lefaives Corners built about 1870. The siding has been added at a later date. The ceiling beams are exposed, and are about 8 inches in the round. There is no provision for a fireplace since this house is quite late. The windows have the upper sash fixed with no parting strip; the muntin bars are quite heavy with plain bevelled sides rather than moulded.

A typical house in Lafontaine, built in 1870, follows the usual three-room plan with a stair in the rear left corner and has either one or two chimneys beginning at the first-floor ceiling. The ceiling joists are done in the English manner, being fairly closely spaced with a thick plank floor above. (The Continental method spaced the beams widely apart with secondary joists of lesser dimensions framing at right angles into the primary ones, called 'summers' by the New Englanders.) The ceiling is 7 feet. The windows are double-hung with the customary twenty lights, four wide and five deep. The muntin bars are rather heavier than usual for the period, and the upper sashes are fixed permanently in the frame without any parting strip. There were no fireplaces, owing to the popularity of stoves by this time.

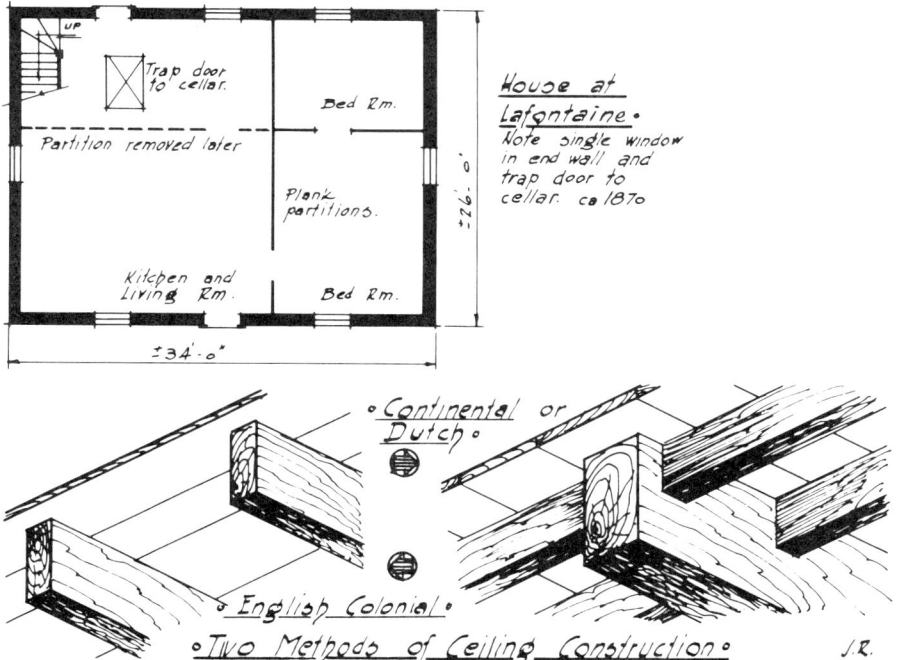

Log construction was not confined to settlers' houses and barns or soldiers' barracks; churches, schools, inns, and jails were also built from logs. Log taverns are frequently mentioned in contemporary accounts. In 1833 Barrie consisted of a log bakery, two log taverns, one of which was also a store, and a log farmhouse. London, two years later, was a settlement of some three hundred log houses with a few more pretentious frame structures[12] and one substantial building built in Gothic style of brick and stucco – the district courthouse. The London jail was of logs, the cells at the rear made doubly secure by a row of logs driven vertically into the ground against the outside walls; in the front was the courtroom, and above it – most edifyingly placed – a schoolroom. The first jail in the town of York was also of log construction. On 12 May 1798, Peter Russell wrote to Sheriff Alexander McDonell: '[in] consideration of the existing Probability that the Town of York would very soon become the Capital of a District ... I judge it my Duty during the present recess of the Council to authorize you to cause a small log building to be erected of sufficient strength and size to secure three Prisoners, and accommodate the Keeper. You will likewise be pleased to provide Handcuffs and other irons for binding gross Offenders, and stocks for punishing those who may deserve such chastisement.'[13]

The log jail on Silver Islet near Thunder Bay before it was turned into a summer cottage. It was the only log jail in Ontario at that time.

The Madill church, built in 1874, is one of the last true log churches of the nineteenth century.

A great many log houses had their life cut short not by natural causes only. Fire was the most common enemy. Not all houses were equipped with the ladders and buckets prescribed by the authorities at York, and doubtless chimneys were not swept as often as they should have been. There was also the possibility of a tree falling on the house: it is often mentioned that a shanty or house should be set in a well-cleared spot. The Radcliff *Letters* tell how one of their friends was enjoying a peaceful rest one afternoon when a tree came crashing down, flattening his house; 'he himself, by a miraculous escape, was taken out uninjured.'[14]

But the logs themselves could render a house uninhabitable or at least make its inhabitants discontented with it. Chinking rarely seemed able to prevent the entry not only of cold air but also of 'bugs' and even vermin. Bedbugs must have been a trial to nearly all the settlers, judging by the frequent references to this nuisance. On one occasion Governor Maitland visited Peterborough; the militia were on parade and guards were mounted before Government House – 'a spacious log home' so full of bugs that a special tent had to be put up outside for the governor to sleep in. John McGregor observed that 'bugs were exceedingly rare in the wooden buildings in America' whereas in England there are 'few old houses that are not infested with those loathsome vermin.' The balance of the evidence is against McGregor on this point, however; he must have been very lucky in his travels!

42  Building with Wood

Perhaps the oldest log school in Waterloo County, now preserved in the Pioneer Village at Doon. Note the door in the end wall and the typical Pennsylvania keying.

This church of the Evangelical United Brethren stands just outside Wallenstein near Elmira. It was built about 1842 and closed in 1935. Churches and schools always had the door placed centrally in one end. A nice touch of refinement is the classic wave pattern at the cornice.

Settlers also heartily disliked the tendency of log houses to dry and shrink over the years, with the consequent warping and twisting of all openings to windward. Today we demand seasoned lumber that has either lain properly out of doors for six or more months or been kiln-dried, but a settler's house was usually up and occupied within a month of the trees being cut down. Log houses contained a great amount of wood. One log house I know of was demolished and its logs sawn into boards of perfectly sound pine up to 24 inches in width: 6000 feet of lumber resulted, enough to frame several bungalows. Rot in the bottom logs, caused by constant exposure to alternate wetting and drying, commonly resulted in settling.

Larch was frequently used in the United States for foundation logs since its wood was supposed not to be as much affected by moisture as were other woods. Cedar and then hemlock were considered by the settlers to be the most durable woods in normal situations. Hemlock was also supposed to possess the peculiar property of preventing iron, driven into it, from rusting, either in the air or under water. Many settlers were quite convinced of

Settling is clearly evident in this log house built about sixty years ago.

the superiority of American timber over European, although it was conceded that American yellow pine was not as durable as Norwegian red pine, but was better adapted, all the same, for certain (unstated) purposes. Pitch pine, red pine, and larch were said to last as long as any similar European lumber.

In order to establish himself, all a settler had to do was pay £20 for his claim, own a few tools, hire several 'choppers' and a yoke of oxen, select the site for his house, and go to work. Logs were cut to length and drawn to the spot in the clearing where the house was to stand. Sometimes, of course, the logs were selected with great care, since logs of a similar diameter made cornering much easier and neater; and sometimes they were not carefully chosen and put together – even warped logs being used in a barn in the Rama Reserve.

All lands were given under certain restrictions, which varied to some extent depending on the district. Generally, the settler had to clear a minimum number of acres, open a road in front of his lot, and build a house of certain dimensions. Such settling duties, if performed within twelve or eighteen months after the location ticket had been issued, entitled the immigrant to a deed from the government, which made the lot his forever. Some of these location tickets bore rather quaint descriptions of the houses. John Clendenning, yeoman of Markham, bought lot 17 in concession VIII in October 1803 and 'built upon the same a good house of hewed and Dough-tailed Logs.' Some built a 'long house,' others a 'sufficient log house,' and others simply built a 'good dwelling house.'

Probably as good a description as any of the general procedure of building an average log house is given by John McGregor:

Habitations which the new settlers first erect are constructed in the rudest manner. Round logs, from fifteen to twenty feet long, are laid horizontally over each other, and notched in at the corners to allow them to come along the walls within about an inch of each other. One is first laid on each side to begin the walls, then one at each end, and the building is raised in this manner by a succession of logs crossing and binding each other at the corners, until seven or eight feet high. The seams are closed with moss or clay: three or four rafters are then raised to support the roof, which is covered with boards, or with the rinds of birch or spruce trees, bound down with poles tied together with withes. A wooden framework placed on a stone foundation is raised a few feet from the ground, and leading through the roof, its sides closed up with clay and straw kneaded together, forms a chimney. A space large enough for a door, and another for a window, is then cut through the walls; and in the centre of the cabin a square pit or cellar is dug, for the purpose of preserving potatoes or other vegetables during the winter. Over this pit a floor of boards, or of logs hewn flat on the upper side, is laid, and another overhead to form a sort of garret. When a door is hung, a window-sash with six or more panes of glass is fixed, and a cupboard and two or three bedstocks put up; the habitation is then considered ready to receive the

This house (TOP) has the logs thinned down to such an extent that it could fall into the class of plank houses. It is a 'neat' log house with dovetailed keying, located near Lake Couchiching on the Rama Indian Reserve. The barn (BOTTOM), with its careless construction, belongs to this house.

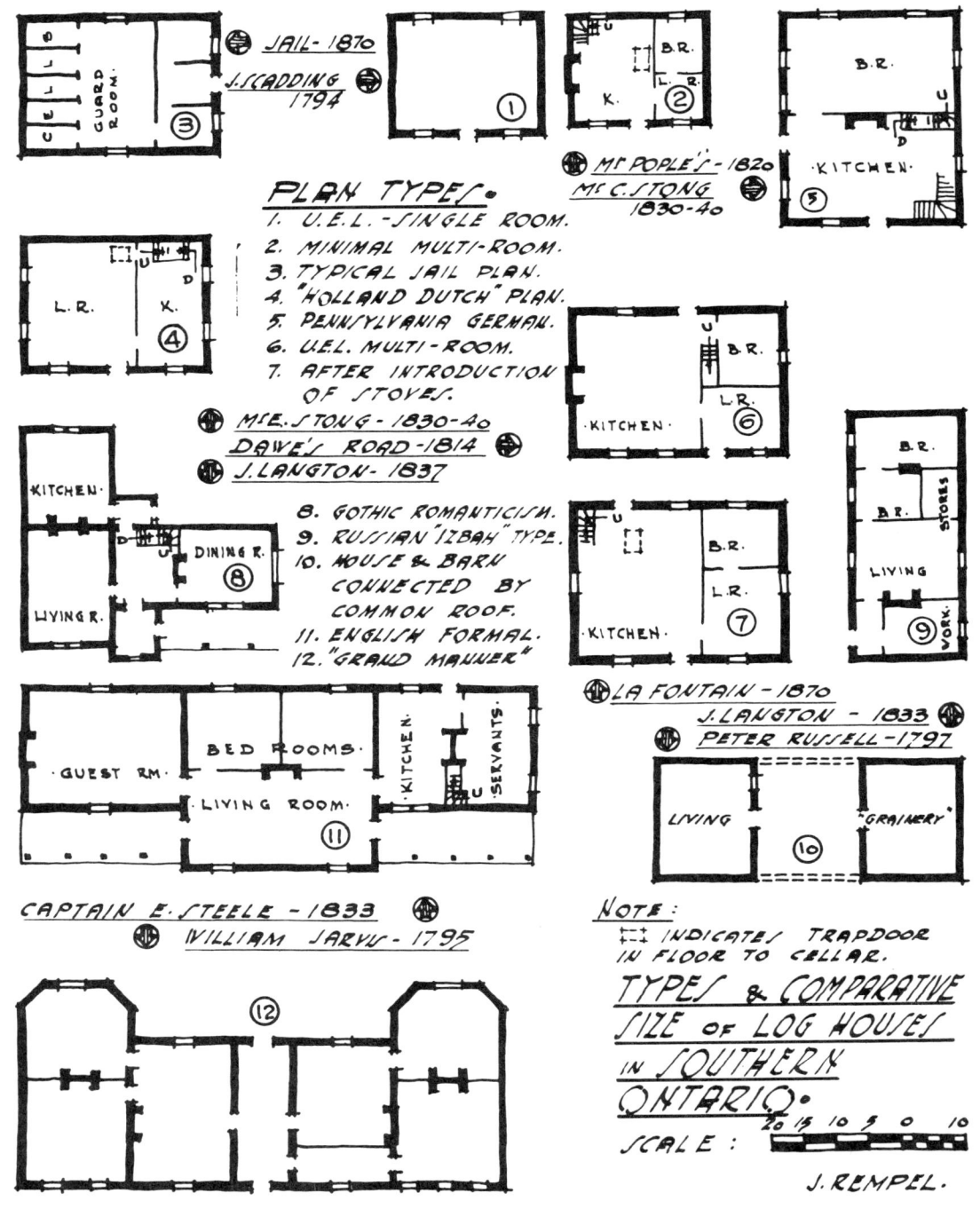

new settler and his family. Although such a dwelling has nothing attractive in its appearance, unless it be its rudeness, yet it is by no means so uncomfortable a lodging as the habitations of the poor peasantry in Ireland, and in some parts of England and Scotland. New settlers who have means build much better houses at first, with two or more rooms; but the majority of emigrants live for a few years in habitations similar to the one here described.[16]

It will be noted that the walls were put together first without any regard to doors and windows. These were cut in afterwards from outside with an axe or a cross-cut saw, and were frequently charged as a separate 'extra' if the house were built on contract. Peter Russell had to pay 4s. for each opening cut into his log houses, according to tender #2 (see below); in tender #3 the charges for cutting the logs, manufacture, and installation of a door were £1/16/0 and of a window £1/18/0. The average log house, built in three to four weeks, cost in the region of £35. Some paid as much as £50, but that figure seems to be rather out of line. The twenty-eight log houses built for the Queen's Rangers at the West Landing at Niagara cost an average of £33/10/0 each; they were of fairly typical internal dimensions – 10 feet wide by 20 feet long. Transcripts of the estimates for the construction of houses for Peter Russell, William Jarvis, and the Rangers are shown on pages 76–82.

Openings in log walls were made by drilling several large auger holes at the top corners to provide entry for a saw to cut vertically and for an axe to split horizontally. From a house in the Brougham museum, Pickering

48  Building with Wood

The wall height of the earlier house was generally eight logs – around 8 feet – but later houses were often eleven or twelve logs high. The ceiling remained at 8 feet, and the extra 2 to 4 feet in the wall allowed for a sleeping loft. The vertical part of a main wall above the first-floor ceiling and before the roof begins is called a knee wall. This trend to higher walls, like the tendency to build more and more with squared logs, admitted a great many exceptions, among which were some of the more notable log houses of the province. John Scadding's cabin, built in 1794, was nine squared logs high, and John Galt's house and office (1827) was probably ten round logs high. The house, dating from 1810–15, which stood on the former Dawes Road, Toronto, was of one and a half storeys, the wall height being eleven round logs.

Now demolished, this house stood on the corner of Dawes Road (now Victoria Park) and Ellesmere, in Toronto. It is a typical, larger-size, round-log house built about 1810–15.

# Log construction

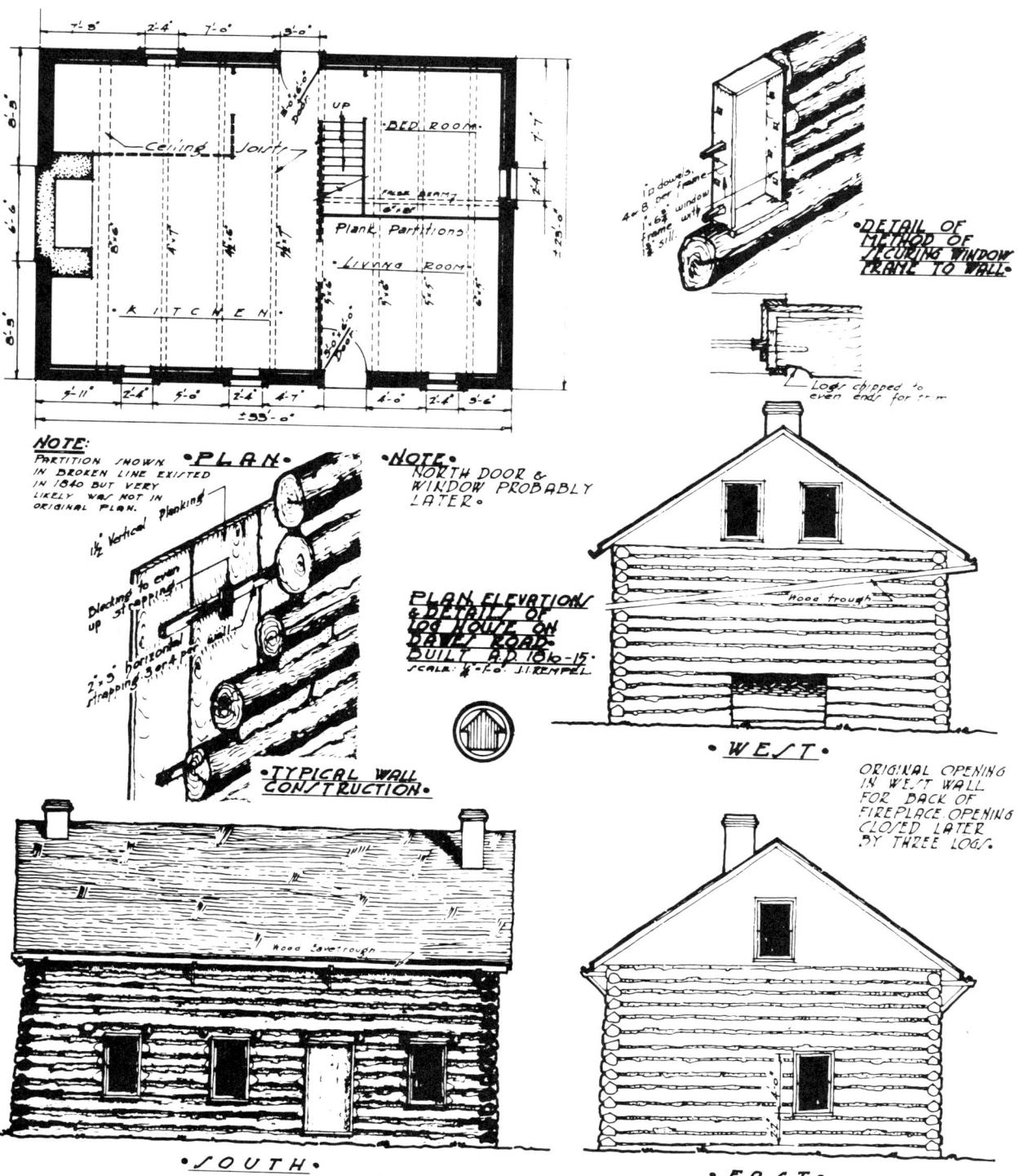

50 Building with Wood

Timbers were frequently enormous.

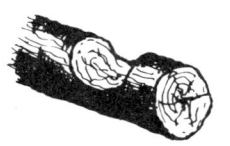

· Probably crudest form of cornering. Shanties, barns etc.

· Military type of cornering · Fort York · Scadding Cabin ·

The most efficient type of construction.
In military log construction timbers would be worked so carefully that no chinking would be required.
In residential work no such care could be exercised.
At times referred to in America as "plank-form" logs with dovetailed corners.

It is virtually impossible to say more than this about trends in log construction. Log houses cannot be dated by their method of construction or by their design, and if there are no records available on an individual house only an approximate date can be given within the sixty or so years of pioneer settlement. It is clearly possible that one settler might have graduated to a frame or even brick house whereas his neighbour, newly arrived, might just be building a log one. In 1795 the Hon. William Dickson, merchant of Niagara, asked for more land from Governor Simcoe, stating that he (Dickson) had erected the first brick house in the province.[17] While Dickson was building his brick house, the Scaddings, Playters, and Coons were settling at the mouth of the Don River, and John Scadding was building his 'neat' log cabin. In 1818 D'Arcy Boulton built his beautiful brick house, now The Grange, in Toronto; Chief Justice Campbell built his brick residence on Duke Street in 1822. Both houses are of the highest order of design. Eleven years later, in 1833, when London consisted of three hundred houses and boasted two newspapers, the *Sun* and the *Advocate*, the Radcliffs pioneered in Adelaide, a few miles away. In Kincardine Township pioneering went on as late as 1851, by which time Toronto had produced such fine buildings as the Bank of Upper Canada on Frederick Street and the Normal School on Gould Street, and Cobourg had the Upper Canada Academy, supposedly the finest building in Upper Canada at the time. Consequently, no attempt has been made here to cite examples in any chronological order.

At all times the size of logs used varied greatly, from the prodigious to small, but with an average of 8 to 11 inches. In the Dawes Road log house, the diameter of the (eleven) logs was as follows, from the bottom up: 10″, 11″, 10″, 9″, 8″, 10″, 11″, 8″, 9″, 8″, 11″. The logs in John Scadding's cabin show the same range: 8″, 9″, 10″, 11″, 11″, 10″, 10″, 8″.

The problem of cornering was generally easily solved provided the logs were all of the same diameter. There were several methods of keying, of which the most common was the round notching of round logs with the ends projecting (usually not so far as in the Swedish manner) at the corners. Several variations were developed from this technique, culminating in the so-called dovetailing of squared logs. This was a very tight-fitting corner, invariably used in later military construction, and sometimes described as 'self-draining' because all surfaces of the dovetail sloped downwards and out, thus preventing any moisture from gathering (and freezing) in the joint. Typical Pennsylvania saddle-notching, used with squared logs, is rather similar to the wedge-shaped notching, for round logs, that occurs in the Woodbridge house. Lap-keying was the most unsatisfactory because it did not really provide a key at all and permitted free movement of the logs. A most unusual keying is shown on page 62, in which the keys are cut so fine that they have literally weathered away – a very unsatisfactory method indeed! No carpenter who knew anything about wood could have produced it.

One sometimes sees drawings of a keying known as double saddle-notching which show a technique that would be quite unsound for a number of reasons: it would provide a seat for any two adjacent logs at only four points instead of a whole surface; it would allow rain to gather and so rot the logs; it would create a large air space in every joint and so make it harder to keep a house airtight; and it would force a builder either to leave extra-wide vertical spaces between the logs or they would have to be cut so thin as to weaken them at the corners. No one has ever found an example of this keying in an actual building, and what seems to have happened is that the structurally sound round-notching (with a notch only on the underside of each log) has not been recognized for what it was. The apparent line of intersection would be the same, but the notching is quite different. It is an instructive example of how an error can insinuate its way into the source material and be thoughtlessly propagated by successive students.

In common round-notching or lap-keying tie-logs were used to prevent the walls from bulging out with the constant movement of the soil during the winter freeze-up and the spring thaw; they were not necessary when proper dovetailing was used at the corners. A tie-log was placed fairly high up in the wall, generally at the seventh or eighth log. In the Dawes Road house, the eighth or ninth log served as a tie-log across the front and rear. John Langton argued against a house of too long proportions because of the difficulty in obtaining long enough tie-logs.

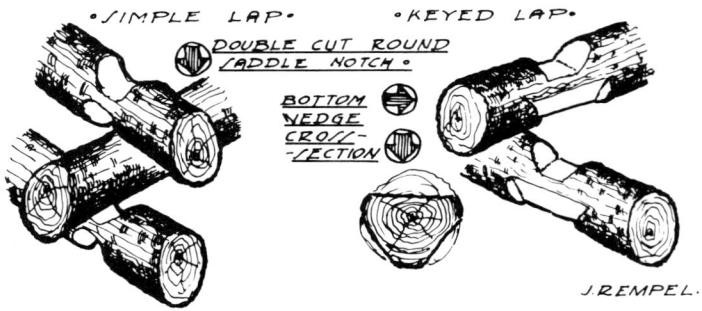

These methods of keying are both unsatisfactory since the upper notches are not self-draining.

Not too frequently used in Ontario. Almost as much work as military keying but with a less neat appearance from the outside. Neat corners and flat wall inside.

Log construction 53

True dovetail keying at its best. Note the careful workmanship as well as the size of the timbers. D. Stong house, 1816.

Lap-keying was most unsatisfactory: in this example near Orillia, spikes have been used to arrest the movement of the logs, obviously without success.

An example of lap-keying with a half-dovetail. It is typical of military log construction with very tight-fitting and bullet-proof logs. Practically no chinking was required. This was the blockhouse, built in 1840 to guard the locks at Jones' Falls near Kingston. It was destroyed by fire some years ago.

The house near Shanty Bay

An example of very poor keying. Note the wedge at the bottom logs and the saddle-notch at the top logs. Near Shanty Bay, demolished

There is a log house near Claremont built of large round logs of about 18 to 20 inches in diameter. The taper of the keys is almost imperceptible, as if done by accident rather than design. In such circumstances a tie-log is essential. It is about the seventh from the bottom and has a proper dovetail key. The ties in this house are across the ends, have a proper dovetail key, and are set at perhaps the seventh log from the ground. (It is not always possible to number the logs, exactly, up from the ground, since bottom logs may have rotted or been covered subsequently by topsoil or sod. It was common practice to bank sod against a log wall for drainage purposes.)

The house near Shanty Bay on Lake Simcoe, unfortunately demolished in 1943, was another interesting example of rather unusual log construction. Logs of 24 inch diameter, although not uncommon, were rarely used in the round, no doubt because of the large amount of chinking that would be required. But at Shanty Bay logs of that size were used at the bottom of the walls, with the higher logs of ever-decreasing diameter. In order to save on chinking, branches were laid between the joints before the chinking was applied. The house is also interesting because two different kinds of keying were employed: the bottom logs had a peculiar wedge-shaped key with the wedge upward, and the higher logs had the common round-notching. Other unusual features of this house were its almost square plan, its hipped roof, and, apparently, its French doors and casement windows. It must either have been built according to the strict directions of a man of means or taste, or both, or have been a builder's 'fancy'; given the squirearchical nature of that settlement, the first possibility seems more likely.

A 16 by 20 foot house, as required by the Dundas Road by-laws, seems to have been about the minimum and, indeed, the most common size. Wealth, wishes, and the size of the available timber imposed the only limits to larger dwellings. The Stewarts built a log house near Peterborough in 1823 that measured 28 feet wide and 42 feet long. The honours for the largest log house are probably shared by Captain Steele and Samuel Frazer. Frazer's house at Midland has already been mentioned as 42 feet long and two storeys high; Steele's house, built in 1833, was about 80 feet long but of only one storey. But Table 1 indicates a sample range of sizes that clearly points to 16 by 20 feet as the most prevalent. There is no reason to think that the house sizes in the townships that appear in the table differed in any way from those elsewhere in the province. We should not conclude, by the way, that these figures refer in any way to the total number of houses built in these townships in these years: the numbers quoted are for houses for which settlement certificates are now available.

The earliest form of flooring for a log house was of 'cleft' planks, smoothed with an adze, and pinned to logs laid on the ground. One of the late pioneers recalls an old log inn as having '… the floor of loose split logs, hewn into some approach to evenness with an adze; … the hearth was the bare soil, the ceiling slabs of pine wood, the chimney a square hole in the roof …' As soon as a whipsaw was acquired or a sawmill erected, however, floorboards were

## TABLE 1

Number and size of log houses according to available certificates of settlement or application of ownership for the Townships of Markham, York, Pickering, and Whitchurch. For some unknown reason, no figures are available for the year 1814 and also prior to 1802.

| Size L × W | 1802 | 03 | 04 | 05 | 06 | 07 | 08 | 09 | 10 | 11 | 12 | 13 | 15 | Total |
|---|---|---|---|---|---|---|---|---|---|---|---|---|---|---|
| 16 × 16 |   |   |   |   |   |   |   |   | 1 |   |   |   |   | 1 |
| 16 × 18 | 1 | 1 |   |   | 1 |   |   |   | 1 |   |   | 7 |   | 11 |
| 16 × 20[a] | 2 | 5 | 5 | 5 |   | 2 | 2 | 2 |   | 1 | 2 |   | 1 | 27 |
| 16 × 22 | 1 | 1 |   |   |   |   |   |   |   |   |   |   |   | 2 |
| 18 × 18 |   |   | 1 |   | 1 |   | 1 |   |   |   |   |   |   | 3 |
| 18 × 20 |   |   | 1 |   | 1 | 1 | 1 |   |   |   |   |   | 1 | 5 |
| 18 × 22[b] | 1 |   |   | 3 |   |   |   |   |   |   |   |   |   | 4 |
| 18 × 24 | 1 |   |   | 1 |   |   |   |   |   |   |   |   |   | 2 |
| 18 × 26 |   |   |   |   |   |   |   |   |   |   |   |   | 1 | 1 |
| 20 × 20 |   |   | 2 |   |   |   |   |   |   |   |   |   |   | 2 |
| 20 × 24 |   |   |   | 1 | 1 |   |   |   |   |   |   |   |   | 2 |
| 20 × 26 |   |   |   |   | 1 |   | 1 |   |   |   |   |   |   | 2 |
| 20 × 28 |   | 1 |   |   |   |   |   |   |   |   |   |   |   | 1 |
| 20 × 30 |   |   | 1 |   |   |   |   |   |   |   |   |   |   | 1 |
| 14 × 26 | 1 |   |   |   |   |   |   |   |   |   |   |   |   | 1 |
| 15 × 30 |   | 1 |   |   |   |   |   |   |   |   |   |   |   | 1 |
| Total | 7 | 9 | 10 | 10 | 5 | 3 | 5 | 2 | 2 | 1 | 2 | 7 | 3 | 66 |

a  This number includes two houses marked 15 × 20, probably by mistake.
b  This number includes one house marked 17 × 21 which are probably inside dimensions.

A type of chinking which is quite rare in Ontario. Note the carefully cut wooden wedges, tapered on opposite sides and driven up one against the other to seat them securely between the logs. This forms an excellent key for the plaster chinking, both on the inside as well as the exterior. Pioneer Village, Toronto

cut rather than cleft. It is sometimes claimed that the establishment of a sawmill brought an end to log building in the surrounding area, but this hardly seems an inevitable process. It may have been so in certain districts, but the presence of sawn lumber in the floorboards, and indeed the doors and windows, of many log houses argues against any such simple statement as 'the sawmill killed the log house.'

The inside of the walls of log houses was sometimes left rough, with more or less attention given to working in the chinking, or sometimes finished in various ways. The face might be squared in a rough sort of fashion, or covered with vertical boarding, or more rarely 'plaistered,' or – uniquely – beautifully panelled as in John Langton's home. Interior partition walls were generally of planks set vertically; as a rule these planks were tongue-and-groove with a beaded edge. In some instances, however, an owner would insist on log partitions, but this was an 'extra' for which he had to pay. Abner Miles charged William Jarvis £8 for such partitions since the logs had to be keyed into another wall at right angles for stability.[18]

  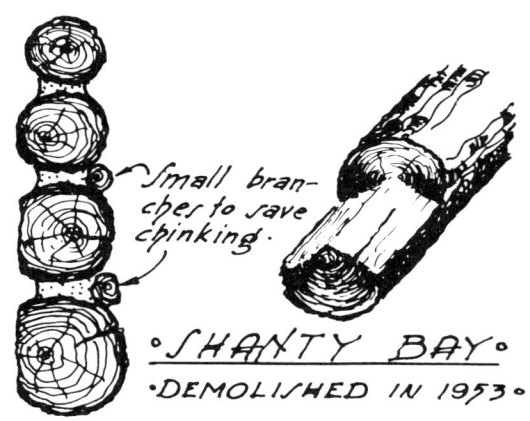

After the walls were up, the gable ends were then boarded up and the whole structure was covered with a roof. The roof could be made weatherproof in various ways. One method has been mentioned: split cedar, basswood, or black ash trunks, hollowed out, and laid in the manner of Spanish tiles with the hollows alternating up and down. Bark or shingles were also used frequently, but I have come across only one reference to clapboard as a roofing material in Ontario – on a schoolhouse in Middlesex County.

The gable roof was popularly miscalled a shed or pent roof by the early settlers. The latter name probably, but not obviously, derived from the German-settled area of America since a pent roof is a typical feature of

Interior finish varied from bare, exposed logs to plaster, paper, or panelling. This was the panelling in John Langton's home in the dining room looking towards the hall.

German and Swiss houses. It is not a roof as such, but rather a porch roof between the first and second storeys, which might run right around the house or across the gable ends or sides only. Its purpose was to protect the log or mud brick walls from the effects of rain, and it was retained on later brick and frame houses, not from necessity but as a decorative overhanging cornice. The Dutch and French also built overhanging porch roofs, but the roof was an extension of the roof proper with logs in the end walls extending beyond the walls and serving as supporting brackets for the overhang.

The smaller houses would, of course, have no ceiling. If ceiling joists were used, the space under the roof was used as storage. Ceiling joists invariably spanned the full width of the house and the ends generally rested on the sixth or seventh log, depending on the diameter of the trunks. The most common ways of seating the ends of the joists in the wall were either to fit a squared end into a square notch cut on the log carrying the joists, or to cut the top of the ends to a wedge shape which fitted in a groove cut into the underside of the log resting immediately on the joist ends. The houses at Beaverton and at Dawes Road are good examples of each method. The ceiling height was generally 7 feet. Mr Pople's cottage at Penetanguishene has a ceiling height of only 6' 8" to the underside of the loft floor, and since the ceiling joists are below the floor the clear head room is barely 6 feet. Captain Spark's cottage in Toronto was 'barely' 7 feet, and in the Dawes Road log house, owing to settling and buckling, the ceiling was only 6' 6" high at the rear and 7 feet at the front. The size of the ceiling joists varied greatly, the most common one for a round joist being about 8 inches, and for a squared one about 5 inches by 7 inches. The selection of joists was frequently most irregular. In the Dawes Road house the sizes of the ceiling joists were as follows: 8" × 6", 4" × 7", 4½" × 6", 5½" × 7", 5" × 6", 5" × 5", 6" × 5". The spacing of the joists also varied considerably, from a maximum of about 8 feet down to 3 feet. Generally the spaces were fairly evenly divided, but there seems to have been no attempt made at a reasonably even spacing. The spacing of the joists in the Dawes Road house from left to right when facing the front of the building was as follows: 4′ 0″, 4′ 3″, 4′ 0″, 3′ 9″, 3′ 3″, 4′ 0″, 4′ 0″, 3′ 0″, 3′ 6″, 2′ 0″. The spacing in a house at Oxford Mills was: 5′ 0″, 3′ 7″, 3′ 9″, 4′ 3″, and 3′ 8″. The spacing of the ceiling joist in the Stong house at Edgeley is equally irregular: 3′ 8″, 2′ 8″, 2′ 8¼″, 2′ 7″, 2′ 10″, 2′ 10¾″, 3′ 0″, 2′ 11¾″, 2′ 11″, 3′ 0½″, 3′ 1″. In the last two houses the large space at the left was reserved for the stairway.

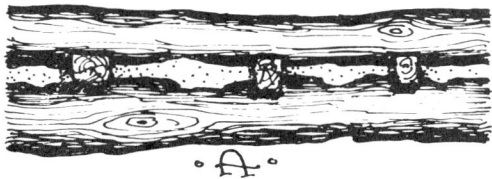
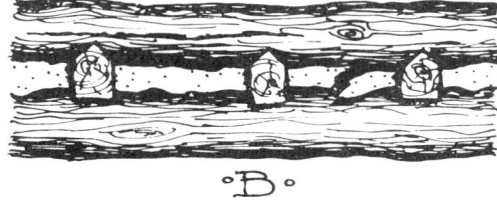

·Methods of securing Ceiling Joists·

·A· - House near Dawe's Rd.
·B· - House near Beaverton.

Unless doors and windows were made on the spot, they had to be brought in from a more or less distant sawmill. One pioneer related how, because the door had not yet arrived, her grandmother had to put a blanket over the door space to deter bears and wolves. John Langton described how he came home one evening before his first log house had its door installed to find that his servant boy had fled to the choppers, frightened by some wild animals roving about outside.

According to early settlers' memoirs, an early log school, 'rough, cold, dark and dismal,' is described as having 'but two windows of six panes of six [probably seven] by nine each.' The window openings of the Dawes Road log house also suggest two sashes of six panes each with the usual glass size of 7 inches wide by 9 inches deep. There are numerous references to panes of this size.[19] The glass was generally about 1/20 (.05) inches thick, but it varied considerably: I measured some old panes and found one whose thickness varied from .042 to .073 of an inch. The number of lights in a window ranged from six to as many as twenty-four.

The type of window in most frequent use was the 'double-hung,' common throughout Europe in seventeenth- and eighteenth-century building. It is no more airtight than the 'casement' window, but it is more weatherproof. The window frame was generally of 1 inch board with no parting strip (the narrow strip of wood separating one sash from the other and forming the centre 'tongue' for the two grooves in which the sashes slide). The frame was secured to the wall by four or eight squared treenails driven into round holes

60  Building with Wood

drilled in the log ends. There is evidence that the top sash, at least in the earlier houses, was fixed. Both sashes had plain meeting rails. The thickness of the sash varied from 1⅛ to 1⅝ inches. Before the American Revolution, window muntins were flat and as much as 1 inch wide, but they were gradually refined and seem to have measured ½ inch wide for most of the first half of the nineteenth century.

The uneven spacing of the ceiling joists as well as their variation in size is seen in the Dawes Road house.

This house near Woodbridge was demolished in 1954. Note the original window frame which was held in place by trunnels. The 'new' frame was inserted into the old one during a later alteration.

It would seem that the more knowledgeable settlers preferred the casement type of window, and occasionally even provided their log house with French doors – really an oversize casement window. Such windows were used extensively in many of the better houses in England. The Langtons used French doors, Captain Steele had French doors and casement windows at least in his living room, and the evidence points to their use in the log house at Shanty Bay. Where such doors and windows were made is difficult to say; certainly there are numerous examples of them in the predominantly frame houses of Prince Edward County.

The officers' mess in Penetanguishene, built in 1830, has casement windows with two sashes and twelve lights each. There is no mullion – the customary vertical dividing bar between two casement sashes – and the windows open inward. These idiosyncrasies appear also in the windows of the old Fairvalley church (1843), established by Captain Steele, as well as in his own log house (1833) nearby. Steele, a member of the mess at Penetanguishene, must have been favourably impressed by this type of window, and this perhaps established one of those regional and vernacular characteristics that are common and easily recognized throughout Ontario.

62   Building with Wood

Unusual but structurally unsound keying. Upper Canada Village

Wedge-shaped keying with round logs is very common.

Log construction 63

It is very difficult to find examples of keying where one interior wall joins another one at right angles. The search for examples leads into strange places: here is part of the pig house of the D. Stong farm before restoration.

64   Building with Wood

To have the porch roof form an integral part of the structure is not typical of Ontario construction. This house, Peter McArthur's now in Pioneer Village, Doon, might show some French influence in this respect. The overhang at both front and rear is especially rare.

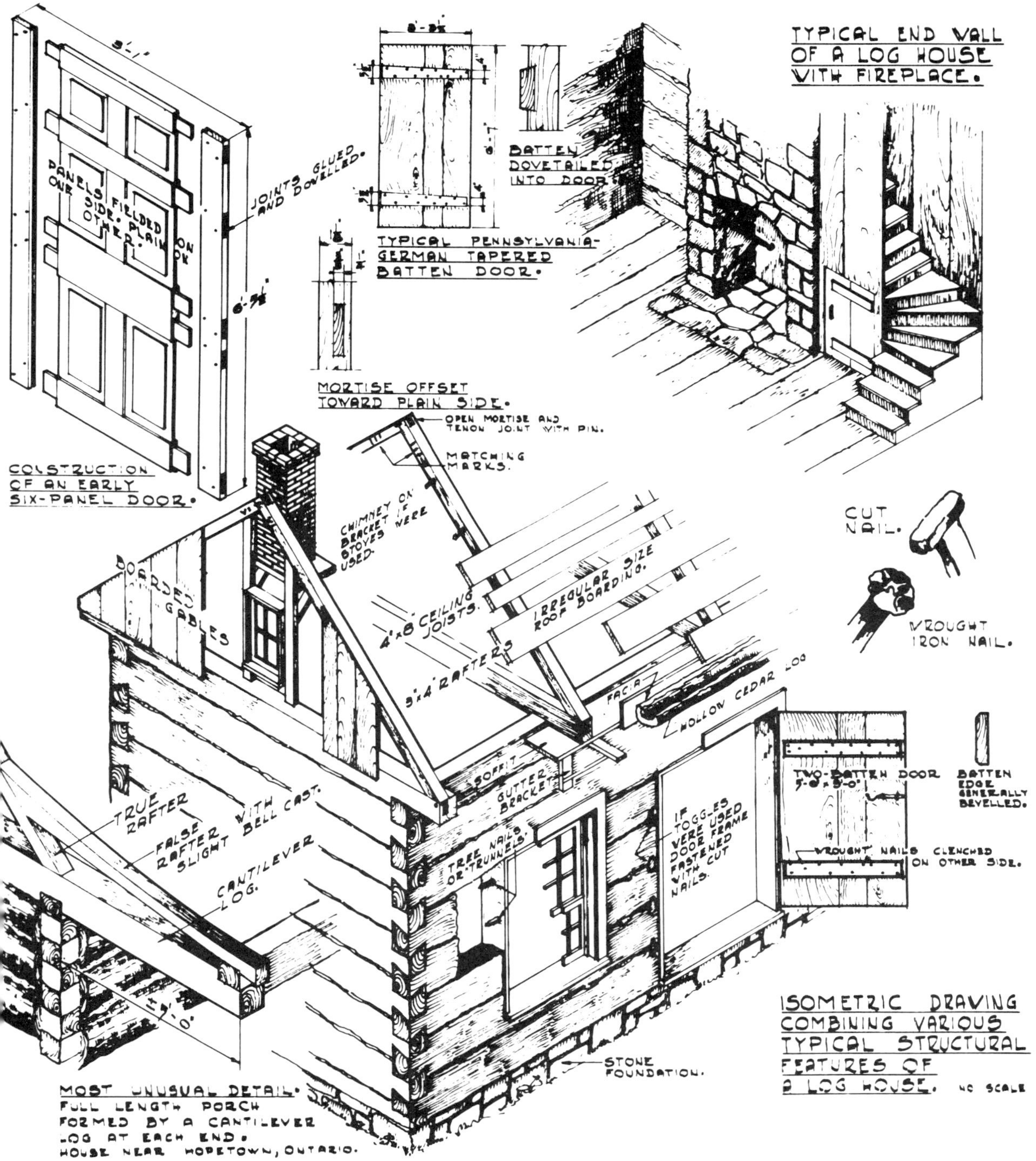
PANELS FIELDED ON ONE SIDE. PLAIN ON OTHER.
JOINTS GLUED AND DOWELLED.
CONSTRUCTION OF AN EARLY SIX-PANEL DOOR.
TYPICAL PENNSYLVANIA-GERMAN TAPERED BATTEN DOOR.
BATTEN DOVETAILED INTO DOOR.
MORTISE OFFSET TOWARD PLAIN SIDE.
TYPICAL END WALL OF A LOG HOUSE WITH FIREPLACE.
OPEN MORTISE AND TENON JOINT WITH PIN.
MATCHING MARKS.
CHIMNEY ON BRACKET IF STOVES WERE USED.
BOARDED GABLES
4"x8" CEILING JOISTS.
IRREGULAR SIZE ROOF BOARDING.
3"x4" RAFTERS
FACIA
HOLLOW CEDAR LOG
CUT NAIL.
WROUGHT IRON NAIL.
SOFFIT
GUTTER BRACKET
TWO-BATTEN DOOR 7'-0" x 3'-0"
BATTEN EDGE GENERALLY BEVELLED.
WROUGHT NAILS CLENCHED ON OTHER SIDE.
TRUE RAFTER
FALSE RAFTER WITH SLIGHT BELL CAST.
CANTILEVER LOG.
TREE NAILS OR TRUNNELS.
IF TOGGLES WERE USED DOOR FRAME FASTENED WITH CUT NAILS.
STONE FOUNDATION.
ISOMETRIC DRAWING COMBINING VARIOUS TYPICAL STRUCTURAL FEATURES OF A LOG HOUSE.
NO SCALE
MOST UNUSUAL DETAIL.
FULL LENGTH PORCH FORMED BY A CANTILEVER LOG AT EACH END.
HOUSE NEAR HOPETOWN, ONTARIO.

An original stone chimney in a log house in Prince Edward County. Date unknown. It was common practice to have the back of the fireplace project through an opening in an end wall in order to gain depth.

The chimneys of Ontario log houses were usually built of stone or local brick. Fireplaces were between 4 and 6 feet wide, with a hearth of stone or brick. Chimneys were entirely inside the walls, but in order to gain depth for the fireplace the back of it was frequently even with the outside face of the end wall. This necessitated an opening in the end wall – a feature common not only in a considerable number of existing log houses but also in frame houses. Some researchers claim that the reason for the opening in the end wall was that originally the chimney had been entirely outside the end wall. The only evidence for this argument is Patrick Shirreff's observation in 1835 that runaway slaves, who had settled near the boundary of the Huron Tract close to London, built log houses with the chimney entirely outside, as was the practice in the southern states from which they came: 'the chimney-stack [is] on the outside ... composed of thin sawn timber, placed horizontally, and mixed with clay.'[20] (In early construction a 'chimney' generally meant our present-day 'flue,' and a 'stack' what we call a 'chimney.') Much the same type of chimney construction is mentioned by John McGregor: 'a wooden framework placed on a stone foundation is raised a few feet from the ground, and, leading through the roof with its sides closed up with clay and straw kneaded together, forms a chimney.'[21] But since it led 'through the roof,' it was clearly not an outside chimney.

Colonel Elliott's house near Windsor showed some interesting detail in its fireplace construction and, indeed, in its walls. Elliott was an American who crossed to Windsor after the Revolution, served in the Canadian militia, and became a superintendent of Indian Affairs in the western part of the province. Three of the walls of his house were of frame construction in the typical manner of his day, but the lower part of the south wall was of squared logs butting against the uprights of the east and west walls. A chimney was built in this wall, half inside and half outside. There was another chimney in the north wall that was entirely outside it, as in the slave cabins at Dresden. This

The end wall of the original home of Daniel Stong, 1816. Note the opening, which unfortunately was closed during subsequent restoration.

house was built in 1784 but has been demolished; it is a pity it could not have been preserved since it was probably the oldest house standing in southern Ontario.

Among later log houses there was frequently no fireplace at all, the woodstove having come into common use. A window in the end wall on the ground floor replaced the fireplace. And about the same time the door began to be made somewhat larger than the old 3 or 3½ feet by 6 feet size. This change from fireplace to stove was, of course, a considerable improvement, a fireplace being a very inefficient method of heating; and since a house formerly warmed by, say, two fireplaces could now be heated by one stove, there was also some saving in expense. Anne Langton expressed amazement in one of her letters at the immense quantity of wood consumed by one fireplace.[22]

The fireplace projects through the end wall in a frame house in Brougham.

It is difficult to estimate the actual number of log houses in Ontario that are still in existence or, indeed, have existed over the last two hundred years. The last census to differentiate wood houses into shanties, log, and frame was taken in 1861, and the next census, in 1891, did not make any analysis at all of the figures for wood houses. The 1861 figures (Table 2) show in general that, compared with the figures for 1851, the number of log houses was declining both absolutely and relatively in the townships nearer to the northwest of Toronto; only in Erin and Caledon townships was there an absolute increase in their numbers. In these two townships log houses still outnumbered all others by two to one during the fifties. This ratio seems to have prevailed in the province as a whole around 1832 and was perhaps even larger in the three or four decades before. The 1832 figure is based on returns given by John McGregor of 42,857 dwellings of all descriptions in that year and of 14,297 superior (frame, brick and stone) houses recorded in the census of 1831, giving an almost exact proportion of two to one in favour of log houses.[23]

The earliest returns we have of dwellings in Ontario are those for the Town of York in 1807, 1808, and 1809 (see Table 3). Log houses increased in number by 25 per cent between 1807 and 1809; but by 1834, when York was incorporated as the city of Toronto, there were only nine log houses designated as such within the city limits. (There are still, according to the Metro-

TABLE 2
Extracts from census returns of houses in Ontario

| Township | Type | 1851 Number | 1851 Percent | 1861 Number | 1861 Percent |
|---|---|---|---|---|---|
| Toronto | Shanties | 89 | 7.7 | | |
| | Log | 367 | 31.8 | 248 | 24.0 |
| | Others | 698 | 60.5 | 785 | 76.0 |
| | Total | 1154 | 100.0 | 1033 | 100.0 |
| Chinguacousy | Shanties | 87 | 7.3 | | |
| | Log | 672 | 58.2 | 496 | 46.4 |
| | Others | 398 | 34.5 | 574 | 53.6 |
| | Total | 1157 | 100.0 | 1070 | 100.0 |
| Esquesing | Shanties | 4 | 0.2 | | |
| | Log | 378 | 47.4 | 290 | 31.7 |
| | Others | 415 | 52.4 | 624 | 68.3 |
| | Total | 797 | 100.0 | 914 | 100.0 |
| Caledon | Shanties | 34 | 7.9 | | |
| | Log | 340 | 79.0 | 427 | 66.4 |
| | Others | 56 | 13.1 | 217 | 33.6 |
| | Total | 430 | 100.0 | 644 | 100.0 |
| Erin | Shanties | 20 | 3.4 | | |
| | Log | 428 | 73.3 | 488 | 63.2 |
| | Others | 136 | 23.3 | 285 | 36.8 |
| | Total | 584 | 100.0 | 773 | 100.0 |

Courtesy of the Department of Planning and Development, Province of Ontario

TABLE 3
Extracts from York's assessment roll

|  | 1807 | 1808 | 1809 |
|---|---|---|---|
| Town lots | 131 | 132 | 172 |
| Round logs[a] | 19 | 21 | 14 |
| Square timber, one storey | 6 | 4 | 11 |
| Additional fireplaces | 8 | 15 | 37 |
| Square timber, two storeys | 15 | 20 | 27 |
| Additional fireplaces | 38 | 44 | 64 |
| Frame, under two storeys[b] | 55 | 52 | 55 |
| Additional fireplaces | 52 | 40 | 58 |
| Stills | 60 | 58 | 58 |
| Billiard tables |  | 2 | 2 |

a No additional fireplaces are mentioned for this type because these were houses of the poorer citizens who could not afford the expense of another fireplace as well as the extra tax which every additional fireplace entailed.
b For some reason no frame houses are mentioned of two storeys in height. The number of stills and billiard tables are included purely for atmosphere and as an indication of a scale of values in those years.
SOURCE: Robertson, *Landmarks of Toronto*, II, 995

politan Toronto Conservation Authority, about three dozen log houses in the metropolitan area, but they are so changed by additions and alterations as to be unrecognizable as such.) The 1834 statistics, however, do not give a completely accurate impression of the number of actual log buildings, since they exclude such buildings as stables, barns, fodder storage sheds, and so on, many of which were built of logs. In all areas except those settled by the Pennsylvania Germans with their huge banked barns, the main outbuilding on farms would be a two-bay centre-door log barn with other smaller log buildings erected as required. Anna Jameson described in her diary how

Log barns on Eric Salter's farm near Franktown

around Colonel Talbot's house, built between 1803 and 1812, there were 'a variety of outbuildings of all imaginable shapes and sizes, and disposed without the slightest regard for order or symmetry.' This was typical of the farms of the English, Irish, and Scots: Eric Salter's farm on Pinery Road near Franktown, for example, contained eleven such outbuildings.

Probably the best known of Toronto's log houses was Castle Frank, the summer home of Governor Simcoe. It was built in 1794 and stood on the brow of the west bank of the Don River near the present Bloor Street Viaduct. Its construction was rather interesting in that the walls were built of horizontal logs, but instead of the usual cornering the French method was used whereby the ends of the log are cut in the shape of a tenon which fits into a groove running the full length of a vertical corner post. The overall measurements of this house were about 30 feet wide and 50 feet long.

Lambeth Palace, the residence of Captain Shaw, standing less than half-a-mile north of Queen Street and several hundred yards northwest of the old

Log construction ranged from the crudest log shanty near Chapleau to the sophisticated 'Beehive' near Fenelon Falls (OPPOSITE).

Trinity College, was another famous log building. So too was the Tecumseh Wigwam, a 'drinking place' on the northwest corner of Bloor and Avenue Road built about 1820 and demolished in 1874. And one of John Scadding's cabins built in 1794 of squared logs has been preserved by the York Pioneer and Historical Society in the Exhibition Grounds in Toronto.

One of the oldest log houses to be lived in within the city limits of Toronto was probably that of old Captain James Spark. His cottage stood just north of Queen and Broadview and was supposed to have been built about the same time as Castle Frank. It stood 'in its own garden, and was designed more for use than ornament. The ceilings are barely seven feet from the floor and the walls, which are of squared timber, are about eighteen inches deep. It possesses no hall, the front door opening directly into the sitting room, which is an apartment about ten feet square, upon which open two decidedly small bedrooms. There is a kitchen in the rear and some sleeping apartments in the half-storey.'[24]

Toronto's first jail was also of log construction; it stood on the south side of King Street opposite Toronto Street. It was built in 1798 – the year of Toronto's first execution when John Sullivan was hanged for forging a note for about one dollar. A well-preserved log jail still exists, however, in the guise of a summer cottage on Silver Islet about thirty miles east of Thunder Bay. Its outside dimensions are 21 feet wide by 30 feet long. The plan provided for a narrow centre entrance at the east end with a small office, 9 feet deep and 7 feet wide with one window, on each side. At the west end were five cells, 3' 9" wide by 7' 4" long with no outside windows. The doors, of solid 2 inch oak planks, were 26 inches wide and 81 inches high, with an opening 16 inches wide by 22 inches high, covered with four iron bars ¾ inch in diameter. Between the cells and the front offices was a common room 10 feet wide, extending the full width of the building; it contained two windows, one at either end. Both windows were 35 inches wide and 54 inches deep, barred with nine ¾ inch iron bars. Cells and common room were lined with 2 inch white oak planks, tongued and grooved, and nailed with square handmade iron spikes. Hinges were all iron strap made from ½ inch stock. The door strap was 24 inches long and the wall straps, slightly curved and two per hinge, were 19 inches long. There were twelve bolts per hinge.

Among the other notable log buildings in Ontario, apart from those already mentioned, were: John Galt's first house and office (c. 1827), now only a few logs in the backyard of a farm near Guelph; the unique log schoolhouse saved by the Waterloo Historical Society; the collection preserved by the Metropolitan Toronto Conservation Authority in its Pioneer Village; and the 'Beehive' near Fenelon Falls, still in excellent state of repair though somewhat mutilated by alterations. We should, I suppose, be grateful that we have as many of these old houses preserved for us and our descendants as we do; but it is still disappointing that efforts to raise a sum of $30,000 required to restore Captain Steele's residence were in vain and that posterity must be content with a small monument of stones and timber salvaged from the ruins.

A derivative of the more conventional log work, generally referred to as 'log-butt' construction, or 'stovewood' in the vernacular, was used at the beginning of the twentieth century. In this method, short log butts, in the round, were laid in lime mortar. Generally 8 to 12 inches long, the butts were laid across the wall with the ends exposed on the outside. Cornering, of course, created a problem, which was solved in one of two ways: either a 6 to 8 inch square post was set upright in the corners, or 3 to 4 foot long squared timber was laid horizontally with the ends crossing each other in the manner of quoins in masonry. In some barn foundation walls the corner timbers were the full width of the walls, perhaps because of the heavy loads imposed on them; in a blockhouse in Hull, Quebec, a double set of corner pieces was used in the manner of cribwork. Both methods provided a stable corner against which the butts were laid. The use of split logs was definitely less common in log-butt construction than that of logs in the round, and the size of the logs does not seem to have mattered at all. Around doors and windows split logs were laid directly against the frames as in regular masonry work. Log-butt construction was not widespread and had a very brief life span indeed; it appears to have been of an experimental nature rather than a traditional method of building.

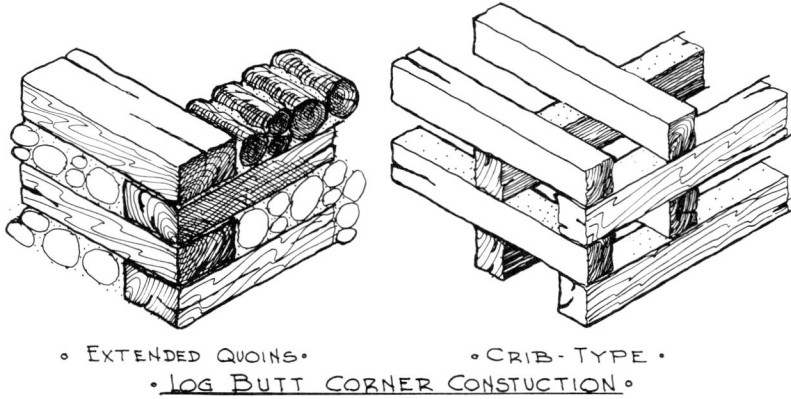

∘ EXTENDED QUOINS ∘        ∘ CRIB-TYPE ∘
∘ LOG BUTT CORNER CONSTUCTION ∘

In the last few generations log construction has been seen more and more in a romantic and sentimental light. Several feeble attempts have been made in this century to revive this method of building, but they have died out after a short duration. The reason for the continuing interest, perhaps, is that log construction is a complete anachronism, entirely out of step with modern planning, building materials, and requirements for daily living. To the pioneer it was purely a matter of expediency, for nothing was further from

Perhaps the most ambitious log-butt construction. Hull, Quebec, date unknown

Longford Mills. Note the posts in the corners which save awkward mitering of logs; logs were generally 12 inches long and laid in lime mortar.

Log-butt construction is a type of building with logs that has persisted into the twentieth century.

his mind than sentiment. It is true that for him, because of an overabundance of wood, it was the most efficient and least costly form of construction. But today the very opposite is true, and the romantic aspect of it is the only reason for its employment. It is also difficult to imagine log construction alongside hot and cold running water, dishwashers, indoor plumbing, and electric heat. The extent to which this sentimental attachment has taken hold of the public, however, can be seen in the fact that several entire summer resorts in Ontario and Quebec have been built with logs. And then there is James McQuat's 'castle' near Atikokan, which would have served an admirable purpose in Anglo-Saxon or Viking days; but in the twentieth century it can be seen only as a novelty or curiosity, like the three-storey 'log skyscraper' in Whitehorse constructed by American servicemen during the Second World War. Who knows but that after a third world war we may have to begin again with the cave, Adam and Eve, and the apple!

'White Otter Castle,' built by James McQuat near Atikokan at the beginning of this century.

## Some structural specifications for log houses

The following tenders, agreements, and bills of materials are direct extracts from the original Russell and Jarvis papers in the Archives of the Metropolitan Toronto Library, and are published by permission of Mr H.C. Campbell, former Chief Librarian. The tenders submitted to Peter Russell are dated 1785 and 1786, and specify neither location nor builder.

Not all specifications were as brief and general as these; certainly those for military establishments and for larger buildings were more specific. But, on average, the construction vagueness and brevity are characteristic. The legal aspects of building contracts and specifications were far more advanced in early Quebec than in Ontario because of the nature of the beginning of settlement in the two colonies; whereas the French simply transported their governmental, legal, and judicial systems into the new land, the settlers in Ontario, more independent and individualistic, tended to follow the precedents set in the New England colonies. By the middle of the nineteenth century, however, a much more businesslike approach was evident in Ontario.

RUSSELL PAPERS

Tender #1

Proposal to Build two log Houses for His Honnour Peter Russel. The Houses to be 16 by 20 foot Each and a Space betwixt of 16 ft more Which makes the Roof 48 footlong, The Roof to be Boarded and Shingled, The Gable Ends to be Studed and Wetherboarded With Rough Boards

   To be 7 joists 5 by 9 Inches for the Grainery floor 20 foot long
   To be 15 pair of Rafters 14 ft long 4 by 6 Inches and 15 Collarbeams 12 ft long 3 by 6
   To be 4 plates 20 ft long 7 by 8 Inches 4 Dto 16 ft long 7 by 8 Dto for the Rafters to Stand on
   To be 2 plates 18 ft long 8 Inches by 9 Dto for the Space betwixt the two houses
   The Gable End Studs to be 3 Inches by 4 Dto

For the 2 houses I propose to Cut the logs and lay them up 12 feet high and put in the joists for the Grainery floor for 20.0.0
I propose to Frame the plates Rafters & Gable End Studs for 16/pr 100 ft
The Scantling to be Sawn at the Mill
I propose to Board and Shingle the Roof for 18/pr Square and the Rough Wether Boarding at 10/pr Square and Barge Boards at 3 pr foot

   *the Bill of Scantling for the Above Work*
   | | |
   |---|---:|
   | 7 joists 20 foot long 5 Inches by 9 Dto | 140 |
   | 4 plates 20 ft long 7 In by 8 Dto | 80 |
   | 4 Dto 16 ft long 7 In by 8 Dto | 64 |
   | 2 Dto 18 ft long 8 In by 9 Dto | 36 |
   | 30 Rafters 14 ft long 4 In by 6 Dto | 420 |
   | 15 Collar Beams 12 ft long 3 In by 6 In | 180 |
   | 150 foot of Scantling for Gable End Studs | 150 |
   | | 1070 |

Log construction

*Value of the Work*

|  | £ | s | d |
|---|---|---|---|
| 1000 foot of Scantling Framing at 16/pr 100 ft | 8 | 0 | 0 |
| 13 Square and a half of Shingling at 18/pr Square Boarding included | 12 | 3 | 0 |
| 4 Square of wether Boarding at 10/pr Square | 2 | 0 | 0 |
| 56 Foot of Barge Boards for the Gable Ends at 3d pr foot Running | 0 | 14 | 0 |
| Cuting the logs for the two houses and laying them up | 20 | 0 | 0 |
| N.Y.C. [*] | £42 | 17 | 0 |

*Value of Lumber*

|  | £ | s | d |
|---|---|---|---|
| 1070 foot of Scantling at 16/pr 100 ft | 8 | 11 | 6 |
| 1300 ft of Refuse Boards at 6/pr 100 ft | 3 | 18 | 0 |
| 6000 Shingles at 40/pr 1000 | 12 | 0 | 0 |
| N.Y.C. | £24 | 9 | 6 |
|  | 42 | 17 | 0 |

*Sum Total*  N.Y.C.  £67  6  6

Tender #2

| Estimate to Build a log House 20 feet long 16 feet Wide and 11 feet High | £ | s | d |
|---|---|---|---|
| Cuting hawling and puting up logs | 6 | 8 | 0 |
| Frameing 428 feet of Scantling at 14/pr 100 feet For Joists Rafters and Gable End Studs | 1 | 19 | 6 |
| To 5 Squares of flooring at 8/ laid Rough | 2 | 0 | 0 |
| 450 Feet of Boarding and Shingling the Roof at 16/pr 100 | 3 | 12 | 0 |
| 150 Feet of Wether Boarding at 10/pr 100 ft | 0 | 15 | 0 |
| To cuting out logs for one Door and one Window at 4/ | 0 | 8 | 0 |
| To making one Door frame and Two Window frames at 8/ | 1 | 4 | 0 |
| To making Two twelve light Sashes at /9d pr light | 0 | 18 | 0 |
| To making one Ledge Door Grove and tongue 10/ | 0 | 10 | 0 |

*Below is Expence of lumber for the above Work*

|  | £ | s | d |
|---|---|---|---|
| 555 Feet of one Inch and quarter floor Boards at 9/pr 100 | 2 | 9 | 6 |
| 500 Feet of Refuse Boards at 6/pr 100 feet for the Roof | 1 | 10 | 0 |
| 200 Feet of Wether Boards at 6/pr 100 for gable Ends | 0 | 12 | 0 |
| 100 Feet of 1¼ In Boards for Door frame Sash frame Step ladder Barge Boards and Ridge Board | 0 | 9 | 0 |
| 3000 Shingles at 20/pr 1000–18 Inches long | 3 | 0 | 0 |
| 428 Feet of Scantling Sawing and hawling at 14/pr 100 | 1 | 19 | 6 |
| N.Y.C. | £27 | 14 | 0 |

Rafting and Halling included

* New York Currency, in which £1 equalled $2.50 (20 shillings to the pound and 8 to the dollar) and exchanged for 10 shillings sterling. Also current, and eventually triumphant, was Halifax currency, in which £1 equalled $4.00 and exchanged for 16 shillings sterling. Add to this the fact that the circulating coins came from the world over and the paper money was mercantile notes. It must have been rather confusing.

### Tender #3

Proposal to Build a log House Twenty feet long and Sixteen[*] feet Wide from out to out the logs to be laid 10 foot high to be one Door and one Window below, and one Window in the Gable end above, The Window below to have 20 lights and the Window above to have 12, the Door to be made of Inch boards Groved and Tongued the lower Floor to be plained Groved and Tongued the upper floor to be laid Roughf To be Seven Sleepers in the lower floor and Seven joists in the upper floor to be 7 pair of Rofters in the Roof to be Covered With Refuse Boards the Gable Ends to be Studed and Wether-boarded and the Roof to be Shingled and Barge Boards on the Gable Ends

|  | £ | s | d |
|---|---|---|---|
| I propose to Cut the logs and put them up for 20 Dollars | 8 | 0 | 0 |
| 480 foot of Scantling at 20/pr 100 ft | 4 | 12 | 0 |
| 500 foot of Refuse Boards at 6/pr 100 ft | 1 | 10 | 0 |
| 700 foot of 1¼ Inch Boards at 10/pr 100 | 3 | 10 | 0 |
| 460 ft of Scantling frameing at 16/pr 100 ft for Roof floor & Gable ends | 3 | 13 | 6 |
| 5 Square of Shingling at 16 pr Square | 4 | 0 | 0 |
| 5 Square of Rough Boarding the Roof at 4/pr Square | 1 | 0 | 0 |
| 2 Square of Wetherboarding the Gable Ends at 10/pr Square | 1 | 0 | 0 |
| 3 Square of Grove and Tongue flooring at 20/pr Square | 3 | 0 | 0 |
| 3 square of Rough flooring plain joint at 10/pr Square | 1 | 10 | 0 |
| Cuting out the logs for the Door making the Door and frame & fixing | 1 | 16 | 0 |
| To making and fixing the lower Window and frame and cuting out logs | 1 | 18 | 0 |
| To making and fixing the upper Sash and frame | 1 | 4 | 0 |
| N.Y.C. | £36 | 13 | 6 |

JARVIS PAPERS

### Agreement #1

Newark 26th August 1794

An agreement between Wm Jarvis Esq on the one part and Abner Miles on the other part which is as follows –

The Said Abnor Miles agrees to build a Log House of Square pine Timber at or near the Town of York on Lake Ontario agreeable to the plan herewith annexed and at the prices hereafter mentioned –

---

* A correction seems to have been made in this figure as the number 18 is written directly above the sixteen.

|  | £ s d |
|---|---|
| Shingles | 28.0.0 |
| Bricks for four chimneys | 48.0.0 |
| Timber | 130.0.0 |
| Underpining the House | 8.0.0 |
| Building four Chimneys | 12.0.0 |
| Persons to attend the Masons | 12.0.0 |
|  | 238.0.0 |
| Log Partitions[*] | 8.0.0 |
|  | 246.0.0 |
| Digging and Walling the Cellar | 10.8.0 |
|  | 256.8.0 |

The logs to be laid up the thickness of [*illegible*]. The said Miles is to find the bricks & fill in between the Logs & the said Jarvis is to find the Lime to make the Morter to lay said between the Logs, to build the Chimneys & point the underpining of the House.

The Logs to be seven (inches) thick and squared on all sides – to be built fourteen feet high sixty eight feet Long, built in three divisions viz. the two wings to be each thirty four feet by twenty four feet – the Center Division to be twenty feet square – The Roof to be shingled on Board the said Jarvis to find said boards and Nails – the Shingles to be 18 Inch & of the best quality & to be laid in the best manner. The House to be raised three feet from the Ground – one foot to be stone the other two feet to be logs below the sills. To build four Chimneys, two at the end of each wing with two fireplaces in each Chimney, the said Jarvis finding Lime and Iron Bars for the Chimneys & the said Miles to find every other requisite. The lower story to be ten feet high and the upper story to be four feet high to the top of the Plate. The Roof to be hipped. The partitions in the Lower Story to be Logs Six Inches thick and to be doughtaled at each end. The Cellar to be under the Center division twenty feet Square and seven feet deep to the sleepers and to be walled up with stone.

The said Jarvis and the said Miles farther agree that the said Jarvis shall be at liberty to add or diminish the said building as occasion may require, at the same time increasing or diminishing the expense of the building in a fair and equitable proportion.

---

* He seems to have raised this price to £10.0.0 later.

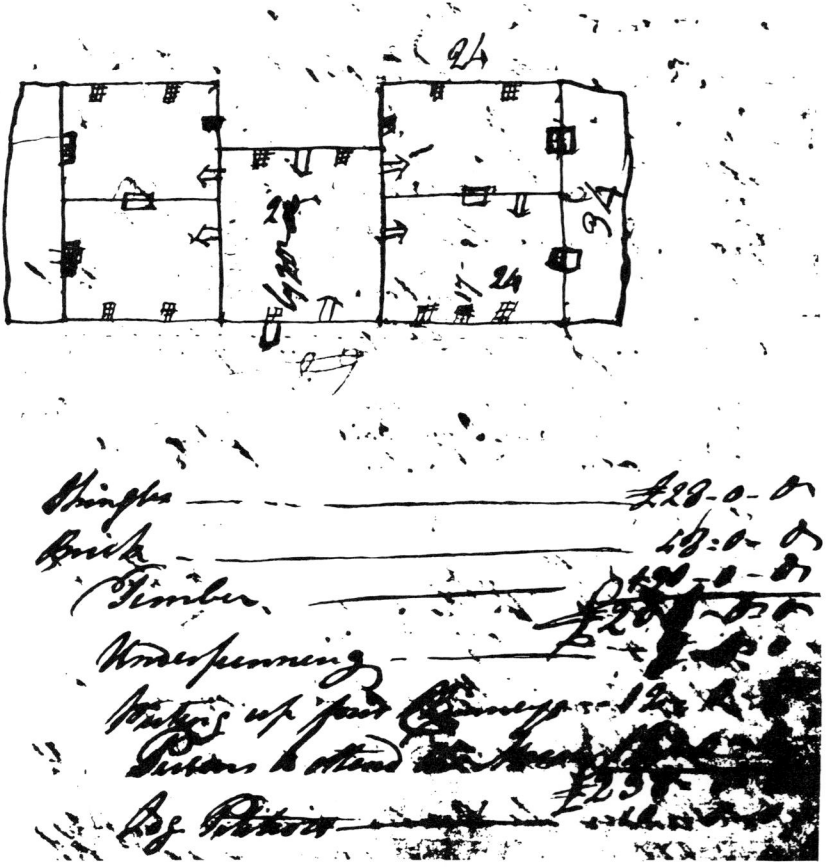

This sketch plan appears on the back of agreement No. 1 between William Jarvis and Abner Miles, builder, dated 1794. The house 'to be built at or near the Town of York.'


Agreement #2

Agreement between Wm Jarvis Esq. on the one part and David Seely on the other part which is as follows – the said David agrees to Dig a Cellor for the said Wm 24 by 22 for the sum of twenty three pounds N. York currensy to find the Stone, & Stone the cellor up, the said Wm to find a pair of oxen to hawl the Stone, upon a droge which the said David is to procure at his own expense – the said David is to complete the above Job in 21 days from the Date hereof, under a penalty of ten pounds lawful Currency of this Province

Newark 7th May 1795                                                  DAVID SEELY
                                                                                                                           WM JARVIS

N.B. the two ends of the Cellor is to be 7 feet high & the sides to be 5 feet high.
                                                                                             WM JARVIS

*Bill of Materials #2*
16th Feby – 1795
   170 th. of Shingle Nails
      One hundred & Seventy thousand Nails for wether Boarding that is by Count.
      Thirty thousand of the same.
   20,000 of flower [floor] brads
   4 pair of Hinges with screws 14 in. long
   9 do rising buts
   2 Iron rim Nob Locks 9 Inches to lock to the left hand.
   1 do to lock to the right
   3 Brass chamber Mortise do to lock to the right hand
   4 do to the left hand – N.B. to distinguish the right and left hand look to the side of
      the lock that sits to the door
   900 Squares of Glass 7 by 9
   600 Cwt white Lead ground in oil in ½ Cwt Kegs
   20 galls paint oil
   100 cwt Yellow Oaker [ochre]
   200 Spanish whiting
   1 Brass Door Knocker
   1 Gross 2 Inch Screws
   1   do   1¾   do   do
   1   do   1½   do   do
   1   do   1¼   do   do
   1   do   ¾   do   do
   1   do   ½   do   do
   1 case 20 py Nails or about 200 cwt

*Bill of Materials #3*
Estimate of the Price of Boards
1440 feet 2 Inch Plank 6 or 7 Inches in width per 100 ft
   90   do   1¾   do   do       7/6      100 feet
   355   do   1¾     do           5/       do
   1300 do   1       do Suffrage[*]   2/6      do
   360 do   1½     do           5/6      do
   225
   300 do   1       do           4/       do
   260 do   1¼     do           6/       do
   200 do   1½     do           5/6      do
   250 do   1¼     do           5/       do
   1000 do          do           5/       do
To be forwarded by Mr McDonell & delivered
at Mr Aitkins house in the Town of Kingston.
10,000 Shingles at 12/6 a Thousand.

ALEX AITKEN

---

\*   Culls or second-grade lumber?

## Building with Wood

RANGERS' ESTIMATE[25]

Estimate of the expense of erecting twenty-eight log houses for the accommodation of the corps of Queen's Rangers at the West Landing (Niagara), as per Captain Fisher's estimate, dated Quebec, 8th October, 1792.

|  | £ | s | d |
|---|---|---|---|
| 600 logs, 26 feet each 9 in. diameter at 5s each | 150 | 0 | 0 |
| 1000 logs, 20 feet each, 9 in. diameter at 5s each | 250 | 0 | 0 |
| 400 logs, 14 feet each, for rafters, at 5s each | 100 | 0 | 0 |
| 950 feet 1½ inch pine plank, at 1s 3d each | 59 | 7 | 6 |
| 600 ¼ inch boards, at 1s 8d each[*] | 30 | 0 | 0 |
| 1,150 1 inch do, at 1s each | 57 | 10 | 0 |
| 6,000 20d nails at 14s pr M | 4 | 4 | 0 |
| 17,000 10d nails at 10s per M | 8 | 10 | 0 |
| 56,000 shingles at 45s per M | 126 | 0 | 0 |
| 84,000 shingle nails at 3s 6d per M | 14 | 14 | 0 |
| 189 barrels of lime at 9s each | 85 | 1 | 0 |
| 5,400 brick at 60s per M | 16 | 4 | 0 |
| 426 panes of glass at 6d each | 10 | 13 | 0 |
| 48 pounds of putty at 10d | 2 | 0 | 0 |
| 19 pieces of flat iron, 6 ft. long each, at 5s each | 4 | 15 | 0 |
| 8 pieces of flat iron, 5 ft. long each, at 4s each | 1 | 12 | 0 |
| 18 pieces of square iron, 6 ft. long each, at 5s each | 4 | 10 | 0 |
| 28 pairs hooks and straps at 4s pair | 5 | 12 | 0 |
| 448 feet 3 in. oak plank, 8 in. broad, at 4d per ft. | 7 | 9 | 4 |
| Total | 938 | 1 | 10 |

Each one of the houses mentioned above were to be 20'0" × 10'0" in 'the clear,' meaning inside dimensions. Eight were to be for the officers, fourteen were for the men; there were two mess and cooking houses for the officers, one bake house, and three hospital houses. From the list of materials required above, as well as from the estimate for materials required for the repair of the buildings after the war, it appears that flat lumber up to 1¼ inch thickness was called a board, above that it was a plank. Scantling was quoted at 4 × 5, or 5 × 6, both 'in the round' which could mean a round log of such dimensions that the above scantling could be cut from them to the required dimensions.

* This should probably read 1¼ inch.

## Cottage and 'izbah':
## an account of two unusual log houses built by John Langton

We are fortunate that the letters of John and Anne Langton have been preserved.[26] In their descriptions of the difficulties encountered in building and living in a log house we have a vivid picture of pioneering. The reason for following the construction of John Langton's houses here is that the structural problems and procedures followed are fairly typical, even if the actual houses in their finished form were not.

Early in August 1833 John wrote to his father in England to say that he was scouting for land in what is now the Peterborough area. There were at this time, he wrote, two 'cities' built on the principal bends on the Otonabee: Cambleton (Campbellford) and Howard, one consisting of a shanty and the other of a log house without windows. John walked upriver to Mr Stewart's place, which he described – it was a log house – as being as comfortable as an 'English cottage.' This concept of the English cottage and its supposed comfort was, as we shall see, an important part of John's dreams, although he was in other ways a most practical and intelligent man.

He had some difficulty in making up his mind what sort of house he would build himself. On 18 August he wrote to his father: 'As to the house I cannot say what it will be as I hear so many opinions, and indeed have not yet settled its nature and dimensions. No two people give the same advice. Some say a shanty is good enough; others talk of log, frame, stone, and brick houses. Franklins, cooking and common stoves and chimneys of different construction have each their own advocate. I incline myself to the regular routine: a wigwam the first week, a shanty till the log house is up, and a frame, brick or stone house half a dozen years hence, when I have a good clearing and can see which will be the best location.'

This was the plan he actually followed. He built a usual shanty with no windows, with canvas for the door and with a hole in the roof as a chimney. No windows were in fact required: the spaces between the logs were so great that when one was outside at night and a fire was going inside the shanty resembled, as he said, a 'tin lantern.'

Sometime during the early part of October that year, he chose a site near Fenelon Falls for his first log house. It was to be about 18 feet wide, 40 feet long, and – judging from Anne's sketches – eleven logs high. By Saturday, 19 October, all the logs had been cut and the walls were raised; John went down to Purdy's Mill near Peterborough to buy boards and potatoes. The total lumber bill for this house amounted to £5/2/0. Next Tuesday the roof was on; on Wednesday the walls were chinked; and on the next day, the 24th, he slept under his own roof. His main concern now was that the frost would hold off long enough to allow the mason to build the chimney – which it did.

By January, however, he admitted that the walls were still so full of holes that they let in both light and wind, the latter sufficiently to disturb the 'equanimity of [his] candle.' Later that winter he wrote that one of the advantages of a cold room is that if one spills some ink it freezes before it can spoil too much paper. And in April he mentioned that the roof was still only boards, nailed lengthwise, which admitted considerable amounts of rain. It was not, as he wrote, 'imbricated' (that is, boards did not overlap, though he might be thinking of tongue-and-groove), so presumably the joints were of the butt type; the existing roof was considered as but the underlay for some future covering. At any rate, there was not much of the comfortable English cottage about this house!

The plan of John Langton's first house is quite unusual in Upper Canada. It is derived from the Russian 'izbah' and shows the general proportions and room arrangements that characterized that kind of house. The plan was a succession of three rooms (kitchen and living room, bedroom, and storeroom) without any connecting passages. John was no doubt influenced in favour of this plan by the advice of his father, Thomas, who had been apprenticed to a merchant in Riga on the Baltic coast. Here Thomas had become well acquainted with the Russian type of log house, its construction, and its heating. He was much impressed by their careful workmanship and their efficient stoves.

After this house was built, John also put up a barn and an ice house. The ice house was half above and half below the ground. The walls were of double log construction with a foot of earth in between; the roof was of cedar slabs thatched with hemlock boughs and covered with earth from 1 to 3 feet thick.

During John's first winter in his log house, his father must have written him (in a letter no longer extant) about the slovenly ways of building in Canada. We have, however, John's reply, in which he pointed out that there was a difference between an old country and a new one and that there was a great urgency for a settler to erect even a temporary shelter. He went on to say that labour was expensive and that everyone had to be jack-of-all-trades – with the proverbial consequence. 'The cornering and hewing of a well built log house is not as nice a work as your Russian mode of fitting the logs, but the one your men have been accustomed to and the other they have never seen.' If men are asked to do something different, they have to be paid more and the work turns out worse. Besides, building a house in England or Russia, with experienced masons and carpenters to call on, with horses and carts and materials all ready to hand, is quite different from building in Canada. 'The ground has to be cleared, the logs have to be cut here and there to be carried on men's shoulders and raised to their places by mere human effort; trees have to be split and hollowed out into troughs to form the roof, boards have to be fetched from a sawmill sixteen miles off and then carried a quarter of a mile on your shoulders; the cellar has to be dug; the stones for the chimney have to be collected and carried by hand sometimes a considerable distance and, if you are unfortunately late in the season, the clay which is to cement and plaster your walls must be mixed with boiling water and

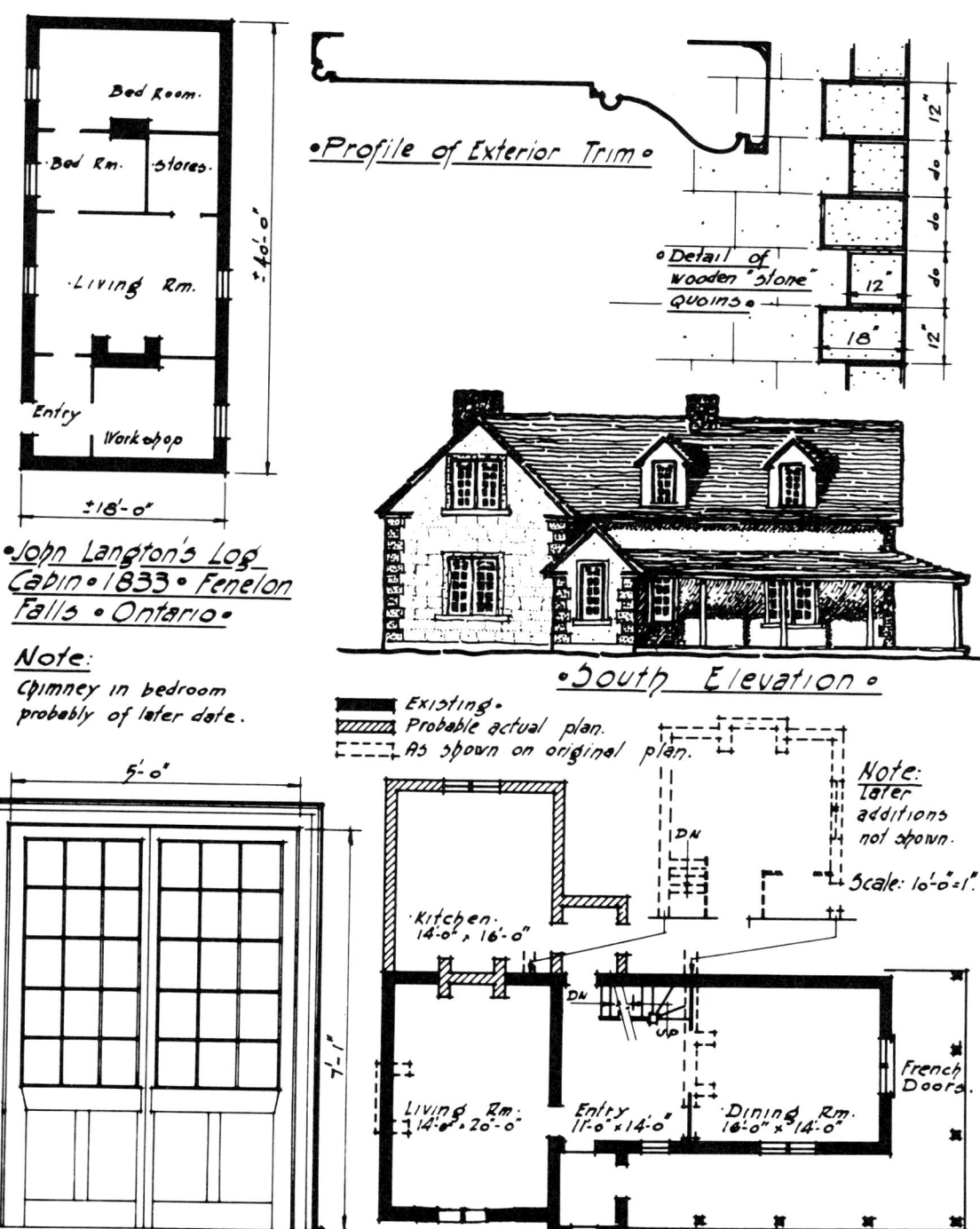

worked before a fire, and you must keep a fire in the chimney whilst building to keep your cement from freezing.' He went on to explain that, although Russian houses could be chinked with pitch, there was no such thing available in the backwoods and moss had to do. As for stoves, the Russian type was quite out of the question because it required fire brick, which was completely unheard-of in Upper Canada.

Four years later John decided on the type of permanent house that he intended to build to replace the 'izbah.' He again discussed his plans with his father, writing thus on 11 February 1837: 'The question must first be decided between log, frame or stone: the latter is too expensive and the frame houses, hardly more expensive than a good log house, are miserable shells which can never be kept warm. I therefore decided on a good log house, raised on a stone foundation to protect the lower logs, and the logs hewn square and bedded in mortar; it may afterwards be plastered or papered inside and roughcast outside. Something outside should be done to protect the timber, and the unsightliness of the rough logs inside might hereafter be obviated the cheapest by paper – not on the logs, but on canvas – though a coat of plaster would be a more effectual safeguard against vermin.'

John Langton also discussed with his father the matter of the number of storeys for his new house. John did not think that a two-storey log house was possible. He was wrong in this, there being in existence in other parts of the province log houses of two full storeys and fine Georgian proportions. But he did not, and indeed could hardly have been expected to, know about them. His house was therefore to be one and a half storeys high, with 9 feet from floor to floor or $8\frac{1}{2}$ feet from floor to the undersides of the beams. The wall height of the second floor was to be 4 feet straight and the remainder sloping, the pitch of the roof being sufficient to permit an 8 foot ceiling height.

It appears that his father must have replied suggesting a one-storey house with a corresponding and consequent increase in floor space. John now argued that such a large floor area would be very impractical from the standpoint of roof framing. It would also be uneconomical because it would require more chimneys, thereby increasing the fire hazard, and much greater roof areas subject to the attack of the weather. It would also be quite uneconomical in space, since too much of it would be lost in halls and passages (this sounds like modern planning). He argued too that structurally a rambling one-story house would meet with difficulties, since several logs would have to run the full length of the building to serve as tie-logs. Here again, he did not know that Captain Steele had built his 80 foot long house only four years before.

He seriously contemplated building a Russian stove, but the very bulk of it worried him. Besides, he was a romantic and he liked the idea of sitting by a roaring fire. However, he did consider putting such a stove in the wall

John Langton's 'English cottage' on Cameron Lake as it was in 1950.

between the living room and the hall, but nothing came of it. The size of the windows was to be determined by the kind of glass available at the time of building. Fourteen feet he considered to be the most practical width for a room, that being the length of log most readily available, and he built accordingly. His foundation walls were to be 3 feet thick, but he did not mention their depth and apparently did not consider the depth of the frostline – or if he did he badly misjudged it. His footings, as we shall see, were to give him trouble.

Work on the house began in the spring or early summer of 1837, sometime after 7 May. His father, mother, and sister Anne arrived at the end of May and moved into the new house during the summer; John insisted on staying in the old one for a while. At the end of October a letter written by Anne expresses her concern about how cold the house might be in the winter because of the lack of double windows. The glass for them had arrived, but the putty had been lost on the way. In January her fears were confirmed, though it was not the windows that caused the trouble. The logs in the walls had shrunk excessively, admitting so much fresh air that during one cold spell water froze only a few inches away from the chimney. They had a thermometer, which one cold and windy morning read 3 degrees above zero (Fahrenheit) while they were dressing. That day they went about the house with a pot of paste and some brown paper patching up the wind holes. The gables, of vertical tongue-and-groove boards, gave them particular trouble with shrinkage. The wind dropped the next day, however, and the temperature in the house rose to all of 20 degrees.

During the next few years they made various improvements, but they also had to repair many defects. In April 1838, for example, stair bannisters were put up, there having been no guard rail at all up to that time; the house was painted outside; and the front steps were built. Until then they had used sawn-off stumps as steps. During January 1841 the house was finally plastered inside, and from then on the house was apparently very warm and comfortable.

Although the house was now warm and comfortable, their troubles had not ceased. In February 1841 Anne noted that they had not been able to get into their larder owing to 'variations in the atmosphere acting upon imperfectly seasoned wood, now swelling it and destroying the perpendicularity of the doorposts, so that doors, not infrequently, will not open or shut.' Later, it was explained to her that it might have been the frost heaving the foundations which was to blame for the warped doorposts. The following year they found that the chimneys had settled so much that they had to be taken down and rebuilt. Nothing had been done about this by September, but at least one of the chimneys was completed by November. Instead of fireplaces they now installed stoves, as had been done in the parsonage of St John's Church at Fenelon Falls with great effect a few years before: water had frozen in that house only *once* during one cold January.

No matter how high the building of this house rates in terms of social history or human interest, from the point of view of architecture it rates very low. The dining room was panelled in butternut, the mouldings were very fine and delicate, and one mantel (found leaning forlornly against the knee wall upstairs) was of good proportion and design. But that is about all that can be said in its favour architecturally. The mouldings, however fine, were Georgian, whereas the house as a whole was in the semi-Gothic revival style. The original window sashes and panes were of the standard Georgian proportions, but the heads of the windows were semi-Gothic. The outside walls were roughcast and marked off in imitation stone joints. To make matters worse, wooden quoins were nailed to the corners. All exterior trim, including the quoins, was painted with a resin-saturated varnish which, when good and tacky, was sprayed with sand from a fireplace bellows; these operations produced a remarkable imitation of real sandstone. This, of course, was a dishonest use of a material, which is considered nowadays as one of the cardinal sins of architecture. But John, with his dream of an English cottage, would not be perturbed by such considerations; indeed, to disguise wood as stone was commonly done in England.

The house has now been dismantled and the timbers are stored in a barn, awaiting reconstruction. The restoration of the house will cost a considerable sum of money, for it had fallen into a very ruinous condition before being broken up. I visited it a few years ago while its remains were still standing, and its tumbled-down, neglected appearance was very depressing. So too was the way in which it had been altered over the years. The west kitchen wing had been torn down completely after the chimney had collapsed, taking some of the roof with it; the living room was a garage, and its ceiling had partly collapsed; the stairway, now leading into nothing, had had to be boarded up; the chimney between the hall and the dining room had been removed entirely, and a new kitchen added at the back of the dining room; some of the window sashes had been replaced by the run-of-the-mill sashes of a later date.

In making the restoration drawings of the house, I have of necessity had to make some conjectures and assumptions. For example, before the building was taken down it had two types of window sashes, one set with a Gothic head and the other a typical Georgian double-hung window of three lights wide by five deep. The plan, the proportions of the elevation, and the pitch of the roof tend to support the idea that the windows were once all Gothic. Another moot point is the number and placing of the fireplaces. In the original plan, three chimneys and fireplaces are shown, though this is hardly in keeping with John's ideas about too many fireplaces and chimneys. However, we know that there was a fireplace at the north end of the living room – its remains could be seen before the house was demolished – and, unless the roof had been altered, which is not very likely, we can reasonably suppose that the kitchen was 14 feet wide, its west wall flush with the west wall of the living room, and its fireplace built back-to-back with the living room one. This back-to-back arrangement was very common in larger houses with inside fireplaces.

Despite the aberrations in the style of its original construction and the unfortunate alterations subsequently made to it, one cannot but lament the disappearance of this house and hope for its resurrection, not so much for its architectural value as for the history connected with it and, indeed, embodied in it. We know so much of the people who first lived in it that it took me, at any rate, little effort of imagination to be back with Anne Langton, going about the house with paper and paste covering up the 'blow holes' and doing her daily chores in the calm and measured manner of the early settlers of Ontario.

# 3
# TIMBER FRAMING

## Theory and principles

In order to have a better understanding of timber framing it is necessary to grasp some of the fundamental principles of stress transfer. It is the mode of transfer that constitutes one of the great differences between log, timber, and masonry construction: in log construction the structural members are generally laid horizontally, thus transferring the stress across the grain; in masonry, whose material substance has remained unchanged since primitive times, every unit is entirely imbedded in mortar, permitting a total transfer of stress from one unit to the next throughout the entire wall. In frame construction, by contrast, all principal load-carrying members are vertical, and the stress over a large area is collected by one member and, in turn, transferred to another member at a given point. This point transfer is of supreme importance in frame construction. There is another basic difference: masonry construction involves solid masses, interrupted only by the lintel and the arch which carry the load over openings; frame construction, on the other hand, resolves into vertical members such as principals and studs, horizontal members such as beams, girders, plates, and sills, and inclined members such as rafters and braces. For these reasons an early frame structure is much more complex – and a far more interesting object of study and analysis – than its masonry and log equivalents.

So long as we continue to 'frame' buildings, primary members such as beams, girders, posts, and columns will be required. These members are basic to the framing of both a fifty-storey skyscraper and a simple refreshment stand. The same principles apply irrespective of the material used, whether it be wood, steel, or concrete. It is in the joining of the members that the greatest progress has been made in timber framing.

Any structural system under load will develop three basic types of stress: tension, compression, and shear. Since any load transfer can take place only at a joint, with the consequent inducement of the appropriate stress in that joint, its design is of prime importance. For our purposes, because the early builders hardly ever took shearing stress into account, we shall examine only the fashioning of a joint in tension and in compression before proceeding to the frame as such.

A joint in tension means that the two joined members tend to pull away from each other. If a simple mortise and tenon are used, the two pieces will simply pull apart. The normal means of preventing this is by the use of one or two pins, variously called pegs, trunnels, or treenails, fitted into drawbores. In heavy framing two pins are used as a rule; in lighter construction one will suffice. Such joints, of which there are a wide variety, rely principally on the effective resistance of the pin. In a compression joint the two members work towards each other, and in this case pins are not necessary by reason of the very nature of the stress. When used, the pins are intended to control tension caused by shrinkage, settlement, or deflection under load.

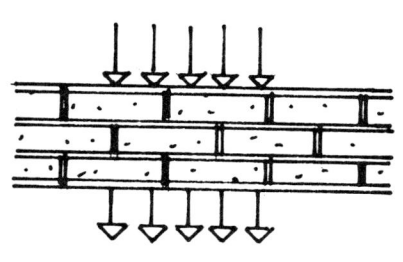 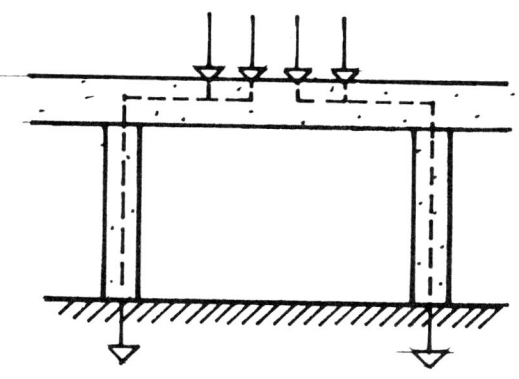

## • STRESS TRANSFER PATTERN •

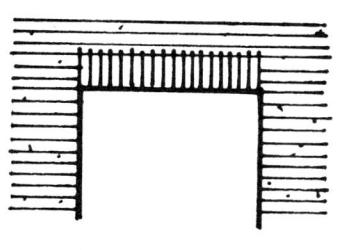 

• LINTEL •      • ARCH •

## • MASONRY OPENINGS •

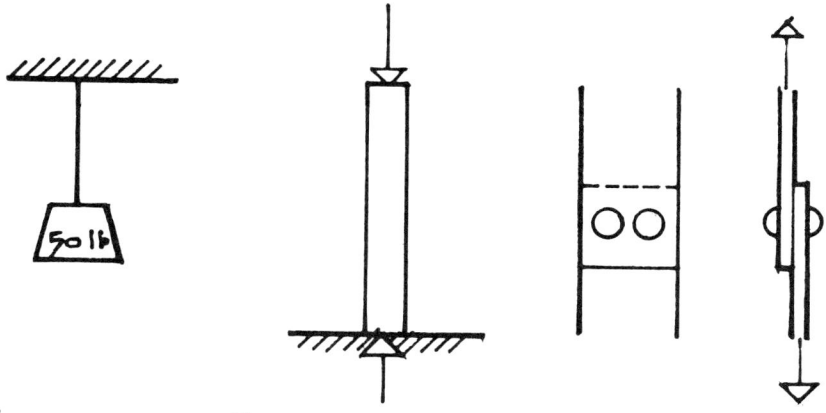

• TENSION •   • COMPRESSION •   • SHEAR •

## • STRESS TYPES •

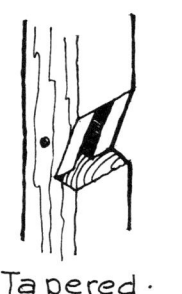 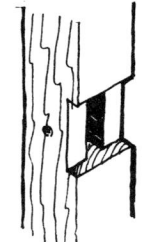

·Tapered· ·Square-cut·

·<u>Full Shoulders</u>·

 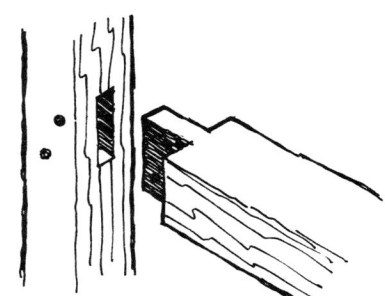

·<u>Tapered Half-Shoulder</u>· ·<u>Simple M. & T.</u>·

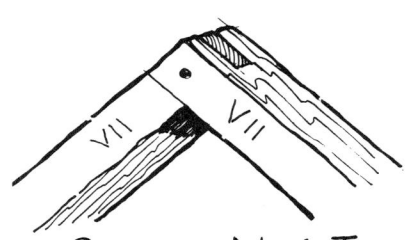 

·Open M. & T.· ·King Post·

·<u>Ridge Joints</u>·

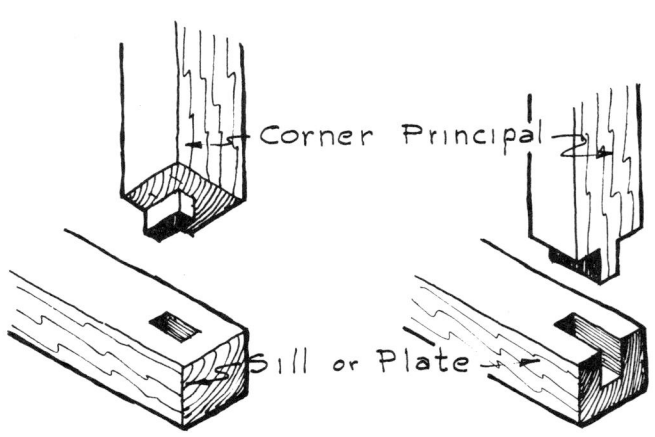

·<u>Correct Corner Joint</u>· ·<u>Evidence of Later Mutilation</u>·

Timber framing 95

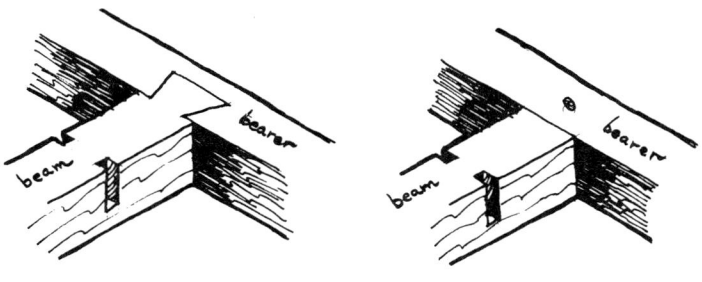

· Floor Beam Connections ·

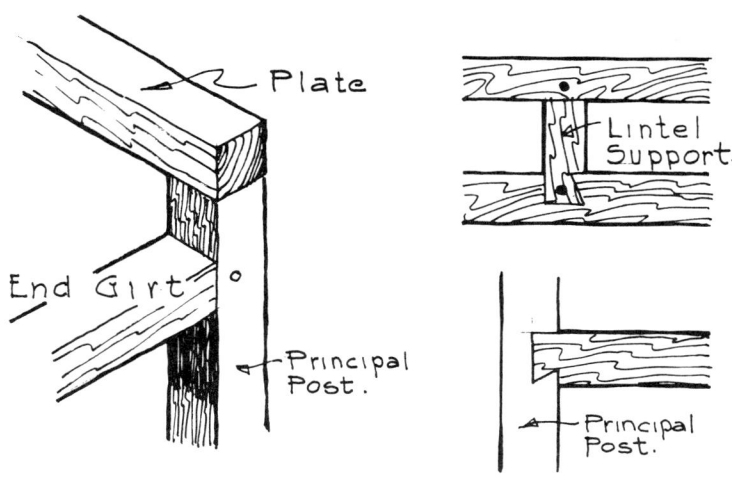

· Corner Assembly ·    · Tie Pieces ·

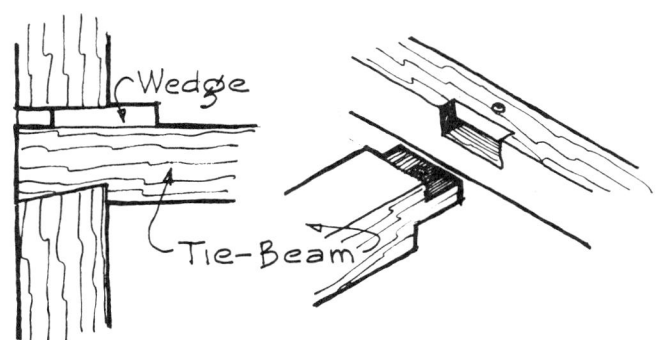

· Tie-Beam Connections ·

96 Building with Wood

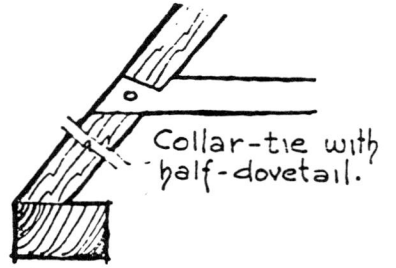

Collar-tie with half-dovetail.

• No support at Plate •

If rafter supported at foot, collar-tie need not necessarily be used.
If not supported, collar-tie is essential.

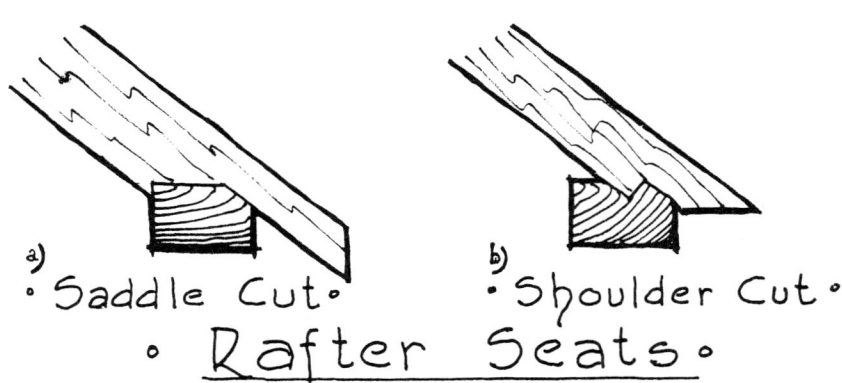

a) • Saddle Cut •     b) • Shoulder Cut •

• <u>Rafter Seats</u> •

• Tension or Compression only •     • Load bearing •
a)                                    b)

• <u>Scarfed Joints</u> •

The dovetail joint is a much more sophisticated device, since it brings a larger area of one member into contact with the other at the same time as its tightness is directly proportionate to the pull exerted on it. Such joints do not strictly require to be pinned. Nevertheless a pin was frequently used, especially in a half-lap dovetail, to prevent the member from sliding sideways. There are several variations of this joint, of which the characteristic feature common to all is the inward taper of the tenon.

One last joint should be mentioned. Although hardly ever used in light construction, it may occur in heavy framing, as in mills, barns, or churches. This is the scarfed joint, whose purpose is to join two pieces of wood when one piece would be too awkward to handle, too difficult to install, or simply not available in the desired length. This joint may also be either in tension or in compression.

Fasteners are an indispensable part of a frame, and should be discussed along with framing principles. The first fasteners were the pin or peg, the nail, and the spike; advanced technology brought in the screw, and the bolt and nut.

Once timbers had been squared, they were cut to size and all mortises and tenons were prepared. Then the drawbores were made – one of 1 inch diameter for each joint in light or house framing and two of 1½ inch diameter in heavy or barn framing. The general rule for the size of the drawbore read: 'a draw bore should be equal to one-half the thickness of the tenon where the tenon is not more than three inches thick. However, in no case should it be greater than one and one-half inches. Heavy timbers may require two pins.'[1] In light frames the hole was made 1 inch from the side and 1½ inches from the face of the mortise, and a hole then bored in the tenons but only 5/16 inches from its shoulder; in heavy framing the holes in the mortise were made 2 inches from both side and face and in the tenon 1¾ inches from the shoulder. This offset of the holes was an ingenious device for securing a very tight joint by effectively reducing the size of the opening; when the pins, always tapered at one end, were driven through the holes, both pieces would be drawn tightly together, hence the term 'drawbore.'

Definite specifications for the size of pins have existed since 1703.[2] Their length was always 2 inches plus the thickness of the timber. The pin was then cut *square* so that its thickness equalled the diameter of the hole that was made for it – that is, either 1 inch for light framing, or 1½ inches for heavy framing, as in Grace Church or the B. Fish mill at Markham (see Chapter 6). The corners were then cut to form a rough octagon and the pin was tapered for about a third of its length. The finished pin was driven through the holes in the mortise and tenon, the taper helping to start it properly and then to pass through the offset hole in the tenon; when driven through completely, the pin so pulled the tenoned timber – given the natural 'spring' in wood – that the tenon was seated perfectly rigid in the joint. This technique usually applied only to joints in tension; joints in compression were frequently left open.

98  Building with Wood

The relative size of pins is clearly shown. They all appear to be of white oak, and their dimensions correspond to those recommended in the standard manuals. Most of them are in excellent state of preservation.

1 This pin is from a church in Markham, built in 1849. It is 12 inches long with a 1½ inch diameter. The taper is about one-third of its length.
2 This pin is identical in size to (1) but the taper is not worked quite as carefully. It is from the B. Fish mill at Bayview and Steeles Avenue. It is dated at anywhere from 1832 through the 1850s. The first two pins were used in heavy framing.
3 This one dates from about 1820 and comes from the Starr home in Bogarttown. It is a true house-framing pin, 8 inches long and 1 inch in diameter.
4 The most carefully worked pins came from the log house on what was formerly known as Dawes Road, dating about 1814. These particular pins were used to hold the window frame in place. There were two pins per jamb.
5 This is a very crude pin from a log house on Jane Street, dating about 1840. It does not follow the rules: it is about 6 inches long and is 1½ inches in diameter.

The main fastener in all early timber construction was the pin. The upper one was made on a pin-cutter, the lower shaped entirely by hand. Both are from the Fisher home, 1836

Since early pins were made by hand, they may have varied slightly in size, but the two basic dimensions remained unchanged for several centuries. Early pins were never turned by lathe; rather, they were shaped to form a rough octagon with the taper being up to one-third of the length. If a turned pin is found in early frames, it must be assumed that it was a replacement for the original. Pins may occasionally be found which seem perfectly round, as if turned out on a lathe, but which may still show the hand-shaped taper and longitudinal striations along their main axis. Such specimens were fashioned on a pin-cutter, a device which took the shape of a vertically mounted, tapered iron pipe. The smaller diameter was at the top and the upper edge was sharpened by an inward taper. The pin was formed by hand approximately to size and was then driven through this pipe, the cutting edge giving it a fairly round form. Not many of this sort have been discovered, probably because a slightly irregular and angular surface had better holding power. An additional reason could be that such pins took much longer to produce.

A plate showing the making of nail rod, from Diderot's *Encyclopédie*.

The idea is prevalent that a building can be dated rather accurately by its nails. This is simply not true. Indeed it is practically impossible to date nails with any degree of certainty since various manufacturing methods were in use at the same time in various parts of the province. Pioneer conditions lasted for a period of about fifty years, and hence the latest cut nails could be found in one area, often near Quebec or the American border, while at the same time, sometimes just a short distance away, a blacksmith was still making nails by hand. Nails are useful in so far as they provide an approximate date when two different types of nails occur in the same building. The De Puisaye house near Niagara-on-the-Lake, built about 1805, provides a good example. In one room upstairs two types of nails and lath were used: one wall was plastered onto handsplit lath fastened with handmade nails, whereas an adjoining wall was built on sawn lath fastened with cut nails. There can be little doubt about the relative age of the nails as well as the plaster surfaces of these walls.

The development of nail shapes is quite well defined. The totally handmade nail (other things being equal) is the oldest, and was formed with the use of a nail rod, which blacksmiths bought in lengths up to 8 feet. It was cut to the required length, tapered on all four sides to a point, and then received its unmistakable hand-hammered head.

The first nail-cutting machine was basically a table with a guillotine knife at one end. A strip of iron, equal in width to the desired length of the nail, was fed against this knife to a fixed stop. The knife was set at a slight angle to the line of feed so as to produce a slight taper cut. The strip had to be turned over after each cut to obtain the typically tapered nail with square edges and a blunt end. At first the heads were still formed by hand; later, machines did all the work. The tapering mechanism was also improved later: the knife was set at a right angle to the line of feed and the strip of iron was moved slightly to right and left after each cut to produce the taper. This process was

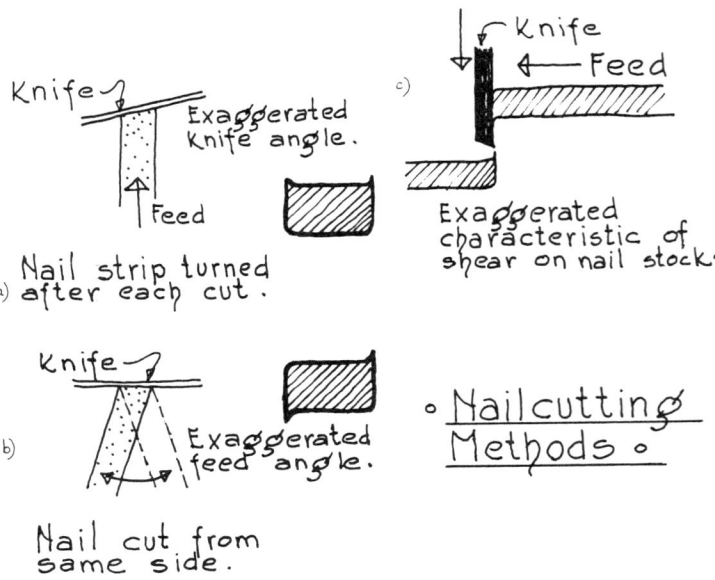

○ Nailcutting Methods ○

# Timber framing 101

speedier since the entire strip did not need to be turned over. Nails made by these two processes are easily identified in that the earlier nails will show two sharp arrises on the same side and the later ones will have them on opposite sides.

It appears that on this continent nail-cutting machines were first patented in 1794 by J. Pierson of New York. In 1807 Jesse Reed of Boston received a patent for a machine that cut and headed nails in one operation (previous attempts had been unsuccessful). Nail technology advanced very rapidly in the United States: in 1807 four nail factories in Pittsburgh produced 100 tons of nails a year and three in Lexington, Kentucky, 60 tons. Later in the century an important technological change in the industry introduced wire nails (that is, nails that were drawn rather than cut).

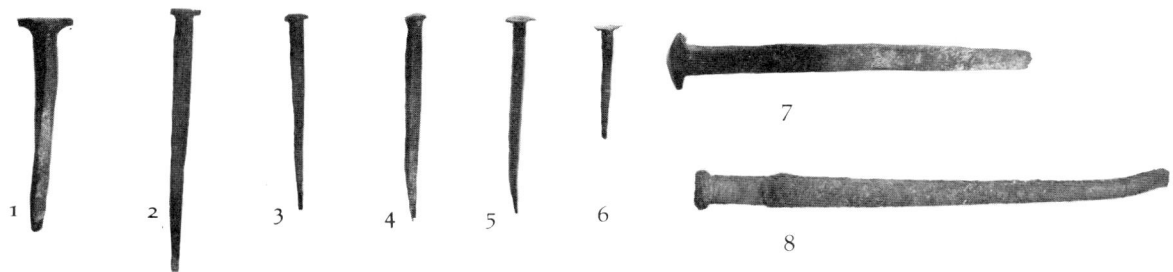

The detailed description of the nails shown is as follows:
1. A handsome nail of unknown date. Used for heavy construction. Note the taper of the point and the flat head. 2¾ inches long
2. A standard, machine-made cut nail. Cut nails always had a stub point. Since the head was formed by one blow, the stem had to be held very firmly by two jaws, so much so that it pinched the end and gave the nail the appearance of being wider in the middle. The taper is on two sides only. Length varies from 1 to 6 inches.
3. Typical handmade nail from nailrod. Taper is on all four sides. The end is always pointed and the head formed by a series of blows which gives it a rounded appearance consisting of a number of flats. This type reached a length of up to 3½ inches.
4. Same type as (3) but with a less carefully made head as well as taper. This might be a home-made nail rather than one made by a blacksmith.
5. The unusual feature of this nail is the extremely flat head. Its length, 2½ inches, makes it too long for a lathing nail, but it is difficult to see any other purpose for such a head.
6. A 1½ inch lathing nail from the De Puisaye home. It was used on an inside wall with handsplit lath. The head is so thin that the nail was perhaps made by an amateur rather than by a professional.
7. This is a spike, 4½ inches long, from the log house in the Sharon museum, dating from about 1840. Note that the spike tapers on only two sides; this was typical of handmade spikes. Outside of several standard lengths, such as the example shown, spikes were, most likely, made to order for specific jobs.
8. A 6 inch machine-made spike from the southeast wall of the De Puisaye home. This wall had undergone some alterations at a later date, and this nail is definitely later than (6).

This assortment of nails came from the Fisher house, built in 1836. These range from a 10 inch spike to a small lathing nail; they are mostly cut nails, but some of the lower ones are handmade from nailrod.

The first machines for making wire nails were introduced into France about 1834, into England about 1840, and by 1850 such nails were being manufactured in the United States. But their overall acceptance by the trade did not occur until later because builders did not trust their holding power.[3] Cut nails were still being produced as late as 1913, though only for special purposes (they are now being reintroduced for restoration work). A great variety of nails was used in some buildings, as in the Fisher house, 1836.

Spikes were handmade almost up to the time of the wire nail, for the simple reason that their demand was not great and they were too expensive to keep on hand for chance sale. Many also had to be made to order for special tasks. Spikes came in various lengths. For domestic use the longest I have found so far is about 10 inches; for heavy construction up to 18 inches. This very long spike, now in the Royal Ontario Museum, came from Fort Albany on James Bay, and is dated between 1650 and 1700.

Scarcity of supply imposed considerable restrictions on the use of bolts and screws. In domestic construction bolts were practically non-existent and screws were used principally for hinges. For the purpose of dating screws, it may be remembered that the cast-iron butt-hinge was patented in 1775. This hinge required a screw with a flat, countersunk, slotted head. Nails made poor fasteners for hinges because of the thickness of their heads. An early screw will always have a blunt, rather than a pointed, end because of the way in which it was made. A cutting machine for pointed ends was not

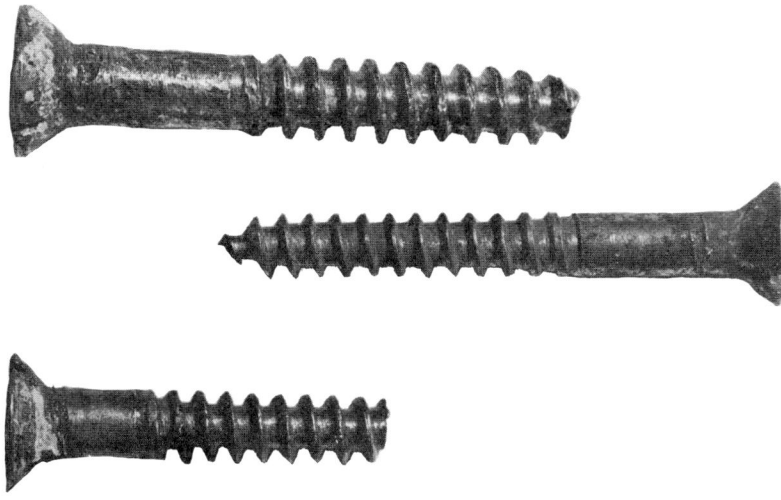

An early screw can always be recognized by its stub point and coarse thread; frequently the slot in the head will be slightly off centre. For purposes of comparison, the middle screw is modern.

patented until 1845, so that if the screws found in a structure are original and have a blunt end, they are likely earlier than 1845. However, the possibility of their having been replaced at a later date must not be overlooked, making evidence of this sort of uncertain value. Yet, in Ontario, if it were not for the wide latitude in the manufacture and use of fasteners throughout the province, nails, screws, spikes, and bolts would provide a much more reliable means of dating structures, since there is little possibility of their ever having been replaced.

## The frame in historical perspective

By the end of the seventeenth century timber framing throughout Europe was almost standardized. Books written in English, Dutch, German, French, and Italian all exhibited common solutions to the problems of the stresses and strains encountered in putting up a structure. This should not be surprising because the same stresses will be found in constructing a lintel over a window in a Renaissance palace as in the entrance-way to a hut in central Africa. By this time books were readily available and translated from one language to another. In addition, an apprentice was required to travel at least one year before gaining master standing; this, no doubt, contributed to the dissemination of construction lore. It is safe to assume that Richards' translation of Palladio's book was in the hands of the settlers who crossed the ocean, and can be regarded as an historic background to timber framing on this continent. One should keep in mind, however, that Palladio probably combined all the elements of construction in his drawing, whereas in actual practice a builder might not have employed all of these features in any one building.

The first step in erecting a frame house is building the foundations. In England, with a relatively frost-free climate, foundation walls were frequently laid dry (that is, without mortar) for the purposes of raising the timbers slightly off the ground and of providing a dead level base for the sills. Cellars were rare in England, and their lack of demand must have been a causal factor in putting up foundations in this way. The Ontario frame houses, discussed later in this chapter, and the mud house at Brougham, originally had no cellar. Settlers had difficulties, however, because they did not realize the extent of frost action. Masonry construction, with little elasticity or rigidity, was most affected (witness John Langton's fireplace); log houses were less so, but doors and windows jammed during the winter; and frame houses were almost not at all since they possessed sufficient rigidity to compensate for any unevenness caused by heaving.

Providing a support for a hearth in a house without a basement was no problem, since the supports could rest either directly on the ground or on very shallow footings. In later houses with a full basement the most popular support was simply a 1½ to 2 inch plank bottom, supported by the foundation wall at one end and by a ledge piece nailed to the first-floor beam.

After the foundations had been prepared, the framers came on the job. The first procedure in framing was to take the 'wind' (rhymes with 'grind') out of the principal timbers.[4] This was necessary because it is almost impossible to spring a heavy warped timber into place and because, should such a timber warp after assembly, there is danger of its splitting the mortise. The wind was taken out of timber by selecting the two best adjoining sides as work sides; one was used for the upper side and the other for the front. A flat surface was then cut on the upper side at one end and a pencil line drawn square across it. A carpenter's square was then placed with one blade along this line and the other hanging down to form a plumb. A corresponding flat surface was then cut on the front side to square with the upper one. Next, a flat was cut at the other end of the upper side of the timber and a second square placed on it in the same manner, except that this flat was adjusted by sighting along the upper blade of the second square until both were in line. The front side of this other end was then squared off too. A chalk line was struck on the upper and front sides of the timber and the timber hewn along it. It was then relatively easy to square the remaining two sides.

A frame wall consists of three main parts: a sill or sole plate, principals or studs, and a plate. The sill and the plate form horizontal bearing surfaces while the vertical members – principals or studs – transmit the roof and wall

Typical seventeenth-century European framing. Redrawn from Godfrey Richards'
translation of *The First Book of A. Palladio's Architecture*, chap. XLVII, first published in
1663.

1 Ground-plate
2 Girder or binding interduce or bressumer
3 Beam to the roof or girder to garrett floor
4 Principal post and upright brick wall
5 Braces
6 Quarters
7 Interduces
8 Prick-posts or window posts
9 Jaumes or door-posts
10 Kingpiece or joggle piece
11 Strutts
12 Coller-beam, strutts-beam or wind-beam
13 Door head
14 Principal rafters
15 Bedding moulding of the cornice over windows
16 Ends of lentels and pieces
17 Furring or shreadins
18 Knees of principal rafters to be of one piece
19 Purline mortices
 (Richards' spelling)

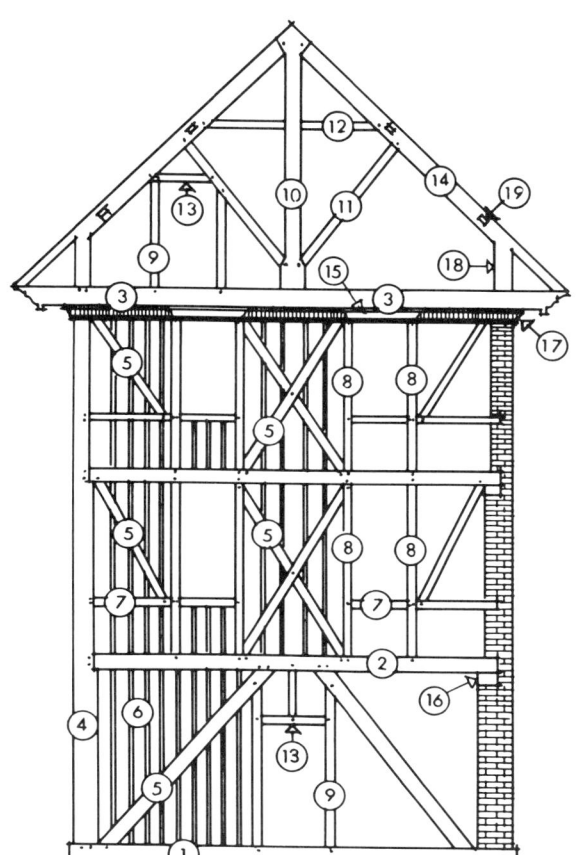

loads to the foundations. A principal post extends the full height of the wall, while studs (or quarters or 'prick-posts') extend only one storey in height, except in balloon framing. Principal posts were used only in side walls, never in gable walls. A small house would have three pairs of principals – two pairs for the corners and one in between – and a larger house four – with two intermediate ones which, as in early New England houses, were frequently placed along either side of a central chimney. Principal posts were always braced laterally by 45-degree diagonals running from near the top of the principal to the plate; sometimes intermediate posts would be braced at the plate in both lateral directions.

No ridge board was used in roof construction. The rafters were joined at the ridge with an open mortise and tenon joint, as a rule, with one pin. The rafters were matched on the ground and each pair marked with Roman numerals for identification on assembly. Roof-boarding consisted of planks which could be of differing width, either closely spaced or laid with a gap between joints. The slatted boarding in the top photograph is most likely of a later date.

The sills were laid first, either dry or in a bed of mortar, and were properly secured by a pinned joint at the corners. If heavy floor beams were required, they were framed into the sills at this time. The bents were then assembled with hookpins, and placed so that when they were elevated, the bottom tenon would slip into its mortise in the sill. The elevation of these bents was the reason behind the customary 'raising bees': their weight and bulk was such that an immense amount of physical effort was required to lift them into position. The first bent erected did not have any lateral support and so was temporarily braced. After the second bent was raised, lateral braces or cross-ties were sprung into place and temporarily secured with hookpins between it and the first. These two bents now formed a self-supporting unit, and no further temporary bracing was required. The hookpins were knocked out when the joints had been checked and then were replaced with permanent pins. Once the frame was secure, unskilled help was dismissed (with the usual liquid refreshment) and the carpenters and joiners completed the building.

## Timber framing in Ontario

The term 'frame' refers to the several horizontal and vertical members joined together to form a structure. The whole frame of a house or barn usually consists of several 'bents,' that is, several members joined together on the ground to form a unit. The unit was then raised and put into place, at first by manpower only, later perhaps by means of a sheer-pole or gin-pole, and still later by tractor and derrick. The bents themselves were then joined to form the whole frame using tie-beams or girders with a pinned mortise and tenon, or a dovetail joint. Members (bents or principal posts) were always prefitted on the ground before raising, and, in order that each might be easily identified, Roman numerals were cut into the side of the members nearest the joint.

Written records of erection procedures anywhere are almost non-existent. Textbooks, even the earliest ones, deal mainly with theory because this aspect of the trade could be learned by the apprentice as 'homework,' whereas the practical application of theoretical principles had to be learned 'on the job.' Here the apprentice would work under the direct supervision of his master, and since this eliminated written instruction, the almost total absence of printed matter dealing with the actual erection of a building is thus perhaps explained. In general, it may be assumed that construction or erection procedures must be determined from the nature of the building itself, and in most cases the building type dictated the order that had to be followed. A typical barn-raising in Waterloo County today is perhaps the last vestige of a building method with a very long tradition. The only concession to modernity is the use of lathe-turned pins, a motorized mortising rig, and a tractor for heavy pulling.

Four principal posts frame

Three principal posts frame

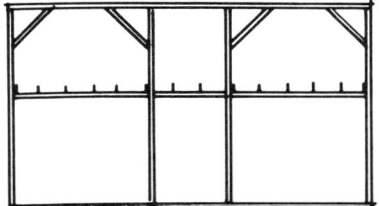

FAIRBANKS HOUSE
DEADHAM MASS. U.S.A. 1637

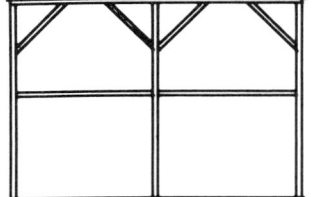

MOULINETTE · ±1825

Multi-post frame

Transition frame

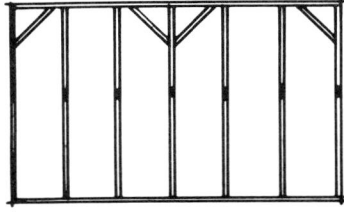

WOODBRIDGE · ±1825

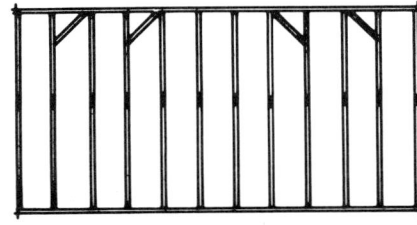

RICHMOND HILL
±1830

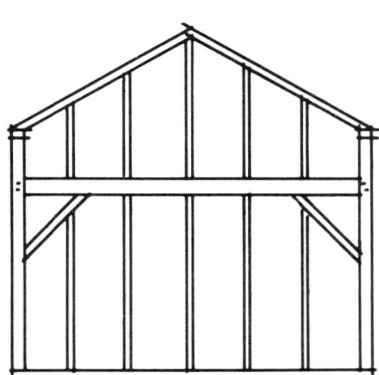

BALLOON FRAMING
±1880 – 1930

VARIOUS SIDE WALL
FRAMING METHODS
· NO SCALE ·

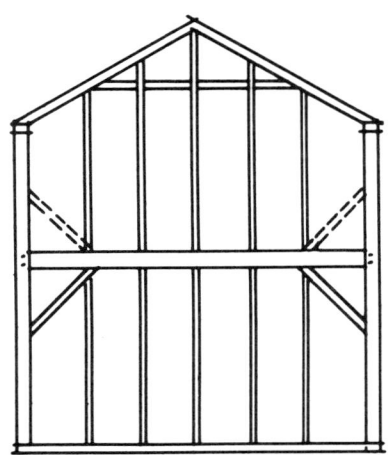

· TYPICAL GABLE WALL FRAMING ·

Timber framing  109

If a frame was held together only by mortise and tenon joints, even with the use of pins the members would eventually dry out and shrink, leaving considerable play in the joint. The frame would likely sway in the wind and could develop a permanent lean in one direction or another. To prevent this, diagonal braces were usually added. They were always set at a 45-degree angle, generally by means of a mortise and tenon joint with, or without, one pin. In heavy framing two such braces were common. The number of braces used in a building varied considerably, as if their use depended entirely on the individual craftsman's notion of good building. The Gleason house in Farmington, Connecticut, had only eight in all, whereas the Fisher house in Toronto had a grand total of fifty. Most braces were employed in walls only; that is, in a vertical plane. Very rarely were they used in a horizontal plane.

Cross-bracing, or transverse-bracing, was always attained by diagonal bracing between the principals and the second-floor beams at the gable ends. Intermediate posts were sometimes also braced to a floor beam if the brace could be concealed in a partition. Such braces were always placed in the lower inside corner between post and beam. In French log construction, however, where the wall below the plate is filled with logs, this was not possible: in the Banwell house the end transverse-bracing is in the upper corner, and in the old Lucier home (Sandwich West, near Windsor) in which the plate and the last cross-beam in the gable wall were at the same height, the braces were placed horizontally across the corners at plate height.

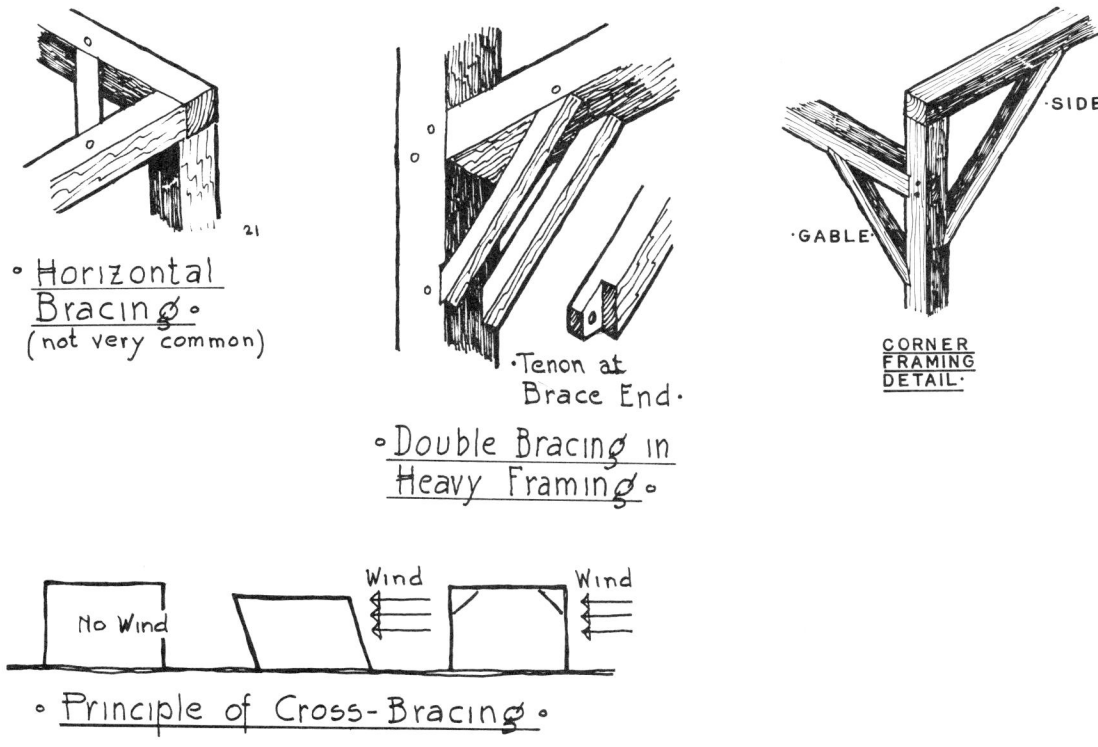

° Horizontal Bracing °
(not very common)

° Double Bracing in Heavy Framing °
·Tenon at Brace End·

CORNER FRAMING DETAIL·
·SIDE·
·GABLE·

° Principle of Cross-Bracing °

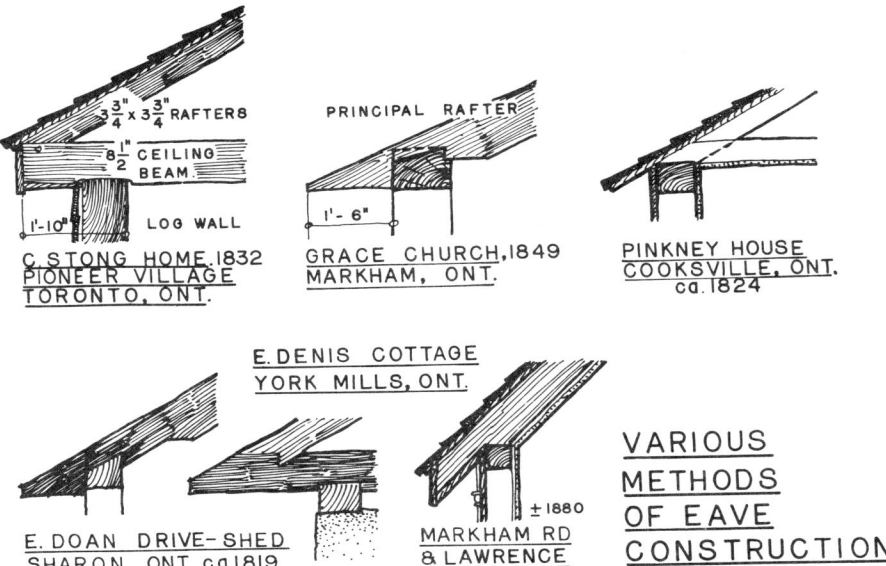

VARIOUS METHODS OF EAVE CONSTRUCTION

Builders were usually anxious to avoid having the plate and the cross-beams at the same height, since this entailed a three-part joint with the principals. Hence in the standard wood framing of one-storey houses in Ontario the plate was always above the level of the floor beams. In houses of one and a half or two storeys, of course, the problem did not arise since the plate was well above the second-floor beams. This three-part joint was common English practice, and raising the plate was one of the simplifying improvements of American builders during the eighteenth century. Isham and Brown[5] show that the three-way joint was employed in many seventeenth-century Connecticut houses and survived to be employed in two houses – the Caldwell (1740) and Sheldon (1750) – as late as the middle of the eighteenth century.

The spacing of studs and rafters was quite erratic in early Ontario houses. The studs in the Pinkney house were spaced at 3′ 2″, 3′ 2″, 3′ 6″, 3′ 0″, 3′ 0″, 3′ 6″, 3′ 2″, and 2′ 11″ intervals. In a house at Richmond Hill the stud spacing was more consistent, varying by only an inch (on the average of 2′ 3″) in the gable walls and being either 2′ 4″ or 3′ 0″ (except for an end space of 1′ 11″) on the side walls; all the 3 foot spaces contained doors or windows. The principals in this house, incidentally, were about 7½ inches square, the studs in the gable end about 4 inches square, the ceiling joists (following the spacing of the principals) about 6 inches by 7 inches deep, and the rafters were joined at the ridge in an open mortise and tenon by one pin, without a ridge board. A house at Woodbridge (to be discussed later) was of a higher order of workmanship and the spacing varied by only half an inch.

Timber framing 111

LEFT  Here the floor beams are seated into the sill. Beams are in the round with an adzed top surface. Because of the spacing, an intermediate floor joist has been inserted to give better support for the flooring.
RIGHT  In early construction, floor joists and beams were housed into the sill either by a pinned mortise and tenon or with an open half-dovetail.

BELOW, RIGHT  Up to the 1880s at least, the studs were still mortised into the sill with a half-mortise. Corner studs, or studs at an intersection of two walls, were 4 inches square.
LEFT  The sill and the floor joists are completely detached from one another.

112

This is the work of an amateur at a later alteration.

Sills were frequently laid on a dry stone foundation. Note that the sill is recessed for a considerable distance from the face of the foundation. I was not able to determine how the weather was kept out of this joint.

In standard framing, the rafters have to be housed in the plate with a compression joint. This requires a shoulder, otherwise the rafter will slip out. Since wood provides a better means to achieve this, a heavy beam is used as a plate even in brick construction. Vintage house, Jordan, early 1800s

A very common method of providing support for the hearth of the fireplace above. House in Dixie built in early 1800s

114

Very carelessly applied fill: crude brickwork mixed with cull lumber, and siding applied directly to the studs. House near Trenton, date unknown

On Highway 2 near Trenton. Date unknown. Here the walls are completely filled, with the siding applied directly to the principals.

Timber framing 115

When the framework was complete the spaces between the studs were frequently filled with brick laid rather haphazardly in mortar. Thereafter practice seems to have varied considerably. Often a horizontal sheathing of one inch boarding was applied to the outside as a nailing base for the clapboard, and in well-built houses, such as the Woodbridge one, similar sheathing was applied to the interior before the lath was put on. In the Parshall Terry house in Toronto, however, siding and plaster were applied directly to the frame without any fill or sheathing whatever; in the Richmond Hill house handsplit lath was nailed to both outside and inside, with the exterior then being roughcast and the interior plastered. (The handsplit lath would date this house at somewhere between 1800 and 1825.) In an exceptional instance, Sandford Fleming's house near Craigleith, lath was sprung into slots cut into the principals and studs; the builder thus discarded the current method of using brick fill and reverted to something resembling the early wattle-and-daub fill of half-timber walls in England and Europe.

Roofs took on a variety of shapes. The earliest forms were the shed or

LEFT This house stood on Yonge Street just north of Richmond Hill. Note that no fill was used in the walls. Handsplit lath was used both for the plaster on the inside as well as for the stucco on the outside. Both were applied directly to the principals.

RIGHT No fill was used in this wall; siding was applied directly to the exterior and lath and plaster on the interior. Parshall Terry's cottage in the Don Valley, Toronto

mono-pitch, gable, lean-to, and the gambrel. Opinions vary as to the order of their appearance, but arguments at this point are purely academic.

The rafters are the inclined members which support the roof sheathing and the shingles. At first the slope or pitch was quite steep, 45 degrees or more, but was gradually reduced to 18 or 20 degrees during the classical revival periods. A number of methods were used for 'seating' the rafter on the plate. A collar-tie was a frequent device. This tie was a horizontal member inserted approximately at the mid-point of the rafter. It was an essential item if the foot of the rafter was not provided with a firm shoulder to brace it and halt the tendency to spread apart under load.

The roof truss was a common structural element all across Europe and in Britain; however, in the transfer of British building technology to this continent, the truss was abandoned for domestic construction almost without exception. The French in Quebec, on the other hand, retained the truss until the end of the nineteenth century.

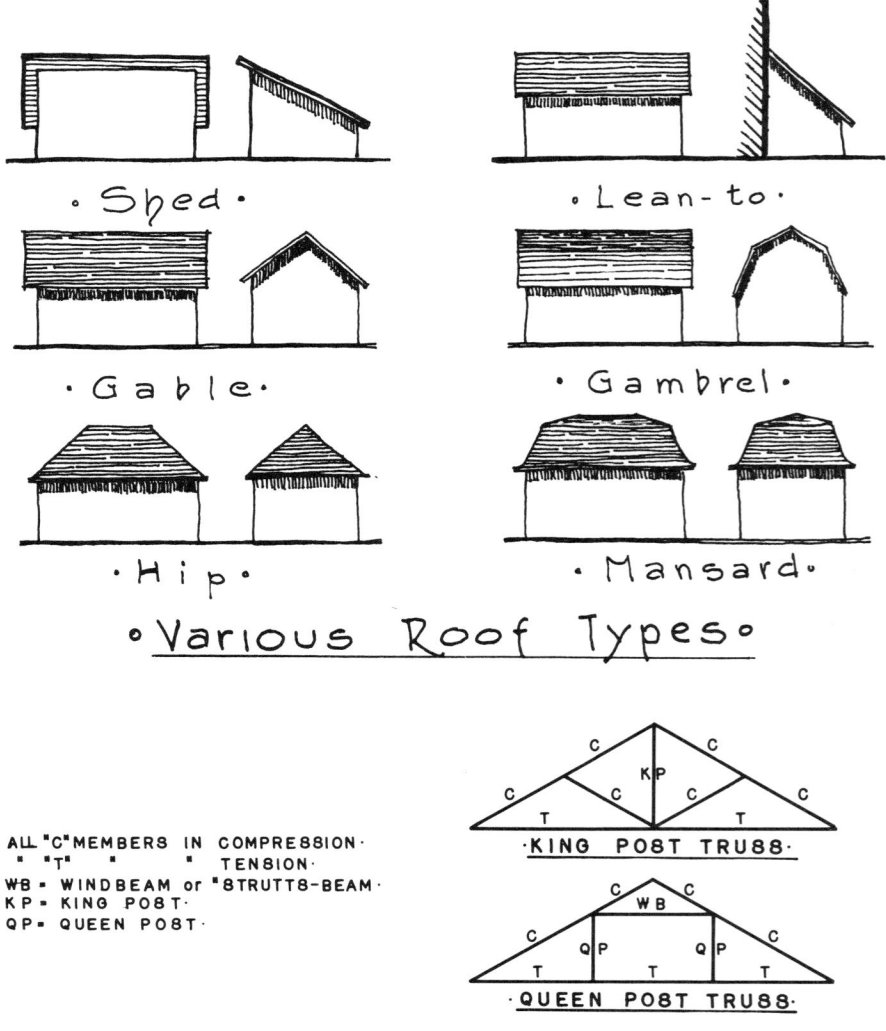

· Shed ·    · Lean-to ·
· Gable ·   · Gambrel ·
· Hip ·     · Mansard ·

° Various Roof Types °

ALL "C" MEMBERS IN COMPRESSION·
  "T"    "    TENSION·
WB = WINDBEAM or "STRUTTS-BEAM·
KP = KING POST·
QP = QUEEN POST·

·KING POST TRUSS·

·QUEEN POST TRUSS·

Board lath (LEFT) consists of wide, thin boards, split with an axe so that the cracks do not run the full length of the board, and then pulled apart while being fixed to the wall to allow the clefts to open and receive the plaster keys. Handsplit lath (RIGHT) was split in both directions; it shows no saw marks, and, unlike sawn lath, is irregular in outline.

Three types of lath were used in Ontario: the fully handsplit, board lath, and sawn lath. Since it was split in both directions, handmade lath has no fixed dimensions. It can be very easily identified since it will show no saw marks and be irregular in outline. It required the same number of nails for the later sawn lath.

Board lath consisted of a thin board of any convenient width and length sawn to a thickness of about $3/8$ to $1/2$ inch. This wide thin panel was then cracked with an axe here and there in such a fashion that no split would run the full length of the board. When it was used it was pulled apart to open the clefts far enough to offer a key for the plaster. Such boards reached lengths of 10 feet or more and fewer nails were required for this type than for the other two. It is generally assumed that handsplit board lath disappeared when the sawn type was introduced. This is, however, quite erroneous, since there is evidence of board lath being used as late as 1879. An account book of Joseph P. Webb, who operated a sawmill at Kettleby, Ontario, shows him charging from 30 to 70 cents per hundred feet for this type and 20 cents a bundle for sawn lath. From the accounts it seems that the hundred-foot rate applied to face measure rather than board measure. There does not seem to be a reason for the difference in cost. An interesting aside is the fact that as late as 1879 this account book adds after 'Ontario' the initials W.C. (West Canada) instead of C.W. (Canada West).

118  Building with Wood

Sawn lath appeared in the 1830s and persisted well into the 1930s, when it was replaced with various types of patented products. It was approximately 1⅜ inches wide by ½ inch thick. Soon after 1830 most sawmills possessed at least one unit for sawing lath. It always sold in bundles until it finally disappeared from the market. It was this type of lath which made the lather's hatchet a necessity. This tool may be described as having a small axe on one side and a hammer on the other. There has been no significant modification of the tool up to the present and it is still used in modern lathing methods.

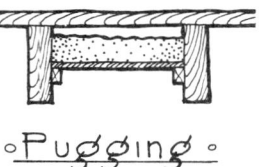

The term 'pugging' can be found in standard textbooks on construction as late as 1904. The function of this structural device is doubtful. Some sources claim that it possessed 'damp-proofing' qualities, others, sound-deadening or 'deafening' properties; or they assert that it will prevent 'the passage of smell from the room below.' About 1879 Joseph Webb wrote to William Ireland in Aurora: '... the floor is to lay and to be deadened by putting inch boards and filling between joists ...' Here is what was done. A board was set between the floor joists. This board rested on cleats nailed to the sides of the joists several inches below the top. It supported a layer of 'dry moss, or a mixture of lime mortar, earth, and smith's ashes; the material might also be slag felt, slag wool, turf, plasterers' rubbish, sawdust, or tan bark. All materials that tended to decompose were of course rejected.'

The earliest means of heat was, of course, the fireplace, a most inefficient device which consumed prodigious amounts of fuel to provide very little comfort. High consumption of fuel presented no difficulty at first in a land of forests. It soon became apparent, however, that a more efficient heating system had to be devised. For this reason, many of the early frame houses in Ontario did not have fireplaces; they had stoves. If a man could afford a frame house, he could probably also afford a stove. Quebec appears to have been the first part of North America to use stoves for the purpose of heating a house. A Quebec regulation of 1673 (for the better class of houses) stated: 'That no one shall erect a new building in the lower town which has not at least the two gables in masonry. That ladders must be provided for reaching the roof. That stoves not be placed otherwise than in fireplaces.'[6] The German settlers who went to Pennsylvania shortly after 1700 introduced the stove to the English, and Benjamin Franklin built his first 'Franklin' stove in 1739 or 1740. By this time stoves produced by the St Maurice ironworks at Trois-Rivières were in use 'all over Canada,'[7] and the only reasons for their absence in Ontario houses of the first half of the nineteenth century appear to be economic.

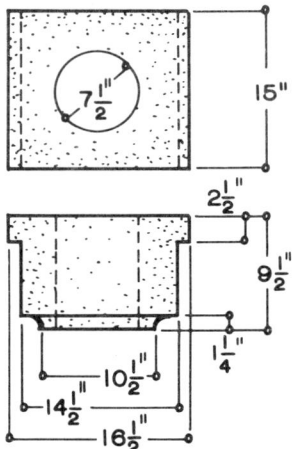

The size of a stone fireproofing block is shown at left.

Timber framing 119

LEFT The simplest fireproofing for the stovepipe, on its way up between the ceiling joists, was a plaster-filled hole in the ceiling. From an old house on Markham Road, now demolished

RIGHT The protection of timber floors, as well as ceiling joists, from the heat of a stovepipe as it passed up through them was a serious problem. One device used was a cut-stone insert; this one is so deep as to permit its use only in floors. From an old inn along the Dundas Highway near Galt, now demolished.

LEFT Stone fireproofing for the stovepipe in place, The old De Puisaye home, Niagara-on-the-Lake, early 1800, now owned by Mr E. Thalmann

RIGHT Another type of insulation for stovepipes was an insert made from clay and burnt to the hardness of bricks; it was thin enough to permit its use not only in floors but also in a vertical position in partitions.

There were attempts to establish iron furnaces or forges in various parts of Ontario in the nineteenth century: at Furnace Falls (now Lyndhurst) on the Gananoque River in 1800, where the indifferent quality of the product forced its closure in 1812; at Potter's Creek (now Normandale) in 1815, which after an unsuccessful start by John Mason was sold to Joseph Van Norman who produced 700 to 800 tons of iron a year until the local supplies of ore and fuel ran out in 1847; at Marmora, where the furnace was in operation from 1830 to shortly after 1867; in Essex County, where bog ore was smelted to produce stoves, ploughs, and potash kettles until the factory was abandoned in 1838 for lack of funds as well as ore; and at Houghton, Norfolk County, where a plant set up in 1854 to produce iron for the Great Western Railway according to certain specifications failed to do so and was closed after one year.[8]

In the United States, the introduction of the Franklin stove is generally taken as an historic landmark. After 1845 fireplaces were often boarded up and the Franklin set in front of them, to become part of the furniture of parlour or bedroom. This encouraged the manufacture of elaborately decorated cast-iron stoves, with nickel-plated trim. A most interesting comment about stoves was made by John Lambert, who travelled through North America in the early nineteenth century, that the stove plates manufactured at the St Maurice forge were *two inches thick*. This seems extraordinary, since the stove would be much too heavy. But his statement is somewhat corroborated in a report submitted on 24 January 1828 by Lieutenant Baddeley (RL Engineers) about the St Maurice ironworks: 'The articles of cast iron furnished by this establishment are stoves and hollow ware of all descriptions. The former are cast thick to resist the cold of the climate and are found to be less liable to crack than those imported.'[9]

Stoves came into use in Ontario much earlier than is generally assumed, but their introduction is known only by casual references in the books and letters of the early settlers. A will probated in Cornwall about 1810 lists 'a stove and pipe.' On 4 December 1811 Sheriff Beikie of York requested, in connection with the local jail, that a stove be installed 'in the Lobby of each range of Cells' to add 'much Comfort of the unhappy persons confined.' In a letter to George Ridout of 22 December 1815, a writer reminisced about the early days in York: 'our sleigh, loaded with backlogs and garnished with stove wood'; 'look what a pile of stove wood we cut today'; 'Frank and Edith are quarrelling like two devils behind the stove.' Basil Hall cites a settler's family in Douro Township, on 1 March 1823: 'got into their house, having put up a stove.' Since stoves were produced in Quebec at least fifty years before the settlement of Upper Canada, their appearance very early in areas close to the border is not surprising.

Although stoves may have been available quite early, they were perhaps not that easy to obtain. But people of means were certainly able to procure one or more from the beginning of the eighteenth century. The Fisher house in Toronto, built in 1836, was heated originally with two stoves, since the structural mutilations around the two fireplaces are proof that the fireplaces were constructed at a later time. However, stoves could cost from five to eight pounds even in the mid-eighteenth century. It is, therefore, not surprising that most log houses retained the fireplace, since an entire cabin would cost no more than twenty to thirty pounds. For most poorer settlers a stove remained an unthinkable luxury.

The unlined stove (that is, one with no firebrick lining in the firebox) becomes so intensely hot as to create a fire hazard. It was never, therefore, placed close to a wall or any piece of furniture. Another danger point was the opening in the ceiling where the pipe passed through to the second floor. Two methods of fireproofing this were in vogue. The first called for a square box framed between the two joists at the point of passage; the pipe was then inserted and the space about it filled with mortar or plaster. A more expensive method was to obtain a square-cut stone with a round aperture in the centre to receive the pipe; this block possessed a shoulder on opposite sides at the top which rested on the two adjacent joists. The Fisher house contained two such stones.

There was a third type of fireproofing, which seems to be a later and cheaper version of the one just described. Clay was moulded to the shape of the stone except that the depth was less. After baking, this form was inserted in the prepared square hole in the ceiling. The shallow depth of this brick substitute had one disadvantage. The stone block was always cut to sufficient thickness to insulate the full depth of the floor construction, keeping the hot pipe away from the ceiling as well as from the floor above it; the clay block, because of its shallowness, safeguarded only the ceiling, and the floor above would still need protection. How this protection was furnished I have not been able to establish.

It is generally agreed that central heating first appeared in North America in Massachusetts at the beginning of the nineteenth century. The medium was hot air. The early furnaces were rather clumsy affairs, consisting basically of a stove surrounded by brick masonry, with a large air space left between the masonry and the stove itself, the whole unit forming a rough cube at least 8 feet in dimension. Ducts in the walls conveyed the heated air to the various rooms. The first patent for steam heating seems to have been obtained in 1831. It is doubtful if any Ontario buildings were heated by either of these methods before the middle of the century. It is also hardly probable that any of these early furnaces have survived to this day, although Upper Canada Village holds one in storage, awaiting reconstruction, and Dundurn Castle in Hamilton contains a similar arrangement for heating one parlour. For the most part these early devices will have fallen prey to 'modernization.' The only evidence remaining of their use will be the ducts in the walls, not to be detected unless the building undergoes great alterations or is demolished.

The last and most significant of the technical developments in nineteenth-century frame building in North America was the balloon frame. Sources differ on who should be credited for the introduction of balloon framing,[10] but they agree on the first building that was constructed in this way: St Mary's Church (25 by 30 feet), built in 1833 at a cost of $400 in the newly founded town of Chicago. After the great fire, which destroyed the major portion of the town, it had to be rebuilt quickly to provide shelter; this necessity for speed resulted in the development of the balloon frame.

The structural principles of balloon framing were the same as in earlier framing except for two divergences: the mortise and tenon joint was replaced by a nailed lap joint and the thickness of the timbers was reduced. The smaller timbers necessitated closer spacing of the principals and thus a greater number of them. But, being smaller, they were easier to handle; and since all joints were nailed, less skill, time, and hand labour were required. The only tools needed to build a house at this time were a saw, a carpenter's

An excellent example of the common fate of a fireplace. The original opening can be clearly seen. It was then reduced in size and still later completely eliminated and plastered over. Woodbridge

square, a hammer – and lots of nails. It was because of the availability of inexpensive wire nails and their acceptance by the trade that balloon framing was made possible.

This technique owes its origin to the prevalence of sawmills as well as nail factories. Grist mills, sawmills, and ironworks were the three most numerous manufacturing units in colonial America. Nineteenth-century ironworks usually contained at least one slitting mill for the production of iron rods, and these could be turned into nails by a blacksmith at the rate of several hundred per day. So efficient and economical was this method of building that it quickly became the standard by the 1880s and continued in use well into the twentieth century before being succeeded by western or platform framing.

An exterior wall of 1880. Note the construction required for a board-and-batten wall. The alterations for a later addition are clearly visible. Carmichael house (see pages 131–2)

124  Building with Wood

The following examples from Ontario illustrate the transition from early to balloon framing.

1 HOUSE AT MOULINETTE

This house was demolished to make way for the St Lawrence Seaway and was razed so quickly that there was not time to make as detailed an examination as the building merited. It was a full two-storey house with three principal bents braced transversely at the three principal floor beams and laterally at the upper corners between the plate and the corner posts. The first- and second-floor joists ran laterally, framing into the principal floor beams; ceiling joists ran parallel to the rafters. There was no evidence of fireplaces, and the second floor was framed around the typical fireproofing stone. The chimney was not on a bracket halfway up the wall, but started at the second floor level and ran up through the roof. The bracket type of chimney was frequently a later addition. All principal timbers were hand-

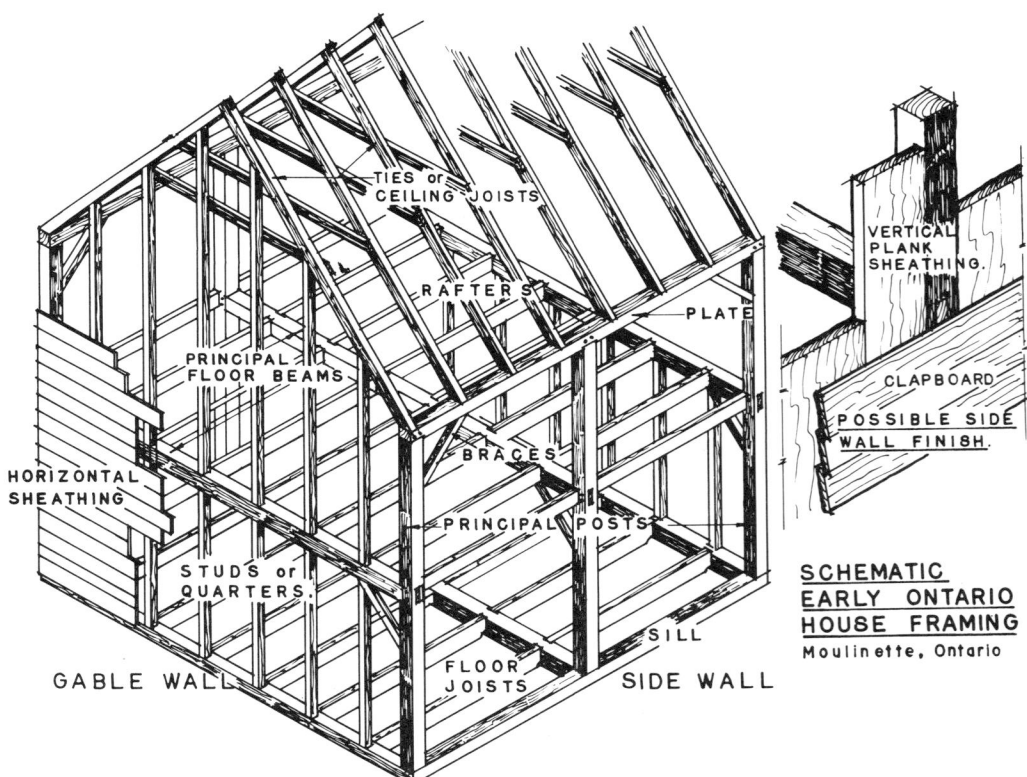

SCHEMATIC EARLY ONTARIO HOUSE FRAMING
Moulinette, Ontario

The framing of the house in Moulinette

hewn and mortised and tenoned, pinned when in tension and open when in compression. There was evidence of vertical planking on the side walls, although the gable walls had studs with horizontal sheathing.

The house was probably built in the first quarter of the nineteenth century, and was originally intended to be heated by a stove. This is early for a stove-heated house in Ontario, but it was near the Quebec border and the St Lawrence, up which a stove could easily have been transported.

## 2 PINKNEY HOUSE, COOKSVILLE

This house stood between Cooksville and Dixie, but was demolished in 1955 to permit the widening of Dundas Street. Local tradition dated the building of the house in the first quarter of the nineteenth century.

Although this house is of much the same size and vintage as the one at Moulinette, a much-improved framing method was used. Instead of three principal bents there were only two, one at each end, where the principal posts were about 8 inches square. Intermediate posts were spaced more closely and were of lighter timbers, approximately 6 by 8 inches. The seven intermediate posts on each side extended the full height of the corner ones, with the second-floor beams mortised and tenoned into the verticals by means of a shouldered joint and fastened with the usual two pins. The spacing of posts and beams was about 3 feet on centre, thus making the connecting beams appear to be oversized floor joists. This spacing, however, required heavy flooring – about 1½ inch tongue-and-groove boards – which was laid directly on the joists. The bracing was still traditional: transverse corner braces at the second-floor level in the gable walls, with lateral bracing in the upper corner at plate level. There was no intermediate transverse bracing.

The house rested on a stone foundation laid dry, and was raised about 12 inches above the existing grade. There was no basement originally under the portion of the building where the ground was excavated to a depth of about 2 feet below the floor joists. The sill was laid in lime mortar; this was the only evidence of mortar in the entire foundation.

Perhaps the most interesting point about this house was the first floor. Its beams, of necessity, spaced the same way as the second-floor joists, were left in the round with the bark still intact except for an adzed top about 4 inches wide at the level of the sill. Now, since a first-floor load is greater than a second-floor load, and yet the beams supporting the two floors in this house were spaced at the same distance, the builder had to compensate for this increased load by inserting an extra floor joist between each pair of beams. These extra joists were sawn, not hewn, and were approximately 2 inches wide and 10 inches deep. They were set into the sill in a shouldered housed joint. This suggests fairly conclusively that these joists were built with the house and were not a later addition; only by radical renovation, of which there is no evidence, could they have been inserted at a later date.

This house is interesting because all the principal timbers were hand-hewn, and yet it exhibited elements of balloon framing in that these timbers were closely spaced – this about ten years before balloon framing became the accepted form.

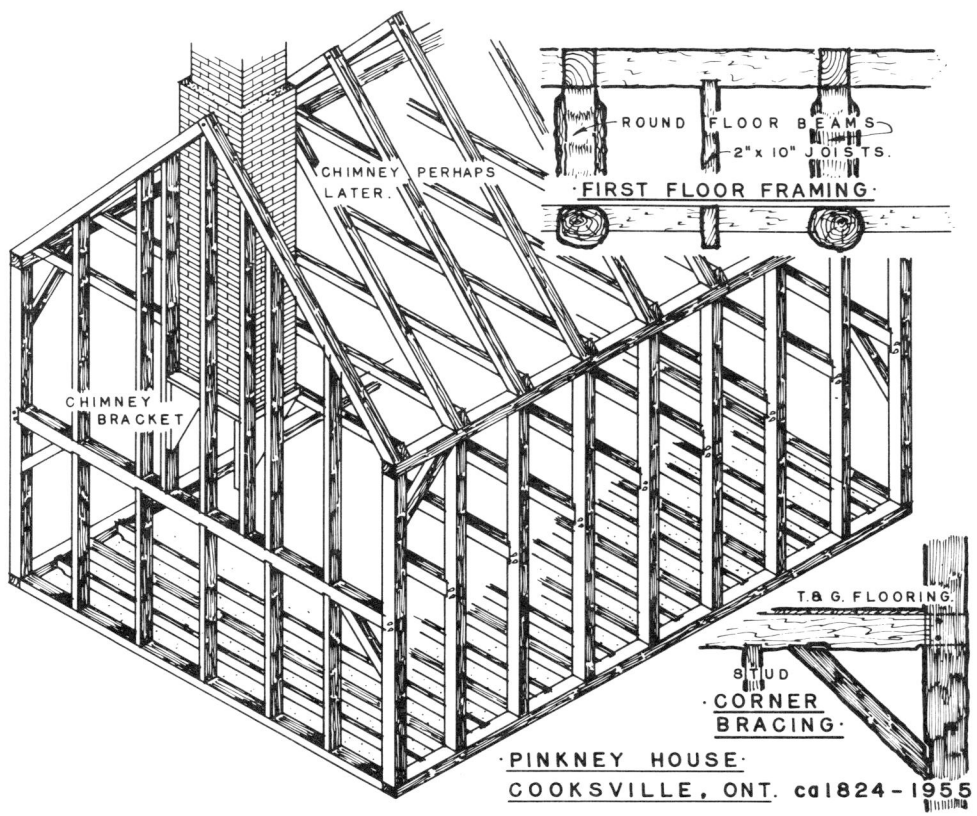

This was the Pinkney house on Dundas Street near Dixie.

128  Building with Wood

3 HOUSE AT WOODBRIDGE

The neatest example of frame construction I have seen to date was a house in Woodbridge, demolished after Hurricane Hazel in 1954. It was so solid and well built that, even though the Humber raged right round it and through it, it never left its foundations. All the workmanship was excellent.

The framed portion of the building was similar to the Pinkney house and, according to local estimates, of about the same age. However, its timbers were all sawn and not hewn, as was more usual at that time, and even its compression joints were pinned. The building was about 20 feet wide and 24 feet long and incorporated an even older building – an old log school that became the living room.

The sill was 10 by 10 inches on a stone foundation. Uprights were 6 by 6 inches with 4 by 8 inch floor beams mortised and tenoned into them. The plate was 7 by 7 inches with 4 by 4 inch corner braces. These braces were also tenoned with one pin in the upper joint and two in the lower; this is most

Excellent construction. Note the outside sheathing, the brick fill with a portion of the board lining still in place under the window, and lath and plaster over wood fill. Woodbridge

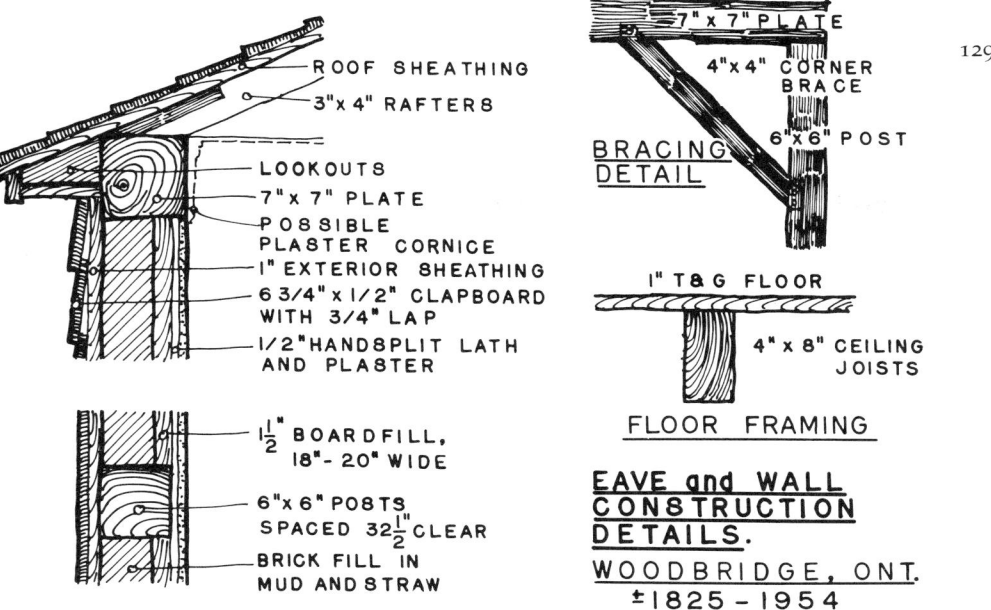

**EAVE and WALL CONSTRUCTION DETAILS.**
**WOODBRIDGE, ONT.**
**±1825 - 1954**

unusual, for these two joints were usually left open. Lateral bracing consisted of the usual corner bracing in the upper corners at the last posts from the end and, in keeping with the solidity of its construction, the middle post was also braced laterally in both directions. The walls were the most solid I have ever known in a frame house: the outside was covered with horizontal sheathing 1 full inch in thickness and up to 20 inches wide. Clapboard, 6¾ by ½ inch, was nailed against this with a ¾ inch lap. The 32½ inch spaces between the posts were filled with bricks laid in mud and straw mortar, and by solid 1½ inch boards placed against the brickwork so that their inside face was flush with the inside face of the uprights. Half-inch handsplit lath was then laid over the whole inside face and covered with plaster.

Another indication of the house's expensive and sturdy construction was a full basement, unusual in houses built at this time, with about 6 feet of headroom under the entire house. The house, being two storeys in height, had the ceiling joists resting alongside the lower end of the rafters and directly on the plate. The ceiling joists were deep enough to permit the underside to be cut in a curve, thus giving the ceiling a slightly vaulted appearance.

Because the top of the rafters were flush with the outside upper corner of the plate, separate lookouts had to be inserted alongside them to permit the construction of an overhang. The rafters were 3 by 4 inches, and the lookouts projected exactly 7 inches beyond the plate. Oddly enough, these lookouts were not fastened in place at all; they were simply laid in a slot cut in the upper outer corner of the plate. The only possible explanation for this, judging by the rest of the construction, is that the roof sheathing was also one full inch in thickness. Since the boards were wider than the usual ones, such sheathing perhaps projected 7 inches beyond the outside face of the plate, the function of the lookouts being therefore simply to form a nailing surface for the soffit. It has been suggested, in view of the fact that the stems of lookouts had been rounded, quite unnecessarily, to a rough circle of 1½ inch diameter, that the lookouts were used as hookpins during construction.

### 4 THE SCHNEIDER HOUSE, KITCHENER

This is by far the most solidly built house I have encountered so far. Joseph Schneider, being of Pennsylvania-Dutch origin, believed in simple but solid construction, a typical characteristic of this group. He came to Canada in 1807 because Pennsylvania was becoming too 'overcrowded' with settlers! He thus became the founder of Berlin, now Kitchener.

The frame of this house consists of three bents only, which is somewhat unusual for such a large house. The most novel feature, however, is the roof framing: although the pitch is not particularly steep and the rafters are not unusually long, Schneider believed in solid support for the rafters and consequently gave them a secondary plate to rest on in the manner of barn framing. The other unusual feature is the size of the corner posts: these are 10 by 10 inches while the filler studs are 4 by 7 inches. In order to avoid a projection in the exterior corners of the rooms, these posts are cut back 3 inches on each side to make both sides the same thickness as the width of the studs. The spaces between the studs are filled with rubble masonry. This type of corner post treatment was also used in Grace Church in Markham – the church, however, was built in 1849, whereas this house was built in 1820.

LEFT Roof framing at the gable end. Schneider house, 1820
RIGHT Roof framing at the middle bent. Schneider house

The Carmichael house, built in 1880, which stood on the northwest corner of Markham Road and Lawrence Avenue

5 THE CARMICHAEL HOUSE, TORONTO

This house, at the corner of Lawrence and Markham Road, was built in the 1880s and was consequently of balloon-frame construction, though without certain later refinements of that method and with some vestiges of the old-style framing. The plan was in the shape of an inverted T, the stem being a later addition which we shall not consider here.

There was no basement but, like the house at Moulinette and the Pinkney house, it had what is now called a crawl space of about 24 inches below the finished grade. The foundation walls were of stone in lime mortar and were about 16 inches thick.

All lumber was sawn but not dressed, and so all measurements are the exact size given. The sill, a 3 by 10 inch piece, was laid in a heavy mortar bed on the stone foundation. The corner posts were heavier than the studs – 4 by 4 inches as against 2 by 4 inches – and all the vertical structural members had 2 inch square tenons mortised into the sill. These are characteristics of the older method of framing. For some unknown reason, the sill for the gable walls was a 2 by 6 inch plank butted against the side sills without any fastening whatever.

An unusual feature was the seating of the first-floor joists. Since the foundation wall projected about 6 inches beyond the back of the sill, the joists were imbedded into the foundation without any connection to the sill. (In later balloon framing the joists would rest directly on the sill beside the

·2<sup>nd</sup> FLOOR LEVEL·

·BALLOON FRAMING DETAILS·

foot of the studs.) The joists were 2 by 10 inches, spaced about 16 inches on centre, and were butted against the sill, their top flush with the top of the sill.

The studs ran the full height from the sill to a 3½ by 4 inch plate into which they were housed to a depth of about 1 inch. This lighter plate was now possible because the spacing of the rafters followed that of the studs. The rafters were 2 by 6 inches and the roof had a Gothic pitch. Handsplit lath was used in the ceiling of the bay window and may have been used elsewhere – I arrived on the scene after all the lath and plaster except this had been removed.

The second-floor joists were supported by a 1 by 4 inch band or ledger board let into the studs to its full thickness. This was a standard method used in all balloon framing. There was a profusion of horizontal bracing or bridging in the walls above the second floor: this was for a board-and-batten exterior which demands frequent points of support to prevent the boards from warping.

Although this was a small house, it was one of the outstanding examples of balloon framing in Metropolitan Toronto. The exterior was elaborately decorated with flat pierced work in the architrave of the front porch, which extended the full length of the building; it had a curved hip roof, carved bargeboards, fishscale shingles on the bay window roof, and an individual cap for each batten. These caps were made out of one piece at the roof line and out of three pieces for the battens in the bay window. The three gables were crowned with elaborately turned king-posts supported by flamboyant brackets at the roof and a turned pendant at the lower end. In spite of this profusion of ornament, it was all in good taste for that period.

## 6 THE GLEASON HOUSE AND THE FISHER HOUSE

A comparison of the frames of two houses, similar in many ways though distant in location and time of building, should give the reader a better idea of the evolution of timber framing in North America and the differences between the 'Early American' and 'Modified American' building technologies. A close study of their construction can be rewarding, particularly the details of the walls, the provision for openings, and especially the intricacies of jointing.

The Gleason house in Farmington, Connecticut, was built in 1650–60, and the details of its construction were recorded by Isham and Brown in their *Early Connecticut Houses* in 1900. The Fisher house, on the Humber River in Toronto, was erected in 1836 and demolished in 1968. The two houses were almost identical in size, and similar in plan and proportion, with centre-hall and two-room construction; both were two full storeys in height. The Gleason house showed an overhang on the front side only, and the two

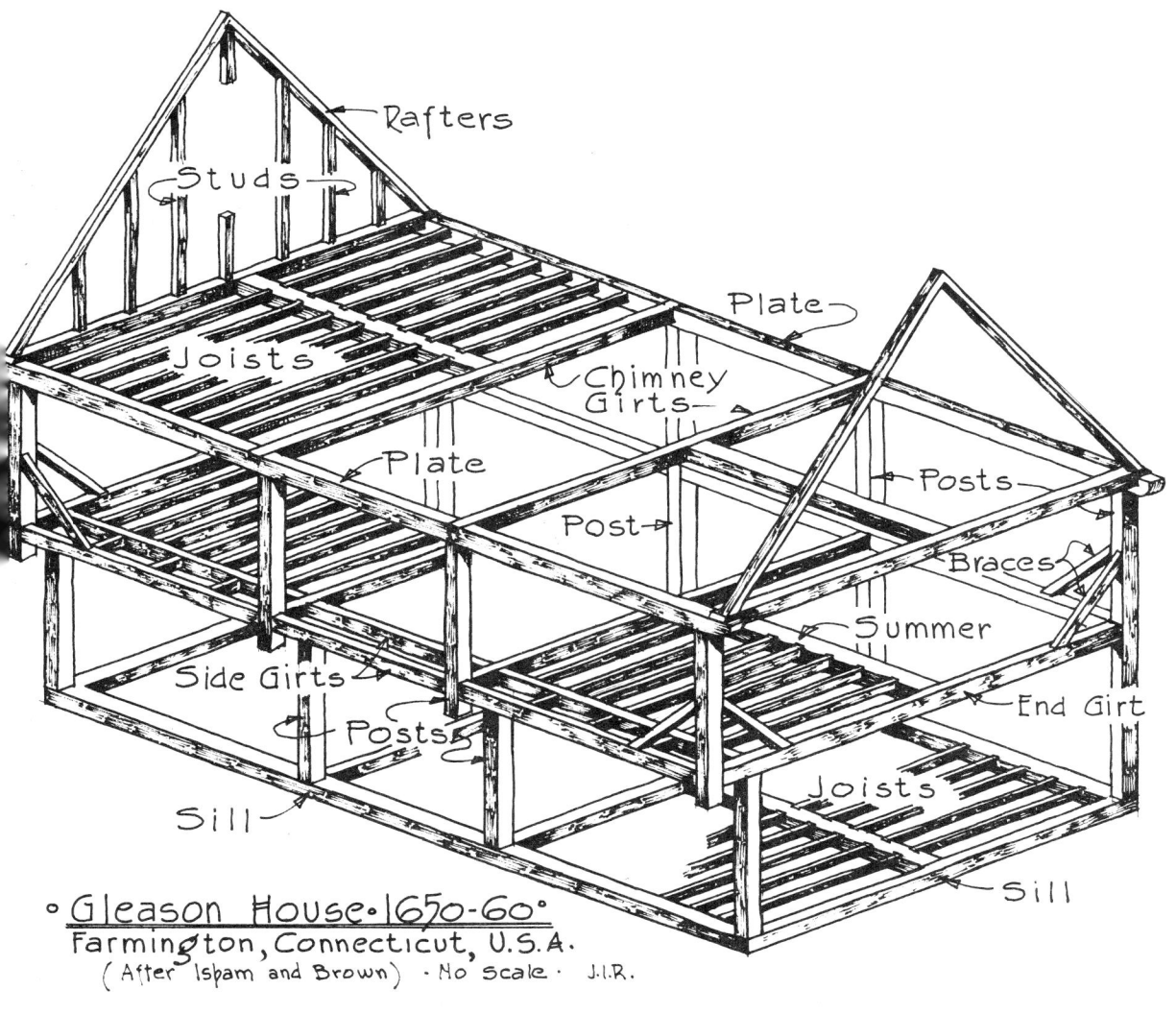

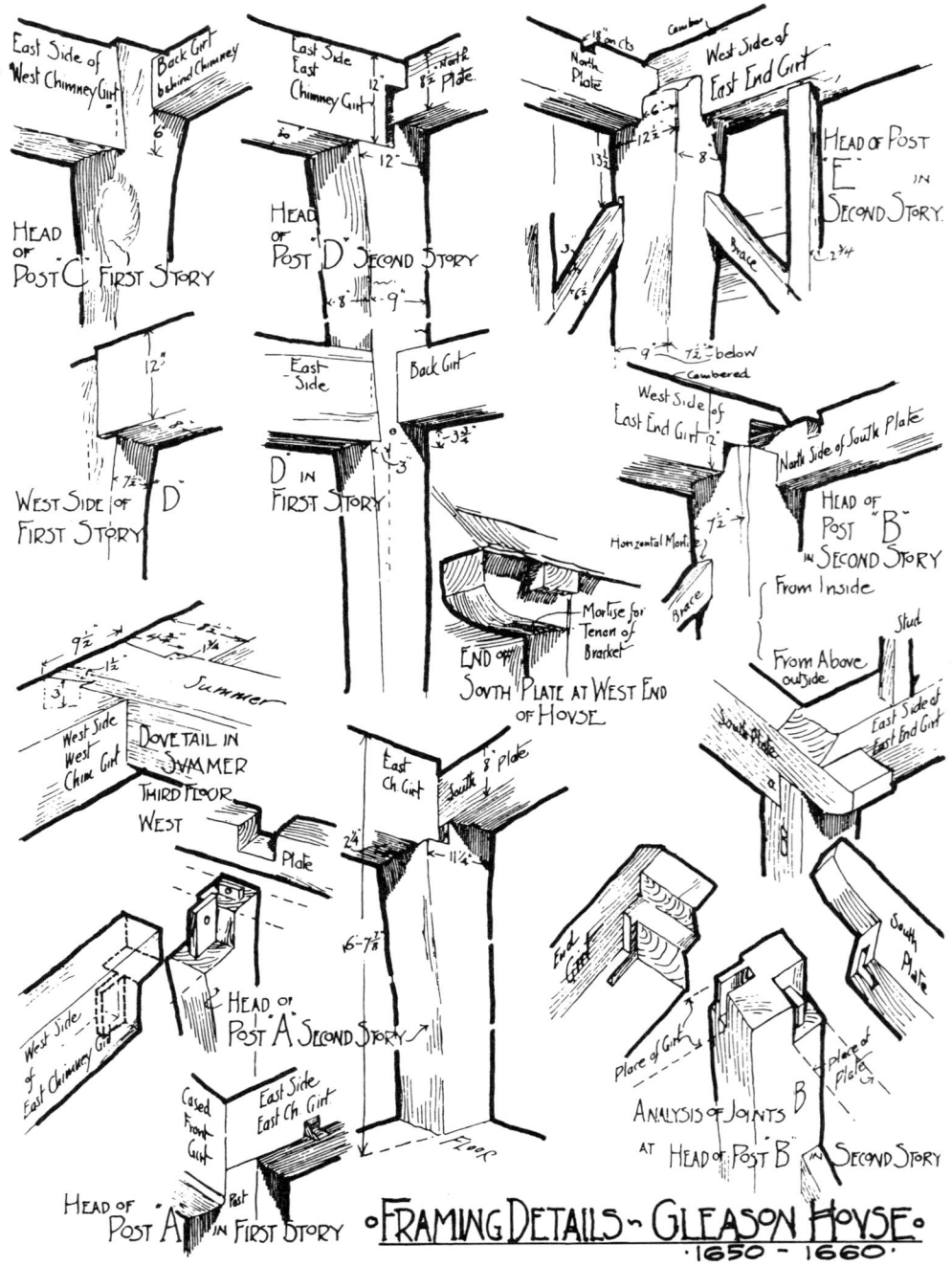

gables projected slightly above the second-floor ceiling. (The overhang need not concern us since this feature had disappeared even in the United States long before the Fisher house was built.)

The Gleason house measured 20' 4" in width by 38' 6" in length. By 1900 it had degenerated, in use, to a wagon shed in one half and a cattle-stall in the other. The centre chimney had disappeared and great mutilations had taken place during the years. Yet 'the very disrepair and ruin of the house were of the greatest service to us, for we were thereby enabled to study the framing with considerable ease.' For the sake of clarity, the drawings omit most joists, studs, and rafters in order to reveal the primary members.

The frame was a typical four-principal or four-bent type. The four pairs of principals would thus demand four girts: two end and two chimney ones. This resulted in a two-room plan with a central chimney and 'porch,' which served as an entry and stair hall. Each of the rooms had a 'summer' (large horizontal beam) running centrally between the end and chimney girts.

The Fisher house was about two feet larger in both directions, the measurements being 22' 2" wide by 40' 2" long. Its frame was also of the four-bent type, resulting in the same centre-hall, two-room plan. The structure was considerably mutilated and added to after its first erection. However, it was demolished rather slowly, making possible a very detailed study of the essential members. For comparison, I have chosen just two details which illustrate the evolution of joining in the two frames. The efficiency and ease of construction of the later frame over that of the earlier one will be obvious, and the method of interlocking the two plates at the corners of the Fisher house is most ingenious in its simplicity.

Perhaps the most significant difference between the two frames was the scarcity of corner-bracing in the earlier one. The Gleason house had a total of only eight such braces, and these were located, not in the upper corners between plates and corner posts as usual, but in the lower corners between the second-floor side- and end-girts and the corner posts. The Fisher house, on the other hand, boasted eight braces in the front (north) wall, fourteen in the rear (south) wall, and six in each of the four bents, making a total of forty-six. In addition, there was a horizontal corner brace between the side and end plates in each corner, to make an amazing total of fifty. Mr Fisher was taking no chances!

It is also interesting to compare the floor framing in the two houses. The older was framed in the standard early method of splitting the width of each end by a summer and running the joists transversely. The summer was always dovetailed into the girts which gave it the property of acting as a tie-beam in addition to its function as a load-bearer. This structural feature was not feasible in the Fisher house, since here all structural members were of lesser 'scantling' or dimension. The need of a tie between two adjacent girts, however, still remained. Since the joists ran longitudinally and were

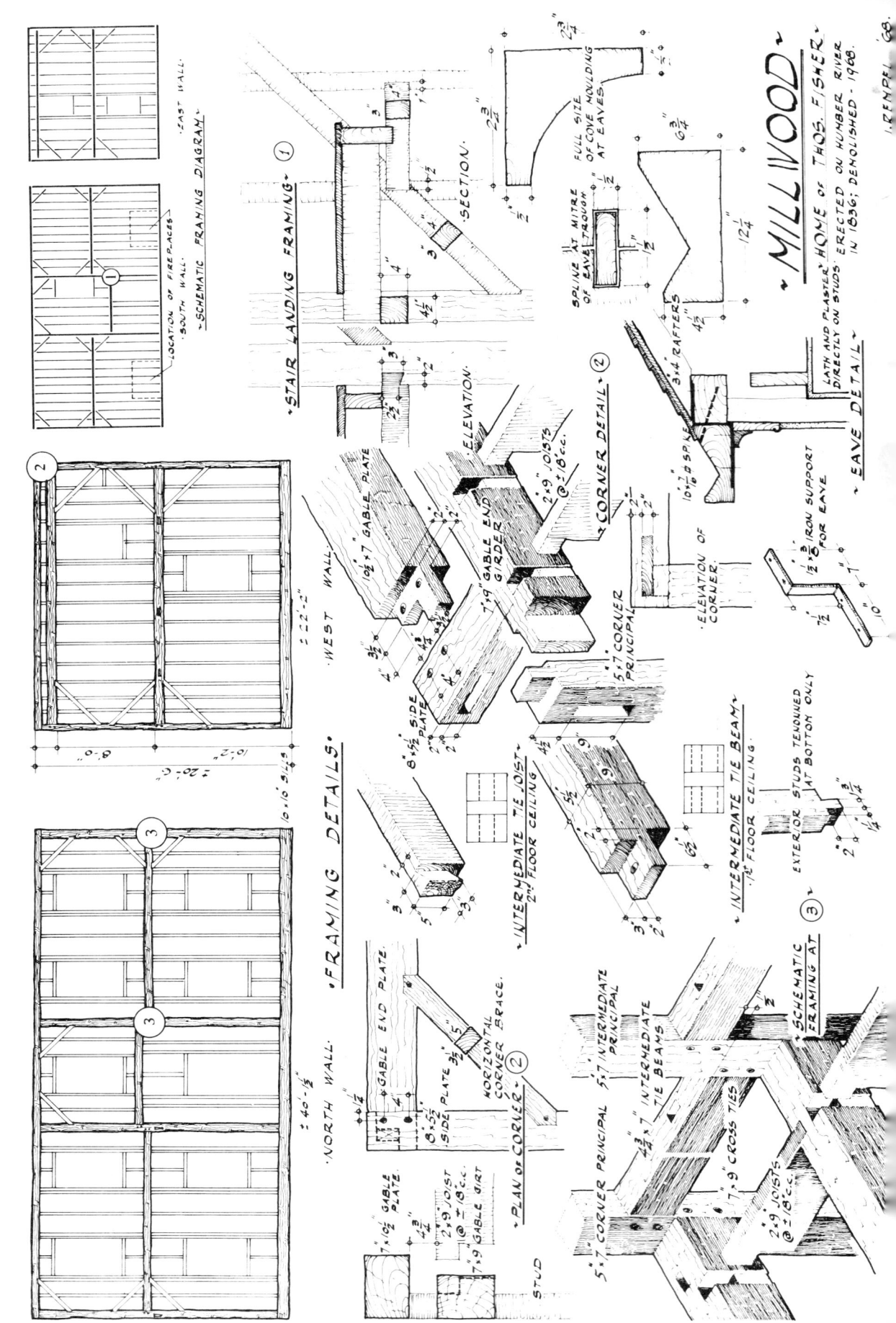

Timber framing 137

set in a shouldered, housed joint at each end, they possessed no tying property whatsoever. Therefore, the summer was replaced by two slightly heavier tie-joists, which were spaced equally over the width of the room. These joists carried a shouldered and pinned mortise and tenon joint at each end at the first-floor ceiling and a half-dovetailed end at the second-floor ceiling. The reason for this change of joint is not clear, unless it was the fact that the second-floor ceiling members were of still smaller size and the builder was perhaps concerned about weakening them too much by employing a mortise and tenon joint.

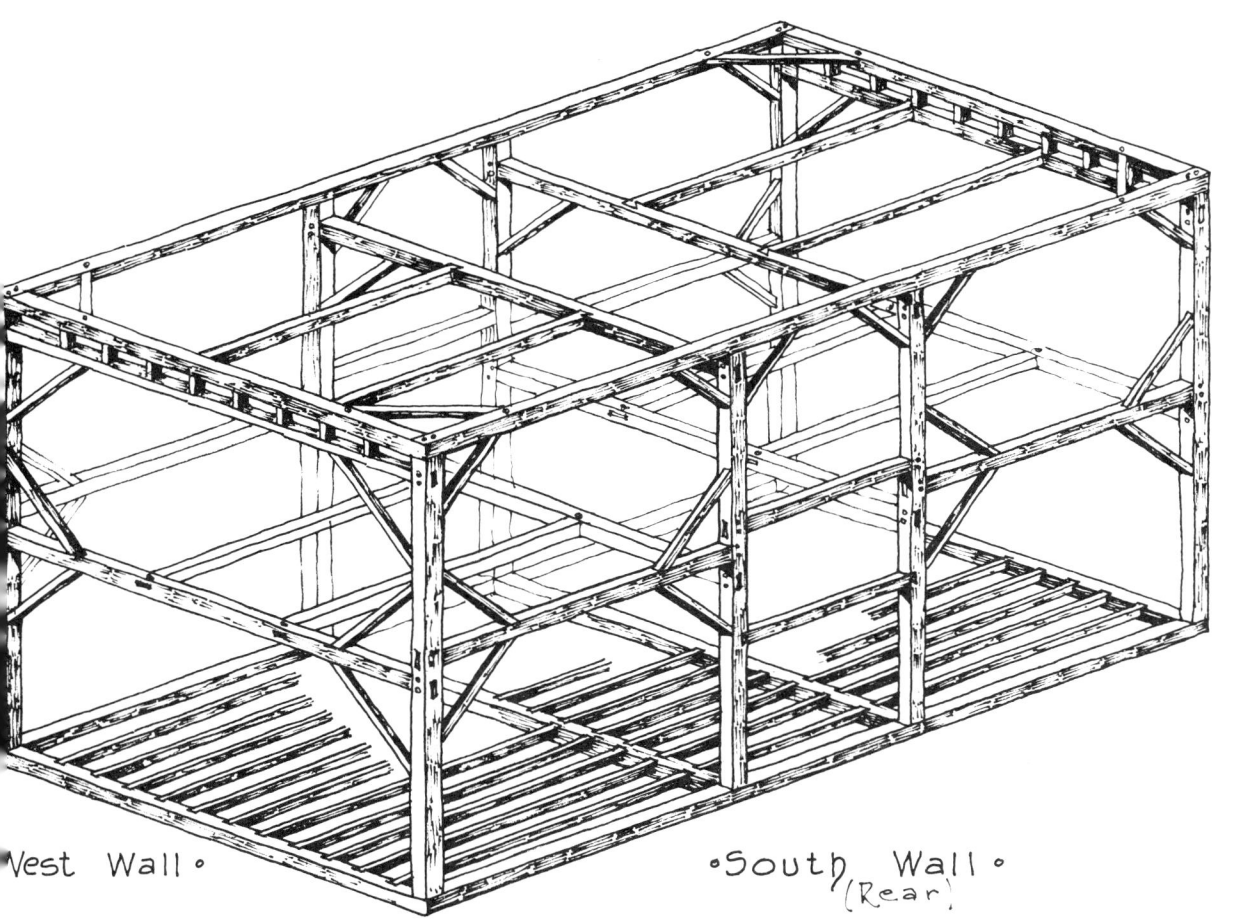

West Wall. •South Wall•
(Rear)
•Fisher House• 1836-1968•
On the Humber River, Toronto, Ontario.
•No Scale• J.I.R.

138  Building with Wood

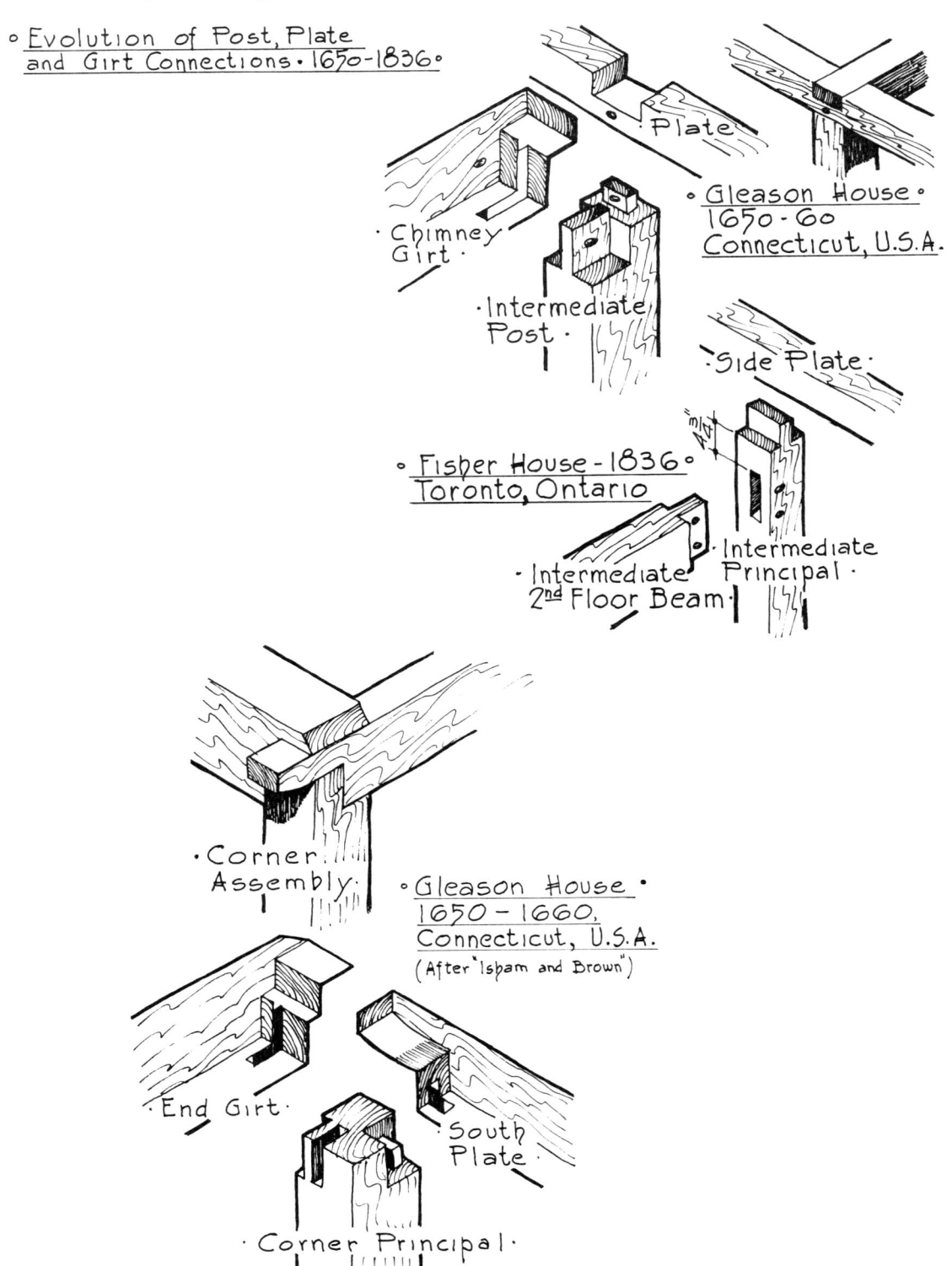

Evolution of Post, Plate and Girt Connections • 1650-1836 •

Gleason House • 1650-60 Connecticut, U.S.A.
· Plate ·
· Chimney Girt ·
· Intermediate Post ·

Fisher House - 1836 • Toronto, Ontario
· Side Plate ·
· Intermediate Principal ·
· Intermediate 2nd Floor Beam ·

Gleason House • 1650-1660, Connecticut, U.S.A. (After "Isham and Brown")
· Corner Assembly ·
· End Girt ·
· South Plate ·
· Corner Principal ·

Timber framing 139

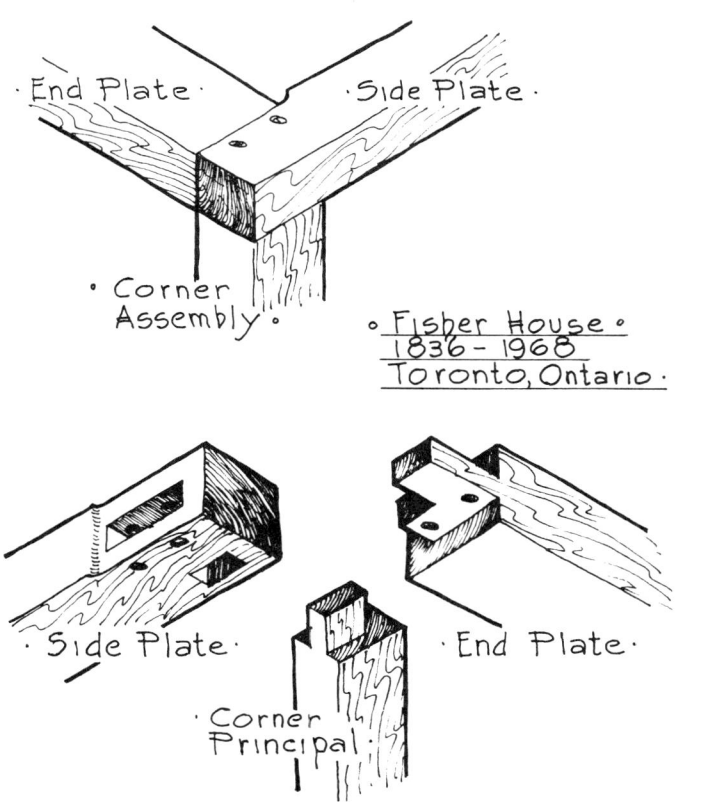

Fisher House
1836 - 1968
Toronto, Ontario.

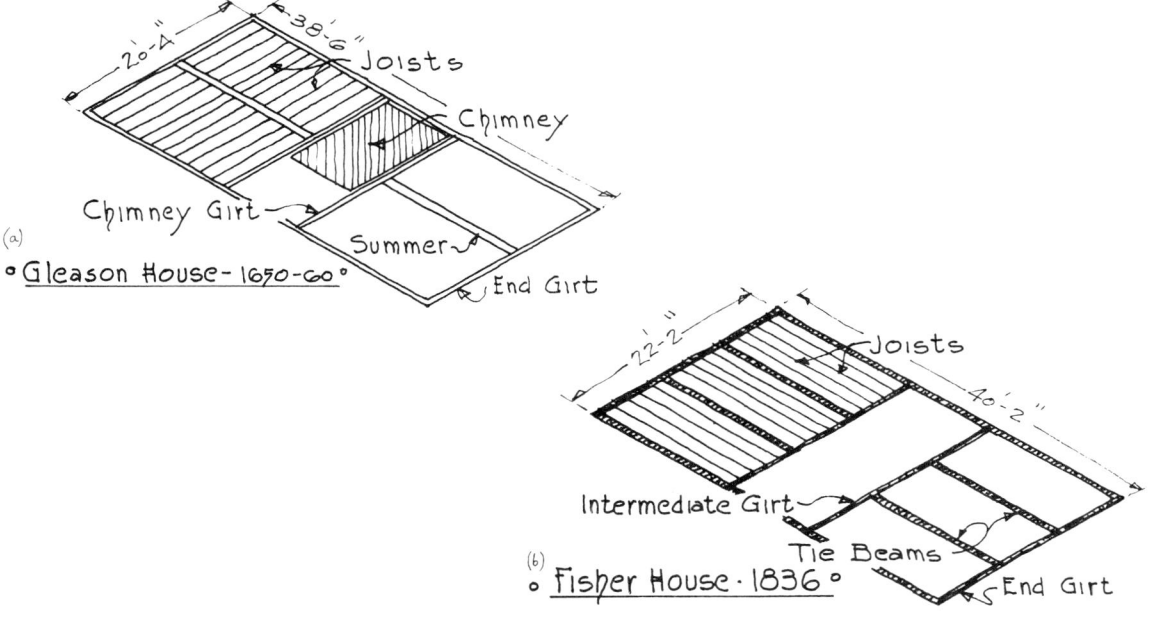

(a) Gleason House - 1650-60

(b) Fisher House · 1836

140   Building with Wood

## Timber framing in Quebec

Technological development never progresses in a regular, constant fashion; there is, often, a long gap between the time when a new method is first introduced and the time it becomes universally accepted. For this reason we shall consider timber framing in Quebec in a technological rather than a chronological sequence.

Basically, Quebec timber construction is of two types: 'poteaux' (posts) and 'colombage' (half-timbering). Originally 'poteaux' construction consisted of logs or posts driven into the ground, spaced fairly closely, and the spaces filled with chinking. The whole structure could then be covered with boards or planks, though it was generally left exposed. Later, the posts were set into sills above ground. 'Colombage' was essentially a wooden, pinned

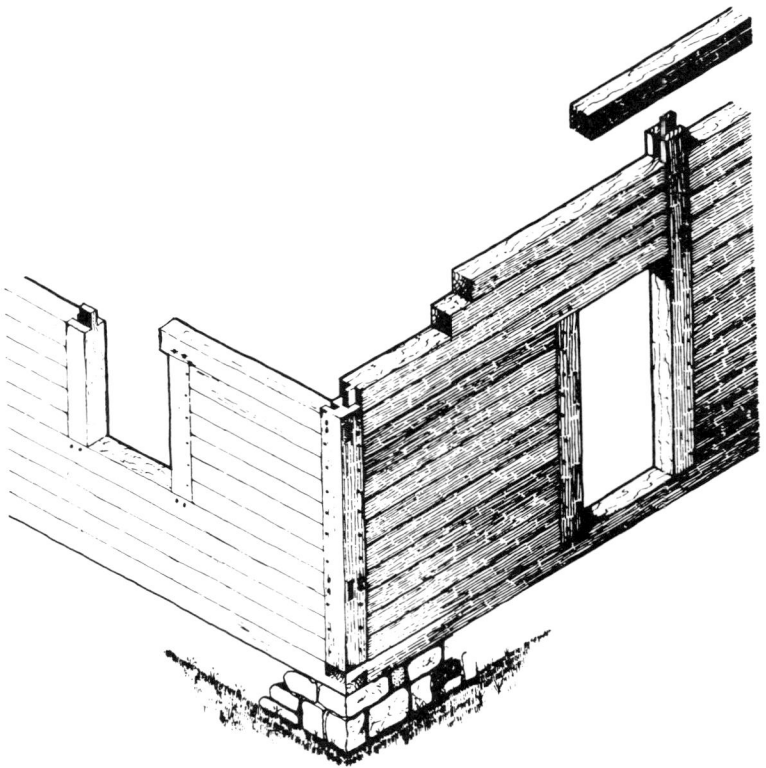

Typical Quebec grooved post construction ('poteaux et pièce coulissante')

Perhaps the earliest French timber construction on this continent consisted of closely spaced posts, set into sills, with the spaces filled with mortar. Cahokia, Illinois, built about 1737 and restored in 1939; compare with the Fafard house, 1720

frame with the spaces filled with stone in mortar; in this case it was known as 'colombage pierroté.' Another type of timber construction was the 'poteaux et pièce coulissante' or the grooved post construction. Typical of this method was the use of vertical posts with grooves along their full length. These posts were appropriately spaced and filler pieces, bearing a tenon at each end, were then dropped into position so as to lie horizontally between each pair of uprights. In France, as well as in other parts of Europe, this method is known as plankwall framing. The more severe climate of Quebec led to the replacement of planks with squared timbers. It is an interesting fact that the filler pieces in Quebec are generally of the same thickness as the uprights into which they fit, making a quite massive wall indeed.

At first, in Quebec, an attempt was made at applying the structural technique typical of Normandy and Picardy. This consisted of closely spaced posts set into a wooden sill and topped with a plate. The spaces were then chinked with rubble stone or masonry fill. This method was also carried into the United States, and the courthouse in Cahokia, Illinois, built about 1737, is the best-known example.

In Quebec the Pichet house, built in the early eighteenth century, is of this type. It is located in Ste-Famille on the Ile d'Orléans and is still being used as a residence. Here the walls consist of 6 inch square pine posts spaced about 6 inches apart. The spaces in between are filled with rubble masonry. This house is of quite rare construction, only three or four similar ones are now known to exist. The most unusual feature is the inward taper, of about 6 inches, of all four exterior walls; no definite explanation for it has yet been given. Another unusual feature is the lateral cross-bracing, which takes the form of a through tenon held against the outside face of the posts by wedges in a similar manner to the Schoharie barn anchor beams, discussed later.

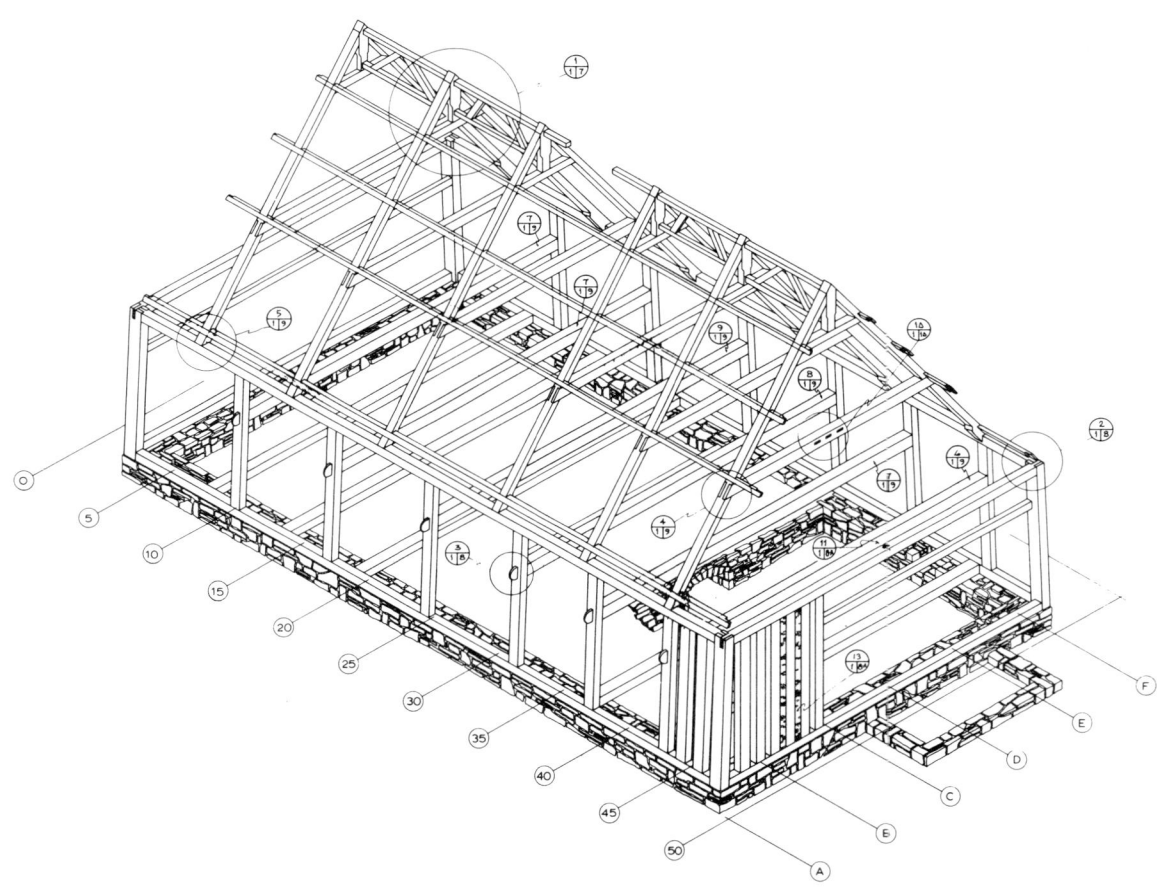

The Pichet house, early eighteenth century

Window construction detail, Pichet house

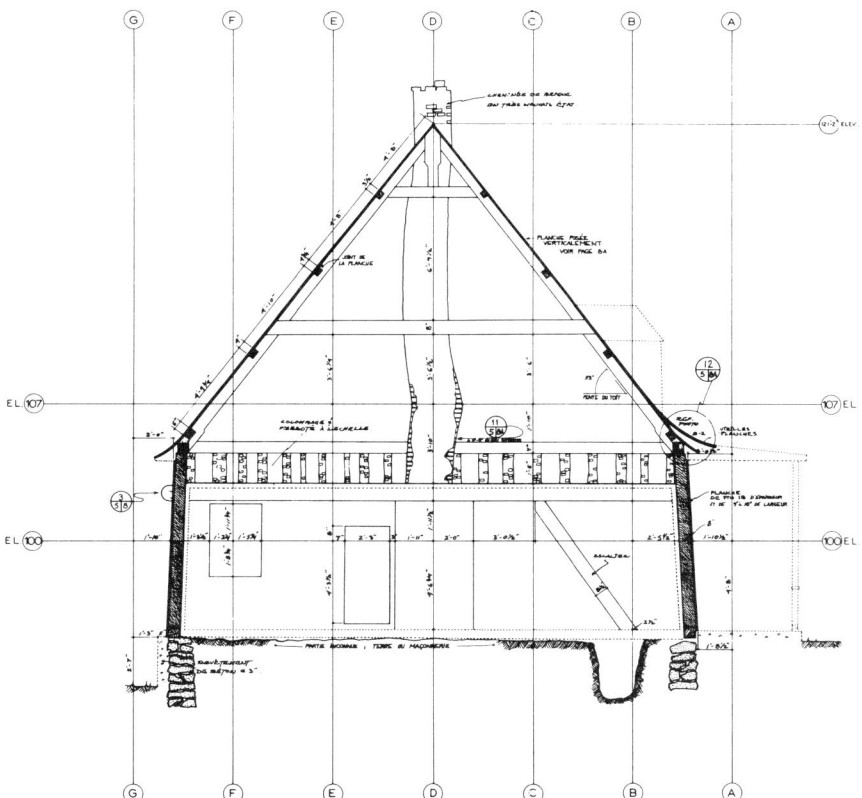

There can be no doubt that the extra work of seating so many studs and the difficulty of filling such narrow spaces with masonry led to experimentation with more widely spaced studs. In 1753 a rowhouse, consisting of three apartments, was built for the widow of Sieur Lartigue, who had been 'baillif' at Isle Royale, Cape Breton. This was a one-storey building and consisted of vertical posts set between sills and plates. Here, however, the timber posts were spaced about 3 feet apart, much wider than in the Cahokia courthouse, but the fill still consisted of masonry – brick instead of rubble.

In the Paradis house in Charlesbourg the spacing is 3 to 4 feet. The significant point in its structure is the horizontally laid timber fill, here covered with vertical siding, typical of grooved post and fill construction. The filler pieces were 4 inches thick and 8 inches deep. The frame consisted of 12 inch square sills and corner posts. The intermediate posts were 7 by 8 inches. The date of this house is uncertain but is probably early eighteenth century. Both the Paradis house and the Lartigue apartments may be considered transitional in a technological rather than a chronological sense.

Apartments built in 1753 for the widow of Sieur Lartigue

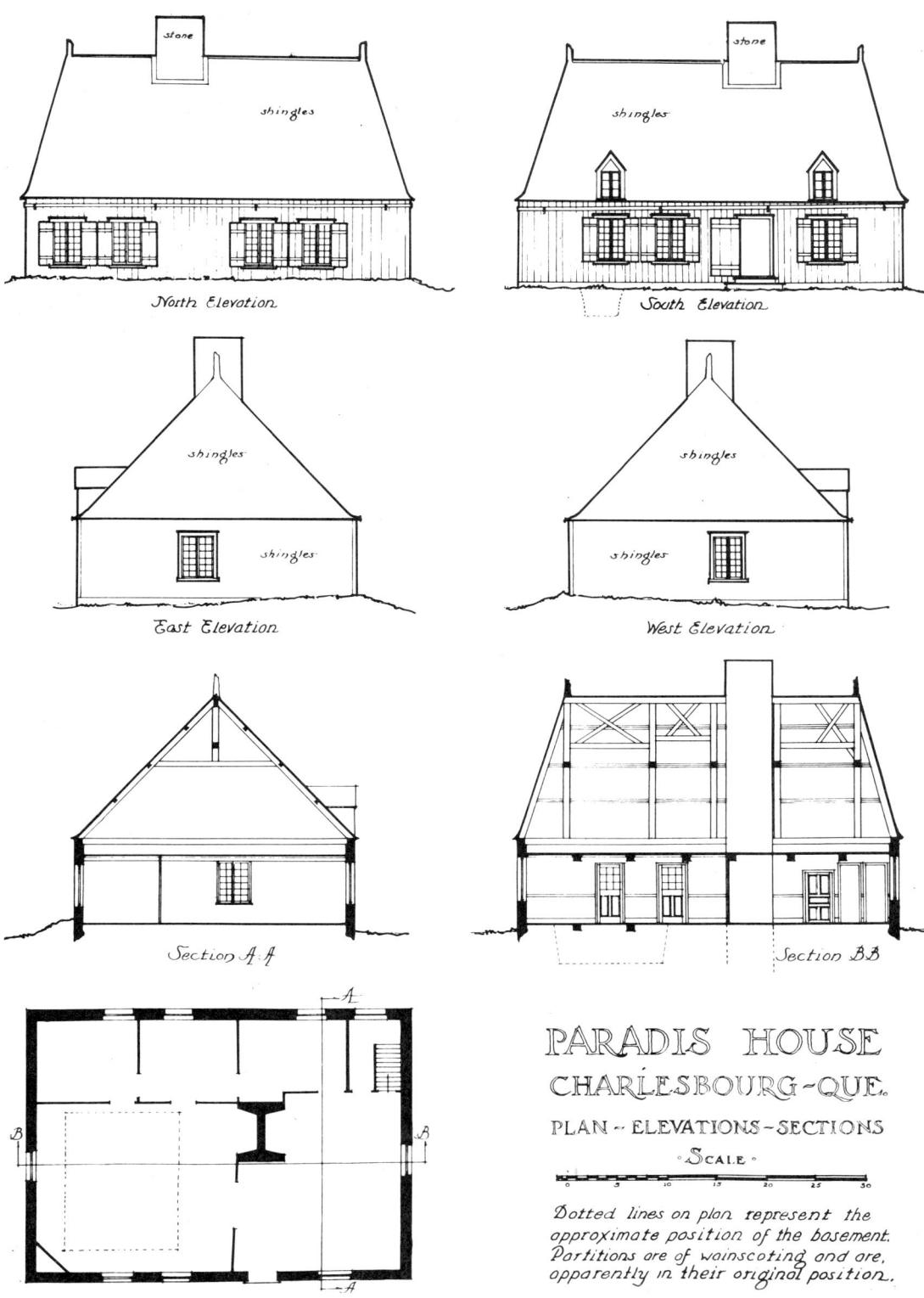

146  Building with Wood

In the Fafard house, which was built about 1720, the posts were already spaced about 16 feet apart. This would appear to be the maximum distance possible; the explanation being, perhaps, that timber fill of this length or greater is awkward to manipulate. Later, the intervals between posts became fairly regular and this produced a wall consisting of a number of equal panels. From available records it appears that, as this method of timber framing moved westward, a 10 foot modulus became more or less the accepted standard. Openings were frequently placed in such a manner that at least one post would also function as a jamb. Heads of doors and windows were generally kept at the same height in order to permit a single timber to function as a lintel at the same time.

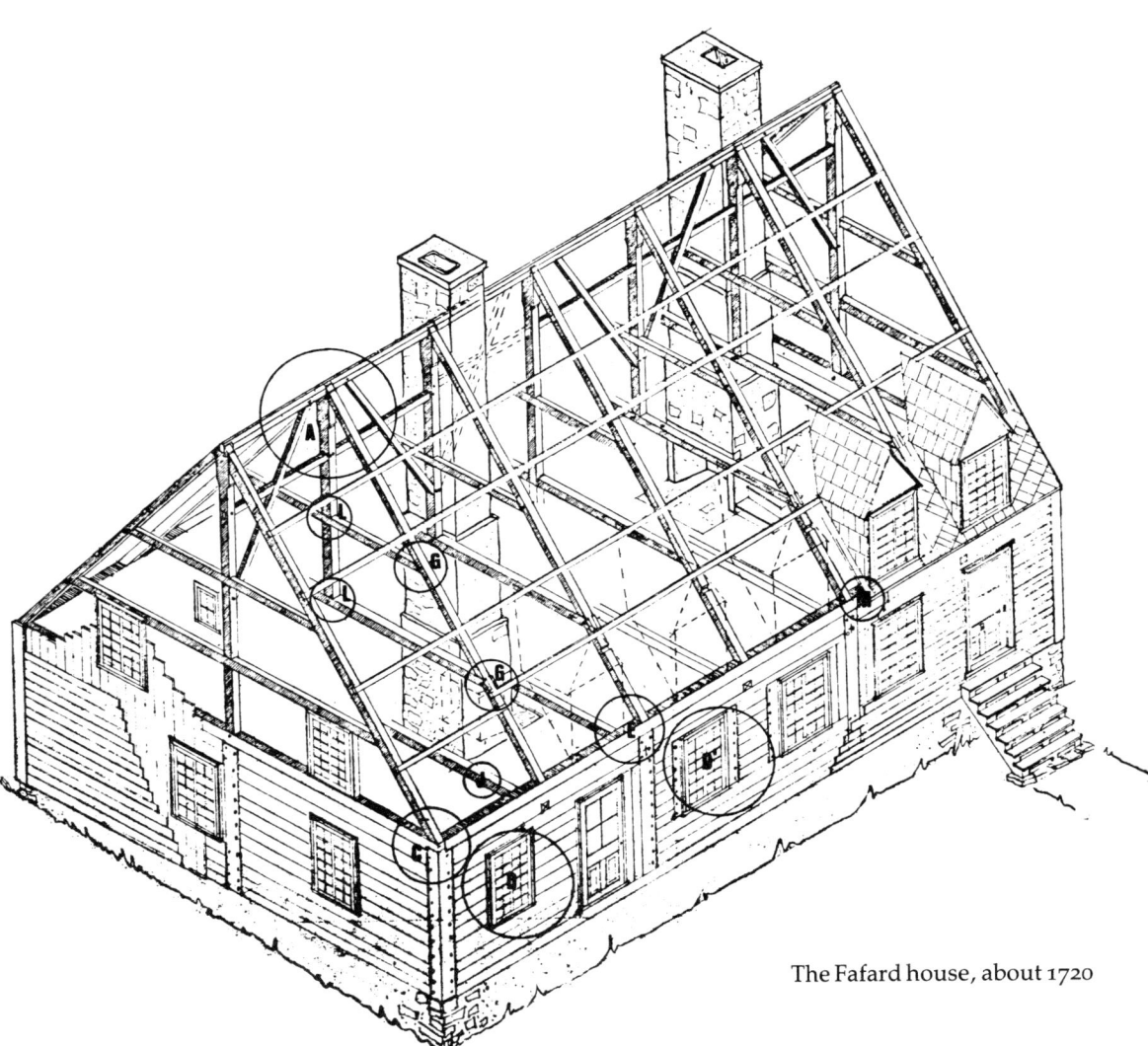

The Fafard house, about 1720

147

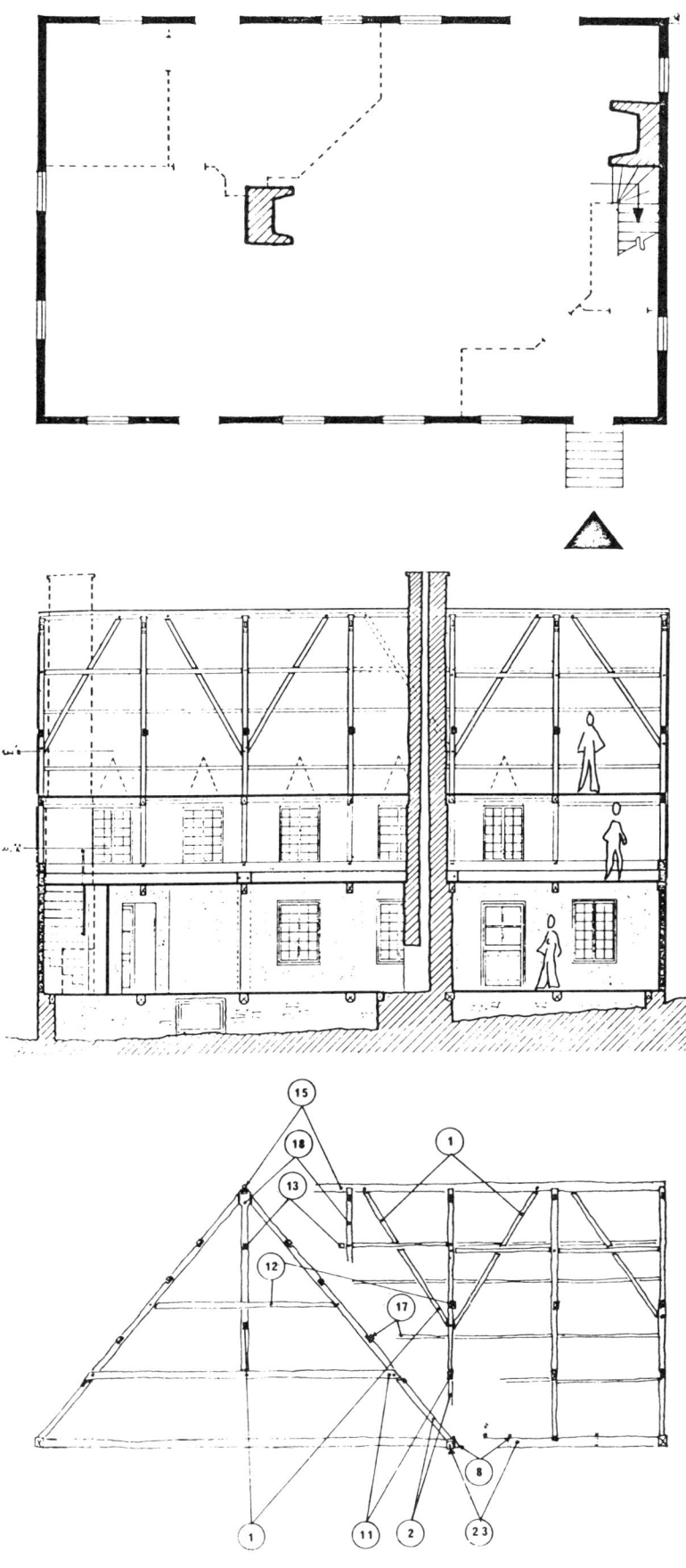

Such construction can also be found in the Detroit area from where it percolated south, at least as far as Monroe County, as indicated by the evidence. In the United States this system was known not only to the French population. Certainly the Palatine German settlers were familiar with it as evidenced by the recent restoration of the old Lutheran parsonage at Schoharie, New York. This building is tentatively dated at about 1750. In Canada, however, this method definitely originated with the French in Quebec.

The Fafard house at Cap Santé, Portneuf County, is a building of great skill and sophistication. It is possible that it is of exceptional quality, but more than likely it is typical. French construction was bound to be of a high standard since it was generally executed by professional tradesmen. The isometric drawing of the house shows all the essentials of the grooved post style of building which a hundred years later would be considered typical of areas several thousand miles to the west. It becomes difficult to question that the style variously known as 'Red River Frame' or 'Hudson's Bay Frame' or 'Rocky Mountain Frame' or simply 'Canadian Frame,' could have developed anywhere but in Quebec and was carried from there by the fur traders.

TERMINOLOGY USED IN CONNECTION WITH THE
FAFARD HOUSE IN QUEBEC

| *French* | *English* |
| --- | --- |
| Aisselier | Bracing |
| Arbaletrier | Principal rafter |
| Chantignole | Cleat |
| Cheneau | Gutter |
| Chevron | Common rafter |
| Colonne | Post, column |
| Contre-fiche | Strut |
| Coyau | Eave prop |
| Croix de St-Andre | Cross bridging, cross bracing |
| Encognure | Angle tie |
| Entrait | Main tie |
| Entrait (faux) | Tie beam |
| Entretoise | Bridging |
| Etresillon | Brace |
| Faitage | Ridge pole |
| Moise | Wale |
| Panne | Purlin |
| Poincon | King post |
| Poteau cornier | Corner post |
| Poteau d'huisserie | Winder or door post |
| Poteau de sous-panne | Queen post |
| Poutre | Beam |
| Sabliere | Wall plate |
| Solive | Joist |
| Tirant | Stringer |

Timber framing 149

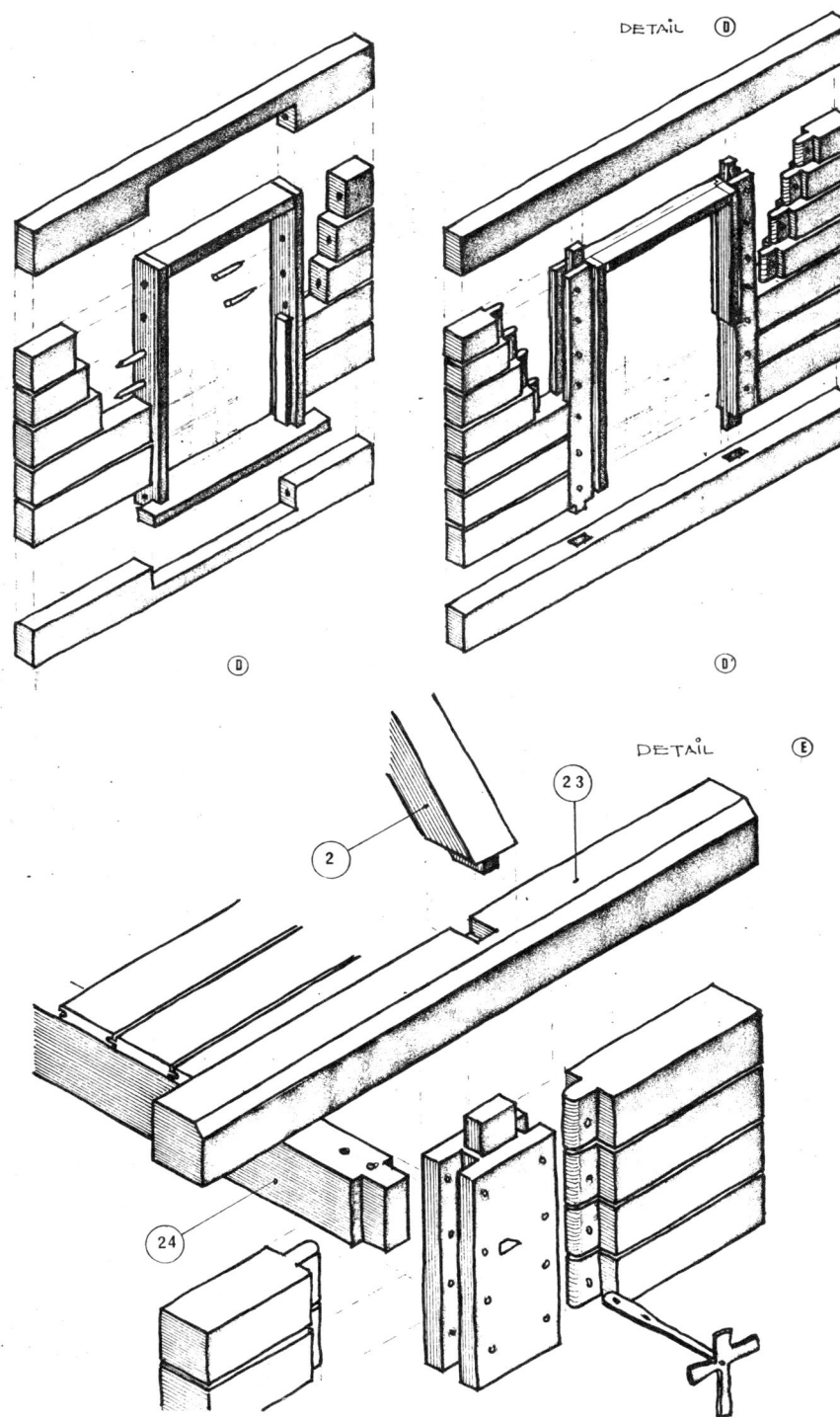

Construction details of the Fafard house (ABOVE AND OVERLEAF)

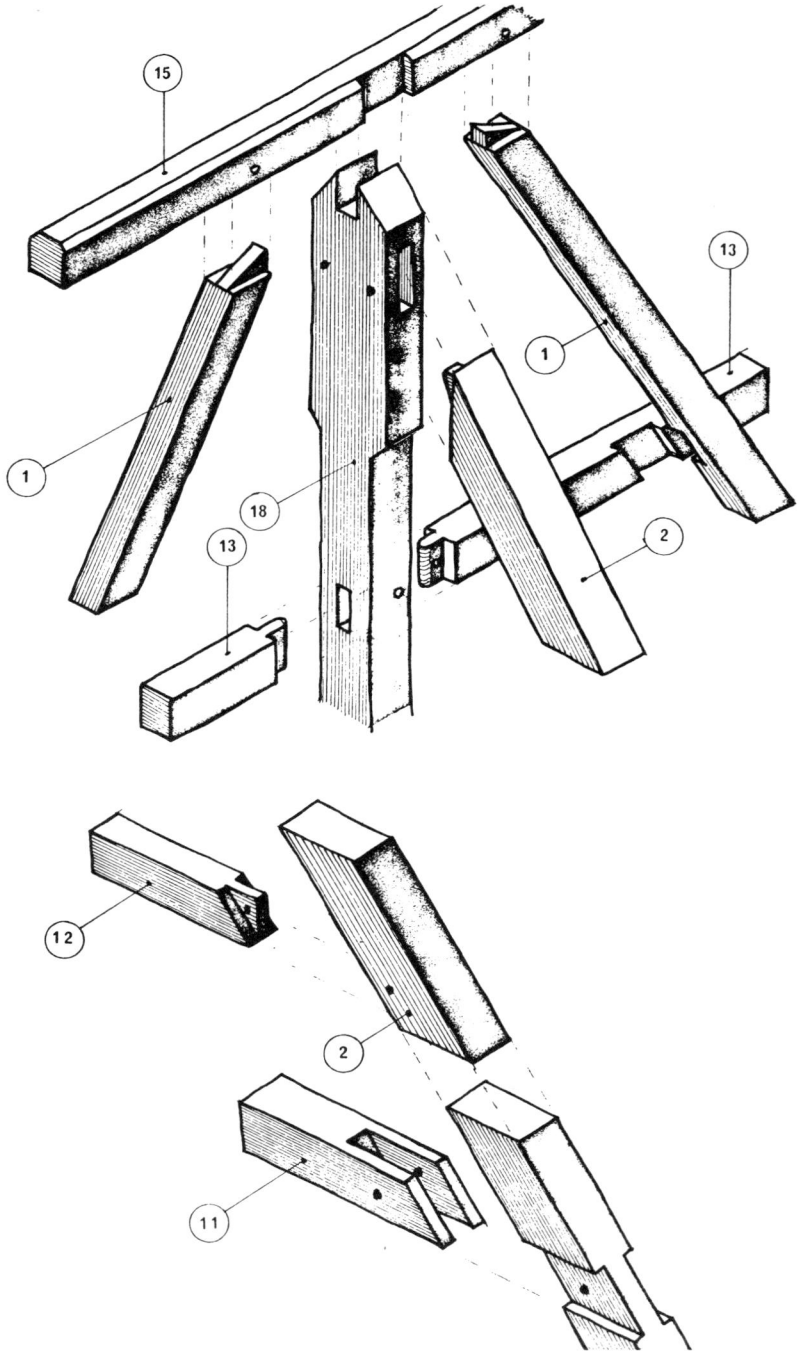

Timber framing 151

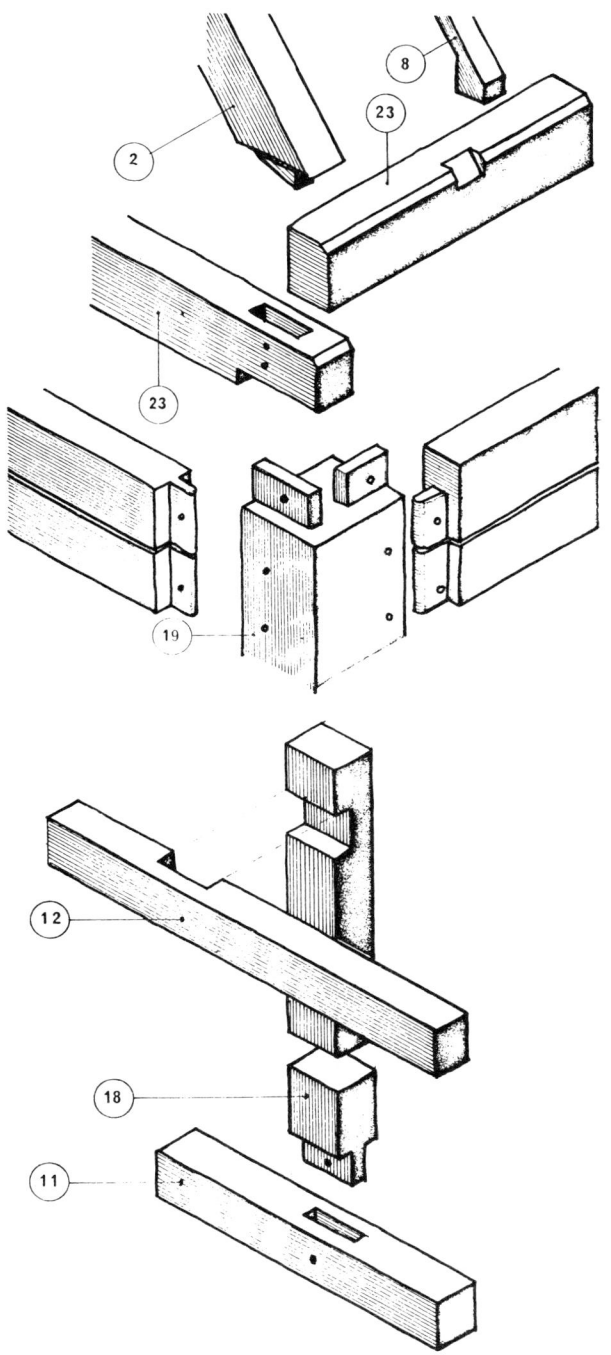

The major difference in construction in the march westward was in the framing of the roof. The typical Quebec roof frame is a most impressive structure which required sophisticated building techniques. As well, the construction of a roof truss with a double collar-tie (as in the Fafard house), king post, ridge pole, and transverse wind-bracing demanded accurate jointing and measurements, all of which would have been too time-consuming for quick erection. For this reason, the intricate French roof truss was replaced by the common rafter and collar-tie method of Upper Canada. The forts in the west were a mixture of French walls and English roof trusses. It should also be remarked that the tall side-hung double casement windows, so typical of Quebec and of France, did not survive the journey westward; rather, the Anglo-Dutch double-hung sash was used in the west, with few exceptions. The fur traders in the west also rarely bothered to provide raised foundations, though these made good sense in Quebec where homes were expected to last for generations; as well, in Quebec every one of the horizontal timbers was pegged, whereas the fur traders frequently pegged only the main framing members.

The roof frame of Quebec is quite distinct from that used in Ontario. The much steeper pitch in Quebec, even in small buildings, meant a much greater wind load and rafters of considerable length, which in turn required bracing at more than one point. The extraordinary amount of bracing meant that the roof was actually framed by regular trusses; these were spaced much further apart than the ordinary rafters thus demanding much more lateral bracing as well as the use of purlins for support of the roof covering. (The 'St Andrew's cross,' as in the Paradis house, was a favourite form of lateral bracing.) The simple collar-tie was one solution to the problem of bracing and is, of course, common to all traditions. But the favoured procedure was to employ a king-post truss with longitudinal bracing.

The complete frame consisted of the truss, with its principal rafters, low collar-tie, a king post, and horizontal tie-beams – in which would be included the ridge pole, and the purlins when present (since the truss was not set as closely as the Ontario rafter, purlins as well as a ridge pole were the custom). The ridge pole and the horizontal tie-beam below it, which also connects with the king post, were braced together with variously arranged diagonal braces. This type of roof structure appears also in areas of French settlement in the United States, and can be shown to derive from seventeenth-century France.

The system of central longitudinal cross-bracing is the characteristic difference between the king-post roof of the French tradition and the king-post trusses common in English nineteenth-century construction. This bracing down the length of the roof is always associated with a horizontal tie, tenoned into the king post between the collar-tie and the ridge pole. This feature is reminiscent of the collar-purlin in the English medieval roof, which always passed directly over the collar and was usually associated with

# Timber framing

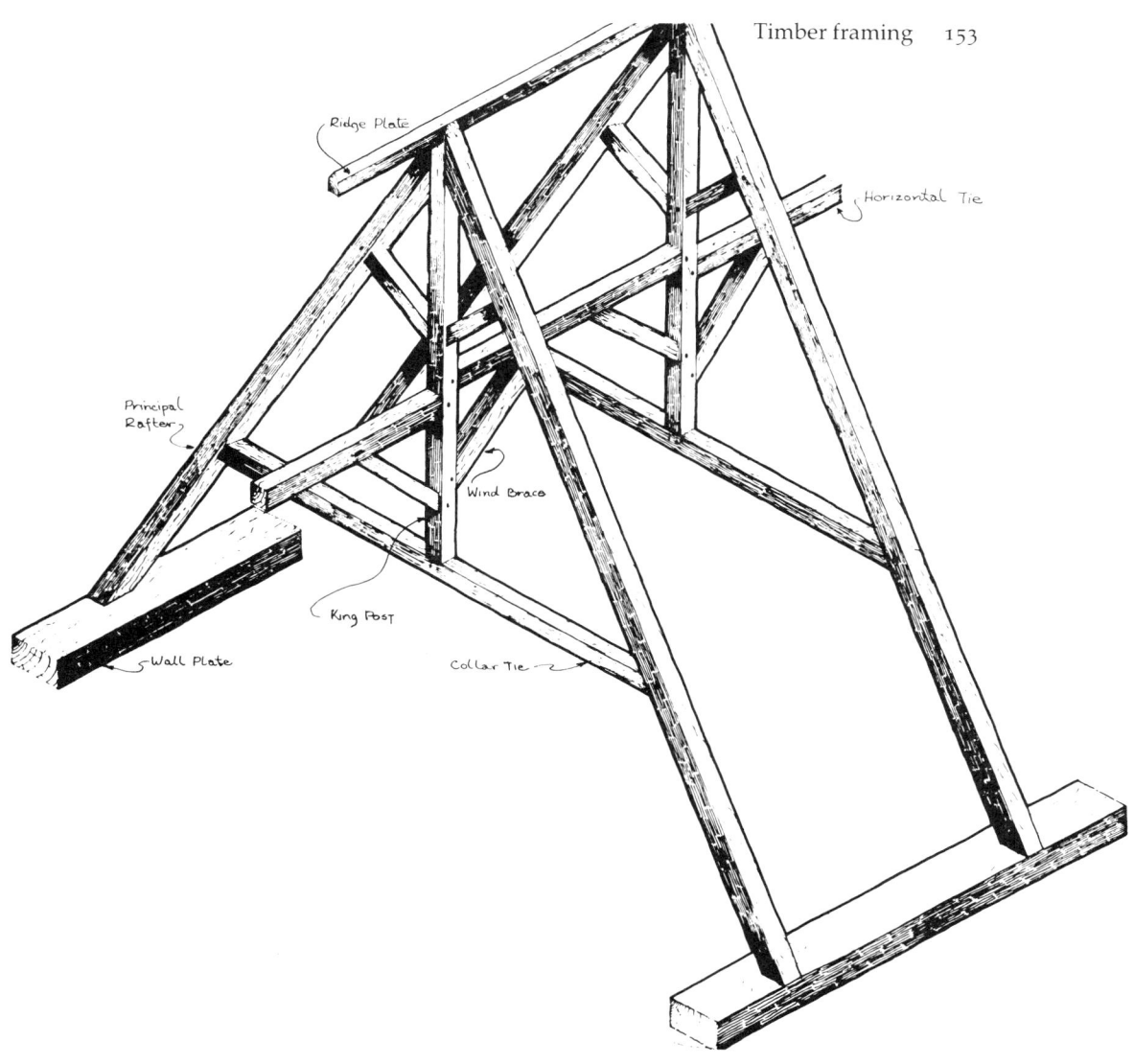

French type roof framing

a crown post (a central post like a king post but stopping at the collar-tie, with bracing out to the collar and to the collar-purlin). It seems safe to say that the French system is a parallel development, continuing and evolving in the steep roofs that remained fashionable in France and necessary in Quebec some time after they had more or less disappeared in England, where Georgian proportions and design became dominant; the Georgian roof pitch was so shallow as to make the use of the roof truss very difficult.

The methods of seating rafters or trusses in masonry also varied greatly. In Ontario the general practice was to imbed a plate in the upper, outer corner of the wall. In Quebec the accepted method was to place two plates, one in each of the two upper corners. Both timbers were then joined by a short tie placed at intervals, and the spaces between the plates were filled with rubble mortar. The construction of the truss in the house at Ste-Scholastique (illustrations on pages 154, 156, and 157) shows a most interesting vestige of a very old tradition dating back to the thirteenth and fourteenth centuries. This is the extra beam-support from the inner plate to the tie-beam. The use of such a beam was common practice in the great tithe barns of Normandy, Flanders, and southern England.[11] The English seem to have abandoned this feature on coming to the New World whereas the French retained it at least up to the middle of the nineteenth century.

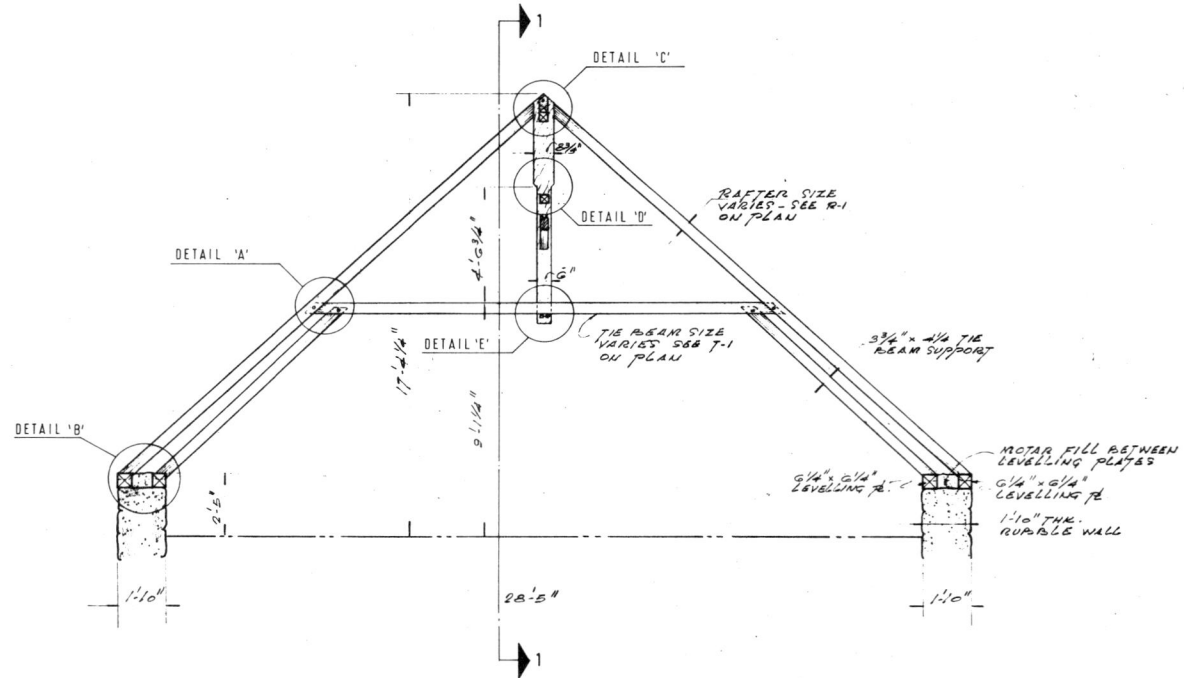

Typical early French construction details are seen here and on the next three pages

Timber framing    155

Two points of refinement should be noted here: the widening of the king post at the ridge and the thickening of the collar-tie where it meets the bottom of the king post. The former can be considered typical in both French and British construction, but there is no precedent for the latter in the British tradition. Several other features should also be noted, namely, the lapped dovetail joint of the collar-tie and rafter; the offset tenons of the diagonal and horizontal wind-bracing; the lap joint of the diagonal and horizontal lateral braces; and the complicated joint at the head of the king post. Ste-Monique

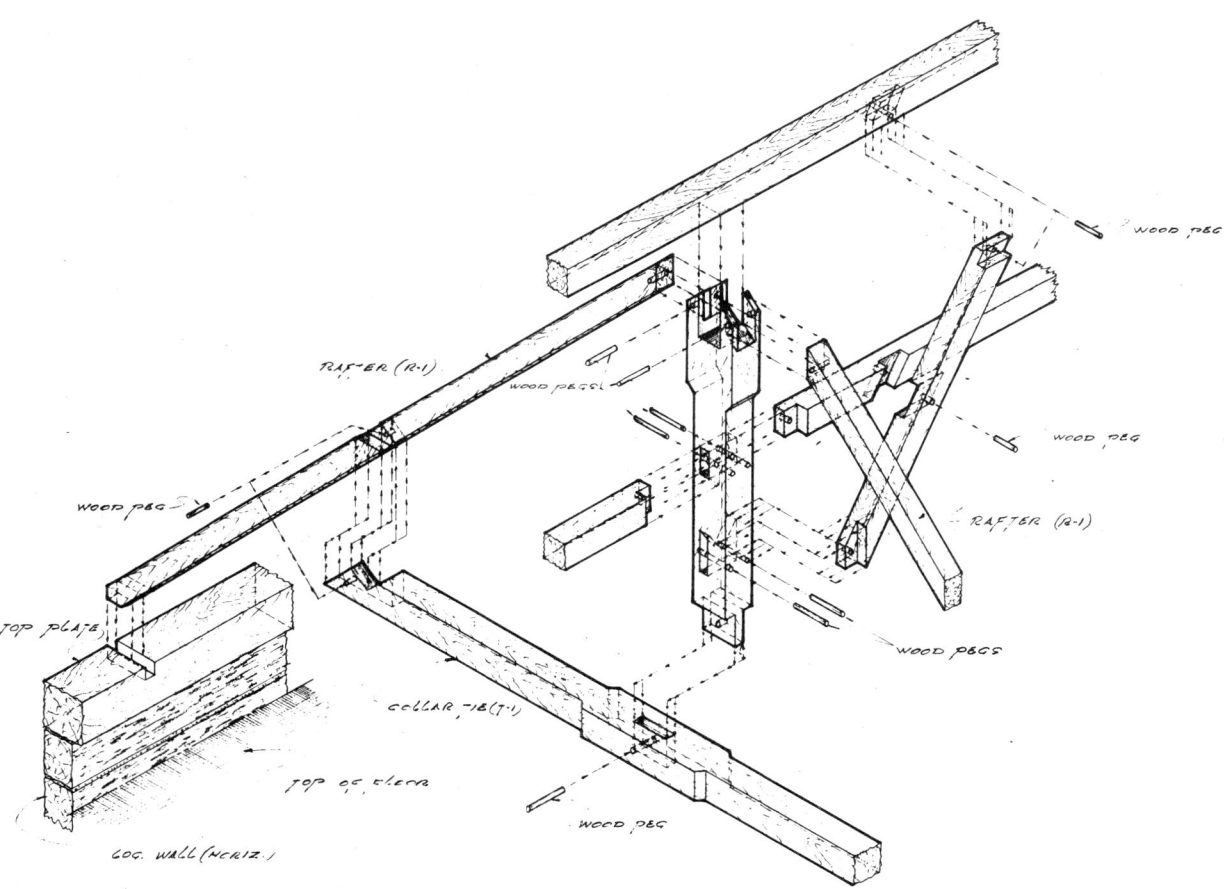

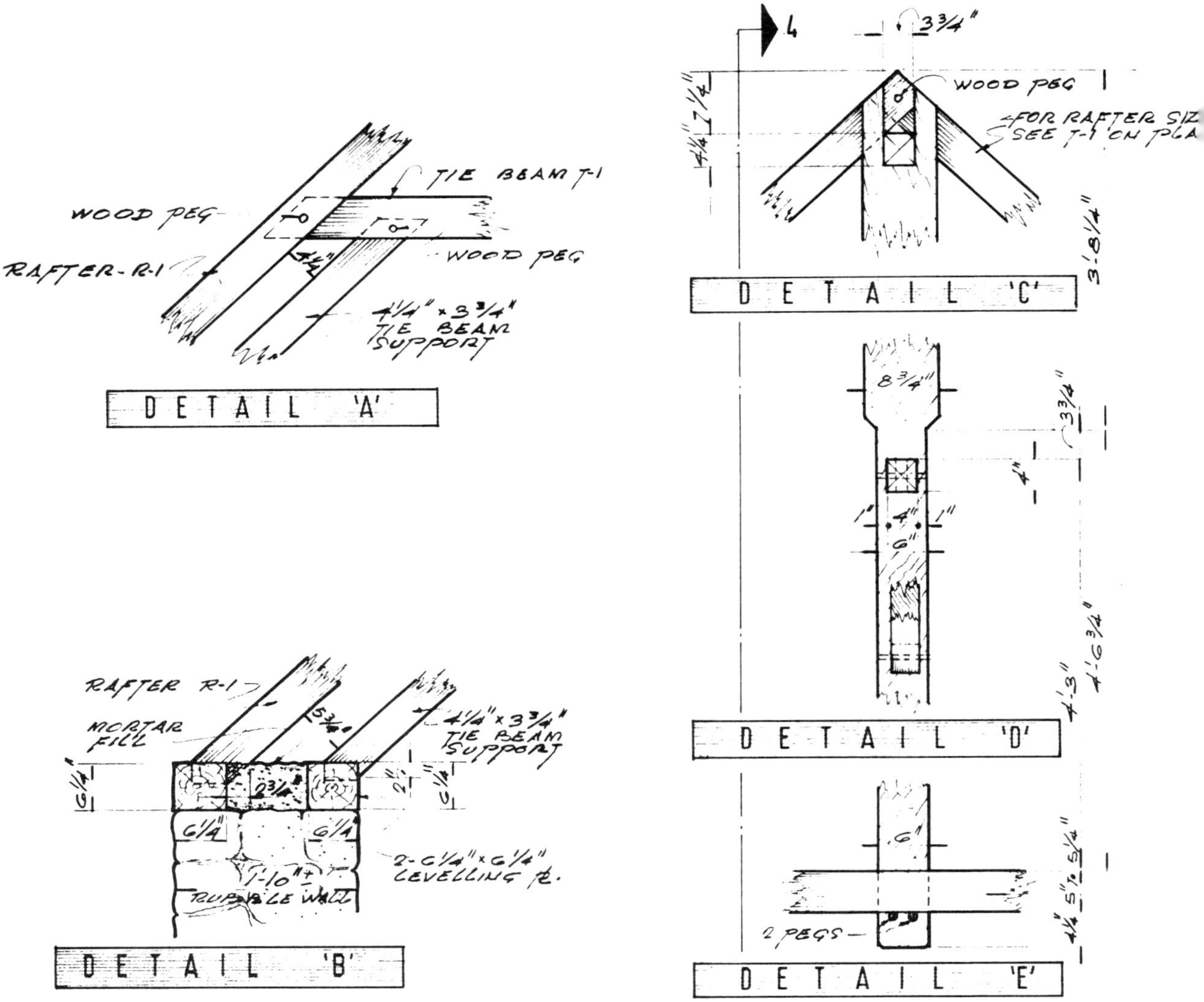

156  Building with Wood

**ROOF FRAMING TYPE 'A' SECTION AND DETAILS**

**TOP OF RUBBLE WALL DETAIL AND ISOMETRIC VIEW**

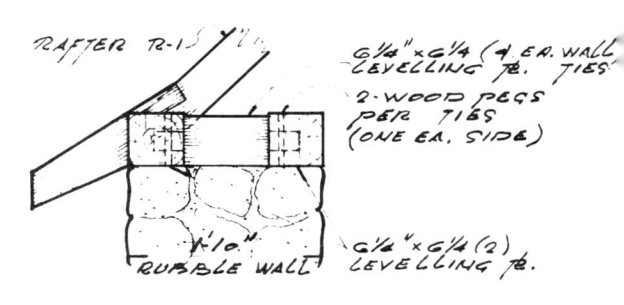

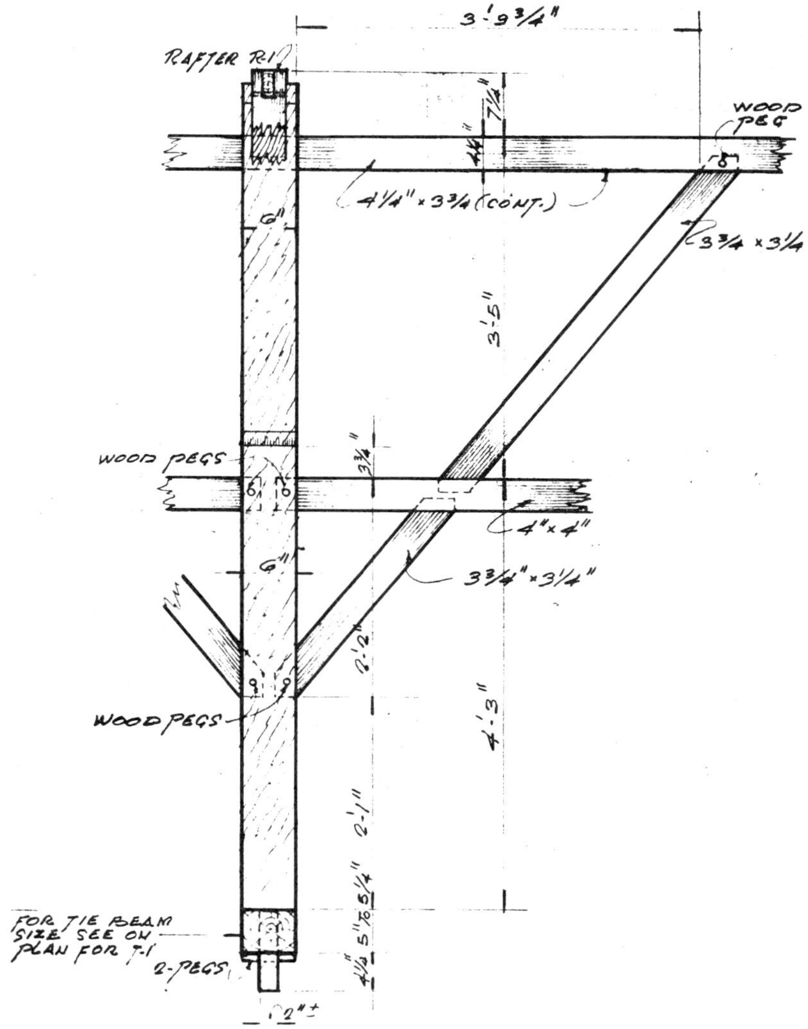

Timber framing 157

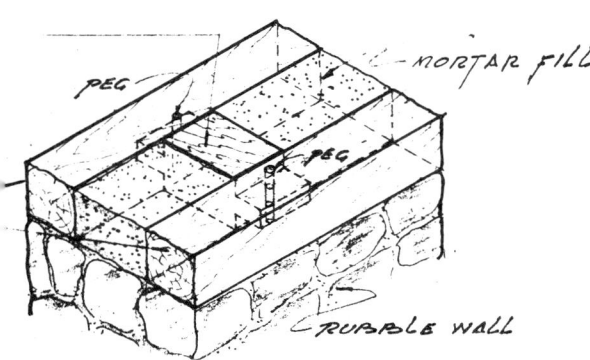

SECTION 4-4

DEPARTMENT OF INDIAN AFFAIRS
AND NORTHERN DEVELOPMENT
Historic — sites — service
1555 COTE ST. LOUIS
STE. SCHOLASTIQUE P.Q.

Building contracts and specifications were more detailed and more numerous in early Quebec than in Ontario, since the established practices tended to be imported from France along with the settlers. Three examples, from Séguin, *La maison en Nouvelle-France*, are given here.[12]

In July 1690 a carpenter by the name of Parent built the frame and roof of a house. This involved the following:

... laying the beams horizontally across the foundation, thereby forming the ground floor. The second storey will be constructed of eleven-foot beams stacked one on top of another. There will be two door frames, one of which will be round and will open onto the street, and four windows, two overlooking the street and two facing the St Lawrence River. A chimney will be erected at one end of the house and a wooden mantel installed on either the first or second floor, whichever Seigneur Charly prefers. The said carpenter will build three dormers in the roof, wherever the seigneur deems suitable. In addition, there will be a window in the gables of the half-timbered house. The roof will consist of two master trusses, the largest being three and a half feet high, one centre truss, a ridge and a sub-ridge, all properly joined together. After the rafters and other supports have been installed the said house will be covered with timber. The said carpenter Parent will begin building the house as soon as he has completed the work for Seigneur St Germain ... for the sum of two hundred and twenty pounds sterling, half in coins and half in bills, in the national currency, which Seigneur Charly promises to pay as the work progresses, and two jugs of spirits.

The following spring (1691) Lacroix would have to supply all the materials needed for Seigneur Chesne's house, except the boards and nails. The carpenter's work would involve:

... constructing the frame for a house seventeen to eighteen feet long by fifteen feet wide (outside measurements) of beams measuring seven to eight feet stacked one on top of another, at a site near Notre Dame de Bon Secours. In addition, he will install three beams, one door frame and two window sashes. The roof will be properly assembled and the house covered with timber. The said carpenter promises to have the said frame and roof, with a chimney mantel, completed in accordance with the aforesaid plans by the end of next May ... for the sum of forty-five pounds sterling in the national currency.

Since house-building was a seasonal occupation, the timber required was normally hewn during the winter. In late October 1691, Jean Fontenelle, called Champagne, promised to do the following work:

... to square, this coming winter, all the timber needed to build a two-storey house with outside measurements of thirty feet long by twenty feet wide, made of beams stacked one on top of another, for Mathurin Moquin. All types of good timber will be used and the house will be finished in deal. The timber will be hewn and the house erected in this town or near Notre Dame de Bon Secours in Montreal. The frame and roof will be properly assembled and eight window sashes and three door frames built wherever M. Moquin deems it appropriate. A porch will be built to rest on five floor joists extending approximately five feet. The said carpenter will build a two-storey staircase in the house and cover the said house with timber. He will begin squaring the timber this coming winter on the banks of the St Lawrence River and will have everything ready so that M. Moquin will have time to transport the timber to the site. As soon as it has arrived, the said carpenter will begin erecting the house and will work steadily at it without leaving to work elsewhere ... for the sum of three hundred and twenty pounds sterling in the national currency.

## French construction in Ontario

French building technology was firmly established by the time Upper Canada came into being, and many Loyalists had to pass through Montreal in order to reach their eventual destination. Therefore, it is only reasonable to expect that a certain amount of absorption of these methods took place, especially in the areas in proximity to early French settlements, such as Windsor, along the Quebec border, and along the north shore of the St Lawrence River.

Slight variations, however, do occur and might be due to New England influences. In the old Dolphis Pitre house in Tecumseh near Windsor (demolished in 1961) the filler pieces between the sill and the lintel tie-beams were inserted in a vertical position, whereas the filler pieces below the openings were placed horizontally. All the timbers used in the house were of white oak, now extinct in the area. According to Mr Pitre's claim that his father was six years old when the house was built, the house should date between 1840 and 1850; since Mr Pitre was himself eighty-five years old in 1961, it is reasonable to suppose this date is correct. The vertical fill used was perhaps, in this case, nothing more than an experimental variation. The basic framing details, nevertheless, remain Québécois.

It should be noted that whereas in Quebec frequently every filler piece was pinned – 'les morceaux sont retenus en place par des chevilles de bois' – in Ontario only the framing members were pinned; the filler pieces were left free to shift without straining the frame. If the Quebec method is compared with that found in Ontario, the difference in wall construction becomes obvious. The low-stud wall above the lintel beam, along with its diagonal bracing, are decidedly un-French. The distinctive corner bracing in the upper part of walls in Ontario was perhaps a vestige of New England framing. The Quebec wall, on the other hand, was almost solid timber, which made lateral bracing impossible.

Another rare type of construction which occurs in Ontario resembles that used in the Pichet house. It is found in 'Malone,' built in 1852–53, originally the home of Charles Dunlop of Peterborough, now owned by Dr R. Honey. The exterior walls consist of vertical timbers about 8 inches by 10 to 12 inches wide. These timbers, however, are set much closer to one another than in the Pichet house; the resulting spaces are close enough to require minimal chinking as in a well-constructed Ontario log house. Unfortunately, no accurate, structural analysis of this house has been possible so far, since the house is still in use and has undergone few alterations. Dr Honey, however, has kindly supplied the specifications for the building of the house.

Specification of Carpenter Work to be done in the erection and completion of a cottage dwelling house for **Charles Dunlop**, Esq., according to the accompanying plans prepared for the purpose and signed Geo. A. Stewart, Auburn, May 1852.

The materials all of which will be supplied by the Proprietor are to be carefully selected and picked out for their several purposes by the Carpenter and no unsound or otherwise defective lumber will be allowed to be used in the building on any account.

The Carpenter is expected to attend on the Stone Mason when bonded timbers, lintels or any other wood work is required by him to be introduced into the Stone Work and to have all door and window cases prepared for the Mason when required.

The cedars which are to support the Ground Floor are to be flattened on the upper side to receive the flooring and to be carefully leveled, to be 2½ from center to center, one end to be notched into a principal sill running through the center of the building and the other resting on the stone work.

The floors to be laid as usual, tongued, grooved and blindnailed.

The floors of Veranda instead of being 4 feet from the Ground, to be 2 feet from Ground line. Supported on Cedar posts. The upper part of veranda to be same as shewn on drawings.

The inside of Stone Walls to be battened. Also the ceilings of principal rooms to be battened.

The partitions to be made of 2" × 4" studs. The studs for door jambs to be 4" × 6".

The doors and windows to be made according to the detail drawings. The doors and windows for the kitchen, for which no drawings are prepared are to be made in the usual manner. Doors to be 1½ Inch 4 panel.

The servants bed room, scullery and pump room are not to be contracted for.

The joists of bed Room floors are to be 2" × 9" and not more than 22 Inches apart. to notch into beams stretching across the building and resting on the Stone Work.

The ceiling joists of Kitchen to rest on the top of the Walls and the feet of the rafters to notch into them. These joists are to be planed, also the underside of the inch flooring which rests upon them for the ceiling of Kitchen.

The Roof of House to be constructed as shewn on the drawings. The principal rafters to be 5" × 7" the Jack rafters 3" × 4". The whole to be covered with inch boarding laid close and well shingled especially the Valleys. A frame to be built to support the Roof as shewn by the dotted line in the drawings.

The verge boards to Gables and eaves to be constructed of 2 Inch stuff and all other parts of veranda to be made in accordance with drawings.

The floor of veranda to be not tongued and Grooved but nailed down on joists. The Whole to be finished in a substantial and workmanlike manner.

The estimate to be divided into sections. Section 1. To contain the laying of the joists and floors. putting on of Roof and making window and door frames. Section 2. to comprise all the finishing of inside work and Section 3. to contain putting up of veranda. Making and fixing vergeboards and ornamental work of outside.

The contractor to commence the work as soon as this tender is accepted.

Geo. A. Stewart<br>
Superintendant<br>
Auburn May 31st 1852

Theoretical reconstruction of the original portion of Sir John Johnson's house, built before 1813, Williamstown

The Dolphis Pitre house in Tecumseh. Note the introduction of vertical timbers in the wall height between window sill and head, and the clear indications that this structure was always intended to have an outer covering to it, probably clapboard; such outer covering was common in Quebec, though the traders of the west tended to rely on chinking the gaps between the logs to keep the cold air out and the heat in.

Wall construction,
Honey house

BELOW A schematic drawing of French construction in Ontario, after the Banwell house, 1849–50, in Sandwich.

This drawing should be compared with the one of typical Quebec grooved post construction on page 140. The chief difference lies in the framed and planked upper part of the wall (here as in the Dolphis Pitre house). Also, the pins are here restricted to the main frame members rather than passed through the tenon of each horizontal piece as was usual in Quebec.

The interruption of the groove at the level of the tie-beams (see detail 'D' of the Banwell house) raises the vexed question of how these grooved post buildings were assembled. Clearly it was not merely a matter of putting all the posts up, then sliding the horizontal timbers down the grooves; the lower timbers might have been placed into the grooves by inserting them at an angle – but the upper tie-beam itself, with its extra long tenons, would have presented certain difficulties!

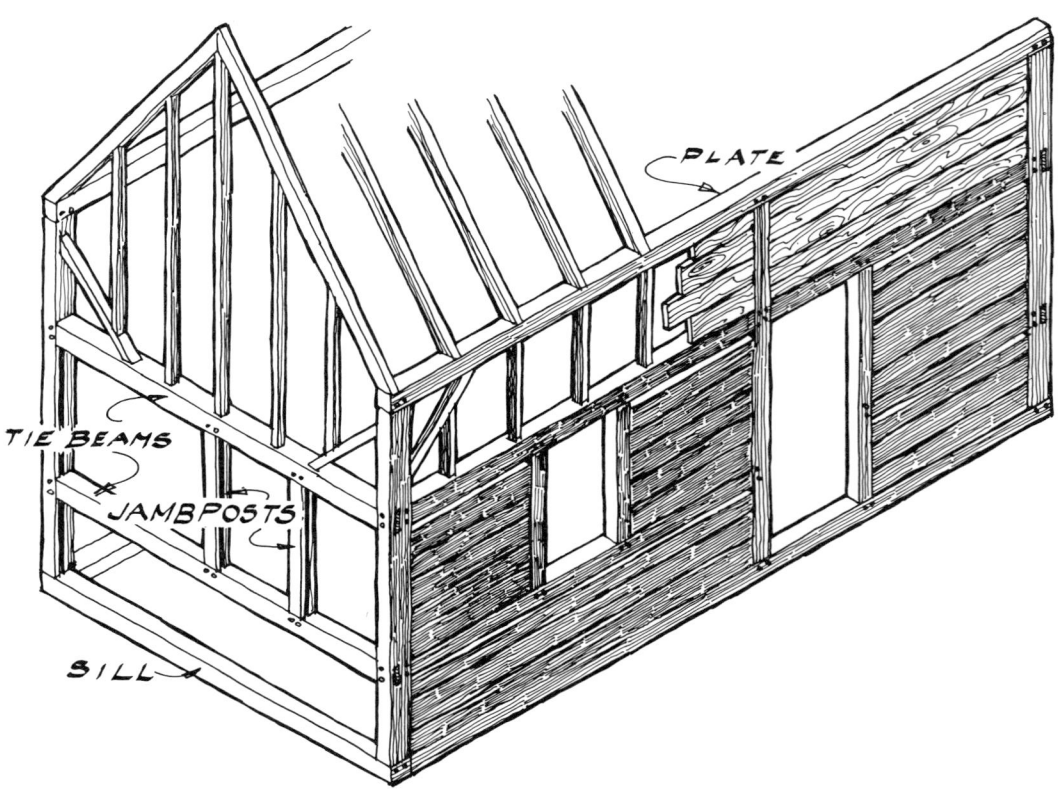

Timber framing 163

An old trading post on the Ottawa River demonstrates typical Quebec grooved post construction, providing a contrast with the method as used in Ontario. In November 1823 the Hudson's Bay Company erected a post about ten miles from Hull named Poste-du-lac-des-Allumettes. It must have been successful for a small settlement grew up around it; in 1848 a post office was established and the fort was renamed Fort William in honour of William McGillivray, director of the company. The post lasted until 1869 when it was officially closed; the land was sold to private holders.[13] Little remains except part of one of the barns, but Quebec building methods can be clearly noted; in particular, each filler piece is pegged, in contrast with the Ontario practice of pegging only the framing pieces, thus letting the filler logs move freely.

Fort William on the Ottawa River, 1823. Note the pegs holding each filler piece, the usual Quebec style.

I have studied in detail the Banwell house, in Sandwich East Township near Windsor, because it is typical of French construction methods in Ontario (there are of course exceptions, but they probably just prove the rule). This house, formerly owned by Mr Hermidas Baillargeon, is one of several of this type still to be found in the area (others have recently been demolished), and it does indeed prove that a transfer of techniques from Quebec to Ontario did occur. It is a small house but in an excellent state of preservation and containing all the typical features of this type of construction. Its only drawback for the present-day local historian is that all nails, screws, hinges, and even shingles were mass-produced commodities bought in Detroit.

The filler logs in this house are horizontal, and I am inclined to regard this as the more common arrangement. Another house in that area, now demolished, had vertical filler logs; there are certain advantages to this arrangement, especially in the assembly of the wall sections. But the evidence of other houses leads me to conclude that the horizontal arrangement was the more favoured.

The Banwell house was built rather late – in 1849 and 1850 – and the workmanship is first-class. All timbers are handhewn but kept to very close tolerances. All main uprights are 4½ by 7¼ inches, the plates 5⅛ by 6½ inches, and the intermediate plate or tie-beam 4½ by 13 inches. The sill could not be measured accurately but was approximately 8 by 11 inches. The tenons are 1¾ inches wide by 4 inches deep, and are slightly offset towards the inside face.

All framing timbers have pinned joints, for the obvious reason that, if they were not secured in this way, the movement of the framing timbers would exert pressure on the window and door frames throwing them out of 'perpendicularity' and causing jamming. All filler logs are free to move with the weather. Since lumber expands and contracts more across than with the grain, spaces are left to permit lateral expansion without fear of straining the frame. There is a 1¼ inch gap below the pinned log forming the window sill and a 2¾ inch gap below the tie-beam. Filler logs are used only up to the underside of the tie-beam; above that are studs and braces. These are recessed one full inch to permit 1 inch horizontal sheathing to be applied so as to lie flush with the outside face of the frame. Vertical board and batten is then applied to the full height of the wall.

The spacing of the studs is about 24 inches, varying up to 2 inches either way. The spacing of the ceiling joists also varies from 3' 6" to 4' 0½". I found such variation in spacing repeatedly in log construction, even where the workmanship was excellent; it would appear that exact spacing was of little or no importance to vernacular builders in the first half of the nineteenth century.

The floor joists vary in their spacing too, from 2' 11" to 3' 4". The floor joists also serve as ties since they mortise into the sill with a half-dovetail joint, thereby making for a very rigid construction. The joists were left in the round, with a diameter of about 12 inches, except for a top, adzed strip about 6 inches wide that provides a level support for the floor boards.

Timber framing 165

The Banwell house, quite unpretentious, but of excellent workmanship and with a well-preserved frame.

166   Building with Wood

The haunched tenon in the tie-beams.


Filler pieces are free to move within the frame. Note the careful workmanship in producing horizontal joints to very close tolerances.

The provision of support for the central chimney is of an ingenious and interesting design. Since a chimney has considerable weight, a single ceiling joist supporting it would eventually sag rather badly. In order to avoid this, a plank partition was placed directly under the load-bearing joist and it, in turn, rested directly over a floor joist, thus providing two structural members for the support of the chimney.

The ceiling joists mortise and tenon into the tie-beam, but apparently with no dovetailing or pinning; they simply rest in position. The mortise is 3 inches wide, 4 inches deep, and 6 inches high. The tenon is 3½ inches long, flush with the top of the joist and the haunch on the underside.

There are eight pairs of roof rafters, including the gable-end frames that are squared. The others are left in the round. The centre pair are only about one foot apart at the eave but spread apart towards the ridge to allow the chimney to pass through. The other rafters are approximately in line with the ceiling joists. The upper wall bracing of this house is shown on page 168.

The reconstruction of the original floor plan caused slight difficulties. I was able to locate the opening to the front room but not that to the rear bedroom because so many floor planks were missing in that area. The door jamb closest to the front was 38 inches from the inside of the front (west) log and the opening was 33½ inches wide. There was once a partition separating the front and back rooms, made of 1 inch plank, with its west face about 20 inches from the edge of the window-framing timber in the south wall. The Banwells seem to have used lots of water to clean their floors for it gathered under the partition and rotted the floor boards there. This rot is 3 inches wide, and, the partition being 1 inch wide, one can deduce that there were originally base mouldings. These may have been a quarter-round shoe mould or a 1 inch plank laid horizontally perhaps with a bead in the top corner. There was no problem locating the stairway. After removal of paint and old wallpaper, the outline of the original stairs against the wall was very evident.

Henry Banwell was a meticulous and methodical person (a school teacher) and kept a complete and detailed diary, which has fortunately been preserved. From this we are able to follow the construction of his house, in some ways in even greater detail than we can John Langton's. But, though Banwell gives all the details, he gives them as laconically as possible. From his terse account the entries relating to the building of his house have been selected; they appear at the end of this section.

There are few enough buildings of this type in Ontario, especially in the eastern part. There was an old homestead on the banks of the St Lawrence about three miles east of Maitland, but it has been dismantled and no record was made. The old Anglican rectory at Cornwall, also in this style, has been dismantled too, but at present the pieces are being stored by the Stormont, Dundas, and Glengarry Historical Society. The Banwell house is a rare and historically valuable building, and one would hope to see it some day restored to its original condition. It would certainly round out Ontario's collection of various types of preserved houses.

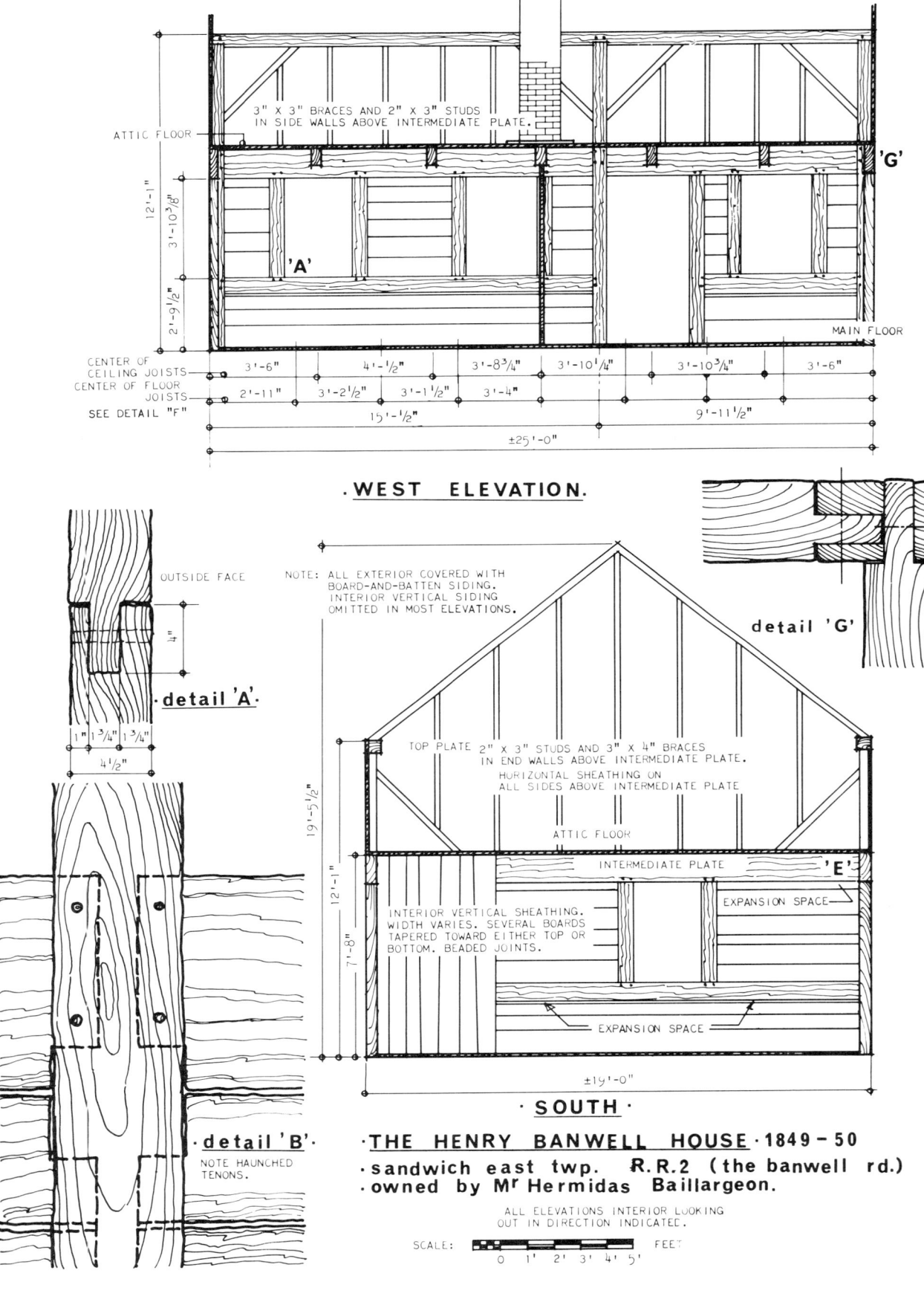

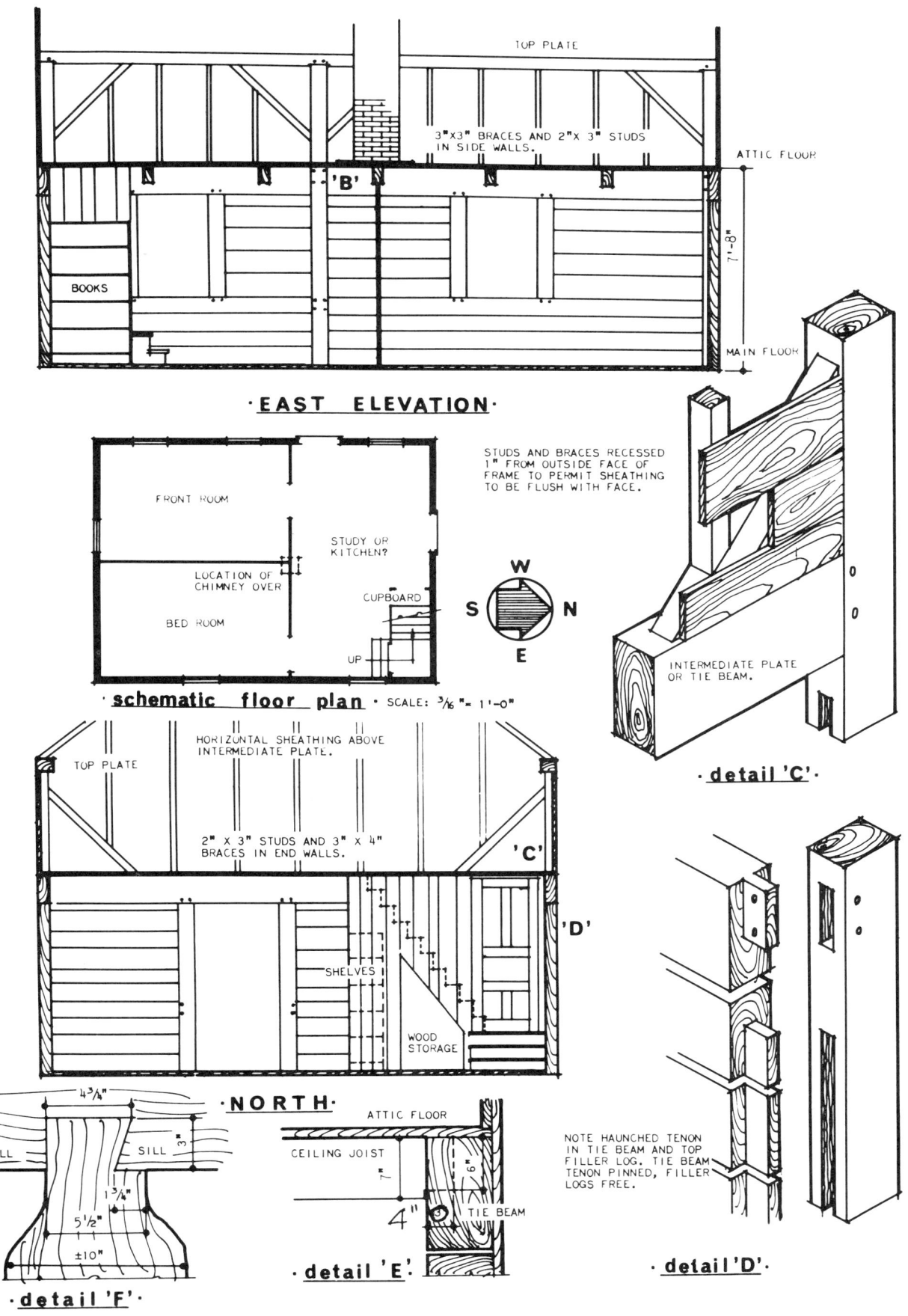

Building with Wood

EXCERPTS FROM THE DIARY OF HENRY BANWELL
(Courtesy of Mr R.A. Douglas, Curator of the Hiram Walker Museum, Windsor)

*1849*

| | |
|---|---|
| Aug. 16 | Jock Ebare agreed with me to put up a block house and find [help?] himself for 35 dollars. Commenced chopping the timbers afternoon. |
| Aug. 25 | 10 pounds of nails. |
| Sept. 3 | Rolling logs afternoon. |
| Sept. 5 | Hauling the house timbers. |
| Sept. 11 | Edward [son] hauled a few pieces of house timbers. |
| Sept. 12 | Augustus and Edward [sons] hauling house timbers in the forenoon. |
| Sept. 13 | Hauling the house timbers. |
| Sept. 17 | Rolling logs. |
| Sept. 18 | Rolling logs. |
| Oct. 1 | Hauling sleepers for the house. |
| Oct. 6 | Hauling the blocks and sills for the house. |
| Oct. 8 | Finished hauling the house timbers and helped Jock Ebare to lay the sills. |
| Oct. 9 | Jock Ebare had his bee and raised the house. |
| Oct. 12 | Boys hauling rafters. |
| Oct. 13 | Jock Ebare went with his wagon to Detroit for 7 thousand shingles for me. Nails 4.75. Shingles $14.00 – Hire $1.50. Duty $1.50 [amount covers other items not listed]. Ferriage 50 cents. |
| Oct. 17 | The boys took 8½ bus. of corn to mill – and brought back a load of shingles. |
| Oct. 20 | I went with Jock Ebare to Detroit for lumber and window sashes. |
| Oct. 27 | I went to Detroit. Bot a stove 5 dollars – paint and glass. |
| Nov. 1 | Pipe for stove 6 feet high 3 feet wide near 6 in – on stove. [evidently the measurements for the pipe required: 6" dia., vertical 6 ft., then horiz. 3 ft. to enter chimney.] |
| Nov. 3 | I went to Detroit – Bot ½ lb. Tea – ½ lb. Snuff – Tape Thread and stove pipe – Molasses – Whiskey – Zinc. |
| Nov. 10 | I went to Detroit – got 400 bricks. |
| Nov. 24 | Paid James Ebare one dollar for bringing 400 Bricks and a barrel of lime from the Ferry. |
| Dec. 14 | I was painting window sashes. |
| Dec. 15 | I was painting sashes. |
| Dec. 18 | Hauled some pieces for steps to the house. Painted the rest of the sashes. |
| Dec. 22 | I went to Detroit. Bot hinges, latches, locks and 1 lb. of Tea – also 260 feet of lumber. |
| Dec. 24 | I was glazing. |
| Dec. 26 | I was painting window sashes. |
| Dec. 27 | I was glazing the sashes. |
| Dec. 28 | I was glazing part of the day. Attending on the road afternoon. [The reference is to present-day Banwell Road.] |
| Dec. 29 | Hauling firewood and glazing. |
| Dec. 31 | Glazing. |

*1850*

| | |
|---|---|
| Jan. 2 | I was glazing. |
| Jan. 3 | I was glazing. |
| Jan. 4 | Glazed one sash. |
| Feb. 8 | Split out some bolts for clapboards. |
| Feb. 9 | Hauling fodder and splitting out bolts for clapboards. |
| Feb. 11 | Sawing and splitting bolts for clapboards. |
| Feb. 12 | Hauling in hay and bolting and barking pieces for clapboards. |
| Feb. 13 | Finished barking the bolts for clapboards and finished hauling hay into barn. |
| Mar. 29 | I was glazing and ditching. |
| Apr. 2 | Heland here splitting clapboards. |
| Apr. 3 | Glazed on sash – Heland finished. |
| May 8 | Finished hauling manure at Noon, then hauling shavings from the new house. |
| May 22 | Jock Ebare finished the house this day. 2 days work more for little matters. |
| May 23 | Moving into the new house. |

*1849*
*Jock Ebare's work on the house*

| | | | | | | | |
|---|---|---|---|---|---|---|---|
| Aug. 16 | ½ day | Sept. 5 | ¾ self | | Sept. 26 | 1 self and Francis and Olivers boys ½ a day |
| | 17 | 1 day | | 7 | 1 self | | |
| | 18 | ¾ day | | 8 | 1 self | | |
| | 21 | 1 day | | 10 | ¾ self | | |
| | 27 | ½ self | | 11 | 1 self | | 27 | 1 self |
| | | ½ man | | 12 | 1 self | | | 1 man |
| | 28 | 1 self | | 13 | 1 self | | 28 | 1 self |
| | | 1 man | | 14 | 1 self | | | 1 man |
| | 29 | 1 self | | | 1 man | | 29 | 1 self |
| | | 1 man | | 15 | 1 self | | | 1 man |
| | 30 | 1 self | | 18 | ½ self | | | |
| | | 1 man | | 19 | 1 self | | | |
| | 31 | 1 self | | | 1 man | | | |
| | | 1 man | | 20 | 1 self | Oct. 1 | 1 self |
| | | | | 21 | 1 self | | 1 man |
| Sept. 1 | 1 self | | 25 | 1 self and Oliver & Boys ½ a day | 2 | ½ self ½ man 1 man |
| | | 1 man | | | | | |
| | 4 | ¾ self | | | | | |
| Oct. 3 | at house a day to make pins and braces | Oct. 4 | ¾ self ¾ man | Oct. 9 | raising the house |
| | | | 5 | 1 self | 13 | 1 self |
| | | | 8 | 1 self 2 men | 15 | 1 self |

On the 25th of October I agreed to give James Ebare $56.50 to finish my house.

*James Ebare's time on the finishing of the house*

| | | | | | | | | |
|---|---|---|---|---|---|---|---|---|
| Nov. | 3 | 2 days | Nov. | 30 | 1 day | | 12 | 1 day |
| | 21 | 2 days | Dec. | 1 | 1 day | | 13 | 1 day |
| | 22 | 2 days | | 3 | 1 day | | 14 | 1 day |
| | 23 | 2 days | | 4 | 1 day | | 17 | 1 day |
| | 24 | wet day | | 5 | 1 day | | 18 | 1 day |
| | 26 | 1½ days | | 6 | 1 day | | 19 | 1 day |
| | 27 | 1½ days | | 7 | 1 day | | 20 | 1 day |
| | 28 | 1 day | | 8 | 1 day | | 21 | 1 day |
| | 29 | 1 day | | 10 | 1 day | | | |

*1850*

| | | | | | | | | |
|---|---|---|---|---|---|---|---|---|
| Mar. | 25 | 1 day | Apr. | 26 | 1 day | May | 10 | 1 day |
| Apr. | 18 | 1 day | | 27 | 1 day | | 11 | 1 day |
| | 19 | 1 day | May | 1 | ½ day | | 14 | 1 day |
| | 20 | 1 day | | 2 | 1 day | | 15 | 1 day |
| | 21 | 1 day | | 3 | 1 day | | 16 | 1 day |
| | 22 | 1 day | | 4 | 1 day | | 17 | 1 day |
| | 23 | 1 day | | 8 | 1 day | | 21 | 1 day |
| | 24 | 1 day | | 9 | 1 day | | 22 | 1 day |
| | 25 | 1 day | | | | | | |

*Expenses of the house building*

| | | | |
|---|---|---|---|
| Raising | $35.00 | Stove with oven | 5.00 |
| Nails | 4.75 | Duty and Lime | .75 |
| Hire and Ferriage | 3.00 | Stove pipe and zinc | 2.50 |
| Shingles | 14.00 | Boiled oil and jug | 1.25 |
| Lumber | 41.50 | Paint brush | .25 |
| Pine lumber | 5.97 | 400 bricks | — |
| Ferriage | .50 | 1 barrel of lime | .75 |
| Duty | 1.18 | Hauling and boating | 1.50 |
| Sashes | 4.00 | 260 feet of Pine Lumber | 2.38 |
| Keg of white lead | 2.25 | Lock, hinges and latches etc. | 2.00 |
| Box of glass 8 × 10 | 2.75 | | |

| Cr. | | Dr. – Jock Ebare | |
|---|---|---|---|
| Finish the House | | | $45.16 |
| | 56.50 | | |
| Bricks | .50 | | 11.84 |
| Lumber | 2.72 | | 23.69 |
| Cash | 10.00 | | — |
| Planning Partition | 1.00 | | 80.69 |
| | — | | 70.72 |
| | 70.72 | | — |
| | | | 9.97 |

*1850*

| | | | |
|---|---|---|---|
| Nov. 1st | ½ a day | | .37 |
| | | | — |
| | | | 9.60 |

# 4
# PLANK CONSTRUCTION

Plank construction is a particular method of timber construction, well known in both Ontario and Quebec, which seems worthy of its own chapter. In this method the outside walls of a timber building are constructed of planks (not boards) which are set either vertically or as 'plank-on-plank' and become part of the structural system. The plank wall may have siding applied directly to its exterior face, and it may be papered or lath-and-plastered directly on the inside. In Ontario this type of construction is not exactly rare, yet it is far from being common. In Quebec the use of planks in this fashion was ordinary practice from the beginning of settlement. The method of securing the planks to the frame, using grooved posts, however, differed greatly from that employed in the New England colonies, which leads one to suspect that the systems are similar in principle but differing in origin. C.F. Innocent makes reference to this form of construction in England, but in such a casual way as to leave the impression that it was never very prevalent. Among the colonists of New England it probably first appeared as the result of successful experimentation, for the Yankees seem to have had the ability to solve almost any problem. The Quebec method can apparently be traced all the way back to early Viking days in Denmark.[1] Thence it spread through Europe, becoming firmly established in northern France before it was introduced into Canada.

What would appear to be a plank-covered house in New England is mentioned as early as 1638. This is Deputy-Governor Samuel Symond's house at Ipswich, Massachusetts, the erection of which was described at the time.[2] Although the covering was supposed to be only temporary, it was to consist of 'very goode oake-heart inch board.' This could hardly mean weather-boarding, the thickness of which was always less than an inch. The term 'plank' is used for the first time in 1639 in connection with the building of the church at Salem, Massachusetts.[3] This church was to be 'covered with 1½ plank and with board upon that to meet close.' This must mean planks covered either with clapboard or weather-board. The first plank frame house in the United States is mentioned by J.F. Kelly as having been built as early as 1690, in Connecticut: it was the Norton house, demolished in 1921, in the town of Guilford.[4] This dwelling was covered with 1½ inch to 2 inch planks, 12 to 15 inches in width. These were set into a rabbet in the sill and plate in such a manner as to make their outside face flush with that of the timbers. The planks were secured by means of two oak pins at each end. For some reason a 2 inch space was left between the planks which was later chinked with daubing. After this, the walls were covered with clapboard.[5] Isham and Brown mention, as an aside, that Plymouth, Massachusetts, and Providence, Rhode Island, abandoned the stud system and replaced it with that of vertical boarding, at least for interior partitions.[6]

From all this it would seem that the use of planks was one of the earliest, if not the first, attempt to improve by simplification upon the traditional methods of building homes that made use of complicated joints, as in frame construction.

The Old Mill on Mississauga Road near Toronto. The lower half of the building is of plank-on-plank construction; note the reinforcing in the walls and the props to prevent bulging.

Three variations of plank construction appear in Ontario. The examples of planked houses that have been investigated seem to indicate that the earlier ones were of frame construction with the studs replaced by planks. A later variation shows heavier planks used exclusively, all vertical posts being omitted. Experiments were also made about the same time in the use of horizontal plank-on-plank construction, but without apparent success because too much processed lumber, too many nails, and too many hours of labour were required. Plank-on-plank was reintroduced towards the close of the century when the new abundance of sawn lumber and machine-made nails put the method within reach of all; its principal use at this time was for silos, sawmills, and grist mills, as well as for coal sheds serving the railroads before they changed to oil. Such wall construction is not stable along the transverse axis unless very thoroughly cross-tied internally (we should note the vertical bracing in the mill on the Mississauga Road near Toronto, now demolished – a later addition to prevent the walls from bulging). There have been sporadic attempts at the revival of this construction in the form of patented systems, but none has ever been accepted.

The earliest system, the plank frame, presented no special problems to the builder. The frame was erected first in the usual manner, after which the planks were applied in a vertical position. In order to achieve a smooth exterior face, each plank was set into a rabbet in the sill and the plate and was cut wide enough to receive its thickness. Generally the walls were then covered with siding. Posts and beams would now show on the inside as vertical or horizontal projections. If the two intermediate posts were judiciously situated where the two transverse interior walls meet the exterior ones, these projections would not be objectionable. It should be understood that in every case the planks extended the full height of the walls from sill to plate, whether the building was of one or two storeys. Such construction was very efficient, since the planks performed a dual function, acting as fill for the walls as well as sheathing. The planks did not need to be more than 2 inches thick, since they were acting only as fill and as a ground for exterior and interior finish. The necessary rigidity was being supplied not by them but by the frame itself.

The upper part of a plank wall in a house in Bolton, similar in construction to the Henry house in Sutton. Note the recessed tenon at the upper end where the plate has eroded.

The lower part of the same plank wall

The second, later method eliminated all posts and retained only horizontal bearing members – sills, plates, and intermediate beams – to carry floor loads. The planks themselves became load-bearing members and assumed a new function. They were therefore increased in thickness to 3 inches at least. The house now had no skeleton, so to speak, only a heavy carapace. Once the firm sheath was in place all was well, but how a building so designed was actually erected is a question not yet satisfactorily answered. The method I suggest later on is decidedly conjectural.

The cheapest type of plank construction consisted of spiking the planks to the outside face of the sills, to the beams carrying the second-floor joists, and to the plate. The method is of dubious value, but this house appears to have remained quite firm. Note the varying width of the planks in contrast to that of a regular 'board-and-batten' house. The planks are about 2¾ inches thick. Note also the row of spikes just above the door hood indicating the location of the second-floor beams. Date unknown; now in the museum in Pickering.

The method of securing the joists, by the insertion of wedges against their upper face, is apparent here (see the drawing of this device, in section, on page 183). The exposed ends of the joists, flush with the wall surface, can be seen here, and just below the joist openings is a long, horizontal scribe mark; this indicates the positioning of the shear pins or edge-dowels, which in some cases can be made out in the gaps between the vertical planks. Note the window frame at the bottom; the opening was evidently cut in the planks after they were assembled.

A typical intersection of two plank-on-plank walls, seen from the inside, in a house in Bolton.

## Plank construction

The third and last method used planks in a horizontal position in the fashion described as plank-on-plank. These were usually 1 inch thick and 6 inches wide and were commonly laid with a ½ inch offset alternately on each side to form a key for plaster or stucco. Lumber, and processed lumber, in prodigious amounts was needed, together with great quantities of nails, which made this method less popular. The amount of material would be equal to that needed for a log house of comparable size. As for the labour required, the amount can be appreciated when one considers that each plank raised the height of the wall by only one inch. Much hand labour was also required at corners, and at intersections of walls, where each plank-layer must alternately lap the lower one. Such work would be extremely time-consuming and costly. Plaster was usually applied directly on the planks inside, while the exterior remained 'roughcast' or strapped and covered with siding. Occasionally siding was nailed directly to the exterior. Pauline Johnson's home near Brantford is perhaps the best-known example of this kind of building.

RIGHT Exterior treatment of plank-on-plank walls consisted either of 'roughcasting' or, as in this case, of strapping and siding. The alternate offsetting of the planks to provide a key for internal plaster can be seen where the siding has been removed.

LEFT Plaster was generally applied directly to the inside face of plank-on-plank walls, using as a key the alternate offsetting of the planks.

~ *Alternate Butt Joints* ~

An interior wall in plank-on-plank construction has to be bonded into an exterior wall in the same manner as at exterior corners, rather like thin brick work. The use of alternate butt joints results in the above exterior appearance. Note that the siding here is nailed directly to the outer face of the planks rather than to strapping. The boards are fastened together not by spikes but generally by standard 3½ inch cut nails.

The two houses which I have been able to examine in detail are the so-called James Butler house at Niagara-on-the Lake and the William Henry home at Sutton. Fortunately each house exemplifies a distinct type of construction. The Butler dwelling, since it is the older, shows the typical frame method; the Henry house, built forty to fifty years later, represents definite structural innovations, although their advantages are questionable.

The James Butler house, built about 1810–15, shows no significant change from the standard plank-covered frame house. About 30 by 40 feet in size, it is a one-storey cottage with a hip roof. The date of construction, at the moment, is tentative; however, the fact that the planks, as well as the siding, are secured entirely by handmade nails, indicates an early date, since it would have been a simple matter to cross the river and secure cut nails in the United States, had these been in ample supply there.

The planks are 2 inches thick. On average they are 11 to 15 inches wide and are held in place at both ends by two or three nails, rather than by pins as in the Norton house in Guilford. Sills and plates are rabbetted in the usual manner to receive the planks. The sills measure about 7 by 9½ inches, the plates 6 by 8 inches, and the rabbet in each 2 by 1½ inches.

The most unusual detail in the house is one that bears no relation to the method we are studying. This is a short post, resting on a ceiling beam. About 10 inches square, this member supports the joint at the ridge where the two hip-rafters, as well as the central common rafter, meet. This joint is an awkward one, in any case, because it develops considerable lateral thrust. The post thus provides a positive support where needed, although decidedly overstrong for this purpose. Here indeed is a most unorthodox detail. The house, at the time of writing, is in the process of being restored by Brigadier W. Moogk, director of the Dundurn Castle Museum in Hamilton.

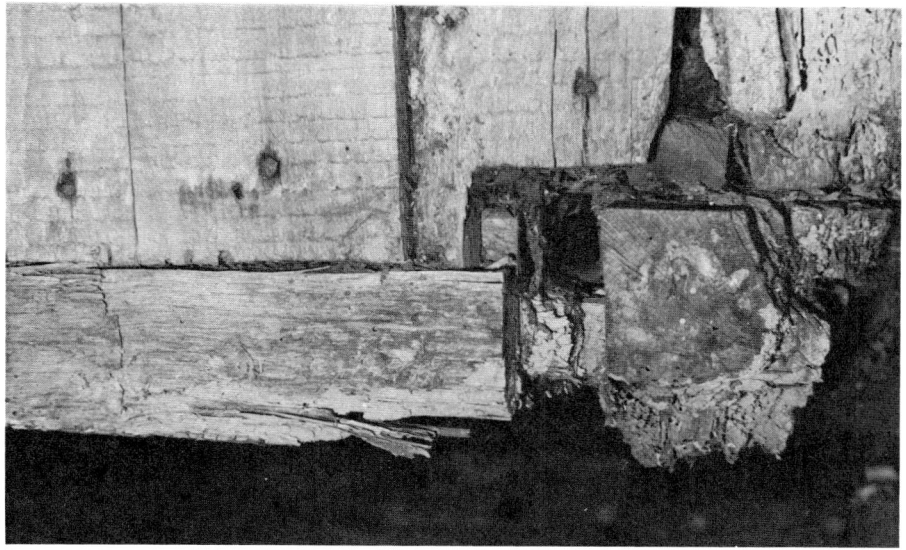

The Butler house, Niagara-on-the-Lake (see also the drawing of the bottom exterior corner). Note the gap between the end and the side sills: this could be the result of inadequate footings, or of expansion and contraction caused by variations in moisture and temperature, or of both.

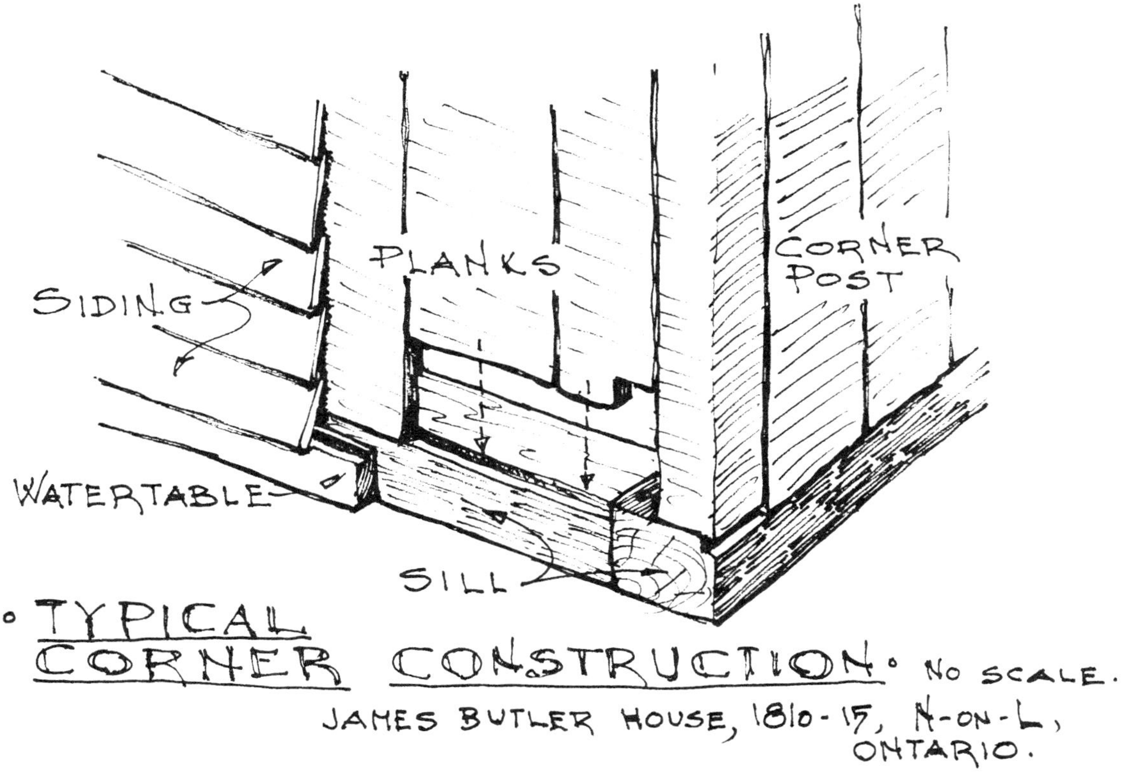
SIDING
PLANKS
CORNER POST
WATERTABLE
SILL
TYPICAL CORNER CONSTRUCTION.
NO SCALE.
JAMES BUTLER HOUSE, 1810-15, N-ON-L, ONTARIO.

The William Henry house, located at R.R. 3, Sutton, and constructed between 1850 and 1860, is by far the more interesting house. It is two full storeys in height, about 22 by 35 feet in size, and is a plank house in the full sense of the expression. No frame is present since all planks in the exterior walls are load-bearing. The only horizontal members are sills and plates together with interior beams supporting the floor joists. These beams run transversely, of course, three in the first floor and two in the second. All heavy timbers were hewn, all other stock is cut on an 'up-and-down' muley or gangsaw. The horizontal timbers number only thirteen in all; four sills, four plates, and five interior beams. The sills are 12 inches square, the plates 7 by 9 inches. The intermediate floor beams in the first floor measure, from left to right, 12 by 12, 7 by 9, and 8½ by 10 inches respectively; the two in the second floor are each 6 by 8 inches. All other structural members are cut from 3 inch stock: the planks varying in width from 10 to 20 inches; joists are 3 by 8 inches; rafters 3 by 5 inches; and all interior studs 3 by 4 inches. Still smaller members may vary in dimension up to half an inch; heavier ones up to 1 inch. The spacing of the secondary members averages 24 inches. In the second floor the centre joist is omitted since it would enter the wall in the middle of the chimney; consequently, there occurs here one space of 48 inches. The flooring is 1¼ inch tongue-and-groove.

This house is furnished with only a half-basement; a crawl space was left under the remaining area. The joists and beams over this area are cedar, for the obvious reason that this wood is less susceptible to the dampness that would inevitably be present. Cedar was all the more necessary since no provision was made for ventilation.

The interior walls were papered first with newspapers directly on the planks. At a later date genuine wallpaper was applied and, still later, lath and plaster.

The most unique feature of the Henry house is, of course, the total absence of a 'frame' so that the method of erecting it, as already suggested, is something of a puzzle. In a framed house the skeleton of timbers will stand quite well by itself; everything else is simply applied to it. But where outside planks themselves take on the function of load-bearing members, while they must also provide necessary stability, it is hard to imagine how builders would begin. Here is my best guess as to what was done.

First, in order to align the planks at top and bottom, a tenon was cut at each end. This tenon was offset towards the inside face. It was half the thickness of the plank and 1 inch long. A corresponding mortise was cut into the sill and plate. This was set back far enough to bring the face of the plank even with the face of the timbers. No nails were used to hold them, since the leverage was so great that even the largest nail could have no appreciable holding power. To align the planks with each other lengthwise, two pins were inserted over their length, each about half way between each floor height. These pins were of oak, about 1 inch square and 4 inches long. Their

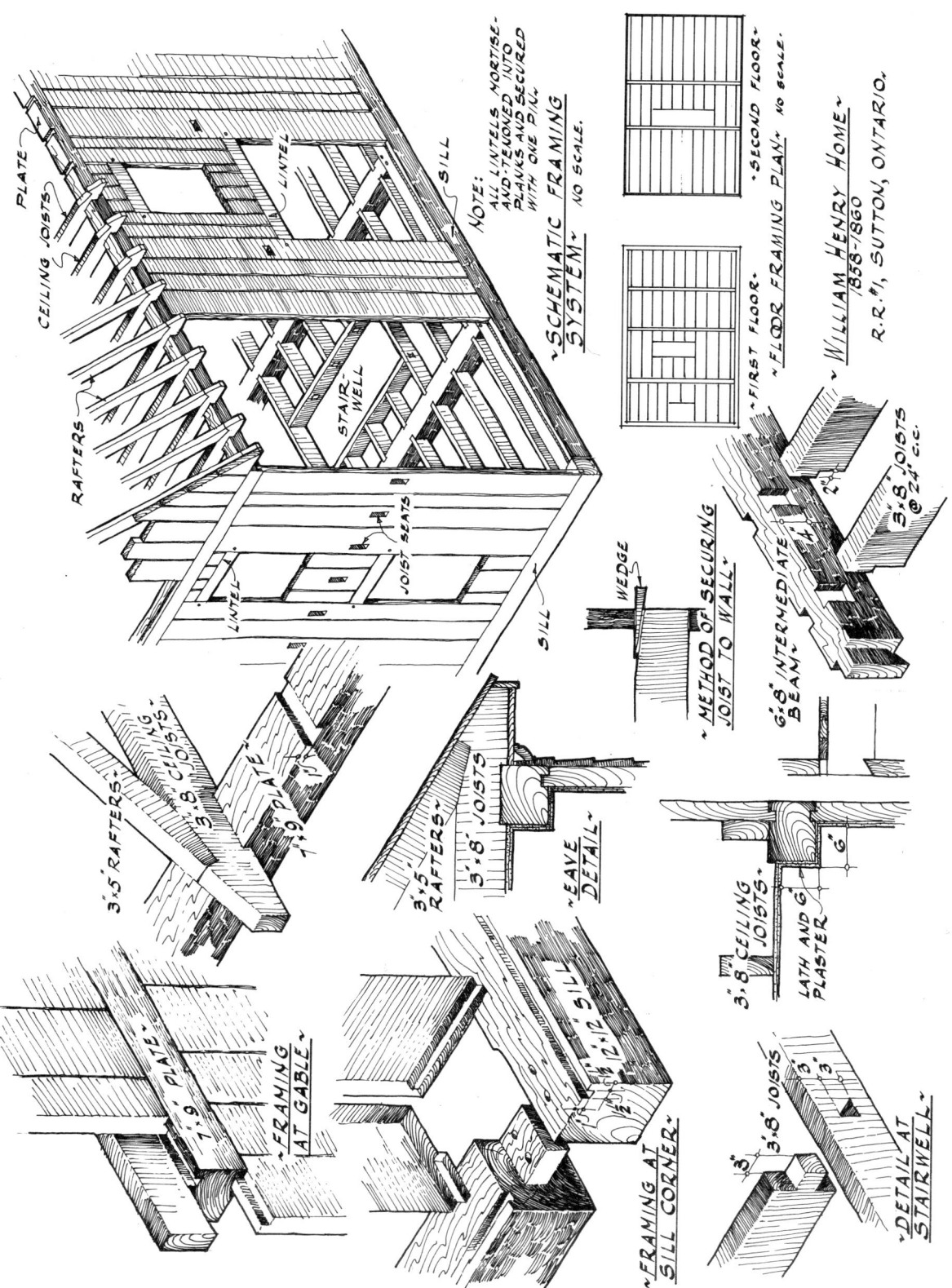

A shear pin from the Henry house – the pin shown is about full size.

main purpose, however, was to act as shear pins, since they would develop a shear stress if the boards tended to move laterally. By this means such shifting was prevented and the wall attained great lateral rigidity. Nevertheless, as it was going up, such a wall would require very strong temporary lateral bracing since it was solid for its entire height and the slightest wind would endanger it. But it could not very well have been assembled on the ground and put up as a unit, since the sill and plate are not an integral part of it and thus the required rigidity would be lacking.

Except for the sill and plates, the only place where a mortise and tenon joint was used was in the lintels over the openings. Lintels were 3 by 7 inches and carried a tenon 1 inch thick at each end, cut to the full depth of the piece. The tenon was inserted into the mortise of the corresponding boards and fastened with a single 1 inch pin at each end. The joists and beams rested in a mortise extending completely through the planks. At the wall end joists were cut with a slight taper and, after insertion into the mortise, were secured with a wooden wedge. The transverse beams, which also acted as ties, were secured to the planks by a wedged half-dovetail joint. At window-sill level the planks were toe-nailed to each other in order to give the spandrel some rigidity. In several spandrels a vertical wedge of very slight taper appears to have been driven between two adjacent planks at the centre, as if to force them together for greater security. In New England examples, spaces between the planks remained wide and required chinking; however, in the two houses under discussion, the interstices were so narrow as to make chinking unnecessary.

There is another sequence of erection that would be possible, but I have not been able to verify it because the structure of the building was not sufficiently laid bare to enable me to make a careful estimate. However, here it is. Let us suppose several planks were put up first at all four corners. The plates were then fitted over, secured properly at the corners, and the whole assembly thoroughly braced. If the groove in the plate were made 2 inches deep and the shoulder at the top of the plank cut back an additional inch, the top of the plank could then be inserted into the plate to the depth of a full 2

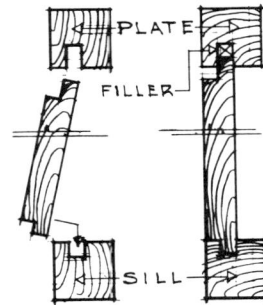

CONJECTURAL ERECTION PROCEDURE

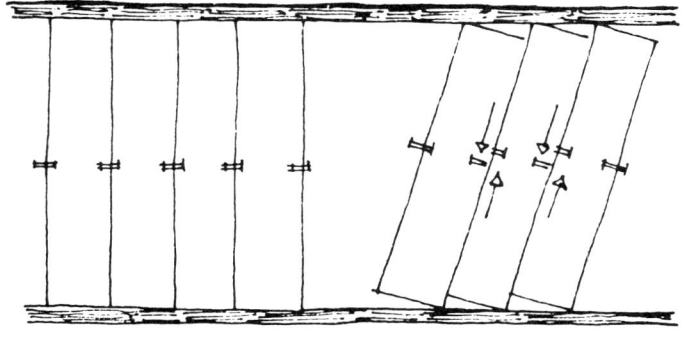

*- Exaggerated Stress on Shear Pin -*

inches. This would raise the bottom of the plank high enough to permit it to be dropped into the mortise in the sill. After having been dropped into the bottom mortise, the plank would still carry an upper tenon with a 1 inch purchase by which the upper end could be secured. A 1 inch space would remain between the upper should and the bottom of the plate, as well as a similar gap between the top of the upper tenon and the mortise. The gap at the face would in any case be covered by the cornice board. As for that between the upper tenon and the mortise it could easily be filled by a separate piece driven into this space after each plank was set into position. This filler piece would be necessary, since otherwise the plate would rest only on the corner planks and would thus give way under the weight of the roof. It must be repeated, however, that this method is entirely conjectural, since no verification of it is possible at the time of writing. The fact that the Henry house is still perfectly true and plumb, after standing over a hundred years, is proof that whatever the procedure employed in its erection, the builders assuredly knew what they were doing.

The principles of plank construction in Quebec are essentially the same as in Ontario, though differences in details of construction do occur and features that have a similar function should be examined closely. Although the table presented here is not at all comprehensive, it does draw attention to some of these divergences.

The drawings of Quebec plank houses reproduced here also reveal some of the details of this form of construction in that province. In the house on Highway 41 near Lachute (page 187) one should notice the method of fastening the beams into the planks, the dropped end plate, and the haunched tenons in the corner planks, which were necessary because the mortise does not extend the full length of the sill or of the plate. The lower corner construction in the house in St-Hermas (page 188) should be compared with the same in the Lachute house and with the lapped joint of the upper corner. This assembly requires a reduced tenon, at the top and bottom of the right corner plank, because it must project across the unmortised faces of the plate and sill in the adjoining wall.

## Comparative plank construction

| Detail | ONTARIO | | QUEBEC | |
|---|---|---|---|---|
| | Niagara-on-the Lake | Sutton | Lachute | St Hermas |
| Plank thickness | 1½" | 3" | 4" | 4" |
| Horizontal corner brace at plate[a] | | | | x |
| Pinned planks | | | x | |
| Shearpin or dowel | | short, single, 2 per joint | continuous[b] | continuous[b] |
| Dropped end plate | | | x | |
| Ceiling beam seat | simple mortise and tenon | half-dovetail, and mortise and tenon | simple, pinned mortise and tenon | simple, pinned mortise and tenon |
| Planks ends | open rabbet, nailed | full rabbet, or continuous mortise, loose | full rabbet, (continuous mortise), pegged at corners and openings only | full rabbet, (continuous mortise), loose |
| Storeys | 1 | 2 | 1½ | 1½ |

a  This feature has been observed in the Windsor area and in the Fisher house in Toronto, but it remains exceptional in Ontario.
b  This is a doubtful feature. It could have been an error of observation on the part of the draftsman.

In the St-Hermas house there is horizontal corner bracing at the plate level. Although I have discovered this feature in the Windsor area, and the Fisher house in Toronto has it, it is less typical of Ontario construction methods than of Quebec. In the Lachute house it should be noted that the end plate is dropped 2'10" below the side plate; this is fairly typical in Ontario buildings, but must be regarded as an exception in Quebec, or at least a relatively late development.

The planks used in Quebec generally seem to have been narrower and thicker, and this fact may explain the use of continuous dowels in Quebec (though I have not had an opportunity to verify this) as opposed to the short, individual shear pins used in Ontario. To drill holes through a number of boards and still have them line up properly is a difficult task and I feel that this is possibly an error due to lack of verification.

The settlers in Quebec seem to have done no experimenting at all with plank-on-plank construction. I do not know the reason for the neglect of this method, but it is possible that the French builders realized how inefficient it was from the outset.

Plank construction 187

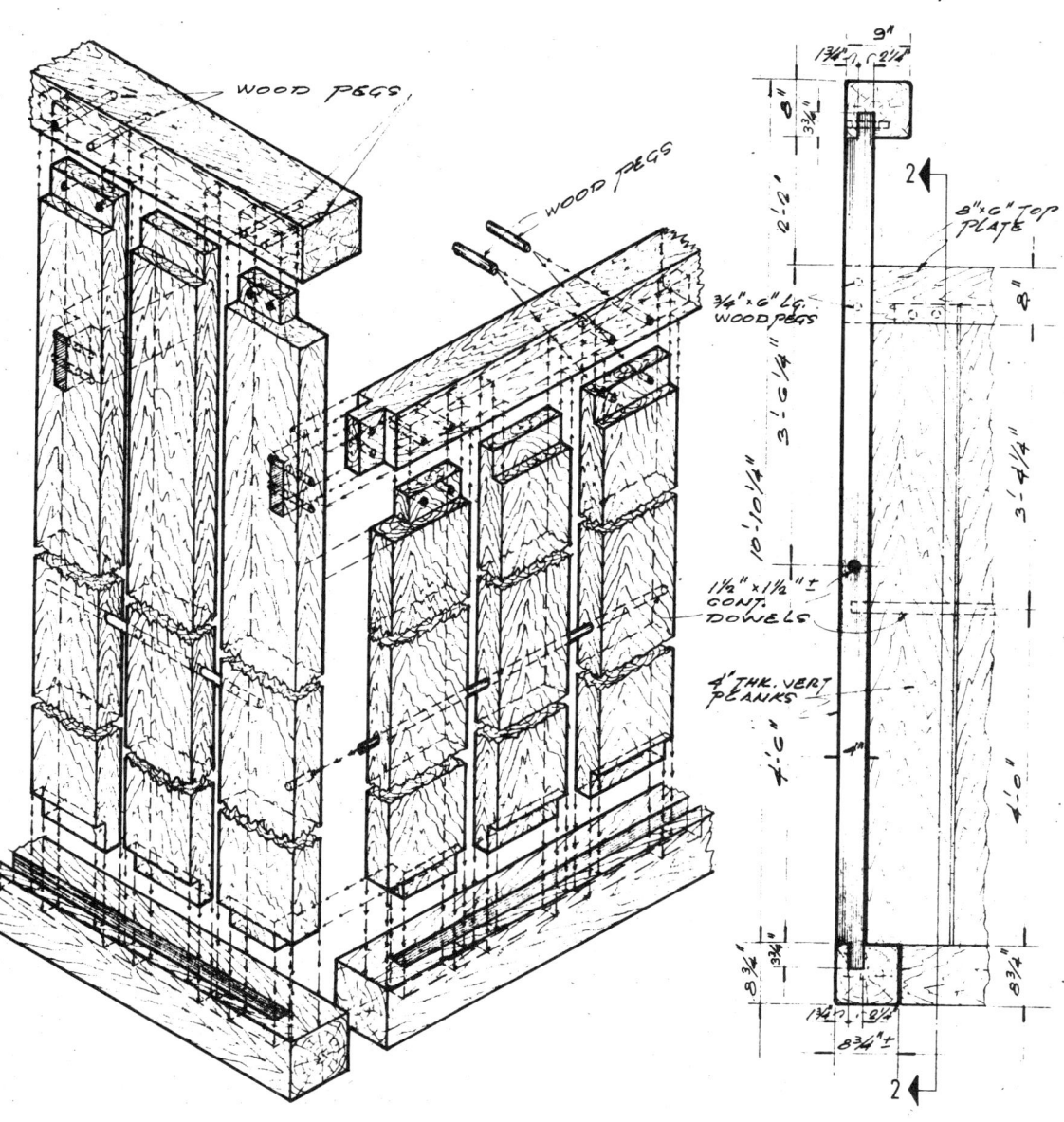

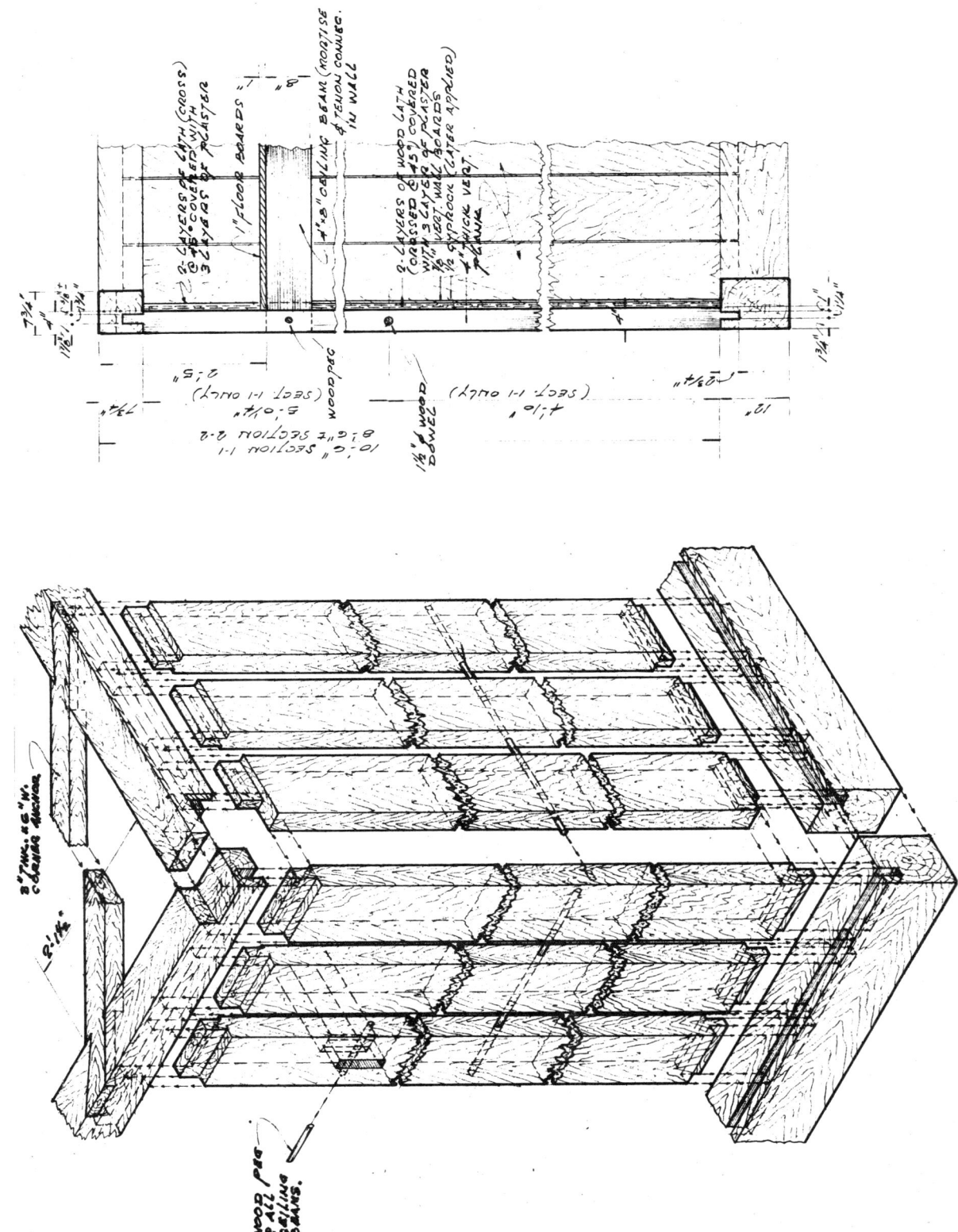

# 5
# BARNS

190 Building with Wood

This brief survey of barns in Ontario and Quebec is intended to be neither thorough nor definitive. If it encourages a more intensive study of these neglected and disappearing structures it will have served its purpose. The Quebec barn has its roots in Normandy; whereas the Ontario barn is the end result of the English or German type, modified or Americanized by progress through New England, and transplanted by the United Empire Loyalists and others into Upper Canada. Although it is an oversimplification to do so, the products of the two traditions will be referred to as the Quebec barn and the Ontario barn.

## Barns in Ontario

Barns constitute by far the greatest number of large buildings in rural Ontario. Many of them enclose much greater space than churches, schools, and halls. Proverbially, his barn means more to a farmer than his house. In

The minimal log barn – one mow, one threshing floor, grain and feed barn. Note that the corners are merely bonded with alternate, overlapping squared ends, unlike a dovetail; the exposed ends of the logs of an interior partition, bonded into the external wall, can be seen just to the right of the vertical boarding.

many instances the barn will contain far more up-to-date equipment, although our present affluence has greatly changed this picture.

As a piece of architecture the barn is perhaps the most neglected of man's buildings. Few historians have troubled to study it and still fewer architects seem to think its structural principles deserve examination. Nevertheless, although the lowest in the scale of architectural and social values, after human shelter the barn is the oldest type of building in history. Its singleness of purpose is never in doubt; it discharges a necessary function most efficiently; and, often enough, it achieves truly monumental proportions.

THE LOG BARN

The evolution of a typical 'English' barn from the days of the New England settler is easily demonstrated. The earliest was the one mow, one threshing floor, grain and feed barn. Next came the two mow structure with a central threshing floor, usualy with a door in each outer side. This barn was in effect

Next up in scale from the one mow barn is the two mow barn with central threshing floor; the ends of the bonding logs of the two interior partitions can be seen on either side of the central double-hung door.

The third stage in the style of log barns in Ontario. The artificial earth ramp is on the other side of the building; on this side, the second of the two great cart doors sits forlornly out of reach.

A typical group of Ontario log barns. In contrast to Pennsylvania-German log barns, 'English' ones were quite small; if more space was required, it was just a matter of adding another building.

two square log structures placed near each other, joined by a common wall plate, and united into a single building by the continuous roof. The threshing floor was the space left between the two distinct structural units of the mows. In many instances, as the farmer prospered, these buildings were later raised and placed on a masonry or stone foundation in order to make room for a stable below. The status of a two-level structure had now been reached, but the higher level required an artificial earth ramp on one side to permit wagons to enter the threshing floor. The cattle entrance remained at the lower level.

When made of logs, barns were of small or medium size. If more room was needed, the farmer simply built additional units. All logs barns in Ontario were of the New England construction, except during a period after the First World War when a large number of Scandinavian immigrants entered Canada. A great many of these were Finns who brought vertical post-and-fill construction into Northern Ontario. This method is indistinguishable from Quebec 'poteaux et pièce coulissante,' but it is not indigenous to Ontario.

Oddly enough, this is not another example of the French 'poteaux et pièce coulissante' method, but rather a type of construction introduced into the Timmins-Kapuskasing area in the 1920s by Finnish settlers.

The outstanding example in Ontario of a full two-storey, Pennsylvania-German log barn is the Johannes Schmidt barn of 1809, now owned by Black Creek Pioneer Village, near Toronto. Here the log walls of the lower floor rest on a stone foundation raised only slightly above grade. The ceiling beams project on either side and form the threshing floor of the upper level. The mow walls are a continuation of the log walls below. This barn has been restored, as has a nearby grain and feed barn.

When a barn was intended to hold only grain or fodder, the lower floor was omitted, as was the case with the barn at the pioneer village. Two rows of very heavy girders run the full length of this structure to form its base. These girders rest on large boulders which raise them a few feet about the ground. The floor beams run transversely, are closely spaced, and project 6 to 8 feet beyond the girders, which are far enough apart to permit the mow walls to rest directly over them, thus relieving the floor beams of any

The Johannes Schmidt log barn, 1809, before restoration. The log walls of the lower level and of the mow above can be clearly seen. The later frame structure conceals the floor beams which project above the basement to form the threshing-floor level. It is worth remarking on the sheer size of the timbers that make up the original structure.

West end view of the Johannes Schmidt barn.

The Johannes Schmidt barn. Here can be seen the floor beams that project above the log basement to support the threshing-floor level above and cover the 'forbay' below; the low, rubble-stone foundation wall is also evident. On the other side of the barn, a combination of natural hill slope and artificial ramp gives cart access to the threshing floor.

A pinned, scarfed joint in the secondary plate over the threshing floor; note also the tie-beam between the two log mows below it.

The two mow grain and feed log barns at Black Creek Pioneer Village. Note the huge girders which form the total support for the structure above; a joint in such heavy load-bearing timbers always has to occur over a support.

additional load. The projection of these floor beams form the overshot, of which the present exterior walls are of frame construction. Their wall plate is lower than the upper log of the mow which, in this case, forms a secondary plate, against which the roof of the overshot 'leans-to,' with a slope virtually the same as the upper part of the roof. (This plate or upper log is frequently and incorrectly called a purlin, though 'purlin-plate' would be an acceptable term.) The whole area is roofed over without the use of a ridge board.

In barns with two mows, when it came to the threshing floor the roof spanned a considerable distance and needed support; the simple solution was to carry the plates of each mow right over the central area as in the one at Black Creek, thus furnishing a means of taking the load of the rafters above. Since these barns were generally of considerable length, the continuous plate thus formed was often made of two pieces joined with a scarfed and pinned joint occurring generally over the threshing floor. If the mows were quite high, another intermediate tie-log might be required. Such a log was also keyed into the opposing mow walls with a half-dovetail joint.

Note the half-dovetail of the piece that ties the wall of the overhang to the log mow wall.

· THRESHING FLOOR ·

· END BENT ·

· GRAIN & FEED ·

· 2nd & 4th BENT ·

· BASEMENT ·

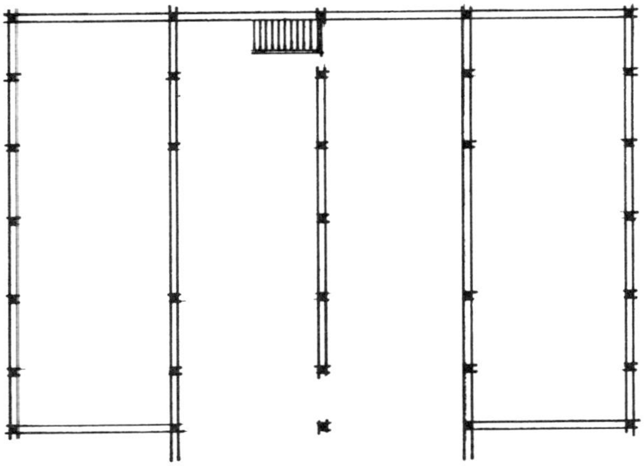

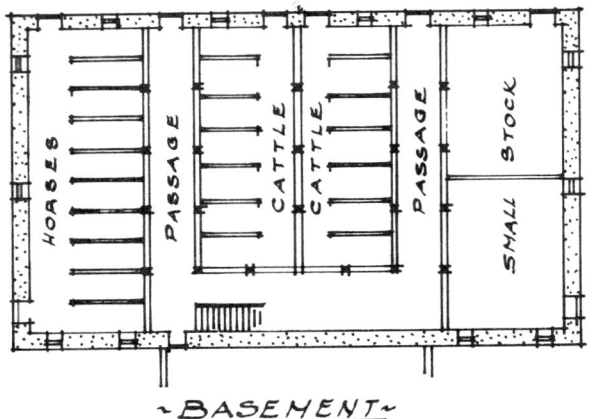

· PENNSYLVANIA - GERMAN HEAVY TIMBER BARN ·
NO SCALE

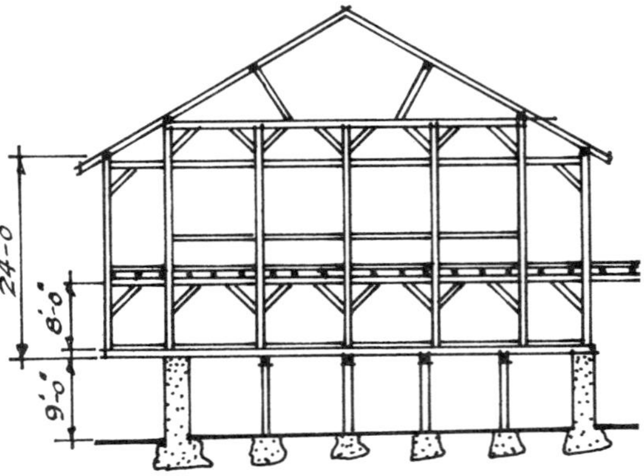

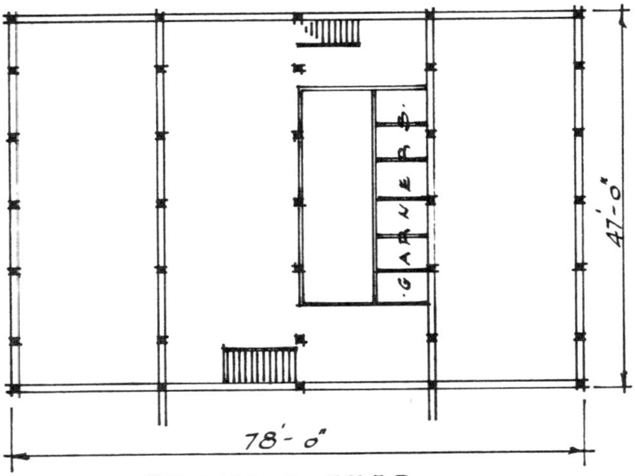

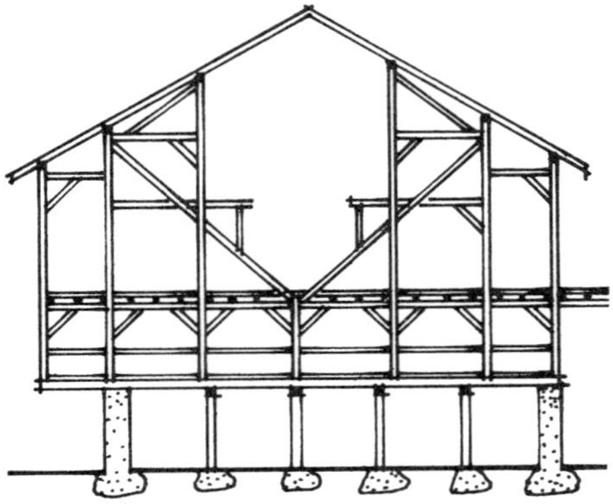

## THE FRAMED BARN

In England the framing principles of the barn are very old indeed and show an unbroken line of development from the eleventh century to the present. Rufus the Red framed the great hall of his Westminster palace (1097–99) in the aisled manner of the tithe barns owned by the monastic orders of the day.[1] For our purpose this early history may be passed over. Suffice it to say that by the time the colonists reached the North American shore barn framing in England had attained great sophistication. After crossing the Atlantic, framing methods were streamlined and simplified just as house framing methods were – and for the same reasons. By the time Ontario was settled the barn frame had become thoroughly Americanized and the rules for its framing, along with those for houses, mills, and churches, had developed into a stable and predictable system. The only new addition to this group of buildings was the relatively small log barn, which quickly developed into what is now the familiar two mow, centre threshing floor barn of one or two levels. We shall confine ourselves to only two types of barn in Ontario, since all others derived from them. These are the typical Pennsylvania-German bank barn, and its 'English' (for want of a better term) equivalent.

A Pennsylvania-German barn is almost always sited on a natural slope. The lower storey will be of brick or stone or even logs. This storey shelters the livestock and is entered at the lower level. The upper floor is level with the higher ground. At least on one side it will project over the lower floor to form the forbay (*forbau* or *forschoos*). These barns may be built totally of logs, or of frame with stone end walls. Even if framed, the lower floor will still be of brick or stone. At present, frame barns predominate, although this was not so in early Pennsylvania: in 1798, out of a total of 15,885 barns registered, 6813 are listed as totally of log construction, 818 as cabin barns, and only 716 as framed (the remainder were various types which have no bearing on this study). Not all barns had a forbay, but since this is a feature which particularly distinguishes the Pennsylvania-German barn, we shall take it into account when the type is considered in detail.

The cabin barn, mentioned above, was the smallest sort of shelter for animals and their fodder, and hardly deserves the name of barn at all. It was built like a log house and was about the same size. Frequently it had served the settler as a home until he became prosperous enough to build a better one. In either case, it was a mere frontier expedient, and hence as an addition to the barn family it is of little significance. Cabin barns can also be found in Ontario.

The barn now thought of as typically Pennsylvania-German had its origin in Saxony, Bavaria, and Switzerland. The Swiss influence is dominant. In early Pennsylvania this barn was called a 'bank barn' (1796), 'Swisser barn' (1802), 'overshot' barn (1813), 'a stone barn with an overshot' (1814),

'Schweitzerscheuer' (1815), and 'Switzer barn' (1819). A report of the Commissioner of Agriculture in Washington for the year 1864 contains the following passage: 'As characterizing States, indeed, Pennsylvania stands prominent in the importance which her people have attached to the barn, as an essential element in the constitution of a farm. Their estimate of its value, in the profitable prosecution of their business, has given to it a form, shape and structure that distinguishes it from a mere shelter for animals or cover for hay and grain, whether they be stables, corn-houses, ricks, or other such devices.'[2]

The size of a Pennsylvania-German barn varied greatly, the smallest measuring only about 20 feet in length whereas the largest 'cow palace' could reach 'cathedral' lengths of 100 feet or more (the most imposing specimens boasted lengths of 140 and 159 feet). Even in Ontario a barn just recently dismantled measured an amazing 80 by 160 feet. The most recent of these giant, three-level barns was built just east of St Jacobs in 1938 by Simeon Martin for Lloyd Farwell of Kitchener, Ontario, the owner at the time of writing.

The fate of the first log house, this one near Orillia, was generally to be turned into a shed or small barn.

Most of the barns in Ontario are framed and are of the two-storey, double mow, and centre threshing floor type. The Walker barn near Coldwater is an example of this type, although the touches of Palladianism in the windows, and the cupola that resembles the steeple of a small church in Essex, England, make it something of a curiosity. The extra aisle on the south side which gives the gable end the appearance of a New England 'salt-box' is also noteworthy. If barns were built large enough, another aisle would be added on the other side but still without an overhang.

In all cases the mows are high in proportion to their width. There was a definite reason for this. After a mow had been filled, the hay or straw would settle considerably. If the mow area was relatively wide, this would mean much wasted space after the settling had taken place. Such waste could be decreased if the mow were made smaller but given greater height. Also, of course, the smaller area plan meant a smaller roof, and therefore a less complicated roof structure.

A small shed or barn on the Rama Indian Reserve near Lake Couchiching, built of rounded logs, trimmed square at the end, and fashioned into dovetail, interlocking corner joints. Note the careful fitting of a warped log into the structure.

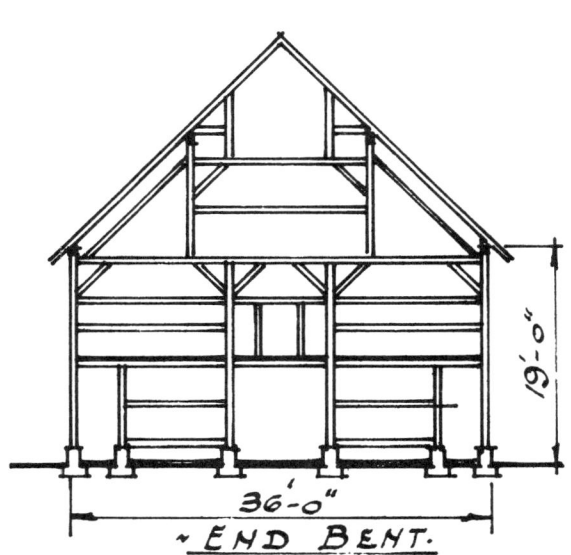
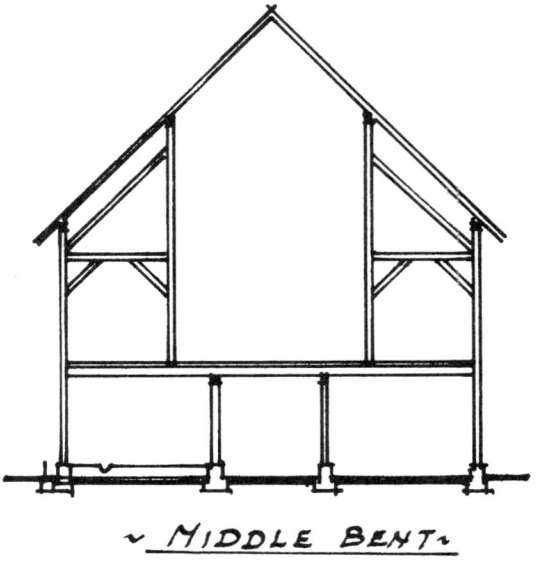
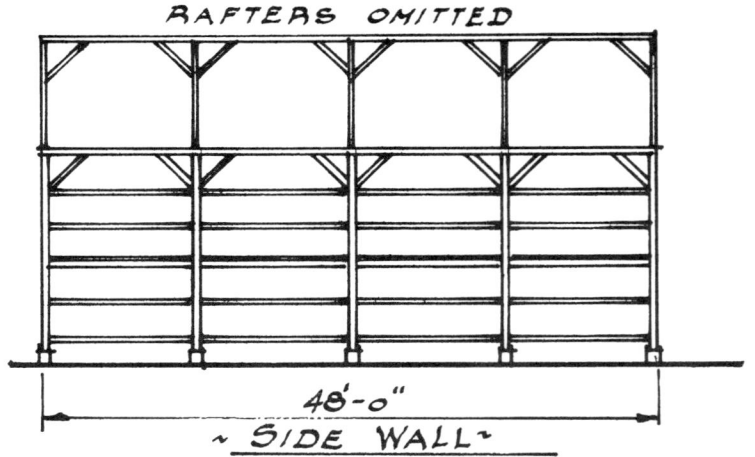

J.I.R. '71.

**SMALL HAY BARN**
ACCORDING TO "RADFORD"
NO SCALE.

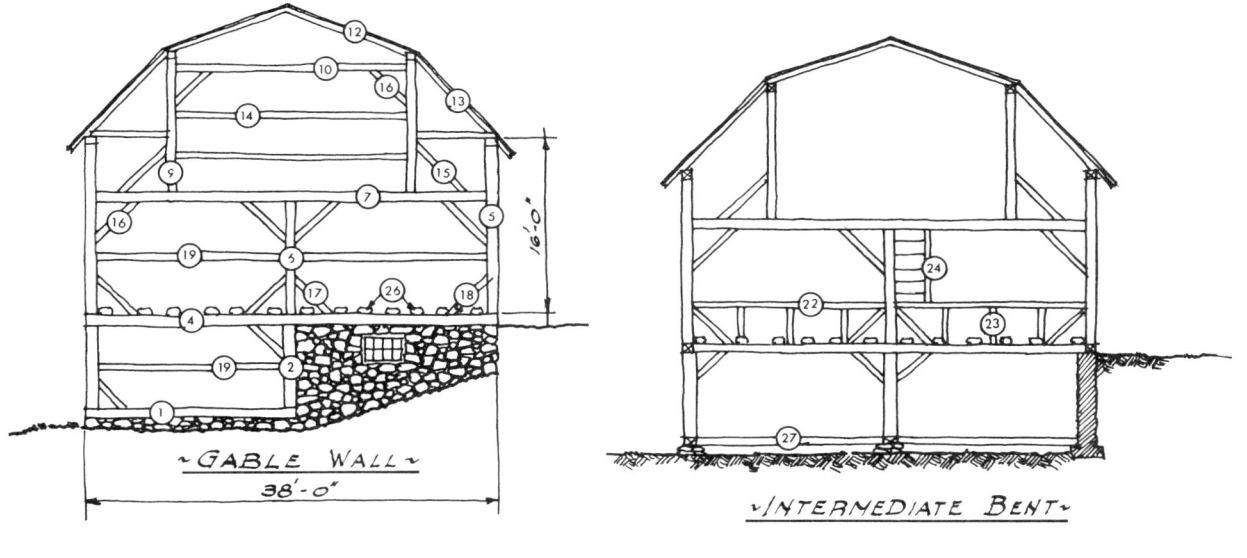

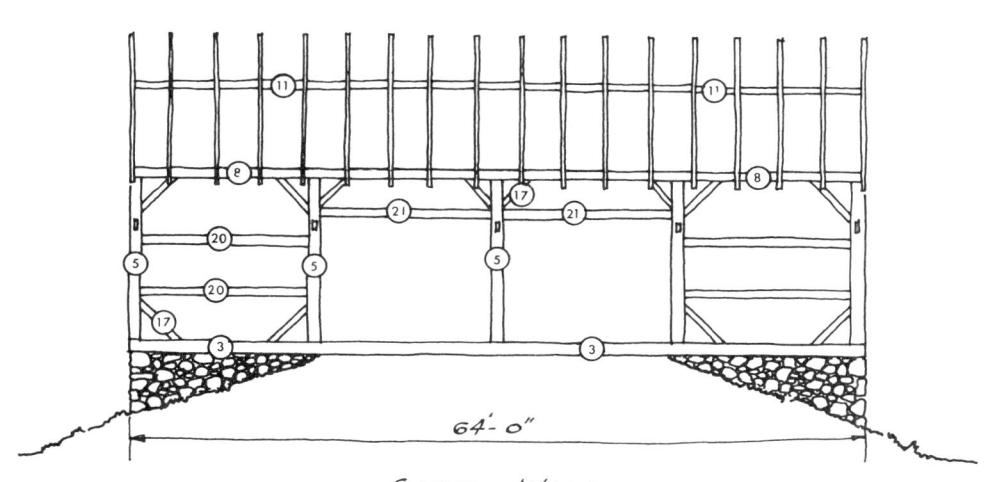

## PARTS LIST:

1. BASEMENT SILL — 10" × 12"
2. " " POSTS — 12" × 12"
3. MAIN SILL — 10" × 10"
4. CROSS SILL — 10" × 10"
5. MAIN POSTS — 8" × 8"
6. CENTER POST — 8" × 8"
7. MAIN BEAMS — 8" × 10"
8. " PLATE — 8" × 8"
9. PURLIN POSTS — 6" × 6"
10. " BEAMS — 6" × 6"
11. " PLATE — 6" × 6"
12. UPPER RAFTERS — 2" × 6"
13. LOWER " " — 2" × 6"
14. PURLIN GIRTS — 4" × 6"
15. PURLIN BRACES — 3" × 4"
16. 3 FT-RUN " — 3" × 4"
17. 2½ FT-RUN " — 3" × 4"
18. 3½ FT-RUN " — 3" × 4"
19. END GIRTS — 4" × 6"
20. SIDE " " — 4" × 6"
21. DOOR " — 4" × 6"
22. BREAST " — 6" × 8"
23. " " GIRT STUDS — 3" × 4"
24. LADDER POST — 3" × 4"
25. DOOR POSTS — 4" × 4"
26. "OVERLAYS"—FLATTENED TOP AND ENDS TO 6"
27. SLEEPERS — 6" × 6"

## "ENGLISH"–HEAVY TIMBER BARN

REDRAWN FROM "RADFORD". J.I.R. '71.

The Walker barn near Coldwater. In shape and construction it is a typical 'English' barn, except for the Palladian window in the gable and the vent that bears a greater resemblance to a Georgian church spire in the manner of Wren or Gibbs than to the functional vents of an Ontario barn.

Ventilation is of the utmost importance in a feed barn, especially after it has been newly filled. In the middle of the last century barn builders advised against cupola vents because, so it was argued, the new hay would produce 'gases and damp fog' which, escaping through such cupolas, would attract lightning. To prevent this, it was recommended that the gable end be covered with boards spaced a fraction of an inch apart; the dangerous vapours would diffuse themselves through these many apertures and the peril would be lessened. After the introduction of lightning rods there seemed no need for such a precaution and the cupola vent became typical, the continuous ridge vent less common.

Framing followed a predictable pattern. Two major considerations governed it: one was the heavy static load to be carried by the structure when filled; the other was the great wall and roof areas that were exposed to wind. Complete and thorough bracing, both lateral and transverse, was essential. It is to the credit of the early builders that so many old structures are still perfectly plumb and true after many years of service. It will be noted that in frame barns the ridge board was generally omitted, the roof being framed in pairs of rafters.

As a rule, the entrance to the threshing floor was located in the middle of a side wall. The double driveway occurred less frequently than the single one.

After 1900, barns began to be made of prefabricated units in the form of trusses built up of lighter members. These trusses combined light weight with the strength of the bulky and heavy timbers.

The smallest framed barn structure is the milk cooling house with a delivery platform. Note that the present platform is only half as high as was the original. The bases of the door-jambs, as well as the propped-up corner posts, declare a structural level beneath them, which is now missing. Obviously the vehicle on which the milk was delivered has changed – at first a horse-drawn cart with a floor perched over a high axle, and now a low trailer on rubber wheels?

206  Building with Wood

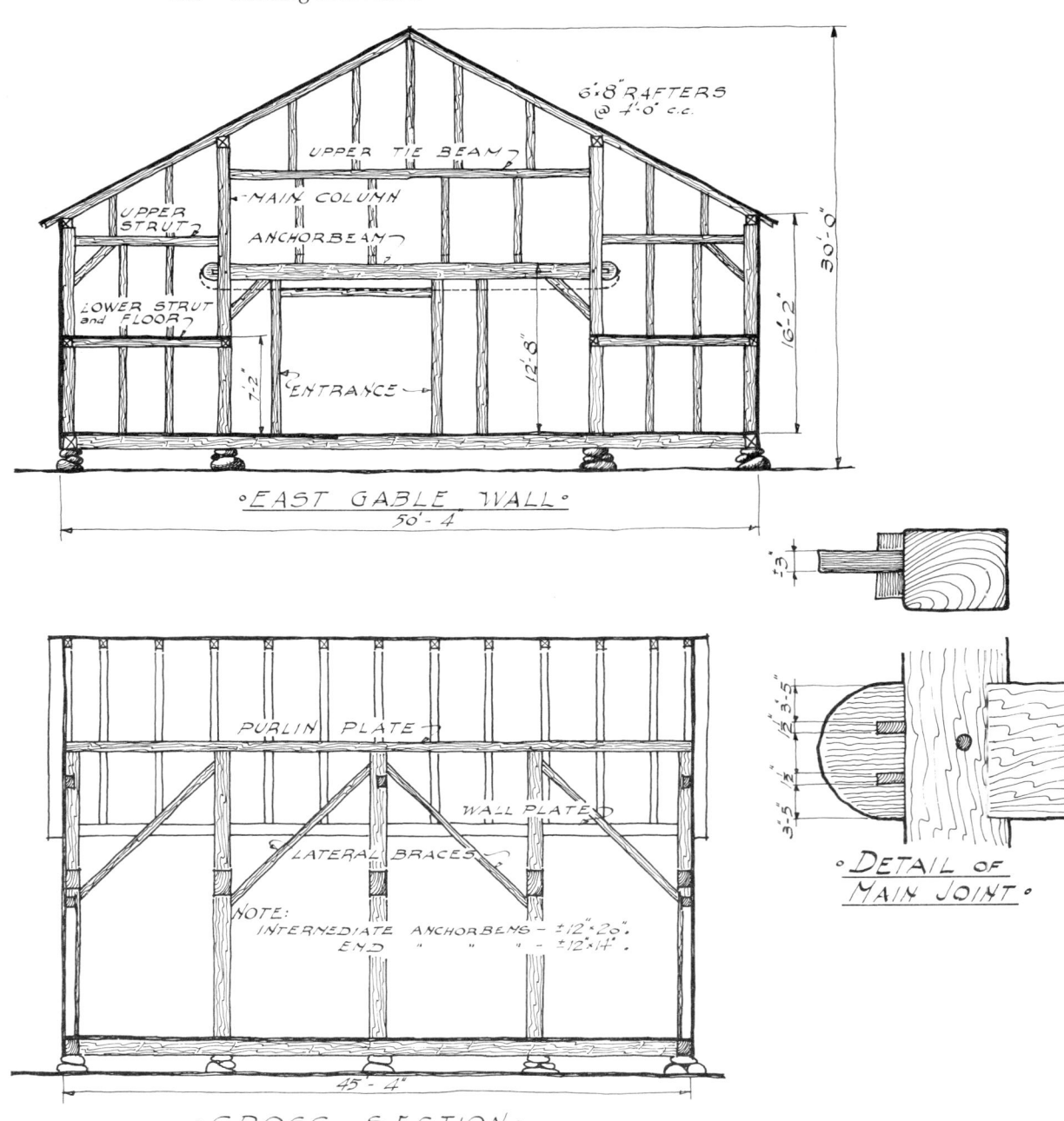

The rarest of all barn types in Ontario is the Dutch or 'Schoharie' barn. These details, showing the massive mortise and 'tusk' tenon, come from one of the two preserved in Upper Canada Village.

Perhaps the most unusual type of frame barn in Ontario is the Dutch or 'Schoharie' barn, which derives its name from a regionally characteristic type of framing practised by Dutch settlers in New York state. Barns of this design followed the Hudson River upstream, spreading westward along Catskill Creek to the Schoharie River. Although this barn is rare in Ontario, two have been preserved in Upper Canada Village. Unfortunately the records of their original location have been lost, and one was badly mutilated during its lifetime.

The two main distinguishing features of the Dutch barn are the framing and the general shape. In plan the barn is almost square. The gable wall is often as long as – and sometimes, as in the drawing, even longer than – the side walls. There is always a wide centre aisle with two side aisles of lesser width (a 'nave and aisles' frame without the great height of the usual Ontario version of that set-up); this makes for a low eave, which in turn permits only one location for the main entrance – in the middle of the gable wall.

The most impressive feature of this barn is the massiveness of the main column and the main central tie beam in each bent, known as the 'anchorbeam.' A remarkable framing detail is the enormous mortise and 'tusk' tenon joint that joins the anchorbeams to the columns. A 'tusk' tenon is one that penetrates right through the mortised member, and is then made particularly tight, with no danger of withdrawal, by the insertion of one or two wedges into the tusk against the mortised member.

ABOVE AND OPPOSITE  The ventilation of barns is of the greatest importance. Smaller barns will have a single vent while larger ones may have as many as three or four; in some cases a continuous vent runs the full length of the structure.

BELOW  Note the double width of the threshing floor in this barn near Stratford, not a typical feature of barns in Ontario.

Another barn from the Stratford area. The unusual feature of this frame is that the central posts extend the full height up to the ridge. Note also the separate post supports under the sill, a rather precarious form of construction by modern standards.

Barns 211

ABOVE AND OPPOSITE Barns must, of necessity, enclose vast open spaces. Since large wall areas are exposed to wind stresses, wind-bracing in every direction is of the utmost importance.

At the turn of the century various methods of barn framing were attempted. This system used light members in combination to form trusses, which could be prefabricated and shipped directly to the site; being light in weight, they were much more easily handled than the heavy timbers of the early conventional frame.

The Fisher barn near Kitchener is a so-called 'slit' barn because of the ventilating slots in the walls instead of windows or louvres.

Stone barns and stable buildings in Ontario are generally associated with Scottish stonemasons. A characteristic feature is the three-centred, or elliptical, archway. This coach house and stable serve the Clarke home in Prescott.

## THE STONE BARN

Stone barns are generally associated with Scottish masons, although the connection is not an absolute one because the Pennsylvania-German settlers also believed in honest, solid, unadorned masonry. The Scottish mason delighted in working with hard stone; he loved shaping stones, cutting and carving mouldings, caps, and finials. In general, he tried to bring a bit of Scotland to Ontario. The Pennsylvania settler, on the other hand, looked with disfavour on frilly decorations. His buildings were four-square, solid, without pretensions. He used fieldstones in the shape the Lord had given them, except at corners or around openings where shaping was a structural necessity. His openings were generally square because a rounded or elliptical head was considered a sign of affectation.

The best Scottish stonework in Ontario can be seen along the shores of the St Lawrence River and in York County, as well as in isolated pockets around Whitby, Guelph, Galt, and Goderich. German work is concentrated in Waterloo and York counties, where some settlements are of German and Swiss origin. Solid stone barns do not differ in plan from framed ones. A typical example is the Fisher barn, built about 1855 between Doon and Blair near Kitchener. This is a 'slit' barn, since it has no louvred vents at the ridge but secures ventilation through slits in the walls. Local legend has it that the slits were used as a defence measure in wars against Indians!

Stonework was used more frequently in structures that served as coach houses or stables and were attached to more important buildings, as at the Clarke home in Prescott. In all countries such additions have shared in the 'polite' architecture of the house itself, expressing the social standing of the owner of the establishment. These grand structures contrast markedly with the straightforward farm buildings we have considered previously, which have been impressive more for their size and structure than for any exterior finish or design (the Walker barn is merely an exception that proves the rule).

The coach house and hayloft attached to the Rockwood Academy (about 1853) is another example of such construction. The structure is built of random rubble laid in a series of 'rises,' at each of which the wall has been brought to a level before beginning the next rise of masonry. The very depressed elliptical arches of the carriage doors are laid with voussoirs, but the windows in general have plain stone lintels – although the square opening in the bottom storey has a sort of 'Cyclopean' flat arch. The corners of the building are made with roughly dressed slabs laid on edge as quoins. The general air of the structure is not so fashionable as that of the Clarke stables.

The only true Scottish barn in Ontario is in a complex of buildings near Brockville known as 'Burnside.' William Freeman arrived from Scotland in 1828, bought 300 acres of land, and erected a stone house on the property the next year; later he added a kitchen wing and a chandlery (he was a candlemaker as well as a farmer), a coach house, and a barn. Still later the property was purchased by William Hargrave who erected a larger barn complex across the road. It has been suggested that since Hargrave had worked for the Hudson's Bay Company his design was influenced by the layout of a trading post. The character of the arrangement as well as the crenellation and the three-centred archway over the gate, however, resemble more the Scottish architecture of the Guelph courthouse, 'Mackintosh Castle' in Kingston, or 'Castle Grange' near Belfountain. Although the present form of the great barn is more typical of Ontario than of Scotland, the concept of the enclosed and gated farmyard is particularly reminiscent of Scotland and northern England (though fairly common throughout the British Isles) – dating from times when, even if raiding bands no longer crossed the border, nevertheless there were plenty of cattle thieves and other rogues to be

The coach house and hayloft attached to the Rockwood Academy

discouraged. The desire to recreate a bit of home seems to be more evident than any attempt to bring a trading post out of the cold north into southern Ontario (though the resemblance to the layout of forts such as Fort Chipewyan cannot be denied). Likely the complex is an amalgam of both influences, as well as a bit of Romantic Revival.

The early buildings at 'Burnside,' dating from the time of William Freeman, who erected the stone house (at the left) in 1829, and later added a kitchen wing, a chandlery, a coach house, and a barn.

The later buildings at 'Burnside,' built by William Hargrave across the road from the earlier structures.

This twelve-sided barn near Thessalon is quite late, but it is one of the very few gambrel-roofed barns in the province. B12

## THE ROUND OR POLYGONAL BARN

These extraordinary barns are rare in central Canada, there being at present only ten known in Quebec and twenty-two in Ontario. They are definitely an American import of the late nineteenth century. There is a good example of a round barn near Hawkesbury, and on Dufferin Street in Toronto there is a gambrel-roofed octagonal barn. The finest example of a polygonal barn in Ontario is the one near Erin, which has three levels of octagonal shapes – the base, the skylight, and the dovecot – all superimposed on one another in a diminishing order, leading the eye inevitably up to the lightning rod with a large glass ball at the top. The shapes relate to each other in an almost perfect arithmetical ratio of one to three; it is likely the builder recognized the proper proportions intuitively, however, rather than by adopting the rules of dynamic symmetry.

Another striking and delightful barn is the twelve-sided or duodecagonal one near Thessalon. Its roof has a remarkably high and steeply pitched gambrel outline, with a bell cast at the base. The upper floor is approached from a higher ground level, the entrance having a large sliding door. Since the individual sides of the plan were short, the entranceway proved to be a difficult problem: when it was opened, it overlapped its face of the building. Thus a projecting screen had to be built to allow it to slide fully open. Lean-to extensions have been erected against the barn, and demonstrate one of the aesthetic and planning disadvantages of such centrally organized, introverted buildings; they are so complete in themselves that they will not accept extensions without visual and structural awkwardness.

Several of these barns are illustrated in the chapter on 'Polygonal buildings.'

## THE BARN-RAISING BEE

The building of a full-sized barn was a task beyond the resources of a typical farmer and his family in the past. Thus erecting a barn was the occasion for a 'bee,' when the able-bodied men of the neighbouring countryside would gather to help the family that needed the barn. A master carpenter took charge, and he was probably the only man who got paid.

No discussion on barn construction is complete without a description of a raising bee. The communal efforts of the Mennonites in Waterloo County, as seen in the accompanying illustrations, is the last vestige of a long tradition. Here is a bit of living history, for the Mennonites have incorporated very few technological changes and have made few concessions to modern methods. It is a thrilling sight to watch a hundred men, young and old, each carrying out a specific task in a quiet, competent manner without any confusion, fuss, or bother. The most dramatic moment occurs when the big bents are put into place with amazing speed.

218

1

2

3

The photographs, more useful than words in describing the process, show the step-by-step erection of this barn near St Jacobs in 1968. All timbers were prepared, sorted, and stacked in a nearby field ahead of time. Most timbers were salvage material from other structures and the missing pieces were cut directly from the bush. Modern technology was generally disregarded, except for the motorized drilling rig (4), which drills holes for the mortise to any predetermined depth and width; originally it was hand-operated but here a motor was substituted. The handmade pegs have also been replaced by machine-turned ones (5). Note the hand auger which has to drill a very precise hole with a tight fit or else the round peg would lose much of its holding power.

The mortises were squared next. In addition to the mallet, two types of chisel were used – the regular straight-edged one and the corner chisel which was used to square the corners of the mortise.

220  Building with Wood

Once the basement walls were in place, the real task began. Manpower was very much in evidence for the simple reason that in such cramped quarters men are much more flexible than machinery. Once a bent was raised, a second one was tied to it by cross-ties and corner braces. Note the absence of ladders. After the framework was completed, the rafters were positioned. As another concession to modern building materials, this barn will be covered with galvanized sheet iron, which requires intermediate supports and a nailing surface in the form of slats across the rafters. The whole process of assembly progressed with incredible speed: the operation shown in (7) was completed on a Thursday afternoon, and by the following Saturday morning the stages shown in (10) and (11) had been reached. When I expressed amazement at such great speed, the only comment made by the foreman, with a sly grin, was 'ya godda geddup early.'

6

7

8

Barns 223

The above barn, replacing one struck by lightning and burned to the ground, is that of Mr Abram Weber near Heidelberg. It was built in July 1966 by a typical old raising bee: all the neighbours, about two hundred of them, lent a hand. The raising 'boss' was David Sherk from near Heidelberg. The raising itself was done in a day, during which the women served about 450 meals, baked 100 pies, and cooked 1000 doughnuts. The whole structure was closed in and roofed within two and a half weeks.

## The Quebec barn

As in Ontario, the early Quebec barn was usually of frame or log construction and was generally small; later ones were larger, especially those that had grown by additions which were built as they were required. R.-L. Séguin, in his book *Les granges du Québec*, tabulated the number and size of barns and stables in two seigneuries, Vaudreuil and Rigaud, which he considered to be typical. These figures, based on the 1781 census, reveal that the average size of the early Quebec barn was about 22 by 30 feet; there were, however, two giants measuring 80 feet long by 20 and 24 feet in width.[3]

The number of barns on a single farm, and their relative disposition, deserve attention. The poorer settler usually owned only a single building, a 'maison-bloc,' which comprised the family living quarters, the hayloft, and the stable, all under one roof. This sort of shelter tended to be long, for the reason that it was easier to set the three units under one roof if they were placed in line. But the farmer of New France usually found himself in better

A typical combination of 'grange-étable'; the two mows and central threshing floor are located to the left and the stable, with a hayloft above, is in the right portion.

circumstances than the neighbours he had left back home. Hence he could often afford several barns, each built for a special purpose. These would be grouped around a central yard or court, and the whole establishment would be known as a 'maison-cour.'

According to function, there were three principal types of barns: the grain or feed barn (la grange), a shelter for livestock (l'écurie), and a stable for horses (l'étable). But during the nineteenth century it became standard practice to combine the first two functions under one roof, with the livestock below and the hayloft above. As in Ontario, this two-storey barn may have been an import from New England.

In upper Normandy, cob or mud walls (murs de torchis) were common in barns. In Quebec, however, settlers soon discovered that walls had to be built of a substance that would provide greater protection from the elements. For this reason mud was combined with a sheath of lath and 'mortier blanchi,' a form of whitewash or stucco. But this type of barn is rare, as are barns of stone, which were considered unhealthy for cattle because in severe

Barn at Cap à l'Aigle, about 1900. Note the thatched roof, the hold-down timbers, the 'encorbellement,' and the combination of log and grooved post construction.

winter weather condensation within the stable caused hoar-frost to form on the walls. The advantages of timber were soon realized by all settlers, French and English. This material was, after all, the most abundant, easy to work, and endowed with good insulating qualities.

The kinds of timber used in barn construction can usually be deduced with great exactness. Most settlements were sponsored by agencies of one sort or another so that legal documents concerning the construction of barns are readily available. From these papers it is clear that the kind of wood employed was never a matter of indifference.

   Sills (soles): almost always hemlock (pruche)
   Posts and stakes (pieux plantes en terre): cedar or thuya (arbor vitae)
   Grooved posts (pieux à coulisse): cedar or thuya
   Logs (pièces): cedar to thuya when used in walls or as 'pièce-sur-pièce'
   Floor in threshing area (aire ou batterie): generally oak; occasionally cedar or arbor vitae
   Planks (madriers): hemlock, lime, or linden when in walls
   Rafters (chevrons): frequently oak if available
   Framework (charpente): pine, lime, or hemock, occasionally oak, walnut, or ash

In early Quebec, threshing was done by flail, the universal practice in Europe at that time. Since this work was generally carried on indoors, a covered threshing floor had to be provided and the natural thing to do was to situate this floor between the two mows and cover the three areas with one roof, as in the examples we have already discussed in Ontario. On large farms more storage for grain and fodder was needed and so a triple-mow barn with two threshing floors was built.

Slight differences are to be found in the design and construction of barns in the three important centres of early colonization, namely, Quebec City, Trois-Rivières, and Montreal. One factor that may explain some of the variation was that it was safer to live in the neighbourhood of Quebec City than in either of the other towns in the early years. One variation found along the shore of the St Lawrence is the shingled barn. It was believed that shingles required less painting than siding, or none at all. The shingled surface was also thought to resist salt air and to be safer in high wind. Along the Ontario border, there are barns with log-butt walls, that is, walls built of short logs mortared together with their cut ends facing out.

A method of construction similar to the well-known 'à coulisse' for houses is that known as 'à calle,' the only difference being that the timbers were sawn along the centre, so that each of the two resulting pieces had one flat side and one in the half-round; the half-round side was then trimmed at each end so that a rough tenon, with no shoulders, was made to fit into the post grooves. Still another method, known as 'à aiguilles,' called for posts to be placed at intervals along the middle of the structure to support the ridge pole; at the same time they offered purchase for the springing of lateral angle braces. The phrase 'avec arcades' means a barn constructed so that the portion of the stable wall containing the entrance doors is slightly recessed from the rest of the side wall. The upper portion of this wall, however, is carried over the recessed section and will contain wide archways without doors. Another type of Quebec barn has a feature – an 'encorbellement' – similar to the forbay of the Pennsylvania-German barn. It is an overhang of less depth, however, than the Pennsylvania one. When the barn is relatively small, this overhang occurs along the entire side, whereas in a larger structure it is restricted to the stable portion only, replacing the 'arcades.' In such a barn one could keep the livestock above and the fodder below. The two-storey barn was quickly accepted because the animals enjoyed greater warmth, could be fed much more easily, and the total cost was lower because of the much reduced roof area.

Barn on the Laberge farm at L'Ange-Gardien. Stone barns in Quebec are not as large as those in Ontario, perhaps because stone barns were once considered unhealthy for livestock.

228 Building with Wood

Finally, there are the round and polygonal barns. These specimens date from the late nineteenth century, generally not earlier than 1880, and all of them are found on the east shore of the St Lawrence, not more than sixty miles from the American border. They were built at about the same time as their counterparts in Ontario and, in both provinces, they are definitely the result of American influence.

The octagonal barn is the most un-French of all. St-Michel, County Bellechasse

# 6
# CHURCH, MILL, AND BRIDGE

In the design of every structure, two types of loads always have to be considered: a 'dead' or static load (the weight of the structure itself) and a 'live' load (a load that varies from time to time). The difference between the framing of a residential building and any other type is chiefly a matter of load-carrying capacity; live loads in a residential frame are almost negligible, whereas those in a mill, a warehouse, or a bridge may be considerable. Since load considerations vary with different kinds of buildings, three types of structures are discussed in detail in this chapter: a church in Markham, a mill near Thornhill, both of which have now been demolished, and a covered bridge at West Montrose.

In a church frame, the live load consists solely of the weight of the congregation, varying from full capacity to minimal attendance. Such loads however, rest on floor beams, which in turn are carried by the foundation walls, and thus do not enter into the design of the frame at all. What has to be considered seriously, however, is the wind load or wind pressure on the building; churches are generally relatively high structures and thus have a

The mill at Woodbridge, built about 1840

large wall area exposed to the wind. What complicates the design is the fact that most church plans will generally not tolerate any interior visual interference such as intermediate posts and bracing; therefore all necessary bracing has to be hidden in the walls and by the roof trusses. The reason for choosing Grace Church as an example here is that the builder has ingeniously incorporated the roof truss into the frame, thus having it form an integral part of the entire structure – a clever design solution that should be studied carefully in order to realize the various fine points of construction.

The frame of a mill is classed as heavy timber framing because of the great strength required to carry the burden of live and dead loads and also because of the resistance it has to offer to a new type of stress, namely, the dynamic stress produced by the constant vibration of operating machinery. Mills also are seldom less than two storeys in height, later ones being up to three and more levels; the great height is necessary because the milling process requires the grain to flow from top to bottom. Since maximum loads are great, single diagonal bracing would not be adequate to provide the necessary

Vivian mill, Oakland, 1842

rigidity to the structure; therefore, double bracing in both directions is standard. Constant vibration may lead to a deterioration of a joint at the greatest stress points, which, at the same time, will reduce the purchase on the shoulder support. To prevent too great a withdrawal, an iron strap is frequently bolted to both pieces on both sides of the joint. An additional supporting piece may also be spiked to the under side of the beam. This condition is a common failure in a heavy timber frame.

All early short-span bridges were simply a pair of timber trusses with a floor in between. A truss is a combination of structural members assembled in a fixed manner so as to act as a unit to span a greater space than would be possible for an individual member. The truss has been known from early medieval times and came into its own during the middle ages when timber framing reached its most sophisticated stage; it was generally used in roof construction but also became the universal method of constructing bridges. In Ontario all the early rural bridges were of this type, except for the most primitive ones. Most bridges consist of a pair of trusses with a roadway in

Church, mill, and bridge 233

between, generally left unprotected from the weather; it was soon realized, particularly in New England, that a protected bridge would last longer, and thus we have 'covered' bridges. The only one in Ontario is at West Montrose; fortunately it is typical, and I was also lucky enough to discover the original drawings as well as the drafting instruments of John Bear, the builder of the bridge.

BELOW AND OPPOSITE Bolton mill. The original part was built in 1822; the mill was moved and rebuilt in 1847. Demolished about 1967

234  Building with Wood

Grace Church, Markham, before demolition began

The church with the siding removed and the frame exposed

The tower was in all probability added later, otherwise it would have been framed directly into the main frame. The tower frame was held to the main frame only by two 1 inch bolts, one at either principal as shown. This is not in keeping with the fine workmanship of the original frame.

## Grace Church, Markham

This church was probably built in 1849 at a cost of about $2000 and with a seating capacity of 225. Its first rector was the Rev. G.S.J. Hill, who occupied the pulpit until 1876. It was sometimes called the Meyerhoffer church, but according to the records the Rev. Phillip V. Meyerhoffer held only one service in the building, and that after his retirement at the start of 1850. A memorial window was added in 1877 and a new lectern and pulpit were installed at the turn of the century. The church was moved in 1927, owing to a widening of the road, to the location it occupied until its destruction in 1963.

The original building was rectangular, measuring about 24'3" by 56'5". Beyond all reasonable doubt, the tower was a later addition; its framing formed a completely separate unit from that of the main body of the church and indeed was joined to it by only two bolts in the front ceiling beams. Had it been built at the same time, it would have been connected to the main frame quite differently. The **L** at the rear of the church was also added at a later date.

The floor beams were pegged into the sill with two pins, thus providing a very secure and rigid base for all the principal posts. The end walls have the usual transverse bracing but, the walls being so large, two intermediate principals with the usual corner bracing were inserted as well. The side walls were framed as one whole unit consisting of four main panels completely cross-braced both at the top and at the bottom. The plate was raised the usual 16 inches above the ceiling beams. All construction members were, of course, quite heavy because of the size of the building.

TOWER
±11'-0"
17'-0"
11'-8"
3'-4 1/2"

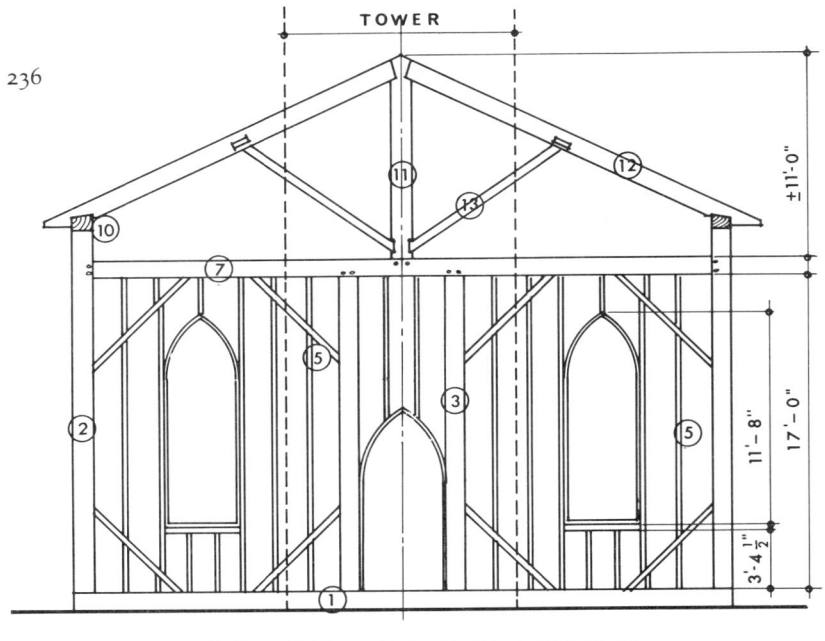

· SOUTH ELEVATION ·

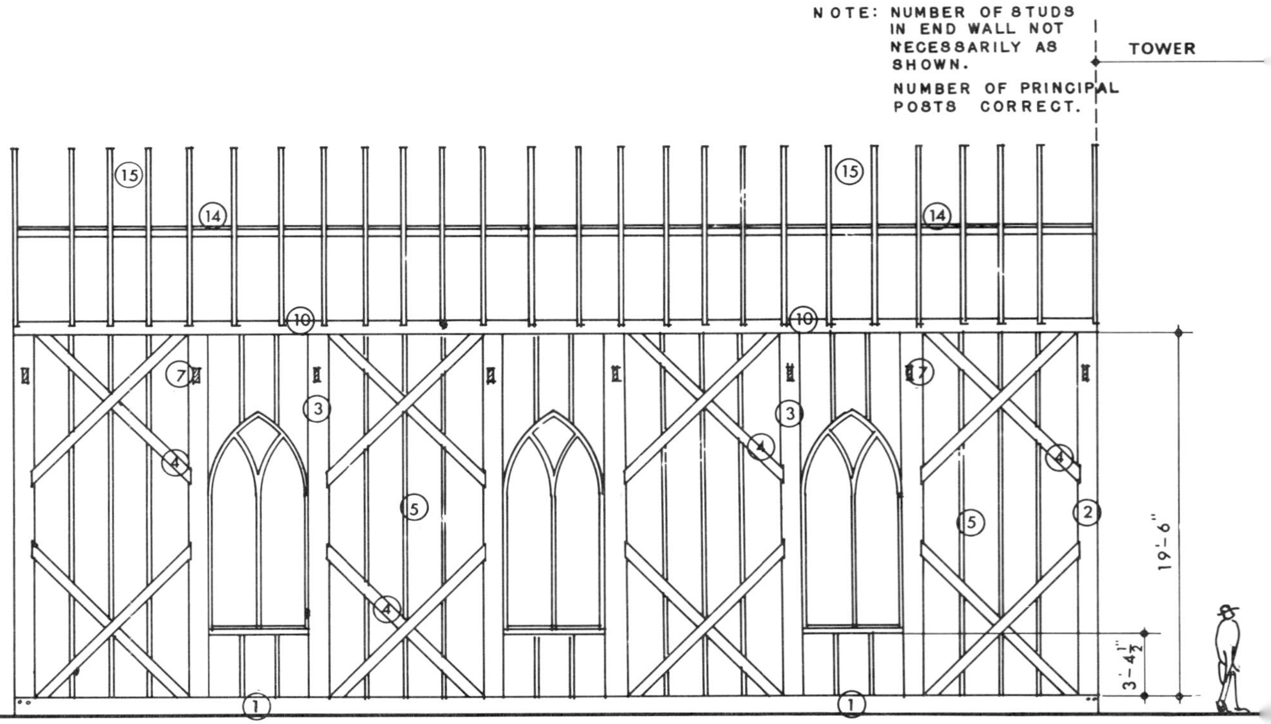

NOTE: NUMBER OF STUDS IN END WALL NOT NECESSARILY AS SHOWN.
NUMBER OF PRINCIPAL POSTS CORRECT.
TOWER
19'-6"
3'-4 1/2"

· EAST and WEST ·
· ELEVATION ·

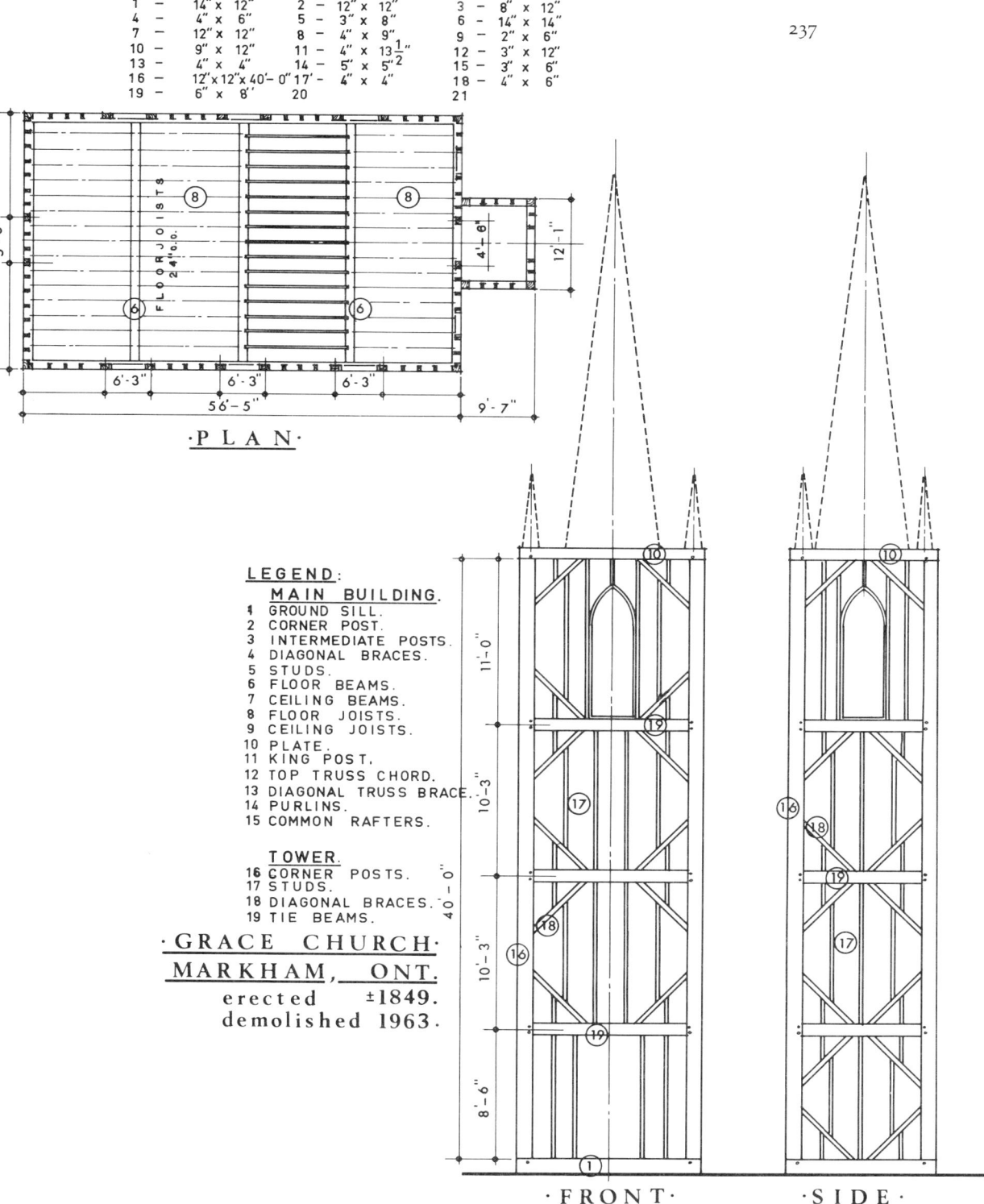

A typical braced panel. Note the cross bracing both at the top and at the bottom, and also the offset mortise in the principal.

As usual, the ceiling beams frame into the principals below the plate. In this case, however, the beams also serve as the bottom chord for the roof truss.

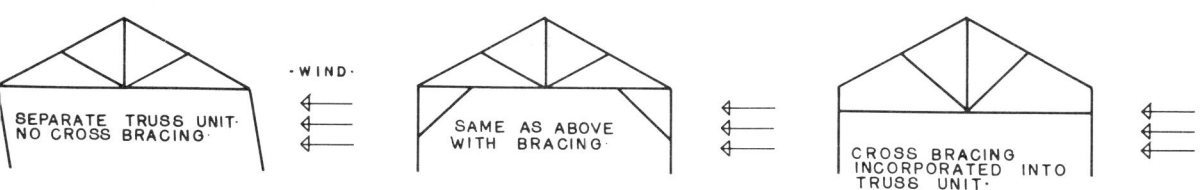

ROOF TRUSS CONSTRUCTION
ANALYSIS · NO SCALE ·
GRACE CHURCH · MARKHAM · 1849 –1963

The studs, for instance, were 3 by 8 inches. This meant that the principals could not be wider than 8 inches if they were not to show on the inside face of the wall. Intermediate principals were therefore 12 inches wide by 8 inches deep, but the corner ones were 12 by 12 inches with the inside corners cut back 4 inches on both sides. This made for a flush wall surface along the entire length of a wall and at the same time provided a solid nailing surface for the lath. Oddly enough, handsplit lath was used on the main walls of the original building.

The ceiling beams, 12 inches square, were of particular interest. For one thing, they formed the bottom chord of the roof truss and were mortised and tenoned into the principal posts. This was quite unexpected since it is contrary to the practice recommended for such buildings in the current books on building. The accepted method was to have the roof truss a separate unit from the main wall structure; the truss rested on the wall plates, and the builder therefore had to ensure that the walls were thoroughly braced and rigid by themselves. But by lowering the roof truss and integrating it into the structure, he added to the rigidity of the building since the beams, while acting as a chord, also provided lateral support for the side walls and wind bracing for the whole church.

Another interesting and unorthodox feature of the ceiling beams was the way in which they were joined to the principal posts. Since the beams, serving as the bottom chord of the truss, were in tension, the builder was not satisfied with the usual two pins to hold the members together but locked both pieces by a tapered tenon which was wedged against a correspondingly tapered mortise. This gave a very positive connection indeed. The tenon, interestingly enough, was not centred as was the custom, but was offset 3 inches to one side. (This same offsetting occurs in tenons in the Fish mill discussed below; the reason for it is obscure.)

A third deviation from the textbook was the joint between the king post and the bottom chord of the roof truss. The books (from as early as 1733 until as late as 1870[1]) generally show this joint as having a strap iron **U** clamp fitted

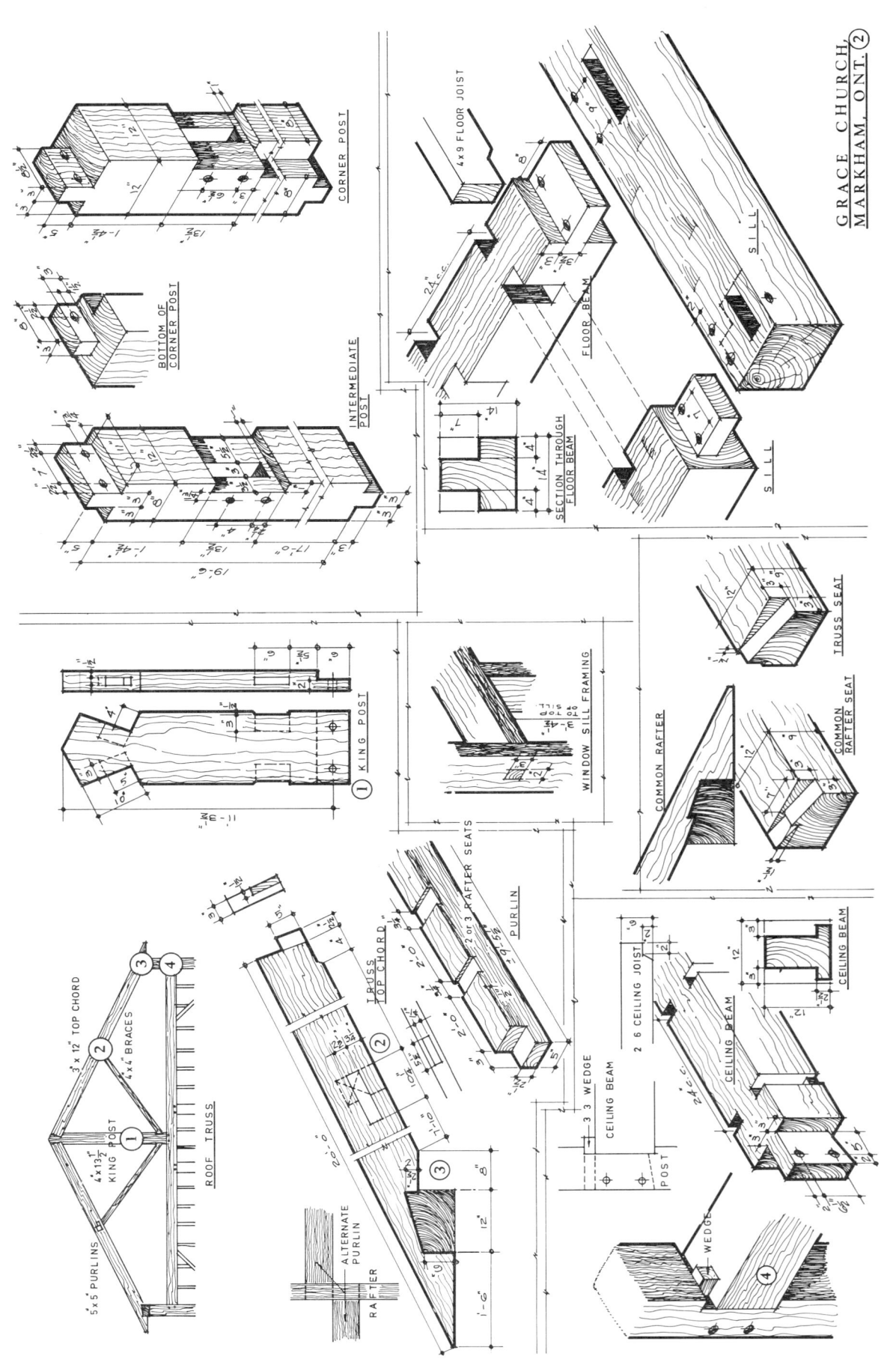

around the chord with the ends bolted to the bottom of the king post. This iron strap was omitted here and replaced by a two-pin mortise and tenon joint.

How common these improved methods were I cannot say. They may have been well enough known practices, though nowhere recorded in words, or they may have been unique. It would be hazardous to attempt any generalizations on the framing of churches since this example at Markham is the only one I have had an opportunity of studying in detail. Perhaps all that can be safely said is that this method of trussing is yet another example of the practical ingenuity of the nineteenth-century builder on this continent.

The bottom of the king post was secured by two pins which are clearly visible.

This shows the top of the king post. Since these joints were in compression only, no pins were used.

## Benjamin Fish Mill, Markham

Lot 1 on the second concession in Markham Township was granted in 1799 to J.B. 'McCulla.' The land changed hands several times before being acquired by Benjamin Fish who erected a distillery on it in 1820 and a grist mill some years thereafter. (Mrs J.C. Bales, daughter of a later owner, dated its construction as 1832.) It is supposed to have cost around $8000, which Fish borrowed from a 'building society' in Toronto. The history of the mill and of its owners and operators has been told in two accounts,[2] which do not, however, entirely agree, one of these sources relating that the mill was burned down and rebuilt in 1866. It appears, then, that its history remains somewhat uncertain for the forty or so years before 1883. In that year it was acquired by J.G. Schmidt who made extensive (but unrecorded) alterations, as did also Angus Macdonald in 1939–40 when he converted the mill into a

The mill before the three eastern bays were removed. Some alterations had already been made, such as the 'picture' window at the west end, the central chimney, as well as several windows at the east end.

Church, mill, and bridge    243

studio and residence and took down three bays to the east. Macdonald's wife, Billy Button, has written an account of their trials and tribulation in converting this draughty old barn into decent living and working space.[3]

The structural evidence at the time of its demolition in 1966 revealed that alterations had very probably been made in the mill in the nineteenth century but it was not possible to say for certain what had been done then. The removal of the three eastern bays in 1939–40 mutilated the framing at that end to some extent, but the framing of the bay now exposed at the eastern end was identical to that of the end bay at the west; this suggests that these three bays might have been a later addition, but there is, of course, no way now of dating it. A witness of the Macdonalds' conversion remembers clearly that the boards on the sides of the grain bins next to the outside walls had bevelled edges. Since the flush siding with bevelled edges was used extensively on the exterior of early New England houses, it is just possible

The three eastern bays being removed

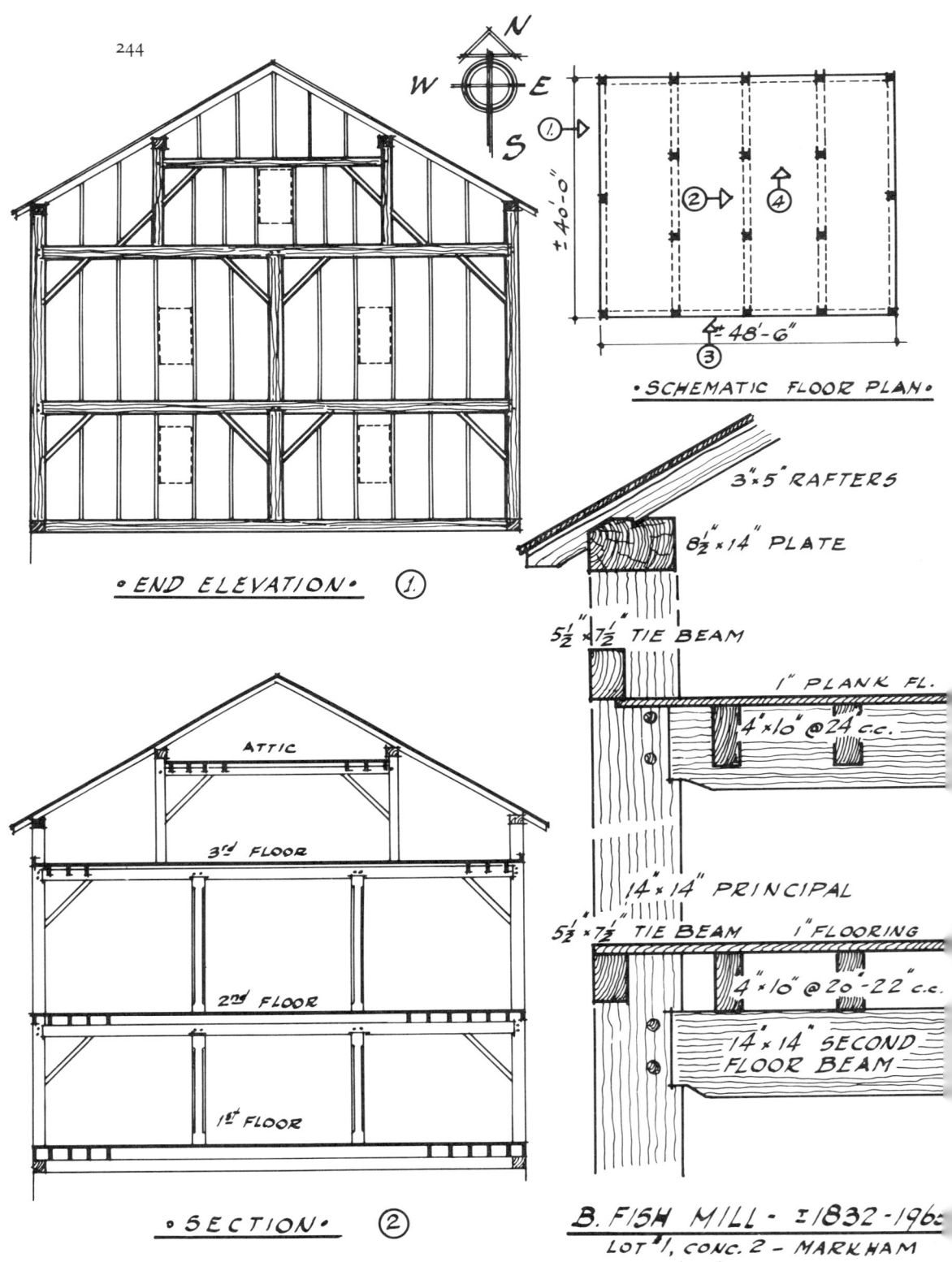

that at some stage these boards were removed from the external sheathing of this mill and used to line the bins. The bevel in such siding, incidentally, ran down and out, the lower bevel of the upper board covering the upper bevel of the lower board so as to form a self-draining and watertight exterior.[4]

In 1832 there were no fewer than 557 sawmills and 504 grist mills in Upper Canada.[5] William Thomson wrote shortly afterwards that the 'flour mills in Canada ... surpass anything of the kind I have ever seen in Scotland – some of them are very large ... Farmers can always get cash for wheat at these establishments.'[6] It seems very probable, given their number, that the construction of mills had come to follow a fairly predictable method by 1832 – or even 1866 – and that we would be justified in considering this mill as a typical piece of mill construction in Upper Canada.

The size of this mill, with only four of its previous seven bays standing when I examined it in 1966, was approximately 48'6" by 40'0". The spacing of the bays from west to east was 11'0", 11'8", 10'4", and 13'5", all measurements taken on centre. Their variation is quite baffling because the builder, whoever he was, certainly knew how to build and would therefore, one would have thought, have been aware of the simplifying advantage of regular measurements. It could be that the size and placing of machinery had something to do with this irregularity although this is not very likely. One can only conclude that here was another builder who had not yet assumed those attitudes that foster repetitive and identical mass production.

Principal posts, beams, and sills were nearly all about 14 inches square with a variation of as much as 2 inches; these members were hewn. Intermediate posts were 12 inches square, again with a fair degree of variation, but they had chamfered edges and were planed smooth. All the other structural members, such as joists, braces, and tie-beams, were sawn.

All diagonal bracing in the exterior walls was flush with the outside face and required an offset tenon. The lateral bracing in the lower external corners consisted of 4 by 8 inch timbers secured by one pin. All other bracing, including interior transverse braces, were 4 by 5 inches and not secured. The lateral tie-beams were also flush with the outside face and held with an offset tenon secured with one pin at each end. The principal cross-beams had a shouldered mortise and tenon with two pins. For some reason, the intermediate posts were not only mortised into the beams but were also housed at the upper end and secured with two pins, although there was neither housing nor pins at their bottom. Strangely enough, the intermediate transverse diagonal bracing under the first-floor beams consisted of two 4 by 5 inch members spaced several inches apart. It is difficult to see the reason for this – one heavier brace would have served just as well. However, such double transverse bracing must have been fairly common practice, for it was also used in the Bolton mill. This mill, originally built in 1822, was dismantled in 1846, then moved and re-erected about 330 yards to the east. It has now been demolished.

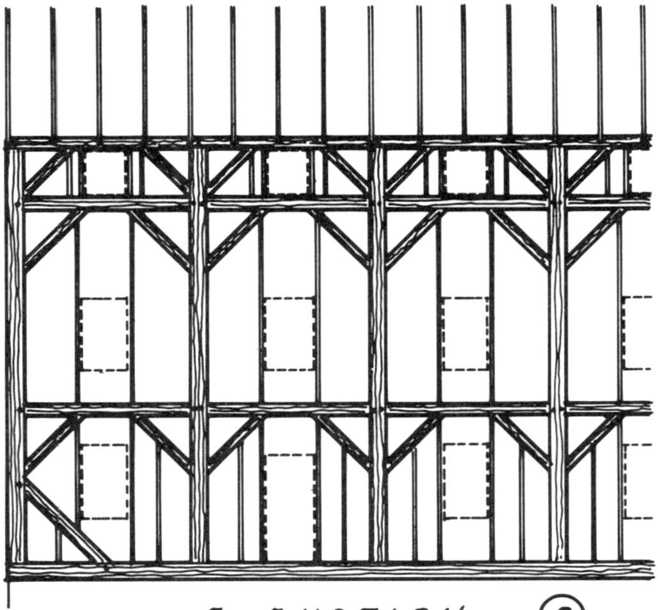

· ELEVATION · ③

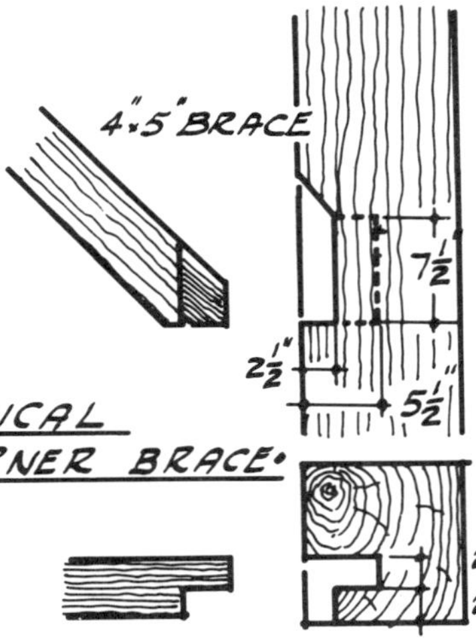

· TYPICAL CORNER BRACE ·

4"×5" BRACE

7½"

2½"  5½"

2½"
2½"

· EXTERIOR FACE ·

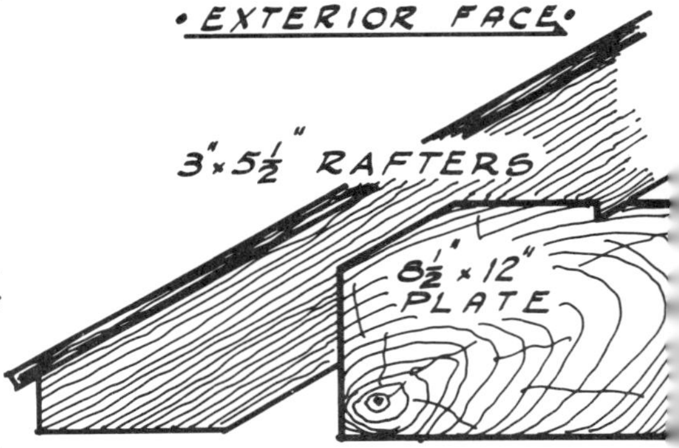

3"×5½" RAFTERS

8½"×12" PLATE

· RAFTER CUT ·

9"×10" INTERMEDIATE PLATE

6"×8" TIE BEAM

3'-3"

4"×5" BRACE

9'-4"

6"×8" POST

3rd FLOOR

4"×10" JOISTS @ 24" c.c.

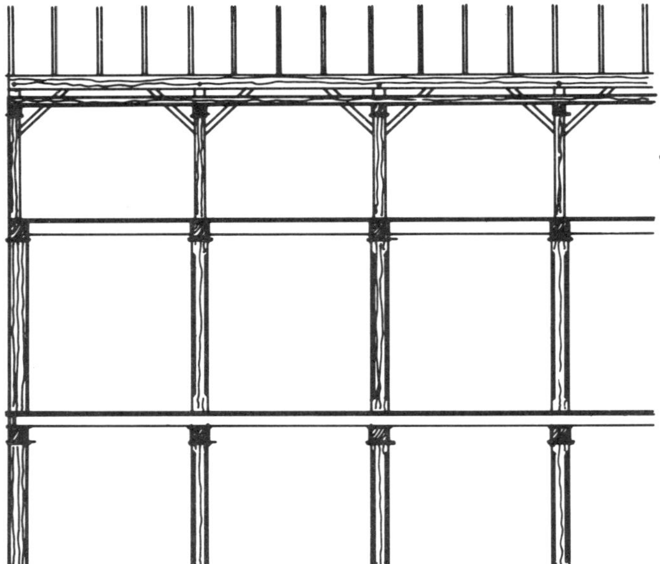

· SECTION · ④

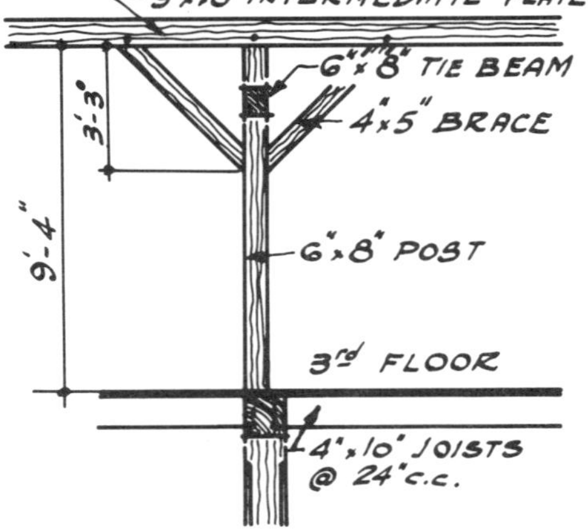

· ORIGINAL MUNTIN BAR ·

1 3/16"
1/2"

· B. FISH MILL, 1832-1965 ·
LOT #1, CONC. 2, MARKHAM.
BAYVIEW & STEELE'S AVE.

Typical framing of the attic floor as well as the secondary plate which gave intermediate support for the rather long rafters.

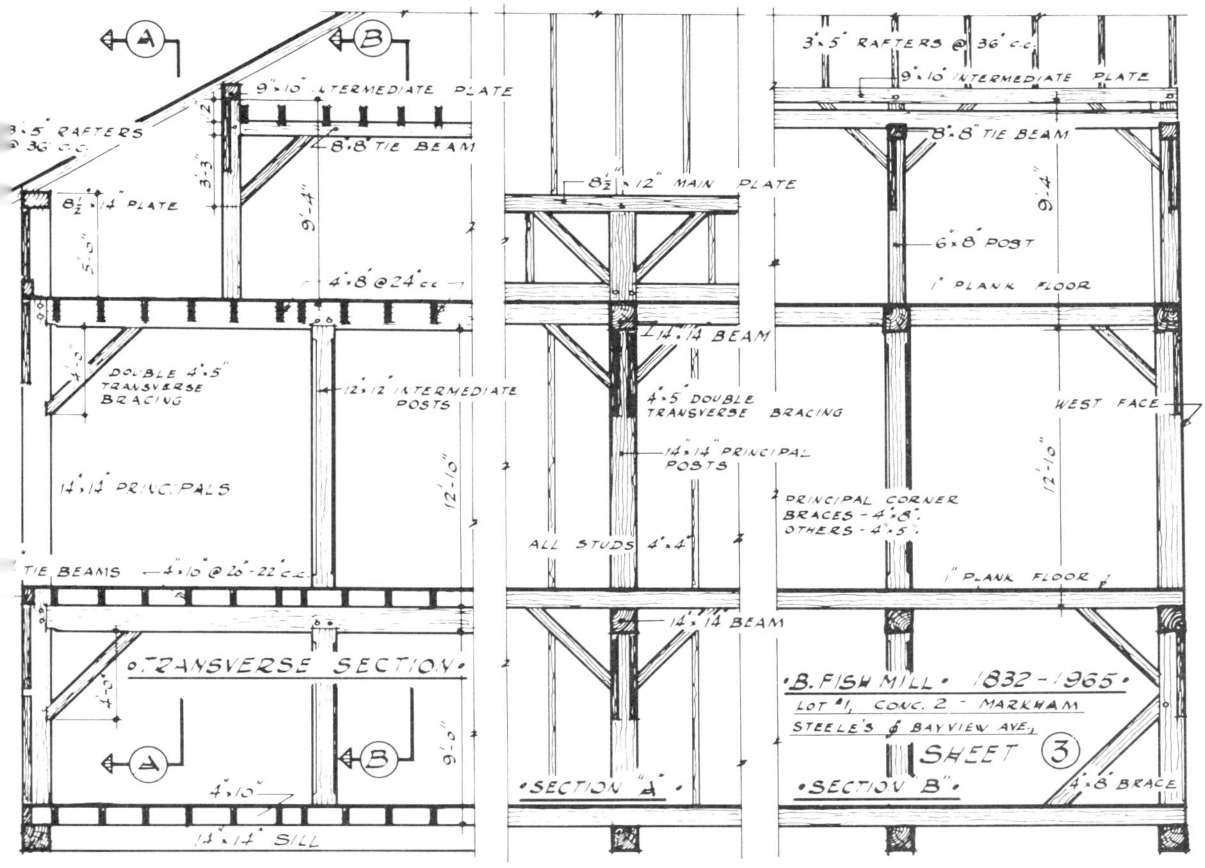

Typical wall framing

Typical framing of the attic floor as well as transverse bracing at an external corner of the mill; all corner braces, tie-beams, and studs are flush with the outside face of the principals.

Church, mill, and bridge  249

All intermediate transverse bracing consisted of double braces at the upper corners of the first-floor beams.

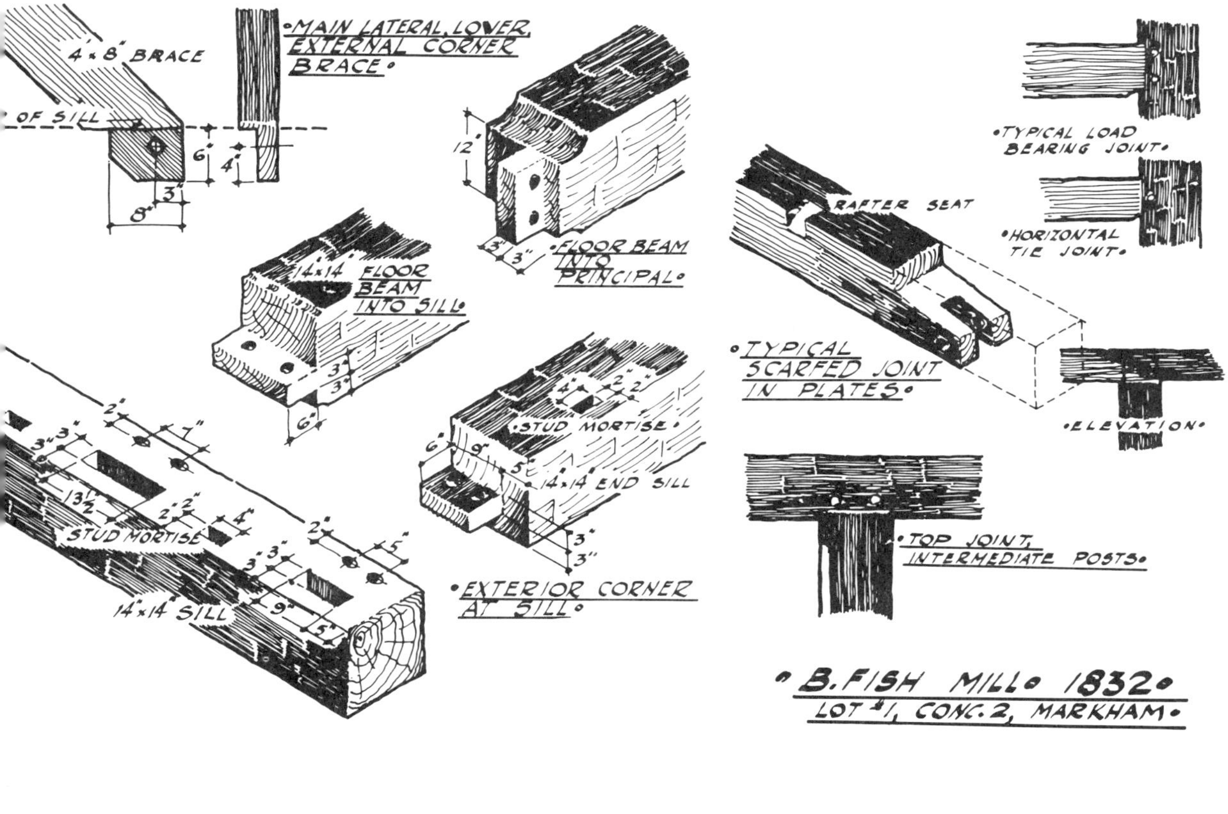

· B. FISH MILL · 1832 ·
LOT #1, CONC. 2, MARKHAM ·

The intermediate posts were pinned at the top, but not at the bottom, joint.

The floor joists of the two main floors were 4 by 10 inch sawn timber; being sawn, they did not vary in size to any appreciable extent. The joists of the first and second floors rested entirely on top of the beams. The third-floor joists, however, were mortised into the floor beams. Such housing of joists into beams reduces their effectiveness, and we can deduce therefore that the main loads in the mill were to be carried by the first and second floor, whose joists, resting on the beams, were permitted to develop their maximum strength.

The spacing of the joists exhibited the same casualness as the spacing of the principal posts. Those for the first and second floors averaged about 20 inches on centre with deviations of up to 2 inches either way; the third-floor joists were much more regularly spaced at 24 inches, centre to centre.

The jointing as a whole was most accurate and snug, and the framework, even after 134 years, was plumb and true. Settling, the bane of many early structures, did occur to some extent under several intermediate posts, resulting in the shearing of several pins in the principal posts and thereby causing joint failure. Heavy iron clamps and bolts were applied later to prevent the beams from pulling out any further. Intermediate posts were not joined at the bottom; the settlement under one interior post resulted in its being suspended by the two pins in the top joint, causing a considerable gap at the bottom. All the pins were hardwood, and were identical in size to those used in Grace Church, Markham.

The sashes were 1¾ inches thick, moulded by moulding planes to this one thickness, with the characteristic bead and tapered stem advocated by contemporary books on carpentry.

The most primitive type of bridge: near Port Arthur, 1937

## West Montrose bridge

In a developing society whose expansion, settlement, and general commerce depended so largely on a network of roads, the provision of bridges was essential. Without them many roads would have been of little use. As were the earlier sawmills and grist mills, so also were bridges built with government money. Wooden bridges varied from the simplest – a few logs thrown across a stream or gully – to such complex structures as trussed spans or the everpopular covered bridge, but they have now practically all disappeared: the remains of several fairly substantial log bridges can be seen alongside Highway 129 from Thessalon to Chapleau, but they will vanish before long; most wooden truss bridges have been replaced by steel and concrete ones, though many of them lasted well into this century; and of the famous covered bridges only one remains in Ontario – at West Montrose crossing the Grand River.

The details of the construction of this bridge have been preserved in the minutes of Woolwich Township council, and are given below in their original form. Preserved, too, are the drafting instruments of John Bear who drew up the plans and specifications; they are in the museum of the Pioneer Village near Doon. John Bear was approached by certan members of the Woolwich council in the latter part of October 1880, and his plans were adopted by the council that December. The township clerk was then instructed to advertise for tenders to erect the bridge, all tenders to be submitted by 17 January 1881. Only one tender seems to have been received – from John and P. Bear submitting a price of $3197.50 – and it was accepted. On 6

Two-span construction: the 'kissing' bridge at West Montrose

June two members of the council were appointed a committee to inspect and, if necessary, reject the timber and materials delivered for the construction of the bridge; this committee also superintended the work of its erection. There is no record of when the bridge was actually finished, but by April of the following year the council was asking for tenders for painting it; Geo. Peppler & Co. won with their offer to paint the bridge for $74.25. It was later decided to relieve the gloom of the bridge at night by having a lantern placed in it, and in 1888, for example, John C. Weber was paid $42.32 for his services in lighting and maintaining it for a year. Another maintenance charge that appears occasionally in the minutes is for hauling snow into the bridge so that cutters and sleighs could pass over (and through) it!

253

Central portion of one span

Detail showing the seating of the tie-rods

Underside of the roadway, showing needle beams

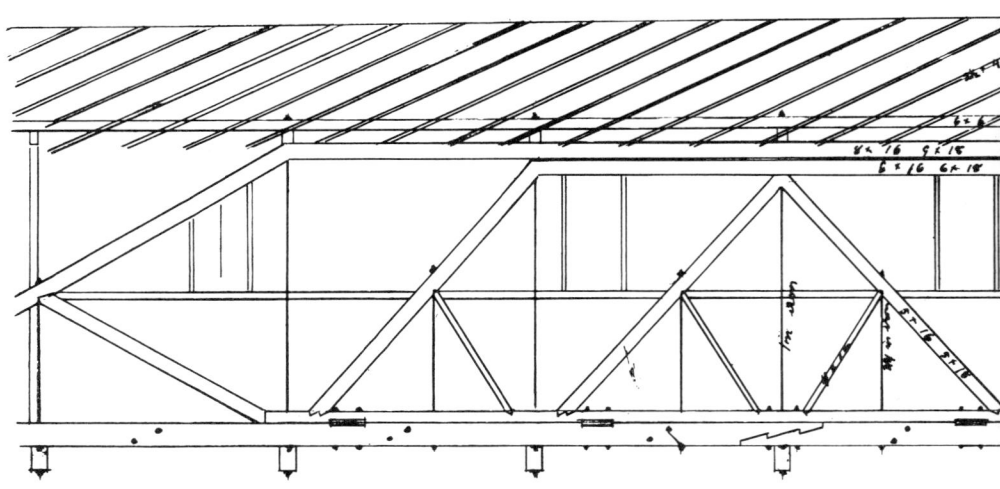

Church, mill, and bridge 255

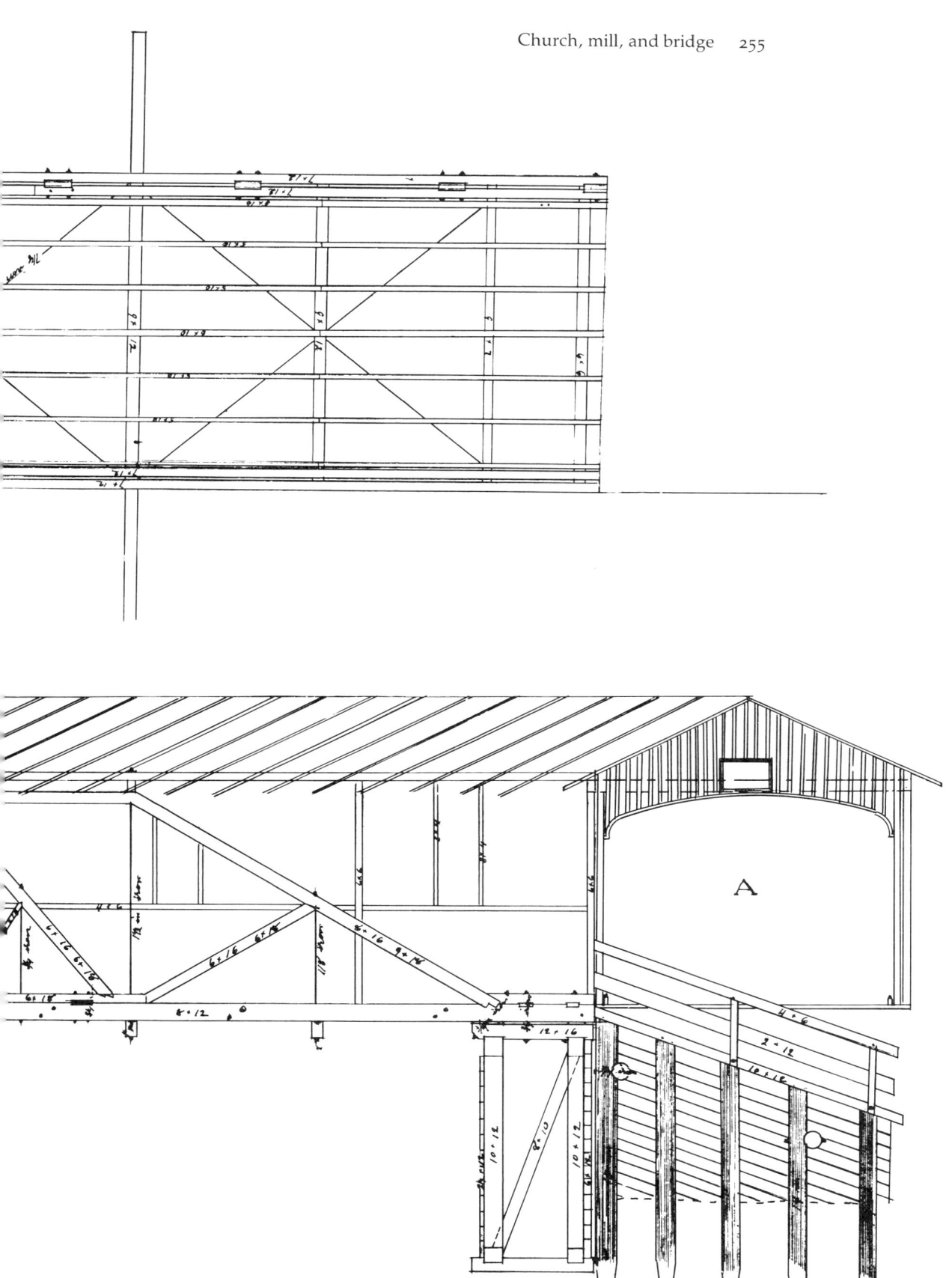

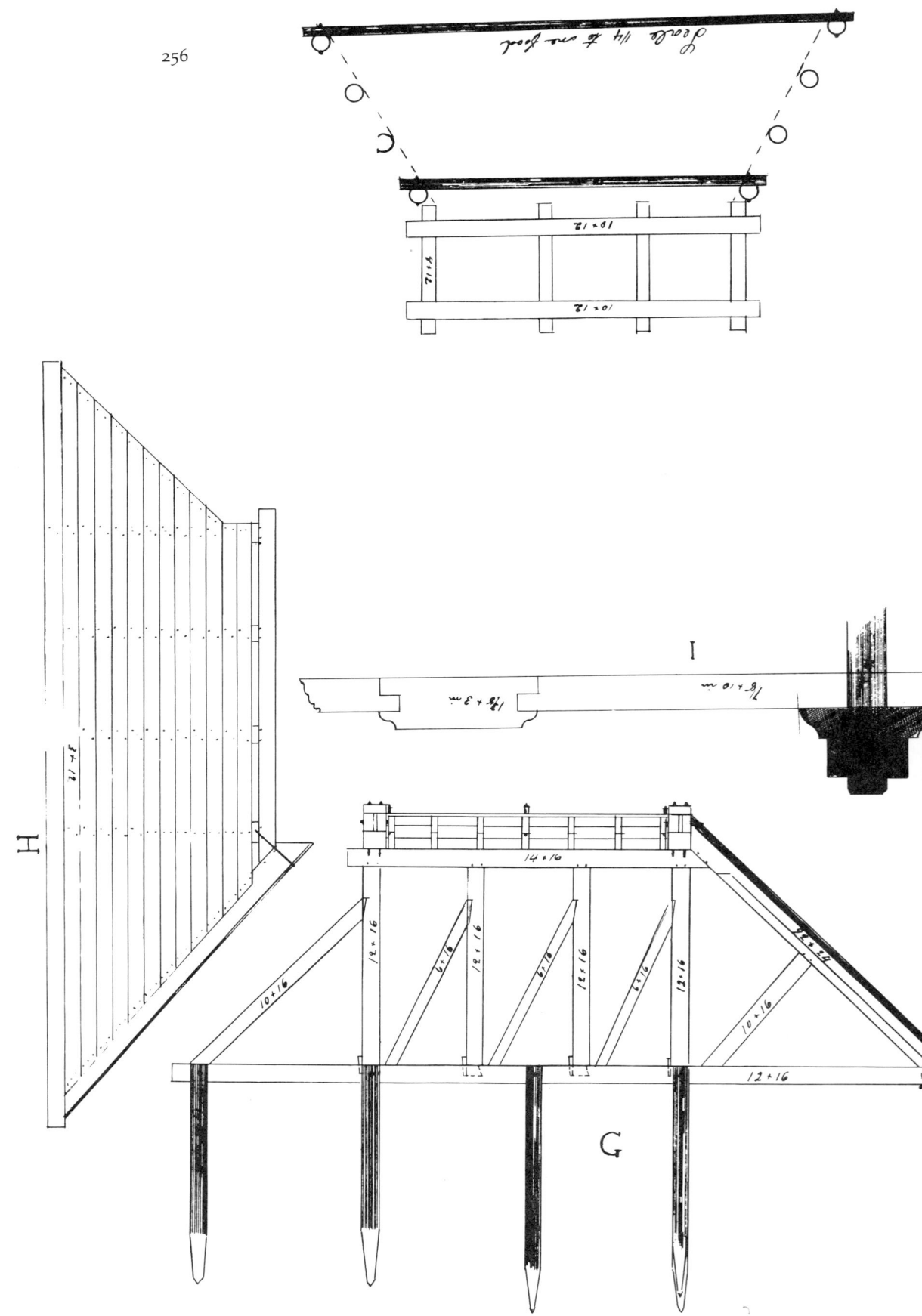

Church, mill, and bridge 257

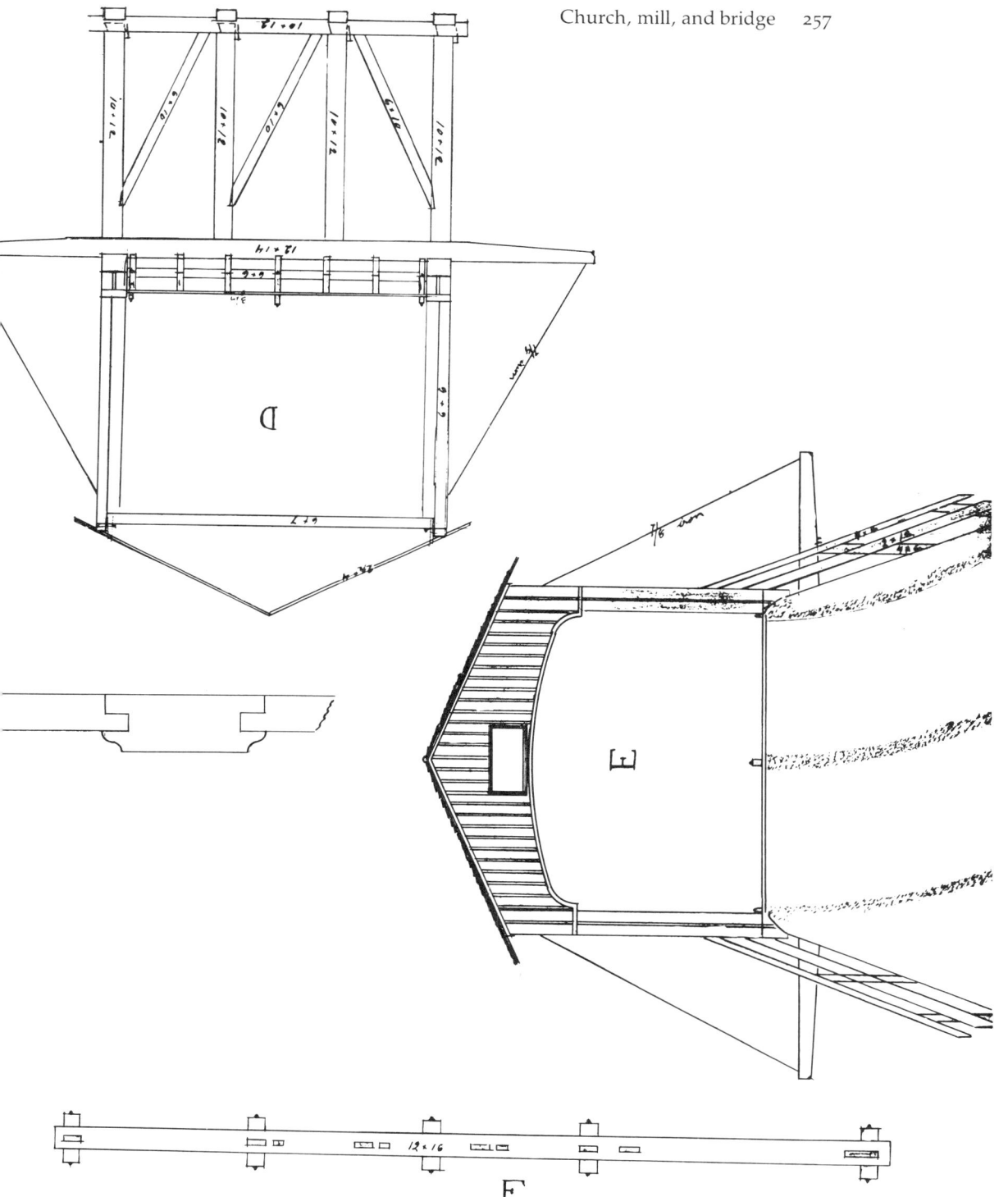

## Building with Wood

### WEST MONTROSE BRIDGE – SPECIFICATIONS

For a Bridge over the Grand River at Westmontrose in the Township of Woolwich in the County of Waterloo & Province of Ontario, Canada.

*Out side measurement*
The Bridge to Be 198 feet long 20 feet wide and 13 feet from the low water Mark to the top of the Corbel.

*Buttments*
Four Bed-timbers as shown on Plan.C. to Be laid two feet below low water Mark as shownCheckeed two inches for the Mudsill to lay in as Shown on Plan.D. Bents constructed as shownon Plan.D. with four Posts and Braces as shown. Corbels to be checked one inch over the Caps and Place as Shown on Plan.A. Plank the front with 2½ in Plank – Oak or Rock Elm well Spiked to the Posts & Braces with six in. wrought Spikes Plant the Back with six inch Ceder Plank as Shown on Plan.A.

*Aproaches*
Drive five Piles on Each side as Shown on Plan.C. to the depth of twelve feet. With two tie Beems as Shown on Plan.C. & A checked half & half to the tie Beem & Pile and Bolt as Shown on Plan.A. with ¾ in Bolts Cut the pile with the Slope of the roadway and frame a cap on as Shown on Plan.A. Place a railing there on as shown well fastened to the Truss and with ¾ in Bolts Bind upp with Cedar as Shown.

*Peir*
Fiffteen Piles are to Be driven to depth of twelve feet or as far as a Hammer of One ton weight will Drive them at the rate of ¼ in to a Blow Three Pile to Be drove side & side as shown on Plan.A. Cutt of two feet below low water Mark The center Piles to be ten inches lower than the Outside Ones for the Mud Sill to lay on The out Side Piles to be Drove Cose to the inside and to Gained or Boxed on the inside to let the Mudsill in Check 2in out of the lower Side of Sill to fitt down on the inside pile as Shown on Plan.A. Bolted with 1¼ in Bolts as Shown on Plan A & E. frame the Pier as Shown on Plan.F. & G with Six inch tenond Bolt Ice Breaker to the Mudsill asShown the top with ann Iron Strap ¾in × 2in Spiked to the Cap as Shown with ⅝in wrought Spike 7in long Plank both sides with three in Oak or rockelm Plank well Spiked to the Posts and Ice Breaker & Braces with 7in wrought Spike as Shown on Plan.H. Rebbitt the Ice Breaker on Each side as Shown to recieve Plank

*Truss*
Build the truss as Shown on Plan.A. The Stringers is built in 5½ Pieces the outside is in two Peices Splicedin the senter as shown on Plan.A. inside Stringers is 2½ pecies or five Peices for the 2 Span one piece 56 feet long and the center will lay on the piers to reach half on one span and half on the other so as to Bind the two together Splices the same as the outside with two Bolts to Each Splice as Shown on Plan A. The twp Stringers are Boxed together with oak Plank 4 by 12in checked into the Stringer 1in so as to leave ann opening of two inches between the two Stringers and to be Bolted as

Shown on Plan. A. The top Stringer is 49 feet long laid with 2 by 16in Oak Plank and Bolted as Shown on .A. the truss is 16in wide for Hard Timber & 18in for Pine Double rods all through as Shown in dots on Plan. A. the Outside suspension rods run upp through the Plate The inside through the tee Beem Needlebemes are Bolted to the truss with Short Bolts between the two Suspension rods so that the Beem can at any time be removeded with out Interfiering with the truss.

### Diagonal

Rods are Shown on Plan. B. Shall cross under the Short Needle Beems and through the long ones as Shown on Plan. A. and to have cast washers bevel to fit the angle and wrought Iron nutts threde the Bolt not less than eight inches at Both Ends so that thay can at any time be tightenned upp

### Lockrails

The lockrails to be checked half and half in the Corbs and Stringers and joice as Shown on Plan. C. Seven joice are Placed in four lengths as Shown on Plan. B.

### Roadway

Plank with 3in oak Plank not over ten inches wide spiked to the joice with 7in wrought Spike two to Each Plank alternately on the joice Apiece of timber 6 × 8in Shall be lade in the center of the roadway the entire length of roadway and Bolted to the joice one Bolt every 6 feet as Shown on Plan. B. & D and. C. the same along both outsides the timber to be 3 by 5

### Stayrods

or Braces Shall run through the Neddlebeems and tye Beems as Shown on Plan. D. with suitible washers for the Different Angles – with ann thread cut Eight inches at Each End and Good Nutts

### Tye beems

The Tye Beems Shall be Checked over the truss one half inch and the Plate one half inch over the tye Beem the Stringers and truss tye Beems and Plate are all bolted together By the Suspension rod as shown on the Plan A. The Plate is carried after leeving the truss is carried on Post as shown on Plan A & D. Framed to the tye Beem and Plate Strait to the cap as Shown with iron rods as Shown on Plan

### Raffters

The raffters to be frameed to Plate with Heels to Project 12 inches and Gained half & half together at the top end Pined with ¾in Pinns and to be well Spiked to the Plate and a Stay of Maple or Oak one by one inch ten inches long boared and Nailed with 3in wrought nail one to Each raffter and Plate

### Roofing lath

The raffters to Be covered with roof lath 1 by 2in laid five well Nailed to raffters

### Cornish

Shall be finished with Plaster board at Rable Ends 12in wide well Nailed to Lath. The Nosing to run all round 3in wide well Nailed to the raffters and Plaster Boards.

*Shingles*
The Entire roof to be covered with No 1 Shingles to be laid 5in to the whether and well Nailed to roof lath Ridge Boards is to Be made of three by four Scantling as Shown on Plan.E.

*Blinds*
As Shown Made of inch Boards Frame 1 × 5 casing 11 by 3 Slats 1 by 5 Size two and half by four feet Placed as Shown on Plan.A. No of Blinds. 24.

*Siding*
To be as Shown on Plan.I. Size and Stile is Given in the Plans Bolts of the truss will come in contact with the Siding as Shown on Plan.I. The Bolts to be long enough to go through Siding as Shown – The Siding to be well Nailed with 3in cut Nail and and the Batton with 3¾ Nail

*Timbers*
The Pier and Buttments Corbles and Plank for the Roadway Shall be Oak The remainder Pine if not otherwise Specified – P.S. the Needle Beems that Project on the outside of Bridge are to be covered with Boards in a roof Stile

*Timbers*
Provided Hardwood be used throughout can be all Hardwood Except Plates & raffters – The difference in size of Hardwood or Pine is Given on the Plans. the Pine with red ink

*Class of timber*
all Timber to Be used in the construction of Said Bridge to Be Good Sound timber free from Splits Shakes large or loose Knots or anything that has a tendency to Impare it Strengths

*Class of work*
All work Shall be Done in a Good and workmanlike Manner and Everything to be carried Out to full intent of Plans & Specification

# 7
# NON-WOOD CONSTRUCTION

By the time prospective settlers began leaving England for the New World the prevailing construction materials were brick and stone. On North American soil, however, the skills and materials involved in masonry building were not readily available. The process of cutting stone or firing bricks is a slow one, and time was of the essence for the early settlers who needed shelter immediately. Forests surrounded them and the most expedient solution to shelter was to cut down the trees rather than find clay or stone. Nevertheless, brick and stone houses are among the oldest found in Ontario and Quebec, and so we may assume that there were wealthy settlers who could hire skilled labour to build them.

In principle, masonry construction in Canada differs very little from the parent traditions of Europe (though perhaps such devices as brick veneer applied to an earlier timber structure are more common). Therefore it needs no more in this chapter than to survey briefly masonry construction in general, with such examples of the various methods as can be found in Ontario. We may note at this point, that of all methods of construction masonry in brick and stone has been the least subject to change in the period of North America's settlement. If only for this reason, the dating of a building by study of its masonry is almost impossible.

## Brick masonry

At various times in history, bricks were used as ballast in empty boats crossing Lake Ontario from certain ports in Canada or the United States. Such ballast was then sold to help defray the cost of a trip otherwise unprofitable. This practice may have led to the erroneous notion that bricks were imported as an item of regular trade. The brick employed in the Fisher home (1836) on the Humber River in Toronto came from the United States, for example, and that used for the McNab church (about 1850) near Welland, came from the Toronto district.

Bricks varied greatly throughout the province both in size and in quality. In many instances they were burned directly on the premises and this fact accounts for the variation, since colour and hardness were determined by the quality of local deposits of clay, as well as by the brickmaker's skill in firing.

A brick may be set in place four different ways, each position bearing its own name: header, stretcher, rolock, and soldier. The manner in which bricks are laid is called a bond. Early brickwork in Ontario is characterized by three bonds: common, English, and Flemish. A fourth type, less frequently found, is that of the 'running' or 'stretcher' bond: it is like common bond with the header course omitted; in other words, it consists of stretchers only. Traditionally this is not a structural bond, for it was used only when the brick was a mere facing or veneer for the actual construction, which may have been frame, log, or log butt. The reason for using only stretchers in this case

Note the different sizes and textures of the four bricks shown. The two on the left were probably made on the premises; both come from Sharon, the one on the extreme left dated at 1828 and the one next to it at 1819. The pair on the right are from the area near Sutton and were made about 1855–60. Note the 'frog' in the two on the right.

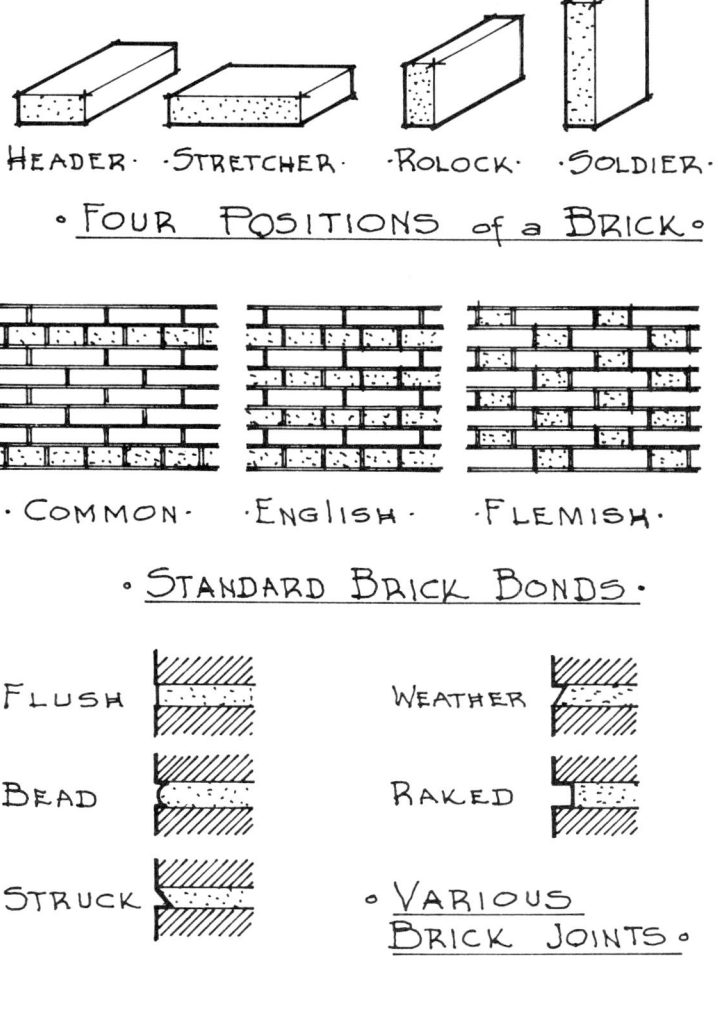

Brick veneer is a common covering for walls, and is easily recognized since the bond will show no headers. It can be applied over any form of wall construction, in this case log.

was that the thickness of the veneer was equal to the width of a single brick and therefore no through headers could be employed. Nowadays, use of the stretcher bond may imply that the wall is of 'cavity' construction; that is, made of two skins, each one unit wide, with an insulating air space between them, bonded together by metal ties placed at regular intervals.

Common bond is strictly utilitarian and functional. English and Flemish bonds are decorative as well. The earliest structures in New England reveal English and Flemish bonds in approximately the same frequency. There is another type of bond used occasionally in veneer work, but it is not recognized by the trade as a type of bond, no name exists for it, and it is not very common in Ontario. It involves the placing of bricks horizontally on edge with the depression showing; this depression, which usually occurs on only one side of a brick, is known as a 'frog.'

By the time Upper Canada began to be settled, however, English bond had practically disappeared from usage. The general practice became the use of common bond for all walls except the façade, for which Flemish bond was used. The reasons why English bond disappeared while Flemish persisted well into the nineteenth century can only be guessed at. One reasonable explanation might be that English bond gives a slightly striated effect, whereas Flemish reveals an overall pattern, which is perhaps more pleasing visually.

Non-wood construction  265

Brick veneer on a log-butt house

Brick veneer on a frame house

A house at Carrying Place, built about 1825. Note the casual alignment of the headers in contrast to those in St Andrew's Church.

An example of Flemish bond, St Andrew's Church, Scarborough, 1848. Note the alignment of the headers.

This house in Baysville shows the most unusual veneer – the brick is placed on edge with the 'frog' showing.

It is of interest that the principle of English bond goes as far back in history as the fourteenth century BC. Amenophis IV of Egypt introduced a monotheistic form of worship with the sun's disc, the Aten, as the principal deity. At this time he changed his name to Akhenaten, and began a great temple to Aten several hundred yards to the east of the now well-known temple of Amun at Karnak. All the inner surfaces of walls, pillars, and pylons were faced with carved stones 10 by 10 by 24 inches in dimension. And all these stones were laid with a row of headers alternating with stretchers, a most impressive antecedent to our English bond except that we use brick in place of stone.

Mortar joints were faced in a variety of ways. When restoring brickwork close attention must be paid to such features, as well as to the size and texture of the bricks themselves. In order to provide a better key for the mortar, most modern bricks have a 'frog.' Many early bricks were manufactured with no frog, although some brickmakers would run their thumb along the middle of one side of the soft clay to form a short groove, which would serve the purpose.

Some excellent brickwork in a house near Kleinburg, 1862. All headers are properly lined up and the traces of an earlier porch can be seen.

For good structural reasons no solid brick wall was ever constructed of stretchers only. Where such a bond is found, the brick can be only a veneer, usually over a timber frame, or, rarely (as in English eighteenth-century practice), over a solid wall of cheap brick. It seems likely that the greater number of early veneered houses in Ontario date from a time (after the Crimean War) when farmers prospered; though they possessed a perfectly sound log house, they would cover it with brick veneer in order to manifest their newly acquired wealth. There is reason to suppose that the number of brick veneered log houses dating from this period is much larger than generally suspected.

In brickwork it is easy enough to detect later alterations or additions because weathering changes the texture of brick, making it next to impossible, at a later date, to match the earlier texture. As well, an inspection of the bond pattern will reveal all vertical joints to be staggered, that is, no two joints are in line. But where an opening has been bricked up, a continuous vertical joint must appear, and this can never be original. The same will happen wherever an addition to a wall has been made. In an original structure, where a wall stands at right angles to another, the one is always keyed into the other by means of alternate stretchers. But when an addition has been made, one wall will simply be butted against the other. Chipping out some of the mortar at the joint will reveal the true state of things.

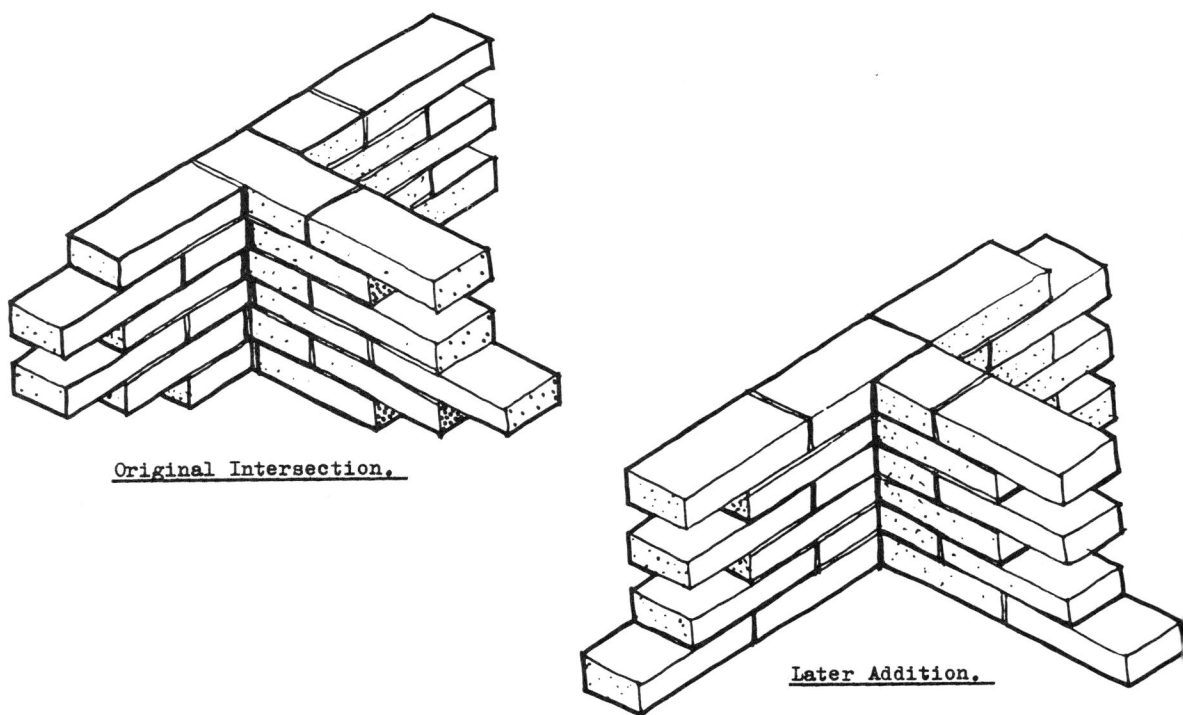

Original Intersection.

Later Addition.

## Stone masonry

The bricklayer handles units of uniform size and shape to be laid in a specified bond, and thus he has comparatively little opportunity to display his skill and imagination – now that such flights of fancy as the twisted chimney stacks of Tudor England have vanished from his repertoire. The same is not true for the stonemason. In rubble work, for example, even if the general pattern is fixed, the appearance of the finished product depends almost entirely on the stonemason's skill, taste, and sense of proportion.

Stone masonry falls into two classes: rubble and ashlar. Rubble is composed of stones gathered in fields, or unworked stones from the quarry; they are used either in their natural shape, or split so that the natural outline of the edge is preserved or the edges are roughly squared. Ashlar is composed usually of sawn and squared stone. The regularity of the size and proportion of the pieces allows for specific patterns, as in brickwork; for the same reason matching is easily done, except with regard to the texture and tinting which are the result of many years of weathering (rubble work is the hardest to match when attempting to restore old buildings).

In Ontario three kinds of stonework are to be found: the grey limestone in a belt running diagonally across the southern part of the province from Kingston through Guelph; the random fieldstone rubble with flush joints,

RUBBLE MASONRY

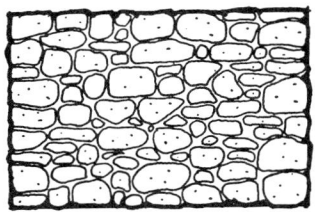

FIELDSTONE

COURSED

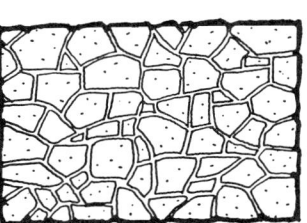

SPLIT FIELDSTONE

COURSED AND SPLIT

## ASHLAR MASONRY

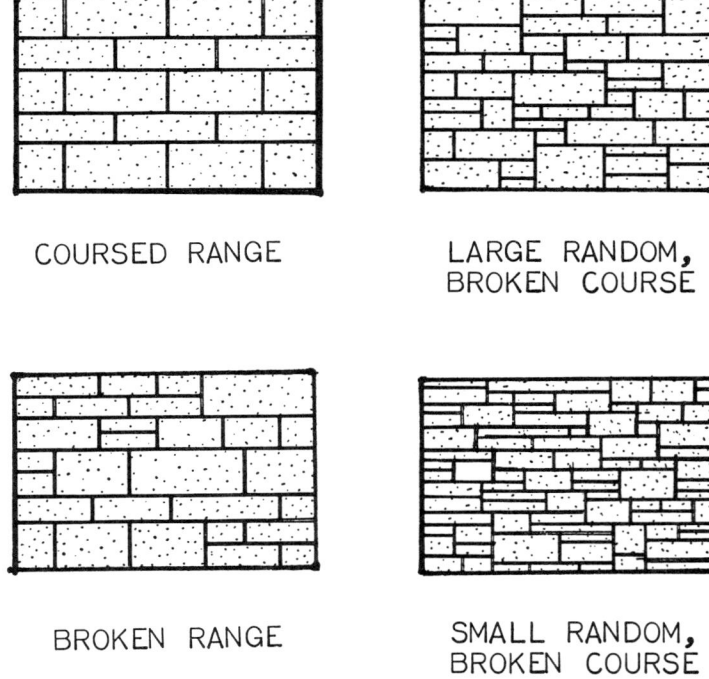

COURSED RANGE

LARGE RANDOM, BROKEN COURSE

BROKEN RANGE

SMALL RANDOM, BROKEN COURSE

typical of the Pennsylvania-Germans, in Waterloo County; the split and sometimes coursed fieldstone of the Scottish variety found in areas other than the limestone belt. These divisions are never clear-cut, of course, and there is considerable overlapping at the borders.

In raising a stone wall, the old English practice was to build up the stone to a certain convenient height, then add to the scaffold in order to construct another layer of stone, repeating this process until the final height was achieved. Each layer was often levelled with smaller flat stones, which are quite perceptible in a wall, but not in any way objectionable to the eye. The method is extremely ancient, dating back at least to the middle of the thirteenth century. It was definitely used in raising the walls of the old English tithe barns.

Old stonework is difficult to match, so that later alterations or additions can be detected without great difficulty. Where the later work has the same character as the old, the difference may still be detected by an examination of the effects of weathering. Stone masonry is expensive so that if a structure is taken down and re-erected in another location, one must brace oneself for a rather stiff bill.

Non-wood construction 271

'Castle Grange' near Belfountain, built about 1860–66. Since this photograph was taken, a fire gutted the interior and unfortunately repairs have severely mutilated the building. Note the smooth ashlar around openings, contrasting with the rough surface of the wall.

'Thistleha' in Pickering Township, about 1855. This is broken coursed fieldstone at its best.

This school near West Montrose in Waterloo County is typical of Pennsylvania-German rubble work. The use of dressed stone around openings would have been a sign of vanity and worldliness.

Ordinary rubble work disguised by artificially raised bead joints to give the impression of more expensive work. Note that this occurs only along the front wall. Cambridge

Non-wood construction 273

The cut fieldstone in this house near Summerville, about 1850, is the least refined type of stone masonry.

Excellent example of coursed stonework, near Mosport, 1869

274  Building with Wood

## Unburnt brick (mud) construction

Walls and houses have been built from mud for centuries. Mud was used for the adobe buildings of Mexico, New Mexico, and Spanish California as late as 1855 (Captain Devenport's house in Monterey). Its use was recorded in England in 1212, when walls were built up in continuous layers of mud alternating with layers of straw.[1] The method used in Ontario was different, however, in that the mud was first formed into bricks.

It would appear that mud-brick building was fairly popular in York County in the 1840s and 1850s; houses, churches, schools, and at least one hotel were built in this way. And the enthusiasts of the day recommended its use for 'sheds and stables for stock, and for every description of out buildings that are desirable for the comfort of man or beast.'[2] Mud-brick buildings are fairly evenly spaced about the county and some of them are still in excellent physical condition.

A house near Maple. Note that the stucco is applied directly to the brick.

The main reason for the use of unburnt brick was that it was cheap: its production required nothing but a bed of suitable clay and unskilled labour, both of which were generally available. An oval pit was dug and filled with (preferably) blue clay and water; after at least twenty-four hours, by which time the clay should have been thoroughly soaked, a yoke of oxen was brought in to tread or 'temper' it. During the tempering, short straw was thrown in the mixture; four bushels of straw were recommended for every hundred bricks. A piece of flat ground near the pit was swept clean; the mud was then poured into moulds of the required size and left in place until the bricks were dry enough to be taken out and stood on end on the clean ground. Once they were thoroughly dry, they were stacked under some protection from the rain in order to season.

Bricks were generally 6 inches thick, 12 inches wide, and 18 inches long for exterior walls, and 6 by 6 by 12 (or 18) inches for interior ones. The mortar used to join the bricks was composed of an equal quantity of pure clay and sand mixed to the consistency of the usual lime mortar. A Mr William Beason in Yorkville charged £1 for a hundred bricks 'made and laid up.' Among the many mud-brick houses built by Mr Beason was a house for Robert Maharfey in the Township of York: in this he used 2248 bricks, for which he charged £22/10/0 laid.[3] The walls of this house were 14 feet high, which would probably mean it was a house of one and a half storeys, and it was fairly large – 28 feet long by 28 feet wide.

'Bond timbers' were an important feature of mud-wall construction. Such timbers served two functions: the first was to attach fixtures to the wall, such as verandas, bases, door and window sills. The timbers for this purpose were planks 1½ to 2 inches in thickness which were laid to within 1 inch of the outer face of the wall; the second function of bond timbers was to act as a plate for the rafters in a two-storey house, and at least 4 inch timbers were suggested for this.

Advocates of unburnt brick suggested that walls be built no higher than 15 feet. This limit was not the result of any consideration for the strength of the wall but rather of the fact that the exterior stucco usually applied to these walls was liable to loosen and fall off, most exterior 'plasters' not being impervious to moisture. A 30 inch overhang at the eaves or a veranda around the entire building was therefore recommended in order to keep the rain off the stucco.

There were 'recipes,' however, for making moisture-proof plaster. The specifications for an original coating called for 'an equal proportion of pure clay, sand, ashes and lime, thoroughly incorporated together, and mixed with a portion of fresh bullocks' blood, equal to one half of each of the above ingredients. The blood should be well stirred to prevent it from coagulating' (this recalls an old British method for making a smooth, hard, dirt floor, in which ox blood was mixed with fine clay[4]). October was considered the best month in which to apply plaster because it would then dry 'by air,' and so more slowly than in the heat of summer, thus producing a better stucco.

Since unburnt bricks are very soft, they would crumble under a heavy, concentrated load. Here a plank, the full width of the wall, serves as support for the ends of the second-floor joists. Note also that the plate has been carried across the ends as well, although no real function is served by this.

The lintel over openings has a longer lug than would be required for hard burnt brick.

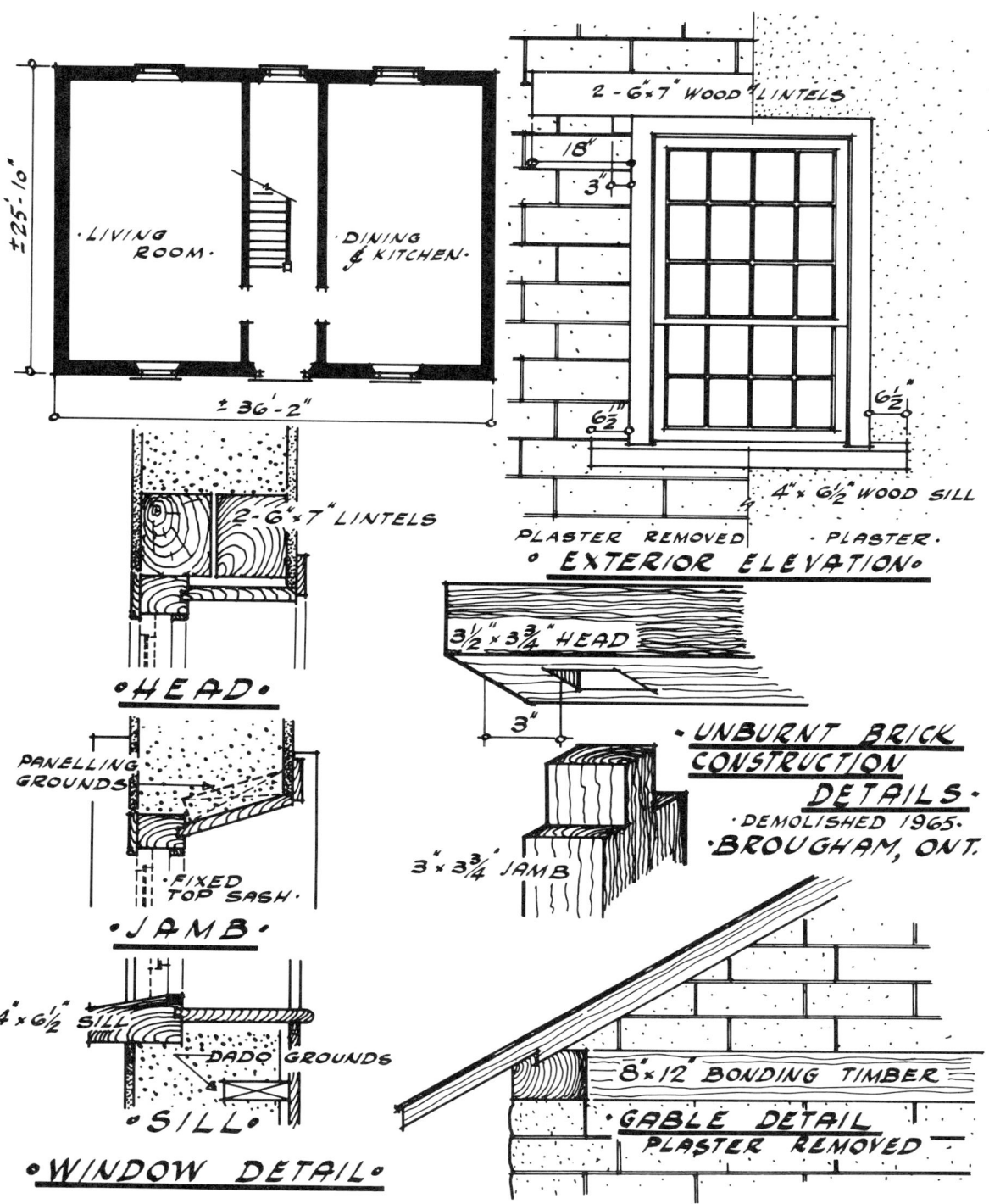

278 Building with Wood

The Helliwell house, Toronto

Mud church at Shanty Bay

For buildings that had already been plastered, but whose durability was in doubt, it was recommended that the owner make a mixture of five gallons of water and five quarts of 'Liverpool' or rock salt; boil it and skim it; 'slack and soft' six quarts of unslacked lime, and add it to the hot brine; then add gradually one pound of alum and finally four quarts of fine pure sand; stir well and apply two coats with an ordinary painter's brush while the mixture was still hot.

The earliest mud house that we have on record in Ontario appears to be that of Colonel G.W. Cruikshank on lot 32, concession 1, in Markham.[5] He acquired the land in 1816 and soon afterwards built himself a substantial thirteen-room house. The walls, of mud brick, were 2 feet thick, four of the six bedrooms are supposed to have measured 16 by 25 feet, and the front door, according to tradition, was secured by a 12 inch wrought-iron lock with a key 7 inches long. The interior trim, shutters, and carved mantelpieces were of walnut.

There is no doubt that unburnt-brick houses could be built to last. Dr Drury's house, located on Yonge Street about twelve miles from Toronto, was cited by the *British American Cultivator* as being 'as sound as the hardest granite.' Among the mud houses that have survived are those in York Mills – notably the Denis cottage and the house of the late C.W. Jefferys, now bricked over – and the Helliwell house (*c.* 1837) in the Don Valley near Pottery Road. St Thomas' Church at Shanty Bay, built in 1838, is also still in use.

Many of the early buildings in Bolton were of mud brick. The first school (built in 1842), the first Congregationalist church (1843), and the first Anglican church (1845) were all built in this way; so too was Hassard's Hotel.[6]

The most remarkable mud structure, however, was probably the house built by Colonel W.H. Berrisford in Bogarttown, near Newmarket.[7] It was built shortly after 1853 in two sections, each section being 40 feet wide and 80 feet long. The walls were three feet thick, 'making wonderful window seats.' The house had 18 rooms, 45 doors, and seven fireplaces. The sections were connected by a large reception hall with an imposing front porch. The entire eastern section was given over to a huge ballroom, with a great fireplace and sliding doors that could divide the room in two if necessary.

The 1½ storey mud house at Brougham, which was demolished in 1965, and which I had an opportunity to examine, was probably fairly typical of its kind. Its size was about average – 26 feet wide and 30 feet long – and it exhibited characteristic construction features in its stone foundation, brick sizes, bonding timbers, and plaster. We have no definite information on its date of erection. The foundation wall was 18 inches thick and terminated about 2 feet above grade. (There was no basement originally.) The mud-brick walls were 12 inches thick, flush with the foundation wall on the outside face, thus leaving a 6 inch ledge on the inside. A 2 by 6 inch plank was laid on this ledge on the long sides, forming an even surface to accept the roughly flattened floor-beam ends; the beams were not secured in any way and their top side was adzed roughly flat to receive the floor boards.

280  Building with Wood

The notation beside the plan reads as follows:

1 vestry and robing room
2 Pulpit
3 reading pew
4 Communion table
5 tower
6 our pew

---

inside length
  37 feet
inside breadth
  29 ft

---

church to contain
  150 people
without gallery

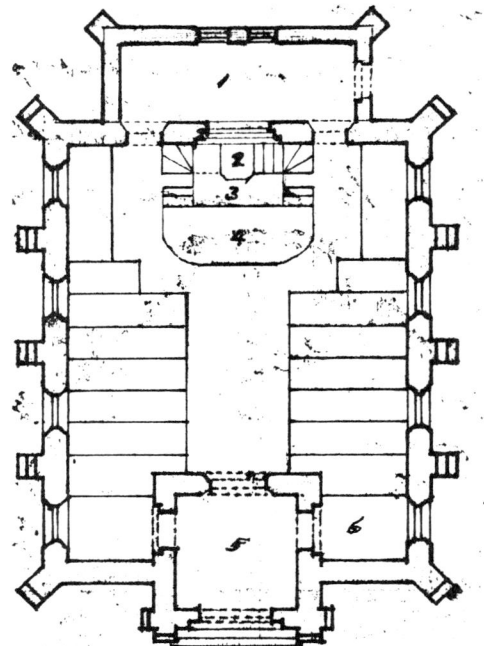

St Thomas Anglican Church at Shanty Bay was planned and erected by Edward O'Brien; commenced probably in 1838 and completed about 1840, it is still in use. Foundation stone laid 29 June 1838. Sketch from a letter of Mary O'Brien, dated July 1838.

Two rows of bonding timber 2 inches thick ran all the way round the inside of the exterior walls, 10 and 28 inches respectively above the floor beams. They had served as a ground for wainscotting, and were removed and plastered over at some later date. There were two intermediate cross-beams at the second-floor level with the joists running laterally. The ends of the second-floor joists rested on a 2 by 12 inch bonding timber extending the full width across both gable ends. The lintels over all openings consisted of two pieces of 6 by 8 inch timber placed side by side and extending about 18 inches past the opening. All lintels and bonding timbers were probably plastered originally.

The specifications for the veranda that surrounded the whole building called for 'four pieces of bonding timber at least four inches thick, sawn or hewn out the exact length and width of the building, which should be laid into the wall for the rafters of the veranda to rest upon and should be laid about one inch within the outer edge of the wall.' The builder of this house, however, made some modifications, for the timbers were 8 by 12 inches, they were laid at plate height across all four walls, and were flush with the outside face rather than recessed.

Non-wood construction 281

The window and door frames being set flush with the exterior face of the wall, a deep reveal was created on the inside. This was frequently panelled. Note the nailing block set into the wall. Plaster was applied directly to the inside face of the wall, omitting all strapping and lath.

Generally the foundation walls were thicker than the wall above, thus forming a ledge. Here this ledge is used to support the first-floor joists.

The rafters had the usual shouldered seat at the plate and were tapered from 3 inches at the ridge to 4 inches at the plate. No ridge board was used. The chimneys were of hard burnt brick, and there was no evidence of fireplaces, which might suggest that the house was fairly late for a mud-brick construction, that is, after approximately 1860.

There is another aspect of its construction that might be mentioned, although it is doubtful if the method was typical. The window and door frames consisted of heavy 3 by 3¾ inch timbers, the jams being mortised into the head which was long enough to form a 3 inch lug at either end. The sill was cut from a 4 by 6½ inch timber, into which the jambs were also mortised and which, again, was long enough to form a 6½ inch lug at both ends. The purpose of these lugs at the head and the sill was no doubt to anchor the frame firmly into the wall. The window frame followed the usual custom of the mid-1800s in omitting the parting strip and having the top sash fixed. Since the thickness of the wall left a deep reveal, an ½ inch square groove was cut all around the inside of the frame, which permitted the window panelling and stool to be housed into it.

## Cobblestone treatment

Another unusual fad besides mud construction, and a very regional one at that, in the story of building in Ontario was the use of cobblestones as an exterior wall surface. This treatment originated around 1825 in the Rochester area of upper New York state and was employed occasionally for some forty years. The reasons behind the appearance of this technique are not known for certain, but it has been suggested that it was an after-effect of the building of the Erie Canal. Between Rochester and Buffalo the canal was blasted through sandstone beds, and it was decided to use the waste stone for building abutments, retaining walls, and other such structures along the canal. Masons were brought into the area from New England and Pennsylvania, but once the canal was completed they found themselves out of work. It was these stone masons who, in finding new work building houses, instituted this new method. At the start the masons built walls in the usual manner, but used smaller stones for the facing. The size of the facing stones was gradually decreased until they lost all bonding value and became simply a veneer with no structural function at all.

In Ontario this cobblestone veneer occurs only in two places: in and around the town of Paris, and at Baldwin on Highway 48. Paris was originally inhabited almost entirely by 'Yankees bound to succeed at any price.' But after the rebellion of 1837 success demanded that they forget their Yankee pride; being shrewd businessmen, they soon became more royalist than the loyalists.

It was Levi Boughton who introduced the fad to Paris. He arrived in 1838 from Normandale in Albany County, New York, and was responsible for

The Norman Hamilton house, built in 1844, is the most dignified of the Paris houses, although its design is an unfortunate mixture of Greek Revival, triple-sash 'French' doors, and a rather overpowering belvedere. Apparently cost was not a concern because even the rear wall has the expensive cobblestone facing.

In Paris, cobblestone was applied quite indiscriminately without regard to style or appropriateness to the design. This is the fairly large, Gothic, Patten house. Note the random fieldstone side wall.

Levi Boughton's house, in which he lived for about thirty years. It is a typical cottage of the period with the usual 'modernized' window sash of the later period. Its cobblestone work is not of the best.

This house is often referred to as the Monteith house although it was built by Charles Mitchell. It is in excellent Greek Revival style, including carved metopes and cast-iron grilles with classical motifs over the eyebrow windows. The stone facing is the best in the area.

several of the cobblestone buildings in Paris. There are two churches and twelve houses built in this manner, but with a detectable difference in workmanship; this suggests that others besides Boughton were engaged in this kind of work, or perhaps that the quality of the hired labour varied from job to job. St James Anglican Church, the first cobblestone building erected in Paris (1839), shows the greatest irregularity and inexperience on the part of the workmen. Boughton's own house, oddly enough, does not have as fine cobblestone work as the Monteith house.

The actual size of the cobblestones on a facing is quite deceptive: they appear to be set flat in the stucco, with their major diameter approximating the visible portion on the stone. However, if this were the case, then how are we to explain that cobblestone work generally shows so little effects from weathering? The answer became obvious upon examination of the Hamilton house. The basement wall, also with a cobblestone veneer, had been pierced at one time for a doorway, revealing that the cobble and stucco veneer was all of 6 inches thick. The stones were also about 6 inches long and of smooth elliptical form; they were laid in a very thick bed of mortar with their major axis at right angles to the wall and with only a small portion of them projecting beyond the outer surface. Hence the excellent weathering of the cobblestone veneer.

There was a small-scale revival of this technique at Baldwin around the turn of the century, when it was applied to several houses and a store. But the workmanship was poor, lacking the refinements of Levi Boughton, and the method was, perhaps fortunately, never attempted again in Ontario.

Ouse Lodge on Arnold Street is an unimaginative Victorian pile making a vain attempt at dignity by hiding behind an expensive cobblestone facing.

Dr Sowden's home (and office) was built in the late 1840s. It has a fine bracketed cornice; the rear wall is of cheaper fieldstone.

This house was built by Osborne Totten at an unknown date. The facing as well as the stone quoins are well executed but the design is indifferent, with the upper storey too large for a belvedere and too small for a proper second floor.

St James Anglican Church (1839), Levi Boughton's first commission for cobblestone facing. The stonework is second-rate: the selection of stones is most irregular and the coursing very uneven. It certainly displays a lack of experience and does not measure up to the fine work around Rochester.

The Paris Plains Methodist Church was built in 1845 by volunteer labour with stones gathered in the nearby fields. Considering that it was built in this way, the workmanship is quite on a par with that in St James. Services were discontinued in 1921. The structure fell into disrepair until restored by a group of interested citizens in 1948. The original cost of the building was about £1000.

This store and residence is in Baldwin, which boasts another three or four houses with rather crude cobblestone facing.

# 8
# POLYGONAL BUILDINGS

Eight-sided buildings have appeared spasmodically throughout the history of Western architecture. The ancient Greeks, conservative and rational builders on the whole, built one that is still in existence – the Tower of the Winds or the Horologium in Athens. Raised in the first century BC, it contained a water clock and had sundials on the outer sides of its walls, which faced the cardinal and intercardinal points of the compass. Its octagonal shape can thus be attributed more to the scientific purpose of the building rather than to any aesthetic or structural reason. The Romans were aware of, and experimented with, more architectural styles, showing a greater interest in polygonal buildings than the Greeks had ever done. The octagonal building that had the greatest influence on future architecture was the Baptistry of Constantine, built in Rome in 430 and the prototype of innumerable baptistries constructed in many parts of the world throughout the following centuries.

Chapter houses and libraries were also frequently built in this form in medieval Europe. So also were steeples and belfries, the latter often separate from the main structure of the church for fear that the vibrations set up by ringing bells would injure the fabric. Polygonal shapes were so numerous during the Gothic period that we have come to consider them part of that tradition. They fell into some disfavour when Gothic was replaced by the classical mode of the Renaissance, but they were far from being unknown, at any rate in England, even before the Gothic revival in the first half of the nineteenth century.

The Butter Market at Barnard Castle in County Durham, for example, was built as an octagon in 1747.[1] It is of two storeys and rather small, each side being 25 to 30 feet wide, and surrounded by a porch. The roof comes to a peak with a cupola and weather vane on top, and a graceful Palladian window is placed directly above the main entrance. This building has a startling resemblance to nineteenth-century North American 'octagons,' but the connecting lineage, if any, has never been shown. In his *Contrasts*, published in 1832,[2] Pugin, one of the great revivers of the Gothic style, illustrates two octagonal buildings, one unnamed and the other labelled 'A Modern Poor House,' but the absence of any comment may indicate that the form was in no way rare or unusual.

The first octagonal building in North America appears to have been a small Dutch church built near Albany, New York, about 1656,[3] which inspired shortly thereafter a number of imitations in the states of New York and New Jersey.[4] The next recorded polygonal building was in Washington, DC, designed by Dr William Thornton in 1789 and now occupied by the American Institute of Architects; it is a hexagon, but was and is commonly known as the 'Octagon.' President Madison lived in it for a while when he was burned out of the White House in 1814. Thomas Jefferson's summer home,[5] 'Poplar Forest' in Bedford County, Virginia, which was built between 1806 and 1819, was also octagonal. He believed that he was the first to use the octagonal form in America, and carried its use to the extremes of consistency: discreetly hidden by flowery mounds, some distance from the back corners of the house, were two octagonal privies, delicately referred to as 'cloacinas.' The octagon survived, however, for higher things, being embodied in the plans for the New South Church in Boston, prepared by Charles Bullfinch some time before 1844.[6]

By this time a man by the name of Orson Squire Fowler was practising in New York City as a phrenologist. He had been born in 1809 and educated in Massachusetts, whence 'he emerged a characteristic product of his day, with a mass of ill-digested information, many enthusiastic theories, and much reformatory zeal.' His success in the writing and publishing of books on the pseudo-science of phrenology encouraged his interest in other similar fields: *Amativeness: or, Evils and Remedies of Excessive and Perverted Sexuality, including Warning and Advice to the Married and Single* had been through forty printings by 1844. He then moved on to the problem of building the actual structure for the happy American home, writing in collaboration with his brother *A Home for all: or, the Gravel Wall, and Octagon Mode of Building ...* which appeared in 1849.

'Fowler's Folly' at Fishkill, New York

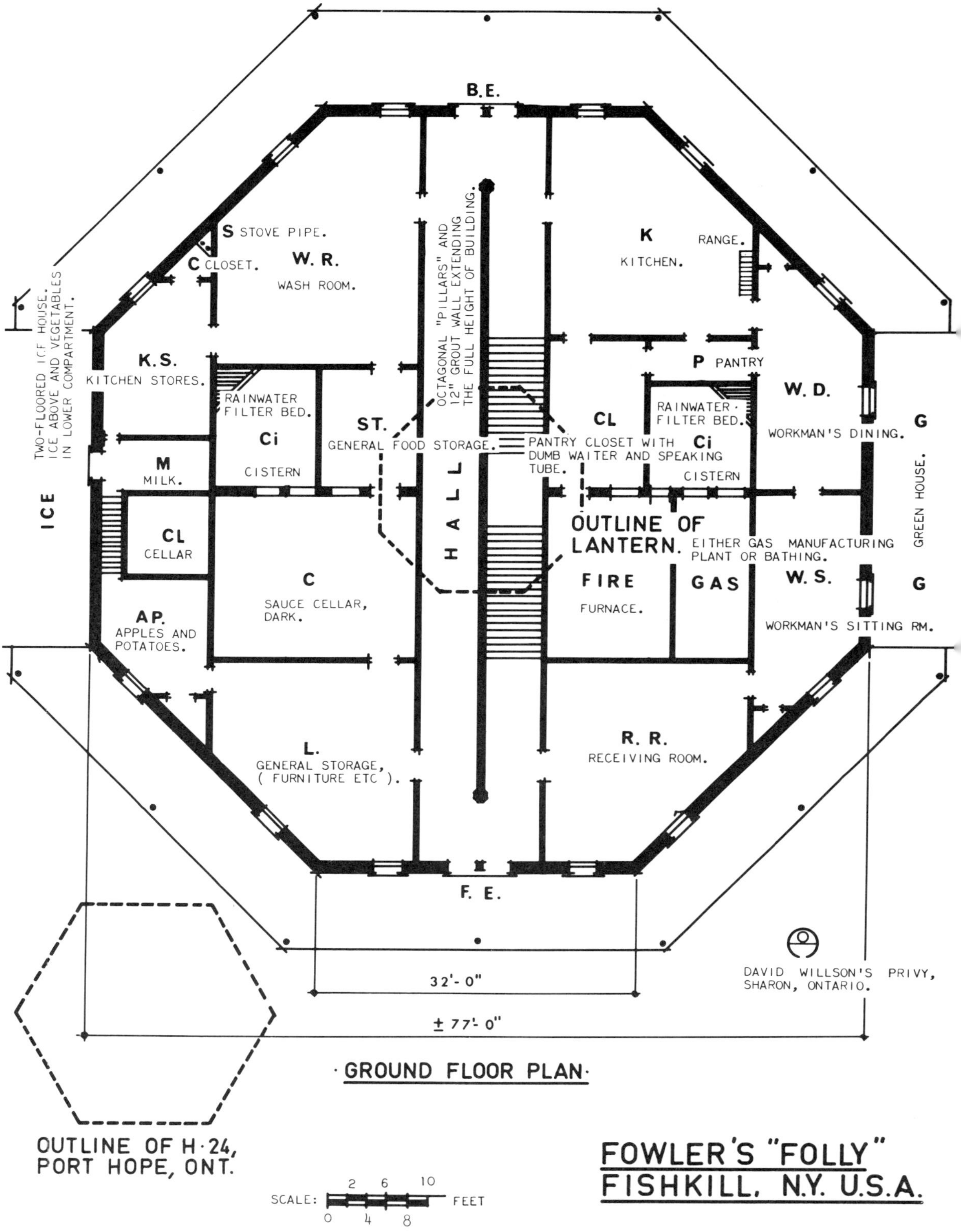

## Building with Wood

**B.E.**

**S** STOVE PIPE.
**W. R.** WASH ROOM.
**C** CLOSET.

**K** KITCHEN.
RANGE.

ICE — TWO-FLOORED ICE HOUSE. ICE ABOVE AND VEGETABLES IN LOWER COMPARTMENT.

**K.S.** KITCHEN STORES.

**Ci** CISTERN
RAINWATER FILTER BED.

OCTAGONAL "PILLARS" AND 12" GROUT WALL EXTENDING THE FULL HEIGHT OF BUILDING.

**P** PANTRY
RAINWATER FILTER BED.

**W. D.** WORKMAN'S DINING.

**G** GREEN HOUSE.

**M** MILK.

**ST.** GENERAL FOOD STORAGE.

**CL**
**Ci** CISTERN

**CL** CELLAR

**H A L L**

PANTRY CLOSET WITH DUMB WAITER AND SPEAKING TUBE.

**OUTLINE OF LANTERN.** EITHER GAS MANUFACTURING PLANT OR BATHING.

**C** SAUCE CELLAR, DARK.

**FIRE** FURNACE.

**GAS**

**W. S.** WORKMAN'S SITTING RM.

**G**

**A.P.** APPLES AND POTATOES.

**L.** GENERAL STORAGE, (FURNITURE ETC).

**R. R.** RECEIVING ROOM.

**F. E.**

32'- 0"

± 77'- 0"

DAVID WILLSON'S PRIVY, SHARON, ONTARIO.

· GROUND FLOOR PLAN ·

OUTLINE OF H·24, PORT HOPE, ONT.

SCALE: 0 2 4 6 8 10 FEET

## FOWLER'S "FOLLY" FISHKILL, N.Y. U.S.A.

'Why is there so little progress in architecture, when there is so much in all other matters?' asks Fowler in his book. 'Why continue to build in the same square form of all past ages? Is no RADICAL improvement of both the external form and internal arrangement of private residences, as well as BUILDING MATERIALS possible?' Indeed, yes. Man, possessing the faculties of 'inhabitiveness' and 'constructiveness,' instinctively wants a house, and Nature has arranged for this, no matter how poor a man may be. 'Ye homeless poor, be assured your mother has not forgotten you. She has provided some cheap and comfortable building material, if you only knew what it was.' Fowler then enlightens the poor with the knowledge that there is an abundance of limestone, sand, and gravel and with advice on using it properly: burn the limestone and make a paste out of it; throw anything – brickbats, stones, slag, slate chips, as well as sand and gravel – into it and mix well; pour it between forms – and almost at once the house is ready to be occupied. Fowler did not explain how the poor could obtain these materials – or how to burn and make a paste out of limestone.

The plan of this 'instant' house would preferably be octagonal. 'How much fretfulness and ill temper, as well as exhaustion and sickness, an unhandy house occasions. Nor does the evil end here. It often, generally, by perpetually irritating mothers, sours the temperament of their children, even BEFORE BIRTH, thus rendering the whole family bad-dispositioned BY NATURE, whereas a convenient one would have rendered them constitutionally amiable and good.' The troubles of the American nation would be over if everyone would live in an octagon!

The fad, naturally, spilled over into Canada and some, though not all, of our octagonal houses can be traced to his influence. The home of the Misses Bird in Bracebridge is one classic example of Fowler's ideal. There are octagonal houses in Ontario which appear to predate Fowler's book, however; and in the light of the Gothic revival and the Jeffersonian fashion one could not claim that Fowler's gospel was entirely new or was being spread to a wholly antagonistic world.

The most perfect form was the circle, Fowler argued, but it was difficult to build; polygonal structures were therefore the next best, and of these the octagon was the most efficient and practical. It permitted greater 'receptivity' of sunlight and air, it eliminated unsightly internal corners, and it reduced the distance between any two points in the house, thus eliminating much of the toil and drudgery of housework. Apart from such dubious arguments for the octagonal form, Fowler also managed to propose certain worthwhile improvements: good ventilation, central heating, dumb waiters, and inside plumbing. This last innovation, however, was only for the benefit of the sick; the healthy would still have to go outdoors. He also advocated a number of tanks scattered throughout the house, which would be filled by rainwater and would supply sinks and washbasins with running water.

To prove his point and as an example to the nation, Fowler began to build an immense octagonal and gravel-walled mansion. Situated at Fishkill on the Hudson River, it was four storeys high, 77 feet from side to side, and contained nearly one hundred rooms and closets. The costs of this monument were such that Fowler had to make several lecture tours in the United States and Canada during the 1850s to raise the money; in 1858 it was completed, but within a few years the admiration of the fickle world was no longer fixed on octagons. It was probably just as well, since before long the celebrated limestone grout walls began to crumble and disintegrate. Fowler sold the house, and it changed hands about thirty times, until in 1897 – ten years after his death – it was declared dangerous and unfit for human habitation. The apotheosis of the happy home was dynamited.

But all over North America there are buildings still standing that bespeak Fowler's influence. In the United States octagonal houses, schools, churches, and barns can be found in many cities and large villages from Vermont to California and from Wisconsin to Mississippi; complete towns were sometimes laid out octagonally. Similarly in Canada the fad left its traces from Vancouver to St John's, with its greatest influence in Ontario. The prairies were too close to the pioneering stage to be able to afford any such experimentation, and it had little effect in the province of Quebec which had its own strong cultural and architectural tradition. There are, however, about a dozen octagonal barns in Quebec, all in the region of Lévis and in other locales between the St Lawrence and the American border, and all built between 1890 and 1910. There are differing opinions on the provenance of this style,[7] but the distribution of the barns suggests, at least on the face of it, an American origin.

In Ontario octagonal buildings can be found from St Joseph Island and Thessalon in the west, to Dalhousie Mills in the east, and from Kingsville in the south, to Fort Albany and the Attawapiskat River in the north. It is intriguing how a Cree council house could come to be built octagonally in the early years of this century, for Fowler's influence on houses, schools, and churches seems to have disappeared in the 1880s. Not so with barns, however: like those in Quebec, the octagonal barns of Ontario that I have examined were all built in the late nineteenth and early twentieth centuries. But I do not yet know the reasons for this revised interest in the octagonal form.

Fowler's arguments for the octagonal barn were quite reasonable. He advocated a banked barn with the cattle entrance on the low side. The cattle would all face inwards, and the floor of the stalls would be dropped several feet below that of the barn. In the centre would be a feeding station at which all the cattle could eat together and which could easily be filled through an opening in the floor above. The lowered stall floor kept the manure off the feeding area and made it easier to collect. It was important, according to Fowler, to collect it daily and plough it under at once since 'the bad smell from it is caused by the escape of the nutritious elements.' He also recommended the use of glass in some parts of the roof to let in sunlight, 'which

295

This church at Dalhousie Mills is situated at the very eastern tip of Ontario: although the church is in Ontario, the caretaker, who lives just a short distance away, lives in Quebec. It is very plain inside, and the ambitious steeple has since been removed. C1

The Indian council house at Fort Albany, a most fascinating structure although quite late, definitely post-1900. Fort Albany is about seventy-five miles northwest of Moosonee, and the intriguing question is: how did the Indians hit on this shape or who took the idea all the way to James Bay? M18

will be found useful for a great many ends of which we do not now dream.'

In his 'reasoning' for the octagonal school, Fowler rises to fervid heights. 'Parents, on your love of your dear children I ground this appeal. PERFECT YOUR SCHOOL-HOUSES. No longer suffer them to RUIN so many fine children – some by breaking down the life-power, and leaving them sickly and inane for life, and so many others by burying them in the very dawnings of humanity. Inattention here is child-murder; for in almost every schoolhouse these death-inducing causes are silently, insidiously but most venomously at work, dealing out disease and death to children, and heart-breaking agony and desolation to bereaved parents.' 'The nearer we can approach the [circular] form the better ... To have a truly agreeable chit-chat, we require to form a CIRCLE ... As in magnetic and electrical experiments we must complete a CIRCLE, so, that several MINDS may act in concert, it is requisite that they form around and face a common center.'

Fowler was not, however, the first North American advocate of octagonal schools. In their appendix to *The School and the Schoolmaster*, Alonzo Potter and George Emerson had given detailed arguments in their favour and provided an illustration of one such school. Among their reasons for the shape were its lower cost per given area (owing to the smaller total wall length: maximum area with minimum walls is attained in a circle), its central roof illumination, which prevented shadows and left plenty of wall room for blackboards and so on, uniform temperature, and excellent ventilation. Fowler added windows to the walls, but repeated Potter and Emerson's arguments. *The School and the Schoolmaster* was considered a most valuable contribution to the educational literature of its day, and was distributed free to all school districts in New York state and Massachusetts by public-minded citizens; it no doubt found its way also into Ontario. It probably did more for octagonal schools than Fowler's books.

Compared to his emotional utopianism about schools, Fowler's reasons for octagonal churches are quaintly realist. This form

facilitates the congregation's SEEING ONE ANOTHER, and thereby the interchange of friendly and benignant feelings toward one another ... [T]he benign smile of recognition and good feeling enkindled by this freedom of seeing each other, and expressed in the countenance, will spread from 'face to face' and soul to soul. In short, what a world of meaning is embodied in this 'FACE TO FACE' – exactly what our form secures ... This form will also accommodate those who attend church 'FOR LOOKS,' or to 'see and be seen.' I once asked a lady what were her reasons for attending Grace Church: 'Sympathy of doctrine?' 'No,' she answered frankly; 'to tell the whole truth, I chose it because of its EXTRA GENTILITY. The fashionable all go there, and of course I must go too.'

Now, ought not our churches to be built so as to satisfy the wants of this class of attendants? If a genteel woman wants to exhibit her dress, or tinsels, or paddings, why do not let her? She may be brought thereby within the reach of good.

Strangely enough, despite his assertion of the beneficent effects of the octagon and his general preoccupation with the purifying influence of Euclid, it did not occur to Fowler to expose criminals to the therapy of the octagon. The polygonal centre-core block so prevalent in nineteenth-century jails owes nothing to him. It was derived from the 'Pennsylvania system' originated by the Quakers in Philadelphia: each prisoner would benefit from the *restauratif* of silent meditation during his sentence and therefore required an individual cell and exercise yard. This led to the standard plan of a centre block with radiating wings – a plan first developed by John Haviland of Philadelphia in 1821,[8] and used in all parts of Europe and even in China and Japan. The plan has the great advantage of allowing for expansion. The Guelph and Goderich jails were originally true octagons, Barrie was a semi-octagon, and the third Toronto jail (now demolished) also had a dominant centre core of octagonal shape which rose one storey higher than the wings.

Jails are difficult to photograph because, for obvious reasons, they are always surrounded by high walls or other buildings. This one, at Barrie, is actually a semi-octagon. A reporter once compared it enthusiastically to the Mosque of Omar in Jerusalem. J4

The best preserved and most complete jail stands at Goderich. It has escaped demolition by a hair's breadth. J2

One other institutional building that occasionally had eight sides might be mentioned: the 'dead' house (or vault or body house) where bodies were stored in early cemeteries during the winter when it was impossible to dig graves. There are seven or eight such buildings in the region north of Toronto, many of which are, notwithstanding their purpose, rather charming in a quaint way. They are discussed in more detail below, under example 5.

As one would expect, however, the most common octagonal buildings left to us from the nineteenth century are houses. Although the outside shape of their plan is, of course, always the same, the internal arrangements are different in nearly every house, reflecting partly the individual ideas of owner or builder and partly, no doubt, the fact that it is all but impossible to divide an octagon into the rooms wanted by an average family without causing some wastage or absurdity. Some plans make an attempt at squaring rooms; others accept the geometry and make triangular sectored rooms. The latter arrangement, which is more sensible given the basic shape of the octagon, demands a centrally located hall and stairway leading up to the lantern which provides the light for this interior room. Without this centre stairwell and lantern, unpleasant dark halls are inevitable unless the halls and stairs are shifted to one side in order to get light; but this results in a problem of traffic circulation between the rooms on each floor – people have to go through one room to reach another.

Fowler argued that an octagonal plan eliminates 'unsightly' corners. In some rooms, it is true, the corners could all be larger than 90 degrees, thereby possibly conferring some psychic benefit on the inhabitants; but then there would have to be other rooms where the corners were less than 90 degrees, and quite apart from any feelings one would have about living among acute angles there would clearly be a less efficient use of the available space. In a really large plan it is not so difficult to have some well-proportioned rooms, but in smaller houses this is almost impossible. Some builders made the exterior 'corner' walls less wide than the main walls in an attempt at reducing the size of the triangular spaces, but this can only have a limited success. It can safely be asserted that in *all* octagonal houses the plan becomes laboured, awkward, and even 'pokey' in places; such ungainly arrangements might well be expected to induce qualities exactly opposite to the emotional stability and contentment preached by their propagandist.

Wall construction was of three types: brick or stone, frame, or grout. Brickwork followed the fashion of the day in its bonding and polychrome decoration, with occasional pilasters at the corners and attempts at brick cornices at the eaves. Even interior bearing walls were sometimes of brick. If the walls were of stone, usually fieldstone rubble was used which was frequently stuccoed. Frame construction followed the usual methods, with a few instances of plank walls for interior bearing partitions. There were three possible places for chimneys: either perfectly in the centre running straight up through to the roof, or along one side of the centre hall, or on the outside walls. If two chimneys were wanted, they were frequently placed on opposite outside walls.

Roof framing was comparatively simple and standard, coming to a peak that was either a flat deck surrounded with a cast-iron railing or crowned with a lantern. If the flat deck were wide enough it could be used as an outside gallery, and similarly a large enough lantern could be used as an interior observation gallery.

1 'WOODCHESTER,' BRACEBRIDGE

This house was built for Henry James Bird in 1882 and named after his family's large rambling Elizabethan manor in Yorkshire, England. It has so many features of Fowler's octagonal plan that it could be considered the classic example of that form in Ontario, and the presence of his book in the library suggests it was built according to his ideas. The house has undergone very few structural changes, so that one can easily describe the original plan. The house is also one of the largest of its kind in the province, being three storeys high with a basement that originally contained the kitchen. The basement walls are of squared random-width fieldstone, as were the original walls above; however, some settling necessitated repair and they were subsequently stuccoed. The walls are 16 inches thick on average.

Situated high above a bend in the Muskoka River, the house is approached by a steep winding drive. It stands on a sloping lot, with the west or main entrance level with the grade at the front and the basement kitchen entrance level with the grade at the rear. Four of its sides are 16 feet

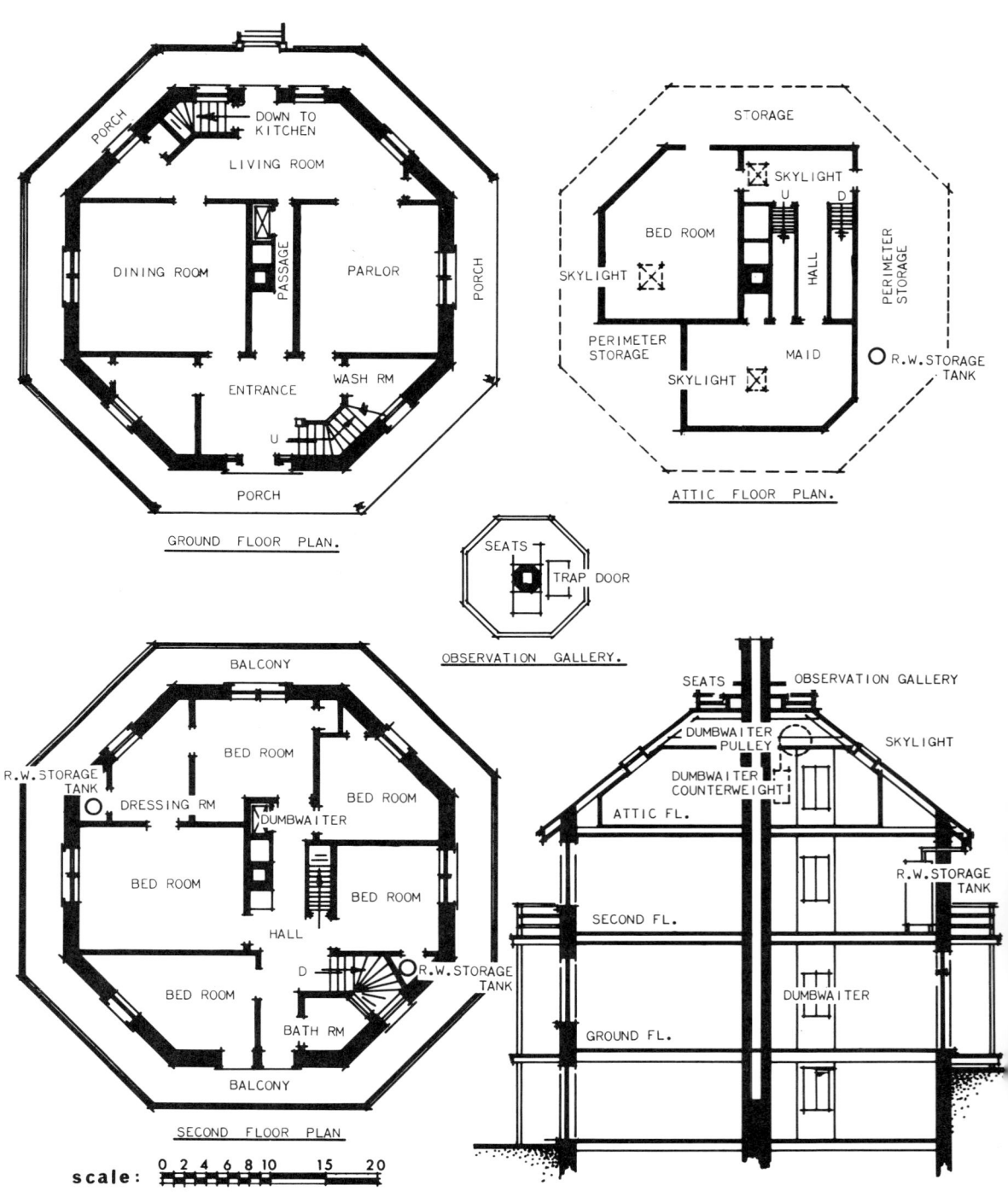

This is the classic Ontario example of Fowler's philosophy in action. Designed very carefully and deliberately from Fowler's recommendations, 'Woodchester' in Bracebridge contains many innovations of the time, such as ventilating shafts, water-pressure tanks, inside plumbing, speaking tubes, and observation galleries.
H10

wide, and the other intermediate four 14 feet, probably to cut down the size of the inevitable triangular rooms. The first floor contains the usual parlour, living room, dining room, and hall. The stairway is open, with an octagonal newel post, so often found in these houses. A small triangular study to the left of the front door was balanced by a washroom and the stairs to the right. An unusual feature of the floor plan is the 2 foot wide passage allowing direct circulation from the hall to the living room at the rear. Originally the house contained no fireplaces, stoves being in common use when it was built. The second floor contained no unusual features, except that there was originally a bathroom as shown in the plan; it is now removed. The attic is as one would expect, but with a crawl space all round the building between the kneewall and the eaves, which is used in several places for storage. A very narrow and steep stairway leads up to the trapdoor in the observation gallery. The gallery itself is about 3 feet wide and forms a walk around the chimney, which is octagonal above the roof. Two seats are built against opposite sides of the chimney, and the view over the low railing and across the countryside must have been magnificent before it was obscured by the present growth of maples and elms.

Like many other houses of its kind and period, 'Woodchester' has a porch surrounding the entire building. The porch might be more accurately described as a walk-around, since it is only 4 feet wide and has no railing at the west side where it is close to the ground. A balcony of the same size encircles the house at the second-floor level, with French doors opening onto it at the front.

The house is remarkable for its time because of its plumbing. Not only did it have indoor lavatories but also a water-pressure system. There were two tanks on the second floor with a direct connection to an outside rainwater leader through the wall, with perhaps an overflow; one tank was above the kitchen sink in the basement and the other fed the washroom on the first floor. There was also a water tank in the attic for the bathroom on the second floor, but I have not been able to discover how it was filled.

One could well expect to find a dumb waiter in this house, but perhaps not such a solid installation as there was. The shaft was divided into two separate 'lanes,' one for the dumb waiter and the other for the counter-weight. The shaft ran from basement to attic, the pulley being at ceiling level in the attic, and measuring some 4 feet in diameter and 18 inches wide. The pulley is still there, although the system has been dismantled, because, when the attic stairs were enclosed, the carpenter forgot to bring the pulley down first and it is too large to be removed now through any existing opening.

There are two other rather extraordinary details to this house. Two ventilator shafts run up on opposite sides of the chimney, with openings just below the ceiling at each floor, and terminate at louvred openings under the seats on the gallery; thus the 'foul' air was conveyed to the outside. Secondly, a speaking tube was built into the wall and connected the kitchen, dining room, and master bedroom. If one blew into it, it made a whistling sound – and doubtless the maid came running.

2 BARRETT HOUSE, PORT HOPE

The exact date of this house is not known, but one might assume that, since it is a house of some pretension and is now near a railroad, it must have been built before the railroad was put through between 1850 and 1855. This would predate the publication of Fowler's book, and indeed the local lore about the house ascribes its design to an English architect who brought the plans with him. There have been minor changes in the plan over the years, but the plan shows the main floor as it existed in 1892. The original owner was Mr William Barrett, a man of some substance in Port Hope who owned a saw and grist mill, the Barrett 'Terrace' (a group of town houses), and had a street named after him. It was acquired by the parents of the present owner in 1892.

Construction is supposed to be of 4 by 4 inch studs with brick 'nogging,' cement stucco on the outside, and lath and plaster on the inside. It is

An outstanding example of early octagons is the Barrett house. The slender posts are indicative of the refined treatment of the interior. It has an air of spaciousness about it which is due, to a great extent, to the large, very light, central hall. H25

interesting to note that the pattern of the lath shows through the plaster on the outside walls; this is because of the lack of insulation and the consequent heat loss, which discolours the plaster and darkens it to a greater degree where there is no lath. This sort of x-ray effect reveals vertical lath at 18 inch centres and horizontal lath at 34 inch centres, the horizontal lath being staggered at midpoint in each alternate row.

The most striking and impressive feature of the plan is the curved stairway with an oval stairwell placed diagonally in a large square hall. Above, and of the same size as, the hall is an octagonal lantern with a 3 foot walk-around enclosing a large octagonal skylight. Square quatrefoil windows in each side of the lantern provide abundant light both to the monitor and, through the skylight, to the entrance hall below. A narrow stairway leads up to the gallery from the hall below.

The most unusual feature of the plan is the shape of the main rooms with French doors at the corners rather than at the centre of the wall area. The drawing room and the double sitting room are both six-sided, but the right angle between the two corner end walls and their overall symmetry make one less conscious of their unusual shape. The French doors at the corners are paired, thus providing ample light and also considerable wall space for furniture arrangement. The French doors themselves are somewhat unusual in that they have transom windows above them. The gentle slope of the

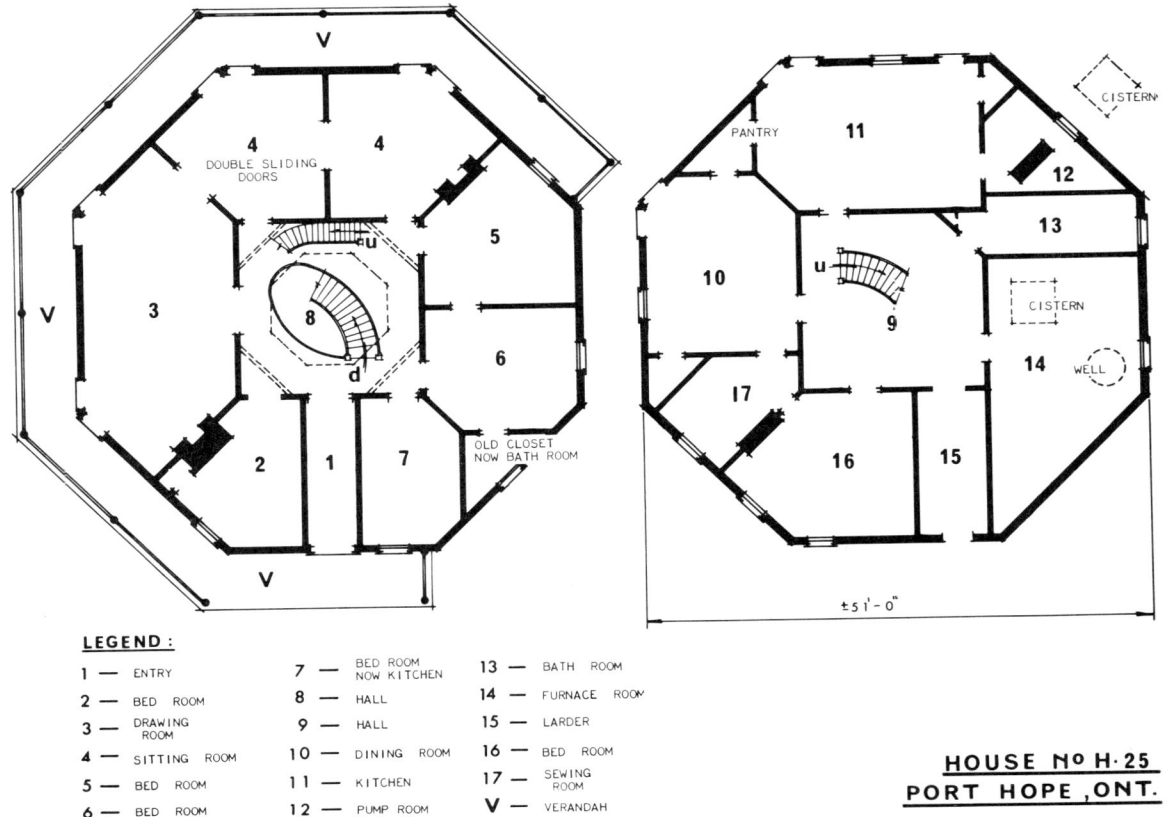

**LEGEND:**

1 — ENTRY
2 — BED ROOM
3 — DRAWING ROOM
4 — SITTING ROOM
5 — BED ROOM
6 — BED ROOM
7 — BED ROOM NOW KITCHEN
8 — HALL
9 — HALL
10 — DINING ROOM
11 — KITCHEN
12 — PUMP ROOM
13 — BATH ROOM
14 — FURNACE ROOM
15 — LARDER
16 — BED ROOM
17 — SEWING ROOM
V — VERANDAH

**HOUSE Nº H·25
PORT HOPE, ONT.**

porch roof permits such windows between the roof and the eaves above, and thus the rooms are bright from the direct 'unshaded' light that comes through them. These windows are also square in quatrefoil design.

The house is remarkably rich in cast plaster ornaments and decoration, particularly in the drawing room. An elaborately struck medallion adorns the centre of the ceiling, an equally detailed plaster cornice crowns its walls, and the main doorways have an ornament above them and mouldings on either side, which extend all round the room along the top of the baseboards. The drawing room also has a fine, well-proportioned fireplace, as does the sitting room.

Mr Barrett must have been enthusiastic about the octagon form, since it seems probable that his influence was responsible for the Port Hope school board's building two octagonal schools in the 1850s. Neither school had a very successful life. In 1856 a certain teacher was transferred to the old but still then existing plank school; shortly afterwards it burned down. The teacher was then appointed to what was known as the East Octagon, and it went up in flames in 1857. He was then discharged, which no doubt explains how the West Octagon, inauspiciously sited on Little Hope Street, lasted until 1873, when it was torn down to make way for a larger school.

## 3 GRIMSBY PARK TEMPLE

This was one of the minor architectural wonders of late nineteenth-century Ontario. Methodist camp meetings had been held on this site in Grimsby since 1846, but attendance had so increased by the 1880s that this large temple was erected in 1888. It was (probably) a sixteen-sided building, open at the sides, covered by a dome, crowned with a sixteen-sided lantern, and rising to a height of 100 feet – from which eminence that city of godliness, Toronto, could be seen across the lake. Sir John A. Macdonald presided at its formal opening on 1 July.

Benches were placed facing the centre and the inevitable shuffling was muffled by 4 inches of sawdust on the floor. 'The Temple,' according to a contemporary guidebook, 'is truly a marvel of construction and baffles description. It stretches its wide umbrella-like expanse over the place where "the fathers" held their out-of-door meetings, and underneath its ample shade seven or eight thousand people can be assembled. The dome of the unique and remarkable creation is 122 feet in diameter and is constructed without brace or truss of any kind.' From an illustration,[9] it appears as if the dome was built in the Roman manner of horizontal rows of bricks, each row receding and of smaller diameter. This construction makes a very strong but bulky dome. Instead of bricks, however, planks were used in horizontal

The Grimsby temple (from an old engraving). c3

layers and spiked together. The weight of the dome was probably well over 180 tons, and its construction was no mean feat of engineering: over 108,000 feet of lumber and 7000 pounds of nails were used for its woodwork. (This weight of nails is equivalent to 100,000 6-inch spikes or 175,000 4-inch ones.)

In 1922 the building was considered a fire hazard and unsafe for occupation. The columns supporting this 'palace of beauty' were dynamited, the whole structure rising slightly into the air before collapsing into a heap of rubble. Parts of the woodwork were used again: old-timers recognized, in the roof sheathing of a house built in the 1920s, the curved boards of the roof of the old Temple. *Sic transit* ...

### 4 THE OCTAGONAL TOWER NEAR BEWDLEY

This remarkable building on the shores of Rice Lake has long since disappeared, but the farm on which it stood is still called Tower Farm. In 1911, however, it was the source of inspiration to an unknown poet of the calibre of James McIntyre of Paris, reputedly Ontario's worst, and the resultant poetic eruption is appended for architectural and historical reasons alone – with the author's apologies.

#### TOWER FARM

Those who find in history any interest or charm,
There's something quite romantic in the tale of Tower Farm.

Away off in England, very many years ago
A gentleman named B's was plunged in heavy woe,
His wife he'd lost, and what made grief more profound
He had seen before his eyes, his two fair daughters drowned.

The old scenes were too painful, he longed afar to roam,
So he sailed away to Canada to establish a new home.
With other friends he ventured to this our own fair land
And bought a tract of country along Rice Lake strand.

That 'mid strange new surroundings he might perhaps forget
His trials great and many – and might even be happy yet.

Not far from the Lake he selected a fine site,
From where through the trees he could glimpse the water bright.
He found a rounded knoll on a gently sloping hill
And there began to exercise his architectural skill.

I must explain just here, he had a most eccentric mind
And a building such as his – you could hardly find.
It was eight stories high, and in form an octagon,
With woodwork of red cedar, and walls of brick and stone.

And of rooms upon each floor, there was really only one
From the basement a stair ladder led to the upper storey
Which was finished, so we're told – as an observatory.
What was the means of ingress, I cannot now declare
But a subterranean passage led to outer air.

These tower rooms were furnished with rare brick-a-brack and china,
Such silver and quaint furniture are not now found in Mina.

On Sundays when the settlers round came to the Tower to meeting
The host would stop his service to give latecomers greeting.
He fraternized with th'Indians, wore their blanket suit and belt,
With knife or tomahawk attached, and moccasins of soft felt.

But there was one thing in their dress at which he drew the line,
His own good head-gear, he would simply not resign.

He must have cut a figure. One could hardly fail to see
In this peculiar garb, sure proof of his eccentricity,
And when in frosty weather he drove to the nearest town
He wore his high silk topper, with silk kerchief fastened down.

But some years of country living, thus near to nature's heart
Did not bring him satisfaction. He decided to depart
To fresher field and pastures new, so his Tower, land and store
He sold to a wealthy Scotchman and was seen round here no more.

That tarried long at wine – and forgot his estate
In drunken stupor. Thus he almost met his fate
When the tower with all its treasures was burned quite to the ground –

Though he managed to escape. After some looking around
He built a more modern house on some-what level space
And planted trees and made of it a very charming place.

But in this fair Eden came the serpent – Drink – Again
And brought as always in its wake – shame, suffering and pain

At last his wife's fond hope, that if a change he'd make
He might in new environment be able to forsake
His evil habit, and again Tower Farm was sold
And they went to California which then lured men by its gold

Since then the Farm has had its share of changes and reverse
But now 'twill surely prosper – under Mr. and Mrs. Nurse.

August 1911

## 5 DEADHOUSES

Octagonal 'deadhouses' are unique to Ontario. Apart from one of uncertain date at Port Carling, they were confined to towns on or near Yonge Street and were built between the 1850s (in Toronto) and 1914, when the fashion expired on the shores of Lake Simcoe at Sutton (see map, p. 332).

There were two cemeteries found in Toronto in the fifties, the Necropolis in 1850 (D8) and St Michael's in 1855 (D6). They both had octagonal deadhouses or vaults, that of the Necropolis being demolished in 1910 and that at St Michael's still standing, though now scheduled for destruction. Their general design was followed by the deadhouses at Richmond Hill (1863, D7), King City (D3), Aurora (1863, D2), Newmarket (1870–71, D4), Bolton (1890–93, D1), Queensville (D5), Kettleby (1899, D10), and Sutton (D9).

The St Michael's vault is of excellent Gothic design, with pleasing proportions and a fine cupola, though the finial has rotted away. Its only defect is perhaps that the doorway is somewhat too large. The vault is clearly the work of a professional, and one might conjecture that either William Thomas, who designed St Michael's Cathedral and Palace, or Gundry and Langley, who designed the spire that was added to the cathedral in 1866,

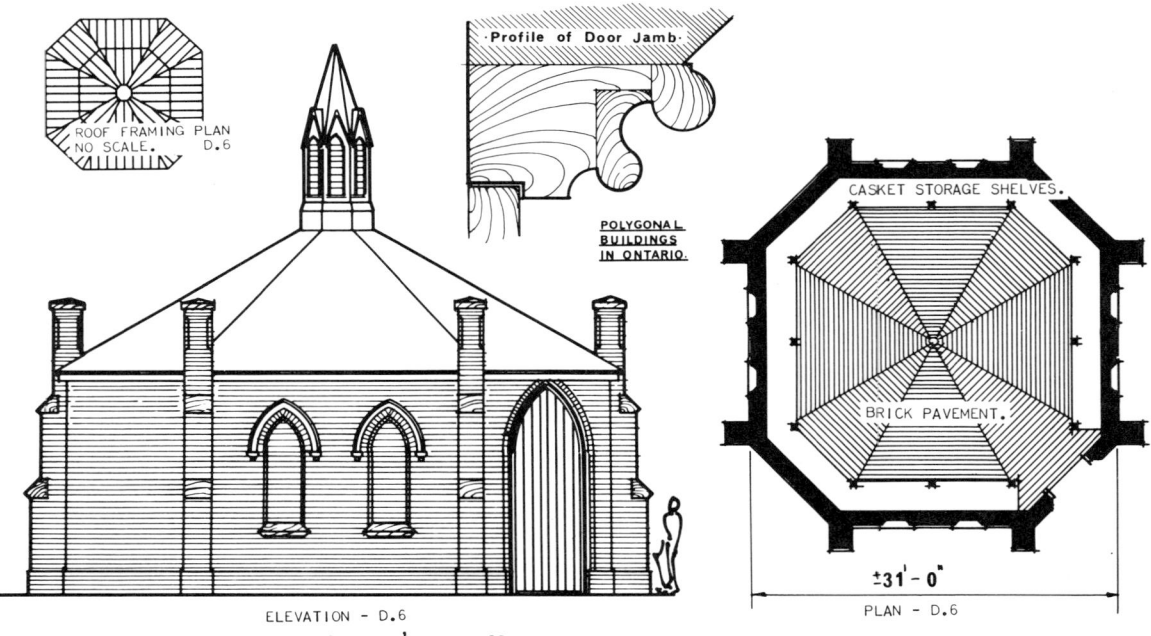

VAULT IN OLD ST. MICHAEL'S CEMETERY. ±1855

were responsible for it. The floor is level with the grade and paved with bricks on end. Some of the casket shelves, running round the inside of the walls, are still in place. The wooden mouldings over the windows are still the original and are applied directly to the brickwork. The wooden trim around the door is particularly well done. Unexpectedly, however, in such a fine structure, the corbels in the buttresses, as well as the buttress caps and the sills in the dummy windows, are all made of wood – an economy not consistent with good construction. There are only two tie beams at the plates, running at right angles to one another along the major axes of the building. The roof rafters make an interesting pattern with a hip rafter at each of the eight corners and with the framework which forms an octagonal opening for the graceful lantern.

The deadhouse in St Michael's cemetery, Toronto. It is the most ambitious of the group and is now slated for demolition. The roof framing makes an interesting pattern which is a pleasant experience – at least to the living. D6

The lantern on the Richmond Hill vault. D7

The deadhouse at Richmond Hill is distinguished by its beautifully proportioned lantern, complete with probably the original finial. The walls are of buff brick laid in Flemish bond, with quoins alternating at the corners. A single Gothic door is the only opening in the structure.

From the minutes of the session book of Richmond Hill Presbyterian Church, we can gain some idea of the social history behind these vaults. On 27 March 1863 the session agreed to appoint a committee to look into costs and plans and to examine the vaults in Toronto. Next month the committee reported 'that they had visited several vaults in Toronto and found the one at the Necropolis would be the most suitable. Its measurements being 19 ft. 6" across inside and of an octagon shape, covered with tin and substantially built of brick floor and stone foundation – 76 pounds, total cost.' The trustees were then authorized to borrow enough money to erect a vault but not for more than $320. 'It was also moved that the tariff of fees for depositing Bodies in the dead house be the same as at the Necropolis in Toronto, but any body taken away from the vault to another church yard would be charged an extra fifty cents. Bodies over 10 years old $2. per month and under 10 years of age $1. per month.' By September, specifications were ready and tenders invited; the lower of the two received, at $368, was accepted. The session also agreed in September that 'fees for the bodies must be deposited at the time the body is put in the vault, and two weeks of a month be considered as a full month, payable before the body is removed from the vault.' The vault was completed that same year, as is evidenced by a letter to the editor of the *Newmarket Era* published on Christmas Day:

Polygonal buildings 311

Dear Sir – Having attended the funeral of a much respected deceased friend last week at Richmond Hill, I was much pleased to observe that the minister of the Presbyterian Church at that place has erected a neat and substantial brick vault, of an octagon shape, covered with tin and surmounted with a neat cupola. The fact that numerous bodies are annually purloined from country churchyards adds much to the importance and necessity for such a building, and all parties who are so unfortunate as to loose any of their relatives will find in this Vault a safe place of deposit until the ensuing spring. I learn that the charges are very moderate – similar to those now made by the Necropolis Comp'y in Toronto.

December 21st, 1863.
Yours truly,
Traveller.

The Aurora vault was built in 1868 by a Mr Doan, for an unrecorded sum. It is still in excellent condition, and the lantern is the best preserved of all. Unfortunately the lantern is too tall for the rest of the building, thus spoiling the proportions of the whole. The Aurora 'repository' served as a pattern for one at Newmarket built two or three years later and demolished in 1940. John Stokes, an English civil engineer who designed, among others, the Presbyterian church at Newmarket and his own (now the Phillipps) home in Sharon,[10] prepared the plans for this vault, receiving $20 for his trouble.[11]

The lantern at Aurora is well preserved, but too tall for good proportion, thus making the building slightly top-heavy. D2

The cemetery records contain the following costs for labour and materials:

| | |
|---|---:|
| W.V. Sutherland, contractor for carpentry | $100.00 |
| Hardware | 1.40 |
| Excavating, levelling and drawing stone | 48.61 |
| Face stone sills and laying some | 49.50 |
| Blacksmithing | 7.17 |
| Mason and brickwork | 68.06 |
| Brick purchased at Mr. Stickwood's brickyard in Newmarket – 14,320 brick @ $5.75 per M | 81.82 |
| Lime | 24.00 |
| Sand | 10.00 |
| Total cost | $390.56 |

Queensville. The best-proportioned of the smaller dead-houses. D5

# Polygonal buildings

The Aurora and Newmarket vaults were visited by members of the Bolton cemetery committee in the early 1890s, and a vault was put up there in 1893–94. Aurora would appear also to have been the model for the one at King City, and it may be that, since the Bolton delegation did not visit King City, we may assume that the vault was built after 1892 or so. At any rate, it has a slightly wider door than that at Aurora, which makes it look poorly proportioned, and it is at present in a poor state of preservation. The Queensville vault, however, is still well preserved, and its steeper roof and shorter lantern, along with four gables on its major sides, give it a more finished and very pleasing appearance. The Sutton vault and the Port Carling vault – of simple frame construction – are of no great architectural significance.

Bolton. This house is rather out of proportion, especially the lantern. D1

**RULES RESPECTING VISITORS To THE LAUREL HILL CEMETERY**

No riding or driving faster than a walk. No Bicycles allowed on the grounds. Drivers of carriages at funerals are required to attend to their horses during funeral ceremonies, and will be held liable for any damage caused by them. No driving allowed upon, or over, any burial plot. Dogs not admitted. Smoking strictly forbidden. Visitors are reminded that these grounds are sacredly devoted to the dead, therefore, quiet and orderly behaviour is requested, and any unruly conduct will be punished as law may direct. BY ORDER

## 6 PRIVIES

David Willson seceded from the Quakers to found his own sect, the Children of Peace, who settled in Sharon and built their unique temple for the rituals invented by Willson. Since he planned all the buildings in the Sharon Temple complex, he may be assumed to have designed this one too. The buildings all date from 1825–32, and we can fairly confidently ascribe the privy to that period. This little structure thus has the distinction of being the oldest surviving privy in Ontario (M7). Apart from its age, however, it is unique also in being the only extant round one. A large octagon, with three 'compartments' for use and one for cleaning out, served the same humble purpose at 'Killiecrankie' in Port Sandfield until burned down several years ago (M13). An octagonal 'two-compartment' privy still stands at Welcome (M8).

LEFT The little round privy at Sharon – the oldest extant in Ontario. M7

RIGHT The unique little two-compartment privy at Welcome. M8

And while we are on the subject – perhaps the only log privy in existence, on the old Monk Road east of Highway 48.

The most sophisticated single seater: at Penryhn house, Port Hope, now demolished

·PORT SANDFIELD·

trapdoor for cleanout.

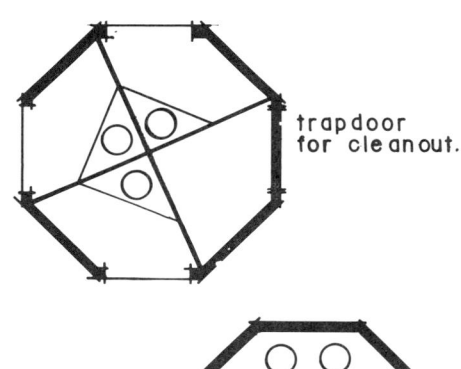

·WELCOME·

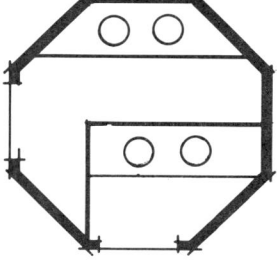

SCALE: 0 1' 2' 3' 4' 5'

## ANNOTATED LIST OF ONTARIO POLYGONS

- H houses
- B barns
- C churches
- D deadhouses
- S schools
- J jails
- M miscellaneous
- \* personally inspected (information on other buildings was obtained from reliable sources)
- † demolished

### H1 *Bowmanville, 1876–81*\*

Supposedly designed by the Rev. W.H. Heu de Bourk as a parsonage for the Congregational church. 42 feet across flats, two storeys high, stuccoed walls, wide but simple roof overhang, square central hall, square lantern with windows on two opposite sides and two-flued chimneys on the others. In excellent repair.

### H2 *Cobden*\*

Two storeys high with an attic, gabled on four principal axes, central chimney, walls of red brick with stone quoins at corners, windows single double-hung symmetrically spaced on each wall.

### H3 *Granton, 1872*\*

Built by Albert Beatson, one of the pioneers of this area. Grout (that is, concrete) walls in main octagon and also in back kitchen, which was possibly added later; on sloping site with front door at one level and rear (basement) door at another; main floor contains living room and three bedrooms, basement contains kitchen and bedroom; only one square room.

### H4 *Norval*\*

Sometimes listed as being near Huttonville. It is of brick construction with the walls of the octagon laid in traditional Flemish bond. Structural differences suggest that the (west) wing is a later addition. Interior bearing walls, forming 15 foot square windowless room from basement to attic, are constructed of 2 by 6 inch horizontal planks staggered to form key for plaster. Very comfortable stair. Design allegedly by Matthew Bird who presumably designed the Maple (H5) and Brampton (H21) octagons, is rather odd: both fireplaces on west wall corners; large windowless centre hall; perhaps Bird's first and experimental attempt?

### H5 *Maple, 1840–42*\*

Locally called the 'round' house and attributed to Bird. Plan shows alterations made over the years: east window on ground flour became a door, house converted into duplex causing the awkward stair, plumbing added. Never any fireplaces. All lumber used said to have been cut on the property, bricks burned on the site, scallops, frets, and brackets of interior trim cut by owner's (Adam or Jacob Rupert) daughters. Supposed to have cost $3000.

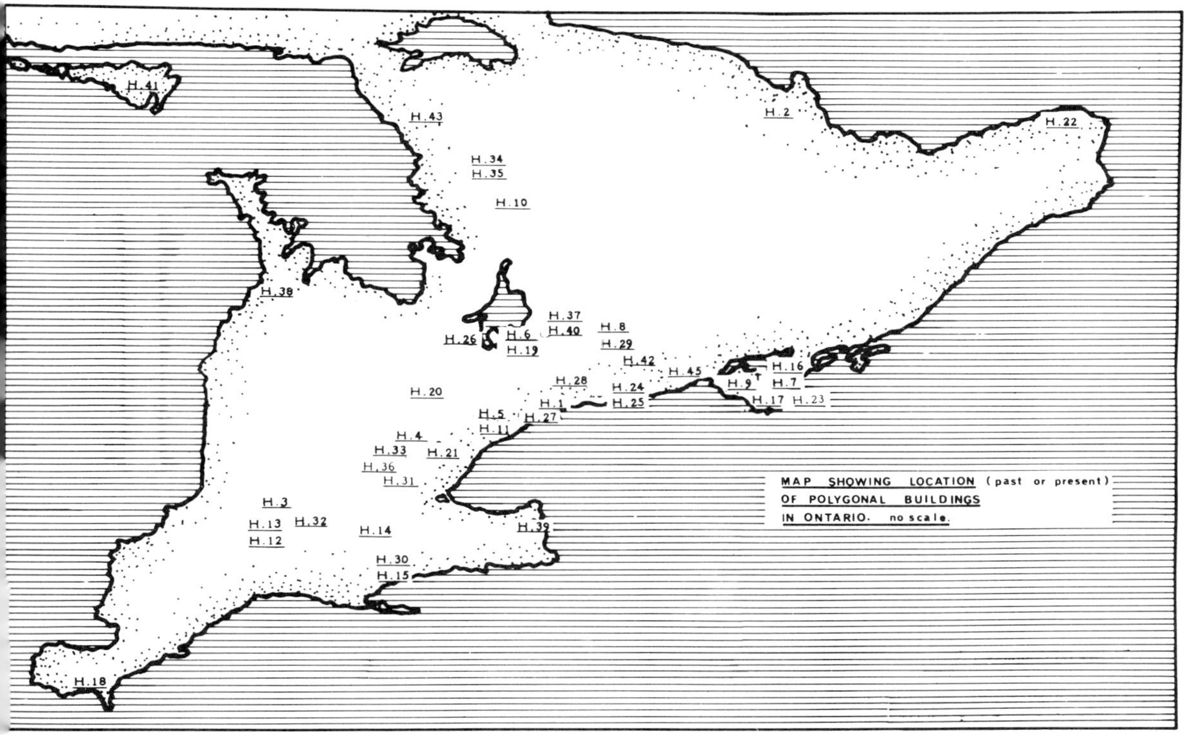

MAP SHOWING LOCATION (past or present) OF POLYGONAL BUILDINGS IN ONTARIO. no scale.

Granton.
One of the smaller octagonal cottages. H3

Maple. This house has been severely altered inside, but fortunately the fine front door has been retained. The lantern is in good proportion. H5

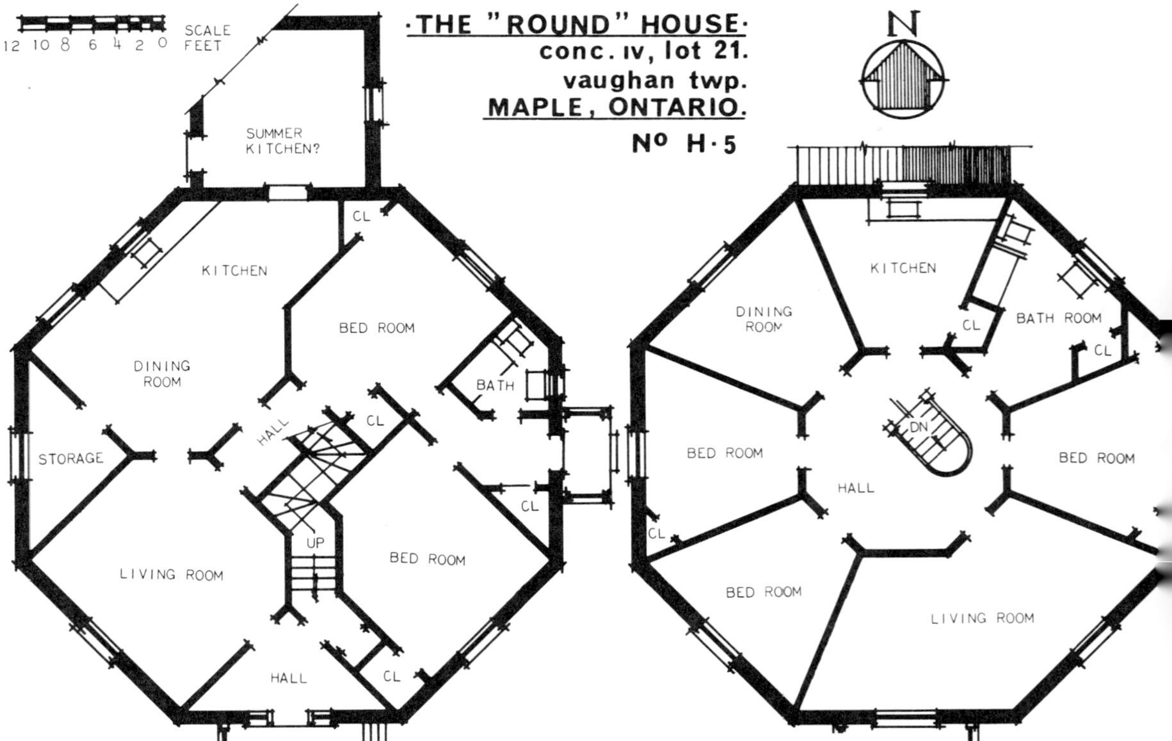

·THE "ROUND" HOUSE·
conc. IV, lot 21.
vaughan twp.
MAPLE, ONTARIO.
Nº H·5

·GROUND FLOOR·

·SECOND FLOOR·

Polygonal buildings 319

H6 *Duclos Point, 1888\**
Built for present owner's father (Richard Cransberry) by James Turner from Wilfrid, Ontario, using bricks from Edward Arnold's brickyard one mile to the south. Walls 12 inches thick composed of 4 inch brick veneer, 2 by 6 studs filled with cowhair and plaster for insulation. 1 inch rough sheathing, and lath and plaster. Dumb waiter unusually located: was the door next to it originally a window? Whole plan and appearance very asymmetrical with irregularly spaced doors and windows.

H7 *Picton\**
Two storeys high with a central chimney and no lantern. Walls, supposedly of grout, 12 to 13 inches thick, stuccoed on outside. Main floor consists of entry with three rooms of about equal size, elegantly finished with moulded plaster cornice, elliptical arches framing bay windows, and console brackets at the springing of the arches. Two main rooms have marble fireplaces back in internal corners, and third room had alcove framed by elliptical arch, now plastered over but still visible. Extensive alterations made recently to convert it into apartments.

H8 *Peterborough, 1860–70\*†*
Stood at 705 George Street North until destroyed in 1962. Built by William Lee for his brother John, a millwright; walls of thick wide planks piled on top of one another with an inch of plaster between; at one time a verandah and balcony ran round the house; lantern reached by narrow stair. Five rooms downstairs, and four bedrooms upstairs; also a low-ceilinged basement and a probably later addition to the rear.

H9 *Ameliasburg, c. 1860\**
Built by Owen Roblin (whose mill is now restored at Pioneer Village, Toronto) for his son Robert and his wife. Typical octagon with surrounding porch, central lantern illuminating attic, two chimneys on opposite outside walls. Interior extensively changed, so plan shows present layout. Some refinement in deeply shouldered mouldings at head of doors and windows, wide sliding doors with elliptical arch and French doors in main room; trim rather crude, however, being mainly flat fillets in several planes with occasional bevel for depth.

H10 *Bracebridge, 1882\**
See text

H11 *Leaside, 1854\*†*
Built south of Millwood Road near the present Memorial Gardens by William, son of John, Lea who bought several hundred acres and farmed in what is now Leaside, when he set up his own farm; burned down in 1915. Bricks made from nearby claybeds, now used by Don Valley Brick Company, and laid in Flemish bond as was characteristic of that period. Joist pockets for a porch were provided, but porch was never built. Photograph taken just after the fire suggests polychrome brickwork, pilasters at each corner, and stone lintels over all openings. Size of house can be calculated by counting the bricks in the photograph. According to memory of one of William Lea's grandchildren, plan contained circular entrance hall and dumb waiter; there were four bedrooms on second floor, three occupied by hired help.

Picton. A typical octagon with central chimney and no lantern. H7

This house in Peterborough was demolished several years ago. It was a good example of the two-chimney-with-lantern type. H8

Polygonal buildings 321

The Roblin house at Ameliasburg, which was a fine home in its day but has been severely 'butchered' inside since then. It is a typical two-chimney type with lantern. Unfortunately the chimneys are located directly above the windows which gives it a very uncomfortable appearance. H9

Leaside octagon, still smouldering after the fire, is shown in this old photograph. H11

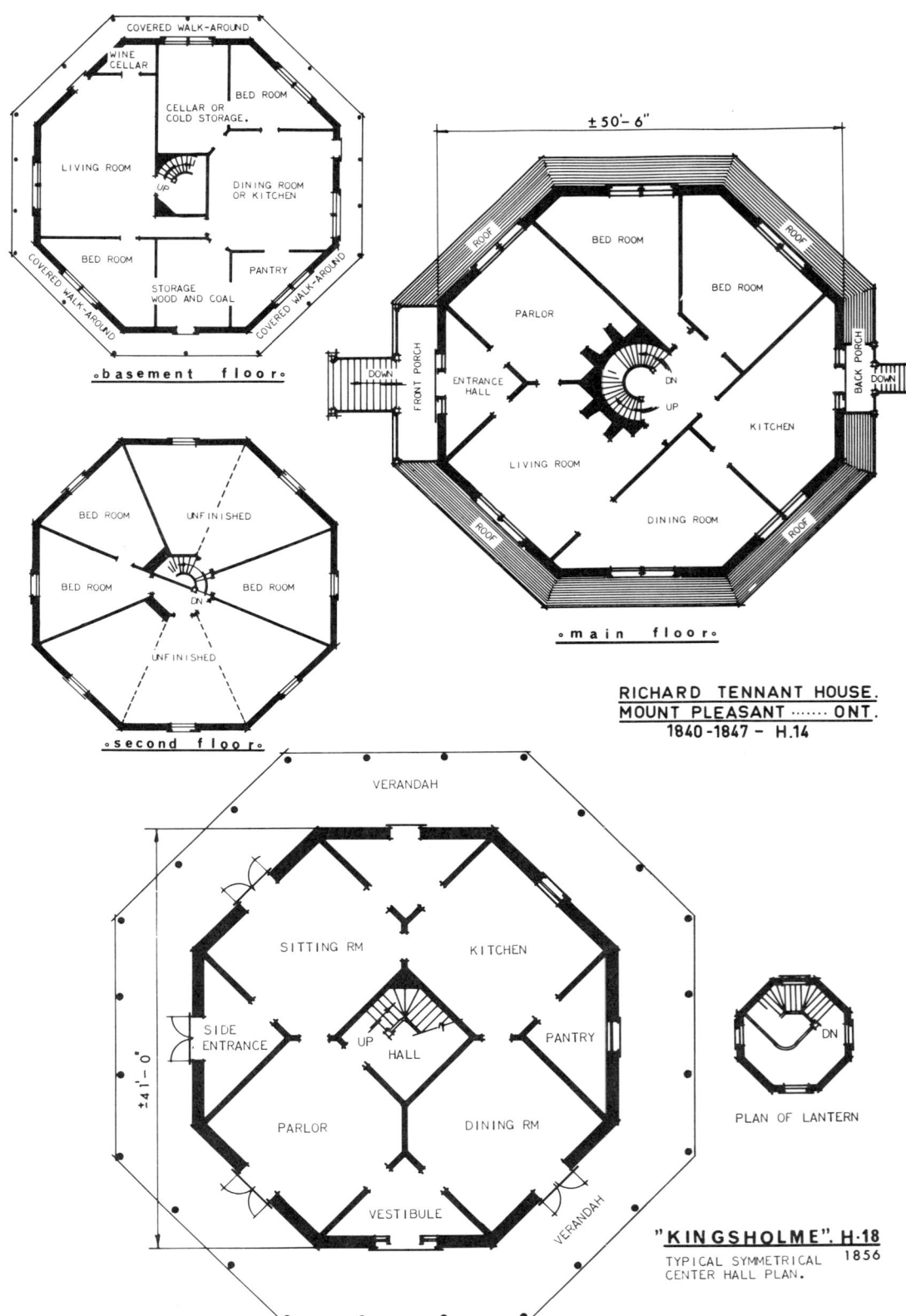

H12 *Lambeth, 1848*†*

Dr Joseph Alexander came from Norwich County in 1848 to Lambeth and built his first octagonal house of frame construction with dormer windows projecting from each gable. The men sent to cut the timbers for the house are said to have used 20 foot lengths instead of 30, so the house was rather queer and patched in appearance. Later used as a barn, when it was burned down.

H13 *London, 1868–78*†*

After a spell in Philadelphia, Lancaster settled in London and built his second octagon at what is now 368–70 Dundas Street. Of brick, with 4 inch air space between inner and outer walls and with fitted corners. Basement contained office and waiting room, store, and furnace room which boasted a coal furnace; first floor, drawing room, dining room, kitchen, and main bedroom; second floor, one large guest room and three other bedrooms (that could be converted into seven bedrooms if necessary). House contained several bathrooms that fascinated crowds who came to church socials held in it later. Circular stairway connected all three floors. Lancaster's son claimed house was easy to work in, his sisters that it was not!

H14 *Mount Pleasant, 1842–48**

Original owner was Richard Tennant. About 30 feet high without the lantern and from 36 to 40 feet wide; the basement above ground for most of its height. Walls of grout finish, the cement having come as ballast in sailing ships from Montreal and Buffalo. Ceiling heights are: basement, 8 feet; ground floor, 12 feet; second floor, 8 feet. Rooms on second floor are pie-shaped, house has eight steep and high gables; rooms on main floor form squares and triangles. Tennant's grand-niece recalls: 'a three-foot stone wall in front with an iron picket fence atop a large double iron gate, and a gravel drive circling the house. The grounds had an old-fashioned garden with lovely flowers and a privet hedge on either side of the circular drive. The steps up to the verandah were directly in front of the main entrance. The porch surrounded the whole house. The steps which are there now seemed to me so stupid because the original steps were so solid-looking and wide. The house looks so out of proportion with the verandah pulled down.'

H15 *Simcoe**

Situated on Queensway East. Originally owned by the Counter family.

H16 *Mountain View**

On concession III of Ameliasburg just west of Highway 14, it is sometimes referred to as the Anderson house. Large octagon with stone walls, now stuccoed over, and a flat octagonal area surrounded by railing instead of a lantern. Chimney slightly off centre, straight-run central stairway, asymmetrical plan with only one square room. Verandah has been removed. Alterations also made to plan, but that shown here is an attempt at the original layout.

H17 *Bloomfield†?*

A bit of a puzzle since records do not even agree that it existed. At any rate, it is now destroyed.

At Mount Pleasant. The most pleasant of the polygonals in the province before several extensive changes for the worse were made. H14

Kingsville. This is a very fine house indeed, as witnessed by the French doors. The porch posts have been replaced. Note the central chimney passing through the lantern; this is unusual. H18

Polygonal buildings 325

H18 *Kingsville*, 1856*
Built for Col. James King, founder of Kingsville, and named 'Kingsholme.' According to tradition, builder was half drunk during its erection, misread the instructions, and so the second-floor ceiling is higher than the first. Apart from that, house is large and solidly built, interior plaster being applied directly onto brick walls and still perfectly dry. Typical symmetrical plan with central hall rising to lantern. Originally no basement. Two wings added in 1881 and probably parlour fireplace at the same time (omitted in plan). Heated with stoves from the beginning. Original posts of verandah replaced. Fine interior trim, with shouldered mouldings around the head of all openings in principal rooms; main rooms also had double French doors to verandah.

H19 *Keswick*\*†
Destroyed around 1960, so plan based on accounts of two former owners. One-storey house, each face about 13 feet; built of 2 inch vertical planks housed centrally in sill and plate; lath nailed directly to planks and plastered; 2 foot square chimney opening at ridge. Square central (and so very dark) living room, similar to H21. Originally a trapdoor opened in floor to small cold cellar, but a basement was added later.

H20 *Bolton*\*
On the west half of lot 21, concession V, Albion Township; a small house, awkwardly arranged, all rooms except one small bedroom upstairs being of irregular shape. Walls of poor-quality grout, mixed too lean (and now full of tiny air bubbles and so porous) and with too much sand (walls crumble when rubbed). Soon to be abandoned. Has been renovated lately.

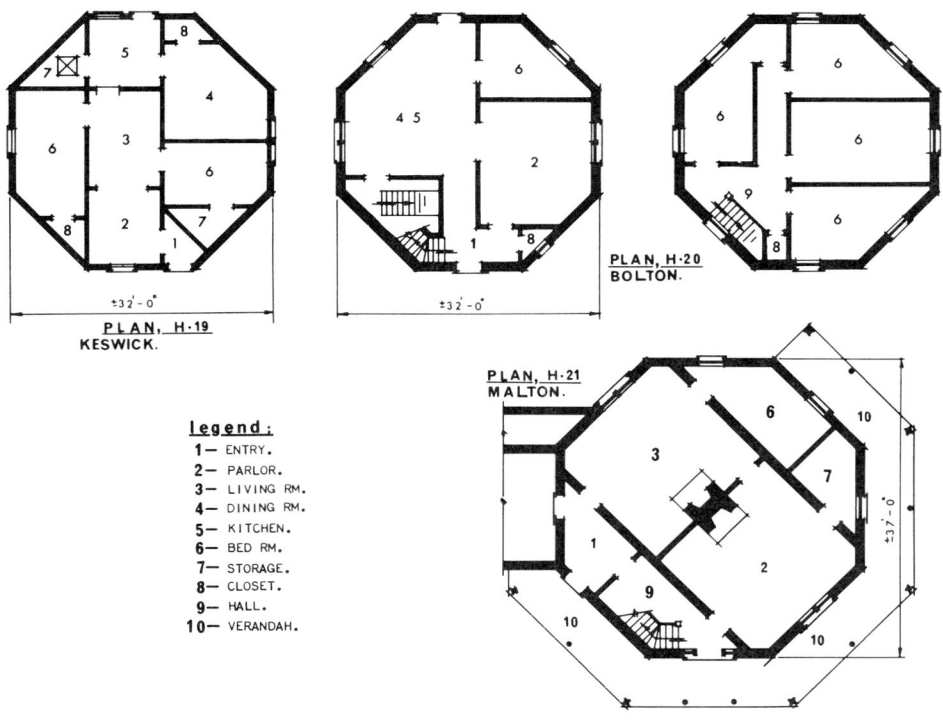

legend:
1— ENTRY.
2— PARLOR.
3— LIVING RM.
4— DINING RM.
5— KITCHEN.
6— BED RM.
7— STORAGE.
8— CLOSET.
9— HALL.
10— VERANDAH.

### H21 *Malton*, 1855–60\*
Probably built for Isaac Bird by George Blane for $3600–3800, and now in the hands of a land development company. Well built of bricks made on the site, with plaster applied directly to inner wall; pilasters at the corners (as in H5) and patterned polychrome entablature running round entire building. Basement has dirt floor, which is very wet, but no rot in the joists; wings probably added sometime after 1863. Hallway has fine stairway with superior turned balusters and a curve instead of a corner at the first turn; central chimney with double fireplace, back to back, on ground floor. Two 12 inch solid-brick interior walls from basement to ceiling with wooden lintels over openings therein form main interior bearing walls.

### H22 *Hawkesbury*, 1860–70\*
Expensively built, with apparently brick-core walls with stucco facing. Fine central curved stairway with turned balusters for full height of building. Roof altered to allow for more rooms in the attic and a wing added to the rear. Plan generally awkward, with little attempt at squared room. Splendid carved 'Jacobean' mantel in living room – bought at Chicago fair in 1891 where it had won first prize.

### H23 *Picton*\*
Well preserved brickwork, red, laid in common bond; Victorian character to windows: narrow, high, with brick mullion; second-floor windows small with top only 5 feet above floor and a mantel-like shelf stretching across the top connecting each pair; ceiling higher than the eaves all the way round. Octagonal newel post. Lantern removed some years ago because of leaky roof.

### H24 *Port Hope*\*
Hexagonal, small, one storey in height; brick walls with suggestion of pilasters at corners; windows central on side with top corners cut at 45 degrees; square central chimney and peaked roof.

### H25 *Port Hope*, 1833–50\*
See text

### H26 *Tollendale*\*†
Demolished in 1960, no other information available.

### H27 *Oshawa*, 1870?\*
On Lloyd Street; of frame construction, two storeys in height, with a rather fine bracketed Victorian eave and cornice. Built by Thomas Kirkland on land bought from Hiram Barber. Two main rooms downstairs and upstairs, according to the owner, 'two decent bedrooms and two funny little rooms.' Stove in the centre, with central chimney out through the roof.

### H28 *Leskard*†
A one-storey frame cottage on a stone foundation, with stucco outside and plaster inside; no attic and no lantern, the roof coming to a peak; verandah right around; basement with outside entrance and lightwells for its windows; tongue-and-groove ceiling (no plaster). Original owner John Kivell.

Polygonal buildings 327

A most stately polygonal house, situated at Hawkesbury. The mansard roof is a later additon. H22

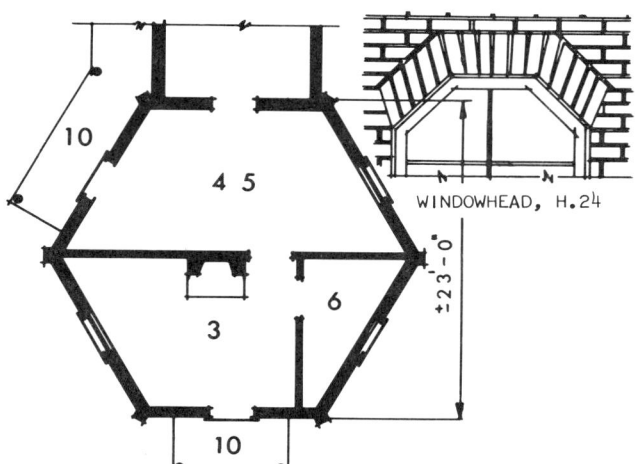

PLAN, H·24
PORT HOPE

### H29 *Millbrook**

About one mile south of the village. Quite small, each side 13 feet, with two storeys; characteristic encircling verandah; roof comes to a peak crowned by small finial; general treatment quite simple; kitchen wing no doubt an addition. Similar to H28 and perhaps built by same builder.

### H30 *Simcoe*, pre-1840?†

One-storey cottage built by Duncan Campbell on northeast corner of Argyle and Norfolk streets, and moved in 1840. Contained entrance hall, combined living and dining room, kitchen, pantry, and three bedrooms; usual porch surrounding the building. Demolished in late 1890s (See also B15.)

### H31 *Lowville*, 1861*

On the Guelph line at Lowville, west of Milton, on the brow of a hill with a good view of Lowville valley. Basement kitchen with large fireplace and bake-oven alongside; rectangular living and dining rooms on main floor; all other rooms (including present kitchen) triangular; central winding stairway to attic, which also serves as lantern.

### H32 *Ingersoll**

About a mile southeast of centre of town; smallest octagonal house I know of; slated for demolition.

### H33 *Brampton**

A half-octagon on Main Street North (see M16).

Ingersoll
Perhaps the smallest octagonal house in Ontario.
H32

## Polygonal buildings 329

H34 *Port Sandfield West*, 1886*

'Killiecrankie,' built as a summer home by W.I. Mackenzie and inhabited by his daughter, Miss E.K. 'Single by Choice' Mackenzie until 1955. Walls of 2 by 4 inch studs, not dressed, 16 inches apart; outside sheathing 6 inch horizontal V, 1 full inch thick, mostly of pine, sometimes of basswood. Corners of two 4 inch vertical boards, mitred with about 1¼ inch bead; sheathing butts against other edge of vertical corner pieces. Verandah 8 feet wide round the building. No lantern, but flat railed observation deck, and no central hall. Four small triangular gables in roof, three of which (except the one facing inland) had a small pane of red glass behind which a candle was put in the evenings as a sign that it was time to come home. Living room occupied front half of ground floor, along with dining room and small study. Very comfortable stairway leads from living room to second floor. Living room is panelled in 4 inch V strips of black ash, as is dining room; both rooms have French doors to verandah. Upstairs four bedrooms, no bathroom; their outside walls of 6 inch horizontal boarding, internal walls vertical V stripping. Doors, four panel type each with small knocker; joints in door are simple mortise and tenon without usual dowels, panels are simple flat fields with o-gee moulding around each; hinges of patterned cast iron. Octagonal observation gallery, supported by posts on attic floor, entered through trapdoor. Kitchen built at same time as house as separate unit butting on to verandah. Octagonal privy, of unique plan with three compartments, but now burned down.

H35 *Port Sandfield East*†

H36 *Guelph*\*

Of red brick, probably from Milton. One storey, with stair to lantern large enough to be a room, as in Lowville (H31) house. No fireplace, so probably built late. Exterior roughcast at one time, then covered with brick siding. Badly mutilated and in poor repair; scheduled for demolition.

H37 *Lindsay*

At Lifford, Manvers Township, Durham County, south side, concession x, ¾ mile east of Highway 35.

H38 *Southampton*

H39 *Niagara Falls*, 1905*

1783 Summer Street, owned by daughter of original owner who has builder's drawings.

H40 *Oakwood*

H41 *Little Current*, c. 1885

Two-storeyed hexagon, originally covered with board and batten; hexagonal lantern. Much altered; fine spiral staircase replaced by conventional one, and outside covered with asbestos shingles. Once supposed an unlucky or haunted house, with bodies buried in the yard: such tales, according to present owner, are like folksongs – 'nothing completely untrue nor pure gold.'

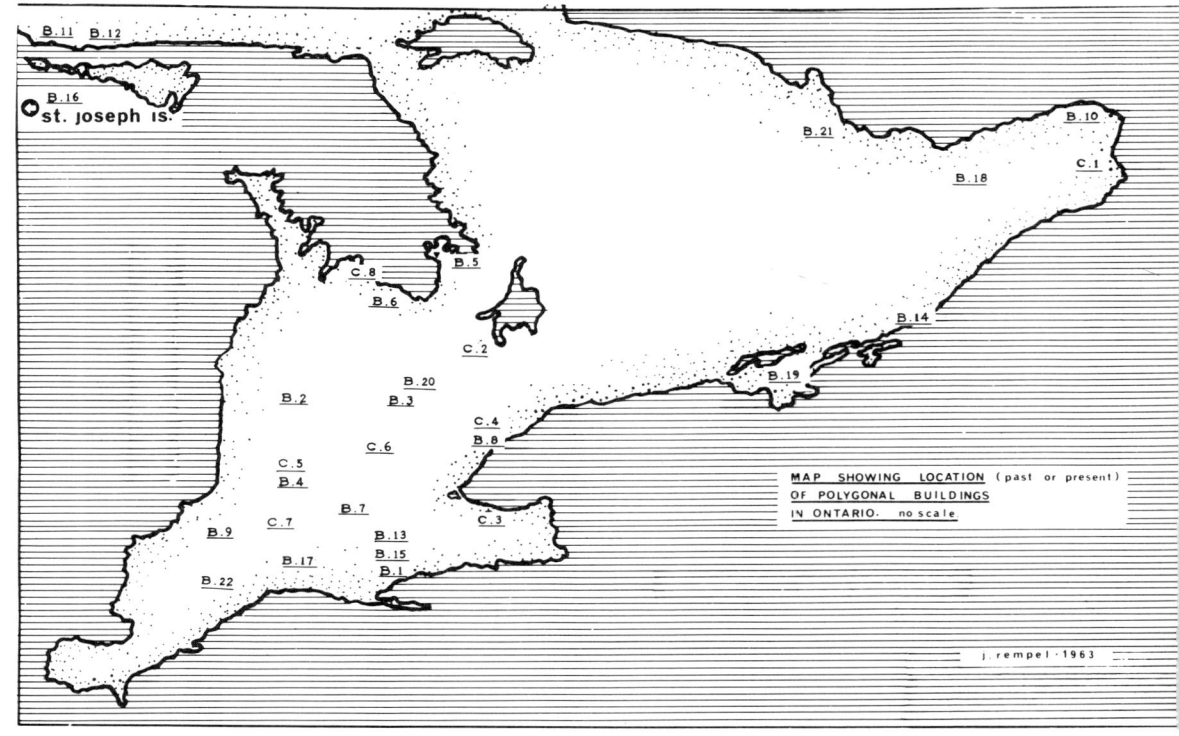

H42 *Tower Farm*†
See text

H43 *McKellar*

H44 *On Attawapiskat River*, post-1900

H45 *East of Colborne*
Owned by Mrs Hattie Gardener, Parliament Street.

B1 *Simcoe*†
Eight-sided brick barn built on RR 4 by Andrew Vandenburg, burned down in early 1950s.

B2 *Lucknow*, 1880–90*
Built 'well before 1900' on lot 7, concession XI, Ashfield Township, by father or grandfather of present owners of Henderson's lumber yard, Lucknow. Twenty foot side, hence about 54 across, with no intermediate supports for roof framing; building thus one large shell. Wall about 16 feet from plate to sill. Plates form hoop in tension, and ridge, forming base for lantern, is ring in compression. One intermediate set of tie-beams between plate and ridge. Joints bolted. A careful piece of work still plumb and true.

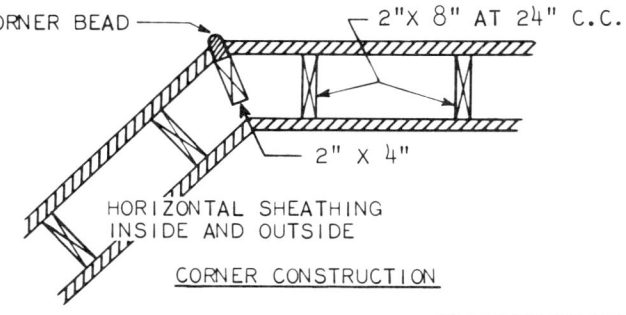
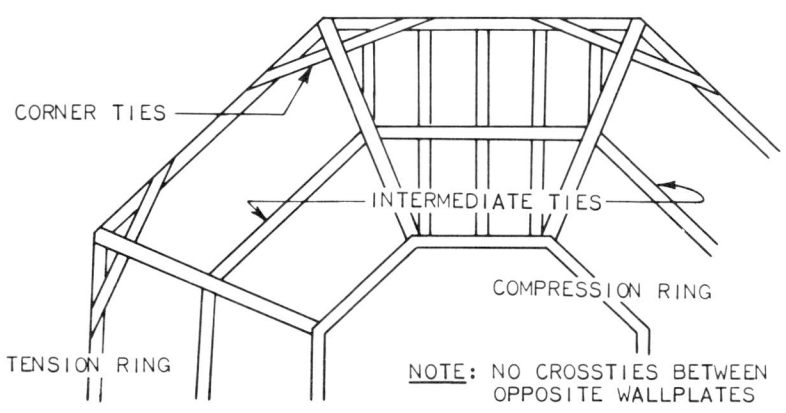

Roof construction of the barn at Lucknow. B2

This barn, near Lucknow, was no doubt raised at a later date on a stone foundation. The construction at the corners is interesting. B2

The octagonal barn near Erin. This is the best-proportioned of all the polygonal barns. The lantern and the dovecot are in good relationship and make for a very pleasant composition. B3

The octagonal barn on Dufferin Street in Toronto, now in the Agricultural Museum, Milton. Another example of a barn with a gambrel roof. B8

A good example of a round barn, a little to the east of Hawkesbury. There are very few of these in existence. B10

B3 *Erin, 1895–1900\**
Built by Mr Leffler (or Loeffler) on a farm on Highway 24 near Wellington County boundary. Proportions good throughout; octagonal dovecot above the lantern adds touch of refinement.

B4 *Fullarton, 1895\**
Built by George Hamilton, Jr, on lot 12, concession VII, Fullarton Township. All timbers of rock elm; raising took two days, with the use of block and tackle since its unusual construction made it difficult to use pike poles. Most interesting feature is two large cranes consisting of huge vertical timber posts from barn floor to roof with horizontal arms attached at the top: each post swivels, and hay can be raised and placed in any part of the barn.

B5 *Lefaives Corners\**
Stone masonry basement built right up to underside of cornerposts but with about 2 feet of log-butt construction below the sills; butts about 12 inches long laid in mortar in the same manner as stone below. Original lantern removed, and its appearance now spoiled.

B6 *Thornbury\**

B7 *Woodstock\**
An octagonal bank barn, with main entrance on grade level and a cattle entrance on the opposite side at a lower level.

B8 *Toronto, pre-1892\**
Built by Isaac Hafenbrack on the old Jack Fraser farm on Dufferin Street. Rather large, on pattern of Pennsylvania-German banked barn, with stone foundation and octagonal gambrel-type roof with lantern. Timbers not original. Now removed and preserved in the Milton Agricultural Museum.

334   Building with Wood

B9 *Watford*†

B10 *Hawkesbury, 1893–94**
A round barn built by Thomas Tweed Higginson, details of which are available in his diaries, edited by T.B. Higginson and published by Research Publishing Company, London, 1960.

B11, 12 *Thessalon, 1910, 1928**
Two twelve-sided barns within half a mile of each other: one at Maple Ridge farm, RR2, built first, probably with a lantern now removed; the second is more interesting. Both have typical layout, with cattle facing central feeding storage.

B13 *Mount Pleasant*†

B14 *Gananoque*
Round

B15 *Simcoe*†

B16 *St Joseph Island*

B17 *Aylmer N.**
Of brick construction, round, quite late; of no particular significance.

B18 *Osgoode Station*

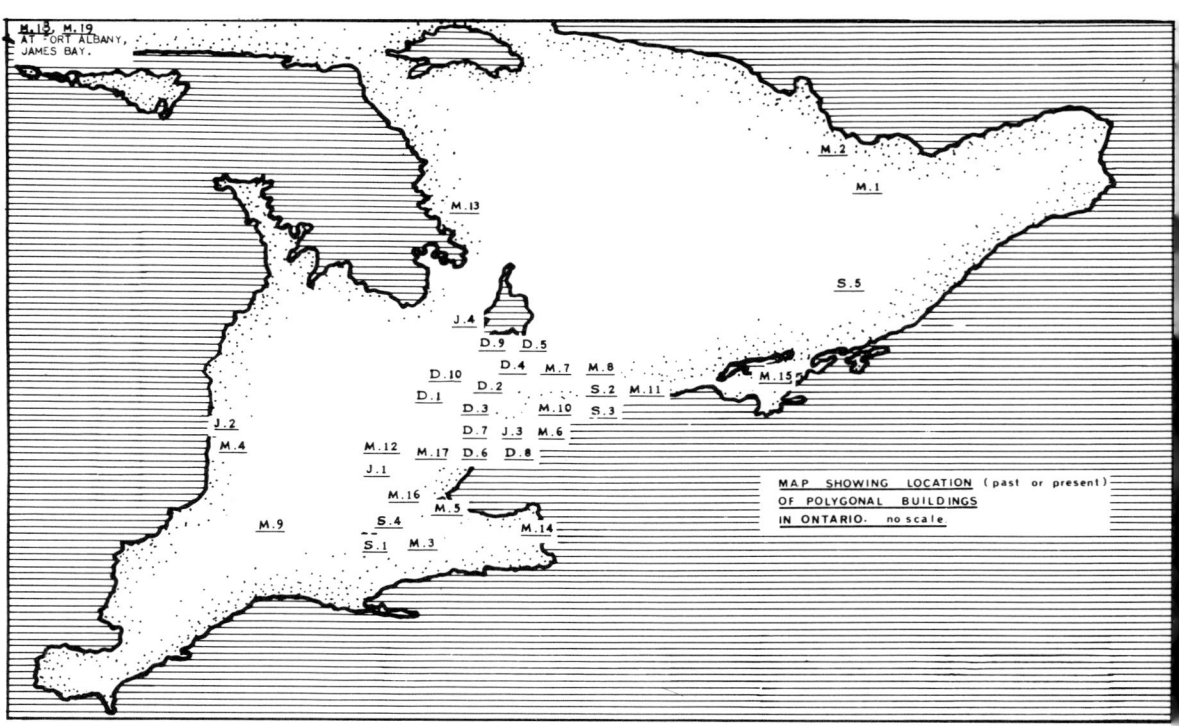

MAP SHOWING LOCATION (past or present) OF POLYGONAL BUILDINGS IN ONTARIO. no scale

B19  *Roblin Lake†*
On concession IV, a mile or so south of the fairground and across Roblin Lake, on the Cunningham farm. A round barn, on a frame of 2 by 6 timbers, with gambrel roof. Dismantled about 1954.

B20  *Caledon East*

B21  *Renfrew*

B22  *Near West Lorne, south of Highway 401*

C1  *Dalhousie Mills, c. 1873**
St Andrew's United Church. There have been changes, including removal of a very ambitious steeple after 1940, but originally was one large open auditorium. Each wall measures about 24 feet 6 inches, and four octagonal posts form the corners of a central square, presumably necessary to support the rafters, since the thrust of such a construction would tend to push the walls out. Local legend has it that the design was imitation of open umbrella! Early church records unfortunately destroyed.

C2  *Stroud, 1909**
Design spoiled by two castellated towers flanking the entrance, but perhaps excusable as Presbyterian nostalgia. Good stone construction in Scottish fashion.

C3  *Grimsby Park, 1888†*
See text

C4  *Toronto*
'New' Holy Blossom synagogue, consecrated on 15 September 1897, to replace 'old' Holy Blossom synagogue on Richmond Street. Cost was over $40,000, and contributions were received from persons of other faiths. Architect a Mr Siddall.

C5  *Fullarton**
Hesitant use of the octagon form in the tower, showing possible influence of Yonge Street deadhouses. To wed this shape to traditional church forms makes strange bedfellows indeed!

C6  *Speedside, 1855**
St Andrew's United church. Dedicated 3 October 1855, Rev. Enoch Baker first minister.

C7  *London, 1861†*
Stood at the Richmond Street V until demolished in 1964. Supposedly designed by Thomas Fuller, architect of Ottawa Parliament buildings, and one might suspect the influence here of his design for the polygonal library at Ottawa, which was not completed until 1877.

C8  *Meaford, 1856†*
Built on north side of Trowbridge Street about 150 feet from the corner of Thompson Street. 34 feet diameter, the first brick church for miles around; plank seats. In use by various denominations for about 20 years, and now utterly destroyed.

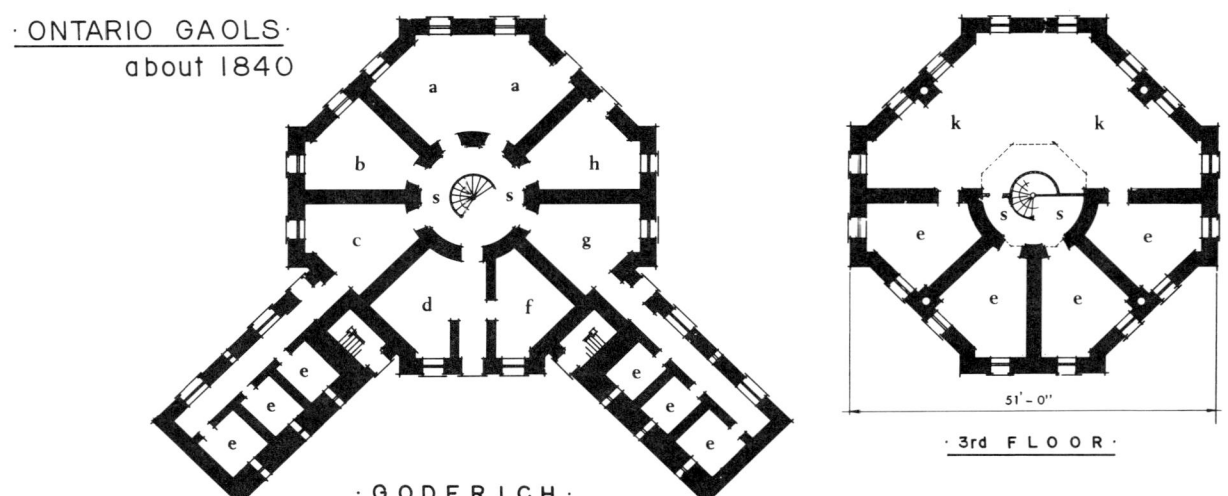

·ONTARIO GAOLS·
about 1840

·GODERICH·
·1st & 2nd FLOORS·

·3rd FLOOR·

s1 *Mount Pleasant*, 1840–50†
Nelles Academy (after first principal Professor William W. Nelles), built about the same time as the Tennant house (H14). Basement completely above ground, and fairly large; pupils remember it as 'huge' with 'big windows.' Supposed to have held 75 pupils at one time. Three storeys (plus basement) in height, first floor being one room for junior students, second two rooms for seniors, third never completed. First an 'Academy for Young Men,' then Brant county grammar school, then village common school. One gable collapsed in 1899 and building then razed. Among the pupils were G.S. Henry, later premier of Ontario, George Bryce, historian and founder of Manitoba College, and John Charles Dent, historian.

s2 and 3 *Port Hope*, c. 1853†
See text on Barrett house at Port Hope.

s4 *Waterford*†

s5 *Morton*
Now a private residence.

s6 *Cherry Valley, Prince Edward County*

s7 *Peel County, near Dixie*

s8 *Cherry Valley, Norfolk County*

J1 *Guelph*, 1840†
After creation of Wellington District in 1837, magistrates were empowered to raise $24,000 at 6 per cent to build a jail and courthouse. Jail was contracted to William Day, courthouse to William Allen of Guelph Mills. It cost £3 extra to anchor the iron beds to the floor so that they would not be taken apart and used as weapons by inmates. James Lindsay was the first inmate, on a charge of stealing cattle.

Polygonal buildings 337

| ROOM SCHEDULE | | | | | |
|---|---|---|---|---|---|
| | GODERICH | | | BARRIE | |
| FLOOR | 1st | 2nd | 3rd | 1st | 2nd |
| a | kitchen | turnkey | | entry | do |
| b | gaoler | bathroom | | living rm | do |
| c | living rm | unassinged | | cell-women | do |
| d | waiting rm | living rm | | cell-male | do |
| e | cells | cells | cells | office | do |
| f | office | living rm | | stair-hall | do |
| g | living rm | unassined | | | |
| h | washroom | hospital | | | |
| s | stair-hall | stair-hall | | | |
| k | | | court rm | | |

WALLS OF EXERCISE YARDS & LATER
ADDITIONS HAVE BEEN OMITTED.
ROOM DESIGNATIONS FROM
OLD PLANS BUT MAY NOT HAVE BEEN
THE ORIGINAL ONES.

SCALE FOR GAOL PLANS-FEET

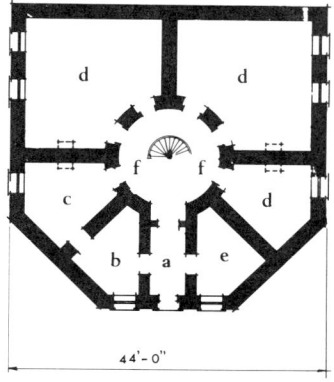

·BARRIE·
FIRST & SECOND
FLOORS SIMILAR.

J2 *Goderich*, 1840–41*
Built for the Huron District, but used only for Huron county since 1867. Designed by Thomas Young; builder unknown. Octagonal in shape, three storeys in height, the third floor containing the court room. Circular stair winds round central post for full height of building. Accommodation for nine male and three female prisoners, but has held as many as 25. Five pie-shaped exercise yards, surrounded by high wall, making the building look larger than it is. First prisoner had sold at auction without a licence; shortly after, a 14-year-old boy spent 15 days in a cell for milking the wrong cow. Jail register copied in its entirety for University of Western Ontario library.

J3 *Toronto*, 1840†
Toronto's third jail, which stood near the corner of Palace (Front) and Berkeley Streets and which was in use until 1860 when the present (Don) one was completed. Central octagon of at least four storeys, gables on all faces, topped by usual lantern, with at least two radiating wings two storeys in height. Architect John G. Howard; builder John Harper; cost around $80,000. Walls of Kingston grey limestone, small barred windows; surrounding walls 12 feet high on which scaffold was erected for public hangings.

J4 *Barrie*, c. 1840*
Some confusion in the building of this jail resulting from local magistrate's proceeding with contract instead of District Council (not formed until 1843). Designed by Thomas Young of Toronto (who also designed Goderich jail) and built by Charles Thompson, a stagecoach and steamboat owner. Built with Lake Couchiching stone (brought by boat). Wing, 64 feet long and 32 feet wide of two storeys, added in 1860, to the design of Mr Horsey, government architect, and built by John Damp after, once again, some confusion. Jail is half-octagon, with the east half squared, but with central hallway, central circular stairway, radiating wings, and octagonal lantern on top.

Built as the office building of a lumber company at Calabogie. M1

The well-known garden pavilion in the grounds of Dundurn Castle; fortunately it is being preserved. M5

## Polygonal buildings 339

M1 *Calabogie, 1875–90\**
Built as an office presumably for J. Francis & Co., the name on what is thought to be the original safe, built by Goldie & McCullagh Safe Works, Galt. Simple interior, with one partition running centrally across the building and a tongue and groove ceiling.

M2 *Carp\**
At the front of an L-shaped series of stalls in the Carp Agricultural Society Fair Grounds; probably built before 1900.

M3 *Mount Pleasant, c. 1846†*
Stowe Bros. carriage shop, near the Tennant house, burned down at turn of century.

M4 *Goderich, c. 1888\**
Gazebo, similar to one at Niagara-on-the-Lake. Doubtless there were many others in the province, but most of them have been removed.

M5 *Hamilton, 1842\**
Garden house in the grounds of Dundurn Castle, dating from 1842; pavilion probably built around the same time. Said to be Sir Allan Macnab's private theatre or cockpit; on occasions women were certainly not admitted. A pleasant if curious building.

M6 *Toronto, 1886\**
A duodecagonal building on Front Street at the foot of University Avenue built by an American company as a cyclorama. About 400 feet in circumference. 'The interior consisted of a large platform and connecting canvasses around the walls, which were lit by an extensive gas system. Patrons who paid 15, and later 25 cents, mounted to the platform and found themselves in the midst of whatever drama happened to be progressing at the moment' (*Globe and Mail*, 24 July 1954). Two bloody dramas were shown, and each ran for two years: the Battle of Gettysburg and the Battle of Sedan. But public interest faded, and by 1891, despite the portrayal of Jerusalem and the exhibiting of famous paintings, the cyclorama was closed. The public, by this time, was watching their own magic-lantern travel pictures. Then the building was used for storing machinery, later it became a car agency and car park, and it has now been demolished.

Toronto. This is the only building in Ontario which was built for the express purpose of exhibiting cycloramas. Now demolished. M6

M7 *Sharon**
Privy. See text.

M8 *Welcome**
Privy. See text on Sharon privy.

M9 *London*, 1861†
A 'crystal palace' standing at the junction of Wellington Street and Central Avenue. It was part of the building complex of the Provincial Fair.

M10 *Bowmanville*†
Privy, octagonal.

M11 *Port Hope*†
Privy, octagonal.

M12 *Guelph**
Judging building. University of Guelph.

M13 *Port Sandfield*†
Privy, octagonal, three doors.

M14 *Niagara Falls*†
Old public washroom (?) north of old museum.

M15 *Roblin Mills*†
50-foot-round building on the fairgrounds south of the Roblin house (H9), with two 10 foot galleries one above the other around the inner perimeter. Demolished in 1928 and framework used in another building.

M16 *Ancaster*†
Tollhouse located at the junction of Hamilton-Brantford toll road and Mohawk Road, later used as a jail. Semi-octagon (see H33) built of brick, but later partially stuccoed; demolished sometime between 1918 and 1939.

M17 *Islington*†
Smoke house, round.

M18 *Fort Albany*
Cree Indian council house. See text.

M19 *Fort Albany*
Hospital isolation ward, now used as a greenhouse.

M20 *Sutton*
Peacock breeding house on Sibbald grounds.

M21 *Ottawa*, 1877
Polygonal library, Parliament Buildings. Designed by Thomas Fuller and completed in 1877.

# 9
# EXTERIOR DECORATIVE WOODWORK

This is a vast topic and we can only sketch it lightly here, though the photographs provide some indication of the endless variety of the decorative touches applied to Ontario houses. The layman often labels fretwork, spoolwork, and pierced wood on buildings as 'gingerbread,' implying that the sole function of exterior woodwork was to decorate. It should be noted, however, that the carving of the ends of beams and rafters and the like had been a common practice for centuries and that the decoration applied to exterior woodwork sometimes had a functional purpose, though more frequently it did not.

The story of the 'bargeboard' is illustrative of these trends. Originally called a 'vergeboard,' it covered and protected the ridge pole, purlins, and plates which, in early English construction, projected out beyond the gable wall. Since roof framing in Ontario did not project in this way, however, there was no functional need for such weather-boarding. Yet it has to be admitted that a bargeboard does give a gable roof a more substantial and pleasing appearance, and therefore it was kept for aesthetic reasons. Traditionally it was a solid board carved decoratively in relief, if at all, and certainly with little or no pierced work, which would spoil its purpose.

A third gable above the front door is a feature generally found in small mid-nineteenth-century Ontario houses. This gable was useful in that it prevented snow from falling off the roof onto the front door step, but it also provided a prime location for a builder to display his decorative talents. In larger houses gabled windows appeared in various forms, and they too, as well as the main gable ends, were adorned with fretwork. The fretted bargeboards would usually meet at the apex, where a king post, with a finial at the top and a drop at the bottom, completed the decoration.

The entablature of the porch provided another opportunity for the display of fretwork or spoolwork, often of the same patterns as the gables. Sometimes, however, the entablature was too narrow and the builder had to content himself with fretwork brackets on either side of the supporting posts. Frequently this bracket extended itself enthusiastically across the whole underside of the entablature, albeit only as a simple board with a patterned outline. Cornices were also favoured as media suitable for decoration.

But it was the gables whose confined triangular shape provided the greatest challenge to the fretworker. Here can be found all varieties of work ranging from the most solid to the most open. In the former the cuts are typically at right angles to the face and quite close together, so much so that from a short distance away the effect of shadow makes the work look like a pattern traced, rather than pierced, on the board. In open work, voids take up so much of the area that the solid becomes the pattern, and is frequently given a sculptured effect by the application of further layers of shaped solids following the basic pattern and enriching it. The extreme of the open type was the loop or drape, where all pretence at function was abandoned and the wood was shaped to curve like a heavy cord with tassels along the

Exterior decorative woodwork  343

This could be a builder's interpretation of Gothic crockets which he inverted to suit his purpose. It is not of sound design for wood, but surprisingly has weathered rather well. The finial does not relate to the design at all and has been recessed from the gable, thus losing significance. Bond Head

underside of the gable, thus repeating on the exterior of the house the interior style of Victorian furnishing. But generally such decorative design shows some regard for its medium; and, in the designs which do not, one often finds a quaintness and lack of inhibition that are at least interesting, if not appealing.

The various patterns are difficult to date or classify, partly because this was a folk art (although there were a number of books dealing with fretwork patterns) and partly because each builder presumably had his favourite designs which he would repeat or vary to suit his or his client's fancy. It is possible to see them as either geometric, composed of straight lines, squares, diagonals, and circles, or free-flowing, with segments of circles, fleurs-de-lis, pendants, and, if in the Gothic style, trefoils or quatrefoils. But such a classification becomes less applicable as the fretwork is supplemented by innumerable turned spools, cylinders, and sheaves, all held together by dowels to form, for example, a large and intricate gable triangle.

As bargeboards and entablatures were reaching these heights of exuberance, the Italianate villa arrived in Ontario with its wide roof overhangs and deep cornices. The brackets 'supporting' these overhangs were thought to be suitable subjects for decoration; some are decidedly robust, others finely constructed of as many as five layers of patterned woodwork; some are unobtrusive, others shriek; some are well spaced, others are in ridiculous disarray. The nadir of poor taste is surely reached by the completely unnecessary application of most ungainly brackets to an early and well-designed Georgian house.

Porches received their fair share of attention. The treatment ranged from exuberant, although frequently in good taste, to the quite timid – as if the porch were ashamed to have been tacked on to an otherwise fine early Ontario home (this porch has since been removed). TOP Belleville; BOTTOM near Palermo

The geometric pattern in which the compass is used almost exclusively. In the 'open' type, the solid creates the pattern, and in the 'solid' the voids become the design. Sometimes the king post does not manage to survive at all. LEFT Lowville; RIGHT Pontypool

Treatment of the porch entablature was, in most cases, of the pierced, solid variety. This ranged from the simple fretwork and cut-outs to the more elaborate, with either a pierced free pattern or a geometric one. LEFT Scarborough; RIGHT Lowville; BOTTOM Pontypool

The free-flowing ornament can be most pleasing if it is on the right house and if well designed. At times the free-flow is carried to such an extreme that it loses architectural significance and resembles the tasselled drapery cord of a Victorian parlour. TOP LEFT near Nobleton; RIGHT near Rednersville; BELOW LEFT AND RIGHT Bowmanville

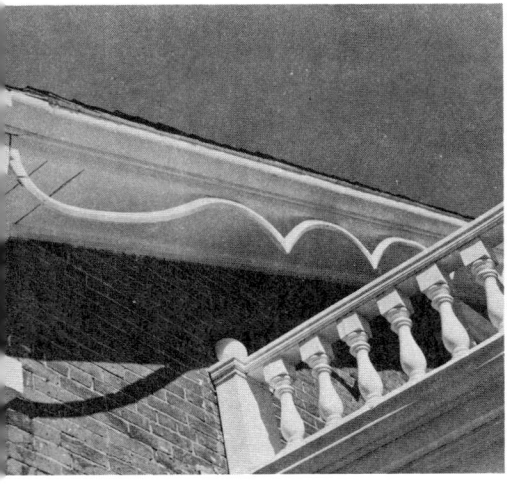

Perhaps the most successful designs were executed in the Gothic style. The reason for this is not too difficult to find: Gothic ornamentation is basically geometric, it had good historical precedents, and it is an integral part of the style (as opposed to Victorian). A builder would frequently display his ignorance; in other instances ornamentation was beyond criticism. The frame house near Sharon (ABOVE) is perhaps the best example of domestic architecture in Ontario, the style being consistently executed both on the exterior and the interior.

Lack of imagination frequently led to quite robust expressions, whereas too much refinement caused trouble later.
LEFT St Mary's; RIGHT near Mosport; BOTTOM Paris

The open Gothic-flavoured gable contrasts sharply with the solid, but not unpleasant, one. ABOVE AND BELOW Scarborough; TOP OF NEXT PAGE Lynden

BELOW This was a carriage-maker's dream (or a painter's nightmare) in Markham.

The 'drop' or 'droop' was a favourite motif of the builders. It ranged from the plain, pierced board to an elaborate attempt at giving it a modelled, three-dimensional appearance. TOP Morrisburg; BELOW Unionville

Exterior decorative woodwork 351

The ultimate in 'droops' is certainly the Duncan home on York Mills Road, built in 1872–74. It is just possible the valance effect was added at a later date along the eaves of the porch as well as the bay window. It certainly makes up in exuberance for what it lacks in taste.

352

**1**

**2**

**3**

**4**

5

6

Cornices were an essential part of architectural design and their treatment varies as much as that of the gables. According to the fashion of the day, sometimes they were treated with restraint, and at other times they displayed typical Victorian ostentation. If an owner had a home of an earlier date, and if he was bound to keep up with the Jones's, the result was frequently tragic, especially if the house was of good early Ontario design, painted white, with the added brackets a brilliant scarlet!
1 Morrisburg; 2 Picton; 3 near Ridgeville; 4 Paris; 5 Hamilton; 6 Duff's Corner

It is not clear just what the builder tried to achieve in this house at Port Hope, except, perhaps, to charge a bit more for applying 'joints' to the front wall. The remaining walls are treated quite honestly.

This house is in Aurora. Note the 'wooden' stone quoins at the corners as well as the rustication in the front wall.

No book on Ontario architecture is complete without the Barnum house near Grafton. This house has all the attributes a good design is expected to have – good proportions, good taste, and a refinement of treatment that speaks of elegance and good manners.

In exterior wall treatment, the greatest attention was paid to the 'front' of the house. In brick masonry, Flemish bond was reserved for the façade only. It was also common practice to imitate brickwork or stone details in wood – a deception that did not disturb our ancestors at all. This 'wooden' brick wall (BOTTOM) was on the front of a small cottage near Baysville. The photo immediately below shows the back of the house, with its uncommon method of roof boarding.

If the wall was of a material that did not lend itself to deception, wood decoration was applied wherever an opportunity presented itself. Trenton

Exterior decorative woodwork must be studied closely to appreciate the effort that went into producing the intricate details of pattern and modelling. On close examination one gets the impression that carpenters delighted in developing new combinations of form and a build-up of patterns, with complete disregard for accepted standards of design. As a consequence, there is no standard, in the full sense of the word. Though some work has a Gothic flavour, and some Classical, often the final result is a horrible combination of many styles. In most of the work the builder's individuality is dominant: it is amazing to what lengths he would go in the making of intricate brackets, caps, rosettes, drops, finials, and applied fretwork, in order to produce the desired effect. Some of the patterns are illustrated here, showing the number of individual pieces and the sequence of steps required to make a cornice, a bracket, or a porch post.

A band of fretwork was frequently used as an overlay on a solid board backing, thus becoming applied decoration. To obtain a more solid, three-dimensional effect in brackets, the patterns for them came in matched pairs, one with a slightly, but proportionately, reduced profile to the other. The bracket was then assembled in three layers, the middle one being of reduced proportions or vice versa, depending on the desired effect.

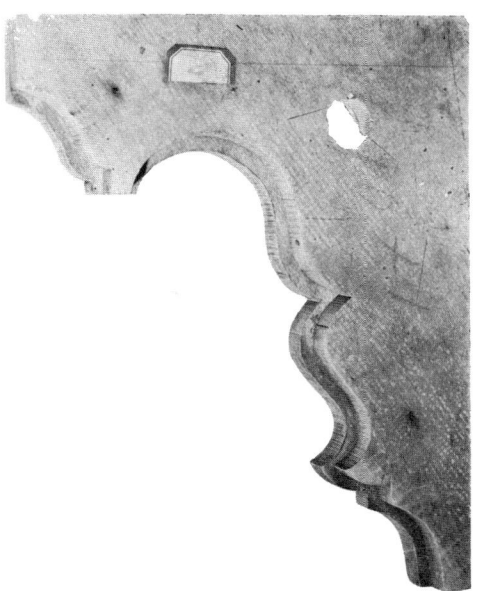

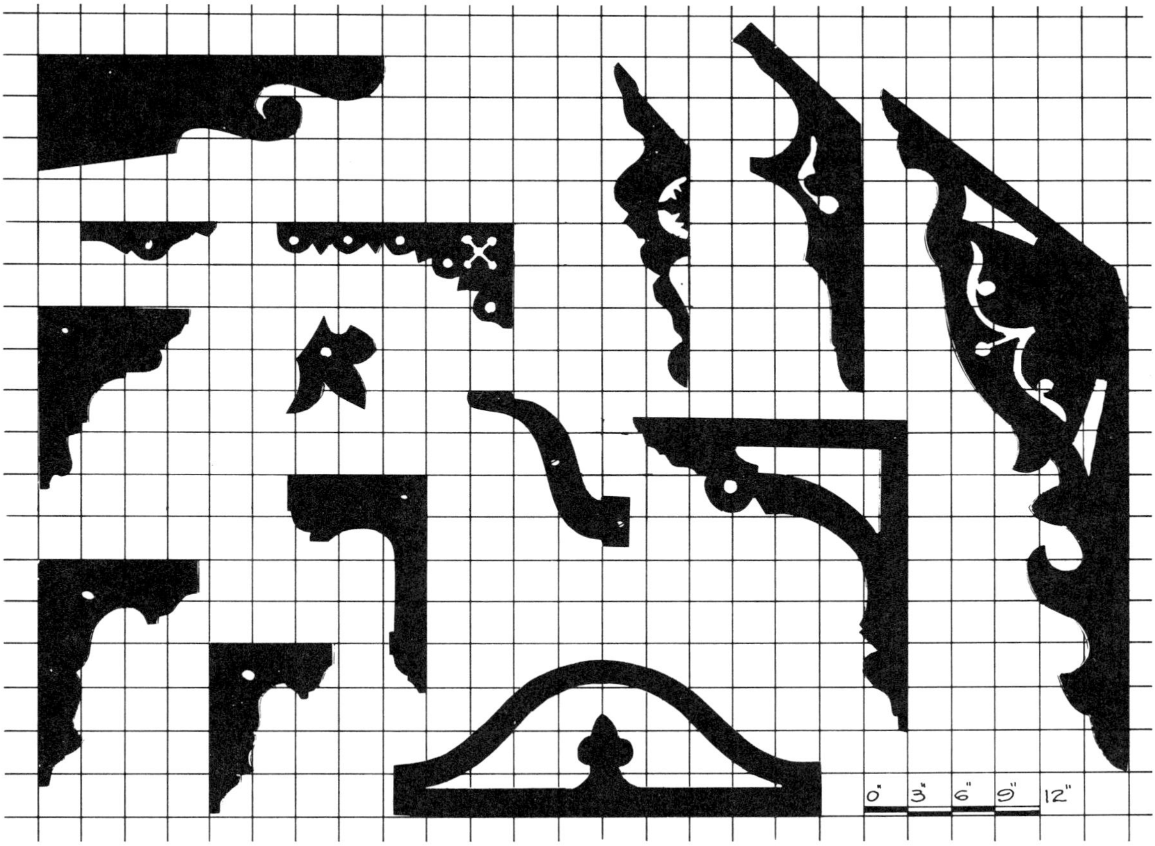

Towards the end of the nineteenth century a number of factories in the United States began to manufacture a variety of architectural components that could be ordered by catalogue. Baltimore seems to have been the centre of the industry, for in 1873 a total of thirteen plants were in operation there. One company listed the items that could be ordered:

Window sashes, doors, blinds, mouldings, brackets, blind hinges, builders' hardware, wood mantels, window frames, door frames, hand railings, balusters, newel posts, bracket shelves, barge boards, paints, oil, putty, glass, lumber, bricks, lime, window caps, door caps, window guards, sand paper, weather strips, sash weights, sash cord, porch columns, tree boxes, pews and church work, ornamental glass, &c.

Although the carpenter in Ontario had to rely mainly on his own set of patterns and his own ingenuity, it seems safe to assume that many of the better built and more expensive houses would have had these ready-made components applied.

Although the art of the wood decorator was most frequently applied to the details of a house, there are instances where entire walls have received his attention. The purpose was to upgrade the appearance of a house by disguising its wooden sheathing as stone or brick. The artifice was often not considered complete without simulated stone joints and quoins – a common practice in New England – but some of the Ontario examples make one wonder if their builders had ever seen masonry.

The most quaint or grotesque (depending on your point of view) example of wood 'transformed' into brick was the front wall of a small farmhouse, now demolished, on the road to Baysville. The other three walls were clapboarded in the usual manner. The front wall was covered with butt-jointed siding, which was meticulously carved to look like brickwork: there were quoins around the jamb and the curved head of the doorway; there were 'brick' quoins at the corner; the wall was apparently laid in English bond with every joint correctly carved; and there was a soldier course over the window. But the 'bricks' were full of knotholes ...!

# 10
# WOODWORKING TOOLS

We tend to take tools very much for granted and to forget that these 'extensions of man' were once few and wonderful and that the development of our civilization has depended to a considerable degree on their reliability and precision. Tools that seem simple to us were once on the technological 'frontier.' The Sumerians had a myth about the invention of the pick-axe, and the Greeks immortalized the name of Daedelus, who invented the carpenter's level as well as building the 'labyrinth' and attempting the first flight, and whose nephew Perdrix invented the saw and the compass. His uncle was said to be so jealous of his success that he threw him over a cliff, but Athene, the goddess of the practical arts, turned him at once into a partridge in order to save him.

Even 180 years ago, about the beginning of the period covered by this book, there was a greater appreciation of the value of tools than there is in North America today. Variety, familiarity, ubiquity, cheapness, have all bred some measure of contempt for tools in an age whose technology is far beyond an individual's understanding. But in pioneer Ontario it was very different: each man required only a few tools and he was intimately familiar with their purpose, functioning, and possibilities. It was on the way a man handled these tools and on their design and quality that much of his success depended. Go back these 150 years in this province, and we are in the age of craftsmen.

The evolution of tools is a subject that has received little attention, but with the recognition of the importance of the technological component in twentieth-century life we might expect this lack of attention to be remedied. It is clear that tools, like so many other things, evolve through challenge and response, and that office records of patents, which have not yet been extensively mined by historians, would provide one primary source material for research and would reveal technological trends well before they became part of economic life.

The role of challenge and response can be demonstrated, for example, in the more recent development of the axe. The axe is a coarse tool, one of the earliest implements of wood technology; its development was halted in Europe during the seventeenth and eighteenth centuries, the attention of innovators then being focused on the development of cutting machines. In North America, however, the axe became the basic tool of the settler, who had to carve a living out of the woods. The challenge of the forests thus encouraged the further development of the axe, and by the time the Loyalists arrived in Upper Canada it was a very efficient tool that they brought with them.

There is a general impression that tools manufactured in England were superior to those made in America, but this was certainly not always true. As early as 1768 Sir Guy Carleton commented on the St Maurice forges: 'There is not much Iron Manufactured here, but for the most common uses, and Edge Tools, Axes and Hatchets, for the Consumption of the Country, and Indian Markets, this being an article in which the British manufactures have not

Woodworking tools 361

A variety of tools are being used in this woodcut from a 1460 French manuscript. Top left shows two carpenters using the hewing axe; one is squaring a timber, while the other one appears to be cutting pins. A tree trunk is waiting to be shaped. In the middle foreground, two men are using the same type of frame saw as was illustrated by Diderot in the *Encyclopédie* three hundred years later. In the foreground one man is using what appears to be a template to mark off a squared timber. On the ground are a square, a hewing axe, pincers, a whetstone, and several pegs made by the man in the background. The lower right corner shows a carpenter using, perhaps, a nose auger. On the ground are a wooden brace with a bit and the common handsaw. It should be noted that the teeth are raked in such a manner that the saw will cut with the stroke away from the workman. It is what is commonly known as a push-saw. There is evidence that until the thirteenth century such saws had the teeth raked in the opposite direction so that the saw cut on the pull stroke. The nose auger and wooden brace were used up to the end of the nineteenth century.

Interior of the carpenter shop in Upper Canada Village, still in active use for restoration work. Note the various tools – on the bench are the mallet, the 'hold fast,' and a special moulding plane. On the wall are an assortment of chisels and gauges, two-handed augers, braces (one modern and one old one), and what appears to be an old iron. It was used for holding small pieces of veneer down while the glue was given time to set; sometimes these irons were slightly heated to keep the parts warm while the glue set. Above the window is a great array of moulding planes.

hitherto been able to hit on the taste of the native or consequently the wants of the Traders.'[1] This situation continued for a long time. Governor Simcoe wrote to the Home Office and to the manufacturers complaining of the quality of British edge-tools, telling them that they were in danger of losing the market. There was no sign of improvement, however, and in the end Simcoe bought an American axehead and sent it off to England in September 1793 with a warning that if it could not be duplicated in size, shape, and weight, England might as well forget about Upper Canada as far as selling axeheads was concerned:

The axes are to be made of the best material and of the shape and size of the pattern sent. The Axe will then weigh rather more than five pounds but should it be found to be less, it must be increased to that weight, preserving still the same proportion. Particular attention must be given to the tempering of the Steel without which the Axe will be of no value as in the case of those already sent over. The little attention given to this particular in England has already deprived her of a great part of the manufactury of edge tools and will eventually deprive her of the whole. Those made in America, tho' not so neatly fabricated are of infinite more value to the several persons who use them. It is customary with the Manufacturers in America to warrant the Quality of the tools they make for six months, and take back or replace those that are found to be unsufficient. This ought to be adopted in England.

Woodworking tools 363

These three machines are in Upper Canada Village. On the left is a mortising machine; note the lever action which exerted great pressure on the mortising chisel. Below is a forerunner of our modern jig-saw. At the bottom of the page is an old treadle lathe with a bow saw leaning against it.

On the left is a two-handed auger for making drawbores or pre-drilling mortises. This is a self-centring auger with a tip at the end. The centre bit belongs to a mortising rig; here the centring tip is clearly shown. The tool on the right is a down-cutting or nose auger. Note the absence of a centring pin. To start this drill the wood had to be dented in order to furnish a bite for the cutting edge; to use, great vertical pressure had to be exerted and, since this is not a self-cleaning bit, it had to be withdrawn frequently in order to clean out the shavings.

Auxiliary carpenter's tools such as a clamp and an assortment of marking gauges.

## Woodworking tools

A week later, on 28 September, he wrote to Evan Nepean:

The axes sent to this Country are so carelessly fabricated as to be totally incompetent to any Service whatever. Those which are constructed in the Country sell at least for two Dollars at Niagara and increase in Price in proportion to the demand – but should they not be of prime quality, I shall be obliged to purchase them in this Country. I have therefore thought proper to have a model made, which should be exactly attended to.[2]

In 1833 the poor quality of British tools was still a matter for comment. John McGregor wrote that an axe 'has not yet been manufactured in England in the form or temper which long experience has proved best. A good chopper will do treble the work with an American made axe than he could do with an English made one.' The vastly superior productivity of American tools was such, according to McGregor, that Philadelphia mill-saws were smuggled into New Brunswick at double the price of British mill-saws.[3]

Such disparity in the workmanship of what we would consider rather simple tools is amazing. It serves to emphasize again the inventiveness and ingenuity in many fields that the size and wilderness of North America elicited among its inhabitants. Some of the technical innovations in tools patented in the United States in the nineteenth century are described in Peter C. Welsh, *United States Patents, 1790 to 1870*. The early patents are mostly for woodworking tools and reveal an urge to increase their speed and/or accuracy and so their profitability. In 1809, for example, Ezra L'Hommedieu received a patent for a double-podded screw auger, a tool that would give speedier and more accurate work in timber framing. In the 1830s patents began to be issued for tools that were part of the new iron-age technology, tools that had to do with nuts and bolts, screws, and nails rather than wood.

Diderot shows this saw being used for cutting veneers. It is a two-handed saw; the bow saw was generally used with one hand only.

366 Building with Wood

Two plates from Diderot's *Encyclopédie* showing several tools being used in the production of heavy framing.

We have already alluded to the importance of the nail in the development of wood construction, and it may be appropriate here to say a little, based on the few references available,[4] on the changes that took place in its manufacture during the nineteenth century. These were changes occurring for the most part in the United States and Britain rather than in Canada. It is this factor which makes it difficult to date an Ontario house by its nails, since in any one year nails made locally by a blacksmith using traditional methods might be used in one area whereas in a neighbouring one the latest imported type of nail might be used.

Woodworking tools 367

Towards the end of the eighteenth century, all nails were handmade from nail rod. Nail rod was produced in a slitting mill attached to an iron works: a strip of wrought iron was fed into this mill, consisting of two rollers with alternately matching grooves and ridges which cut the iron into long thin rods, square in cross-section. These were sold to the 'village blacksmith.' He cut the rod to the length required in the nail, heated it, and tapered each of the four sides at one end to a point with a hammer. The nail was then placed in a heading tool, where its head was hammered out; such nails can always be recognized by their end taper and the irregular shape of their heads. Nails were 'custom-made' in many localities of Canada, but large quantities of American handmade nails were also being imported by this time in order to meet the demand.

Around 1800 a nail-cutting machine was invented. Such a machine could have been used by a local blacksmith, but it is clear too that it provided the basis for a specialized, mass-producing industry. It was quite a simple machine, rather like a table with a guillotine type of knife set at the far end.

The earliest nails were made from square nailrod; the tip was tapered on all four sides and the head rounded by hand.

The later nails were made from strip iron cut by a machine with the head still hand-hammered.

The fully machine-made nail can never be mistaken because it has the typical shape of a cut nail with a flat head.

Spikes were the last nails to be made by hand because of their size. Note that the tip is tapered only on two sides.

Strips (no longer rods) of iron were fed against the blade. The strip, about as broad as the nails would be long, was moved slightly to the left and right alternately after each cut, thus giving to this type of nail a taper throughout its length. It was still square in section, and the head was still handmade.

During the 1820s, improved nail-making machines began to make their appearance. Indeed the second Canadian patent ever issued, in 1824, was for a nail-cutting machine. In these machines the knife was set so as to cut across the strip at not quite a right angle; the strip was then turned over and cut from the opposite side, and so on. A device was added so that the nails could now be headed by machine too, though for about the first ten years the head did not have the regularity we expect in machine-made goods. Cut nails were predominant in the nail industry for about fifty years until wire nails, which are drawn rather than cut, began to be made. The first wire nails in North America were produced in Montreal in 1870. The building trade was slow to accept the new nails, but the prejudice was overcome by 1890, when wire nails ranked fourth in the total steel production of the United States.

Apart from enabling the change from timber framing, with its mortise and tenon joints and treenails, to balloon framing, the increasing cheapness of these mass-produced nails also affected lathing. Sawn wood lath, requiring many more nails than split board lath, was introduced in the 1830s, and although it was cheaper, lathing was still a time-consuming job since each piece of lath had to be sawn to an exact length so that it ended at the centre of a stud. But by 1834 Joel Howe had invented a hammer hatchet – a tool with a hammer on one side and a hatchet on the other – that eliminated this careful sawing: the lather nailed the lath to the studs and, when he came near the end, just turned the tool in his hand and cut the lath in the right place on the last stud with a blow of the hatchet. Later known as the lather's hatchet, it continued in use until quite recently when this type of lath was replaced by various patented lathing boards.

The coming of the iron age was attended by many other humble inventions, of which we shall mention only three in order to complete this brief sketch of the changes in woodworking tools that occurred in the eighteenth and nineteenth centuries. The screw wrench (now called the monkey wrench) was patented by Solyman Merrick in 1835, and a combined screwdriver and hammer by Christopher Dodge in 1866. Planes, which for hundreds of years had remained basically unchanged, with a wooden body but with continuing small improvements in their performance, began to be redesigned in cast iron; seven patents were issued for such planes between 1827 and 1870.

Another important effect of the industrial revolution was that tools became cheaper and more plentiful. One of the reasons, indeed, that the craftsmen of the former era so knew and valued their tools was that they were scarce and expensive. In many government-sponsored schemes for the settlement of Upper Canada, grants of tools and other basic essentials were made to the settlers. Indeed, this had been done earlier, under the French regime: Joseph Gaspard Chaussegros de Léry, a military engineer who accompanied the expedition to found Fort Detroit, recommended in 1749, for example, that the King provide 'one pit-saw, one cross-cut saw and one stone-cutter's saw for every six inhabitants' and for each inhabitant 'one axe, one hoe, one plane, one iron tool [?], one adze, one 1-inch auger, one tomahawk' in addition to a kettle, a four-point blanket, shoes, leggings, seed, guns and powder, and livestock. De Léry claimed that all the Canadians knew 'how to use the above-mentioned tools and possessing them they will be in a position to build their houses, barns and stables and even wooden forts if needed.'[5] The stone-cutter's saw in this list is rather unexpected: in the original French document the word is 'Scio' which may be a form of 'sciotte' – a large saw for cutting stone or marble – but may also and more probably be a mis-spelled vernacular diminutive for 'scie' and so mean a small saw for finishing work.

A good example of an English claim for material assistance in founding a settlement can be found in a petition sent from Sorel to Governor Haldimand in 1784 by 'the Companies of Associated Loyalists going to form a Settlement at Cataroque':

That Boards, Nails & Hinges be found Each Family for Compleating such Building as they shall see Cause to Errect for their Convenience at any time, for the space of Two Years from & after their first Arrival at Cataroque with Eighty Squares of Window Glass to be delivered shortly after their arrival there.

That Arms & Ammunition with one Felling Ax be allowed to Each Male Inhabitant of the Age of fourteen years.

One Plough Shear & coulter
Leather for Horse Collers
Two Spades
Three Iron Wedges
Fifteen Iron Harrow Teeth
Three Hoes
One Inch & half Inch Auger
Three Chizels (sorted)         Be allowed each family
One Gouge
Three Gimblets
One Hand Saw & Files
One Nail Hammer
One Drawing Knife
One Iron for Splitting Shingles
Two Scythes & One Sickle
One Broad Ax
One Grind Stone (be) allowed for every Three Families[6]

The Loyalists also requested clothing, livestock, two years' provision of food, seed, and that a blacksmith be established in each township and provided with tools and iron at the expense of the government for two years. It is difficult to establish now to what extent such requests were met by the government; certainly Haldimand wrote shortly after the date of this petition that axes and hoes were being made for the Loyalists, and a correspondent writing from Cataraqui to Philadelphia in November 1785 mentioned that 'our gracious King gives us Land gratis, and furnishes Provision and Clothing, farming utensils &c until next September.'[7] It seems probable that aid was generally given the settlers, even if not always as liberally as they requested.

The amount and kind of assistance no doubt varied with conditions. The English settlement in Smith Township prospered with practically no help from the government, but the Irish settlers at Enniskillen, about ten miles away across Chemong Lake, received food and grain as well as some tools (axes, handsaws, hammers, gimlets, and nails) from the authorities. A year's assistance to the disbanded 99th regiment around Richmond included one pound of putty, twelve panes of glass, and twelve pounds of nails per man. The average minimum by way of tools provided by the government to an individual seems to have been one hammer, some nails, and four small window panes.

Nails and hardware were particularly precious items for a settler in these days. Supplies of these commodities, as well as putty and glass, often came from England, and because each ship in the trade made on average only two trips per year severe shortages were possible. In 1811, badly needed repairs to the York jail could not be carried out because the necessary spikes could not be obtained in the town; in the end, three months later, they were made by special order of the lieutenant-governor. A curious practice from the earlier years in Virginia reveals the extraordinary importance of nails: if a settler wanted to move on, he used to burn down his house in order to salvage the nails.[8] The custom was widespread enough for the government of the colony to offer a settler a quantity of nails estimated equal to those in his old house if he should want to move on. (This throws an odd light on Lamb's story about the discovery of roast pork!)

Woodworking tools were also an essential part of the pioneer's kit, and each man acquired a varied collection. The five most basic tools were the axe, the saw, the chisel, the auger, and the plane, in that order. The necessary minimum, according to a letter from T.M. McGrath in Erindale to the Rev. Thomas Radcliff in Ireland in 1831, comprised '2 Axes ([cost £] 1 0 0), 3 Iron Wedges (0 10 0), 2 Two-inch screw augers, with all other sizes down to half inch (0 15 0) ... Jack, smoothing and trying planes (0 6 0), Hammer and hatchet (0 3 0), Brace and set of bits (0 10 0), 1 Hand saw (0 7 0), A set of chisels, four sizes (0 6 0).' The prices were 'considerably cheaper' than in

Canada and the Radcliffs were advised to buy their tools in Liverpool or Dublin; there is no mention of differences in quality.[9]

Woodworking tools can be divided into two categories: splitting tools and cutting tools. Splitting tools must have a dull edge since they have to follow the grain of wood rather than a predetermined plane. They tear rather than cut the wood, and so are wedge-shaped rather than sharp-edged. Included among such tools are the frow, the wedge, and the splitting axe. Cutting tools, with a steel blade sharpened at one end, are designed to work the wood irrespective of its grain or grain pattern; they include chisels, gouges, planes, axes, and – in a special way – saws and augers. Planes are probably the best known and most varied of pioneer tools.

It would be more sensible, however, in a book dealing with building, to classify tools according to whether they were used for heavy framing and other such coarse work, or for the subsequent fitting and finishing.

## Heavy framing tools

These tools were relatively few in number and include axes, saws, mallets, augers, chisels, and planes.

There were generally two types of axe used in heavy work, the broad axe and the adze. Three characteristics of the broad axe might be noted: first, when it is held in its vertical working position, one side is perfectly flat with all shaping projecting to the opposite side; second, since this axe has to be worked on a flat surface, the handle is generally straight and is always offset away from the face of the blade; and, third, the working edge is bevelled or basilled on one side only, that is, it slopes away from the workman, and is slightly curved.

The broad axe was used to cut in a vertical plane only, all heavy work on a horizontal plane being done by an adze. The cutting edge of the adze is therefore at right angles to the handle. Like the broad axe, its face is flat with a slightly curved edge which is basilled only towards the flat side away from the worker. It is a two-handed tool, with the handle slightly curved and parallel to the line of the stroke. Both it and the broad axe have a slight 'head,' perhaps for balance.

Among the saws used for heavy work were the pit saw (of either the open or frame type), the frame saw (in various sizes), and later the crosscut saw. The one-man crosscut saw, popular in New England, seems to have been less common in Ontario, perhaps because the regular crosscut saws, either of the two-man or hand variety, were readily available by the time settlement was underway here.

Mallets came in many sizes, the 'grandfather' of them all being the very heavy Beetle or Commander, which was made of a piece of oak or ash trunk 8 to 10 inches in diameter, frequently with iron rings around it to prevent it from splitting. A mallet of this size was used for driving together heavy

Woodworking tools 373

Note the flat side of the head as well as the straight handle of the broad axe. Below it is an adze.

The relative size of various planes is clearly evident here.

mortised and tenoned timbers. Smaller mallets would, of course, be used with chisels.

All pegged joints require drilled holes, and thus augers were essential. Augers were also used in the earlier days in making mortises; after being drilled, the holes had to be squared with chisels. In later years the auger was replaced in this work by the mortising rig. This rig was a wooden frame in which a sliding chuck was driven by a set of bevel gears operated by a double handcrank, the travel of the chuck being adjustable so that it would drill to a pre-set depth.

For squaring an auger hole, a heavy mortising chisel, sometimes called a 'slick,' was used. It was simply heavier and sturdier, with a longer shaft and wider cutting edge than other chisels. It was also useful for smoothing hewn timbers or similar rough surfaces. A special corner chisel, with a 90-degree angle in the blade, was used to give a neat corner to a mortise, if such a tool were available. For the most part, however, chisels were used for finishing work.

The only plane that would be used in heavy framing was the heavy plough and the tongue. This kind of plane was at least three feet long: it made a very heavy cut and needed two (or even three) men to work it. Handles projected horizontally from the body at the toe and at times at the heel, and a heavy iron ring, to which rope could be fastened, was attached to the body so that a helper could pull it. These planes had an adjustable fence and were used for cutting grooves. Tongue-and-groove construction is not common in heavy framing, occurring only in the floor of barns and especially of grain bins (which were sometimes laid double with the planks at right angles to prevent grain loss). Such a plane might also be used to cut a groove in the principals if lath was to be sprung into them (as in Sir Sandford Fleming's house at Craigleith), or in the underside of the plate to receive the upper end of vertical planking, (as in the barn on the Mackenzie farm on Brock Road, Pickering).

The Beetle or Commander was a heavy mallet used to drive framing timbers together in assembly.

There is one other tool that might be mentioned here – the frow, frou, or froe. It was not used in framing as such, but it was essential for the making of roof shingles and clapboard. The frow had to cleave the wood along the grain and was therefore a dull-edged tool.

Pins, pegs, and treenails (or trunnels) have been mentioned earlier in connection with heavy framing, but they were also used as fastening devices. In a window frame held in place by pegs, it would seem that two pegs per jamb were required. In a door frame, I have counted as many as eighteen. In frames where the head might be visible, pegs were frequently squared for a tight fit. Hookpins, which have also been mentioned as an aid to framing, were longer than the standard peg and had an enlarged head at one end. The head acted as a shoulder, preventing the pin from sliding all the way through the auger hole. Being longer, the pin could easily be knocked out from the other side when it was time to make the joint secure with an ordinary peg.

The frow, the standard tool of the shingle maker

## Finishing tools

As far as Ontario is concerned, the first half of the nineteenth century was the great age of finishing tools. The mechanization of woodworking was proceeding apace, however. Such machines as the treadle lathe for turning cusps, finials, balusters, knobs, and chair and table legs; the treadle jig-saw for fretwork; the mortising machine; the planing machines invented in England around 1770; and the mould-cutting machines that appeared on the market between 1830 and 1860 brought this age to an end. In its heyday, the finishing work done for the average home might be on mouldings, doors and windows, handrails and balusters, a mantel or two, and perhaps a panelled dado or window recess with shutters. The tools used included chisels, a brace with a range of bits, handsaws for rough and fine cutting, marking gauges and squares, and – above all – a wide assortment of planes. Because they were the finishing tool, par excellence, and were so numerous and varied, this section concerns itself entirely with planes.

The plane is a tool with a long history. It is impossible to say when it was first invented, but it is interesting to note, bearing in mind the patenting of the first iron plane in the United States in 1827, that metal planes were being used in the final years of the Roman Empire. A plane, with a body of metal plates rather than of cast iron, has been found at Silchester in England and

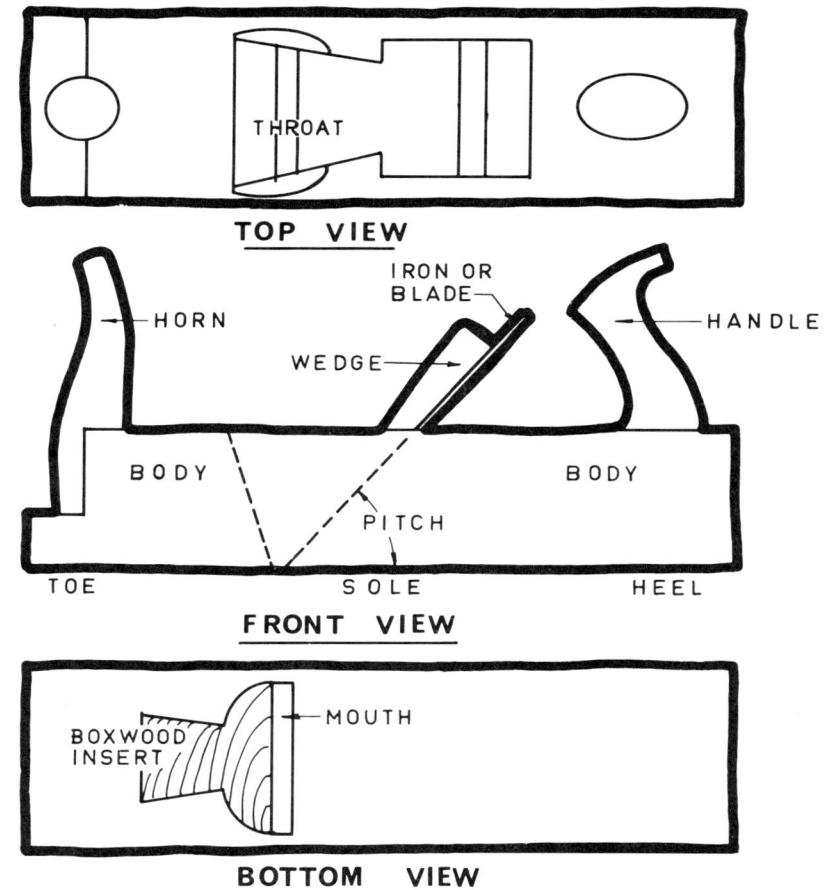

dated at about 400 AD. It is similar to a modern plane, is 13 inches long, with a knob for a horn and another knob at the heel for a handle, but with the blade set at around 60 degrees, which is somewhat steeper than we would find today in this type of plane.

The parts of a modern plane are named in the drawing above. Not every plane contains all the parts shown; a great many American planes, for example, did not have the horn that was usual on European planes. Handles varied slightly, but I have shown only one type; the other most common form of handle was solid with an oval opening tilted slightly forward for the fingers. The body was generally made from beech, apple, or rosewood, with beech being the favourite since it is hard and densely grained enough to take a great deal of use (and abuse) and to become very smooth. The parts which received the greatest wear from the friction and pressure inherent in a plane's use, however, were frequently reinforced with boxwood inlays. This was almost always done in moulding planes; in other types of plane the boxwood was inserted just ahead of the mouth. Here, where the blade raises the wood while cutting it, is the area of greatest pressure on the sole. Without this insert the sole would frequently become slightly hollowed at the toe side of the mouth as can be felt on many old planes by running the fingers across the sole. The pitch of the blade varied from about 45 degrees for soft woods up through 50 degrees for harder and stringy woods to about 60 degrees for moulding planes. There were also a few special finishing planes in which the pitch might be as much as 85 degrees; this puts them almost in the class of scrapers rather than planes.

Planes themselves can be divided into two groups: (a) those designed to cut only *with* the grain and (b) those designed to cut both *with* and *across* the grain. The two groups are readily distinguishable, since the blade of the first is always set at right angles to the longitudinal axis and the blade of the second is set at a slight angle to that axis. This angle gives it a slight shaving action which prevents the tearing of the wood when the plane is used across the grain. The first group comprises most of the familiar planes: the jack, trying, smoothing, floor, tongue, plough, reeding, and moulding planes. The second includes the rabbet and banding planes, the sash fillister or sash plane, the sun plane, the croze, and the howel. The croze is a bastard tool: it is really a saw but it is used like a plane. It, the howel, and the sun plane are special cooper's tools, however, that need not concern us here.

It was general practice to insert boxwood in the plane body at various pressure points. Photographs show an insert in the sole and some typical shaped inserts which extended the full length of the body.

378   Building with Wood

 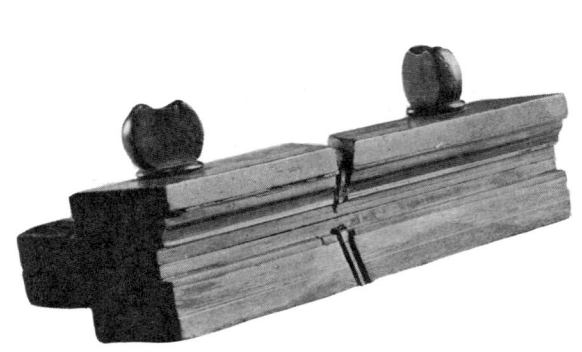

A typical single-iron, single-body paired combination forming a sash fillister or sash plane. Sashes generally came in standard widths with a fixed moulding, therefore planes required fixed fences and stops. One of the pair is a common rabbet plane which cut the rabbet for the glass; the other one is a moulding plane which cut the typical sash moulding.

The smoothing plane was always very short. In this example the boxwood insert has been replaced by a steel plate covering the entire sole in front of the cutting edge.

The basic planes in a woodworker's collection were three: the jack plane, the trying plane, and the smoothing plane. The jack plane was the first one to be used in any levelling work. It was about 12 to 16 inches long with a flat sole. The cutting edge of the blade was slightly concave, producing a slightly convex cut and thus a fine wavy texture on the surface, which can be detected by touch far more easily than by sight. The trying plane would always be used next. Twelve to 16 inches or more in length, it had a straight cutting edge and was used for final levelling. Because of its increased length, at the start of the operation it would ride on the higher points of the board which it would subsequently remove until it could cut a continuous shaving the full width of the blade. Whenever an especially smooth finish was desired, the shorter (6 to 10 inches in length) smoothing plane was used. It, of course, had a straight cutting edge, and because of its shorter length it would tend to follow the contour of the surface, unlike the trying plane. The smoothing plane was also generally used to even out a surface where two boards were butted.

Two special planes of the trying type might be mentioned here. The floor plane was used, as its name suggests, for levelling floorboards. It was long – as much as 5 feet – and consequently heavy, but since it was used only on a floor it did not need to be lifted very often. The second one is the cooper's plane, which was even longer and heavier; it was kept in an inverted position with the toe uppermost resting on some support, and was used by pushing the staves against the iron – not the iron against the staves.

The common tongue and the plough went together in pairs. This is the tongue. Both planes were used to cut the regular tongue and groove for flooring or panelling. Since they have to match, these planes always have fixed fences as well as stops.

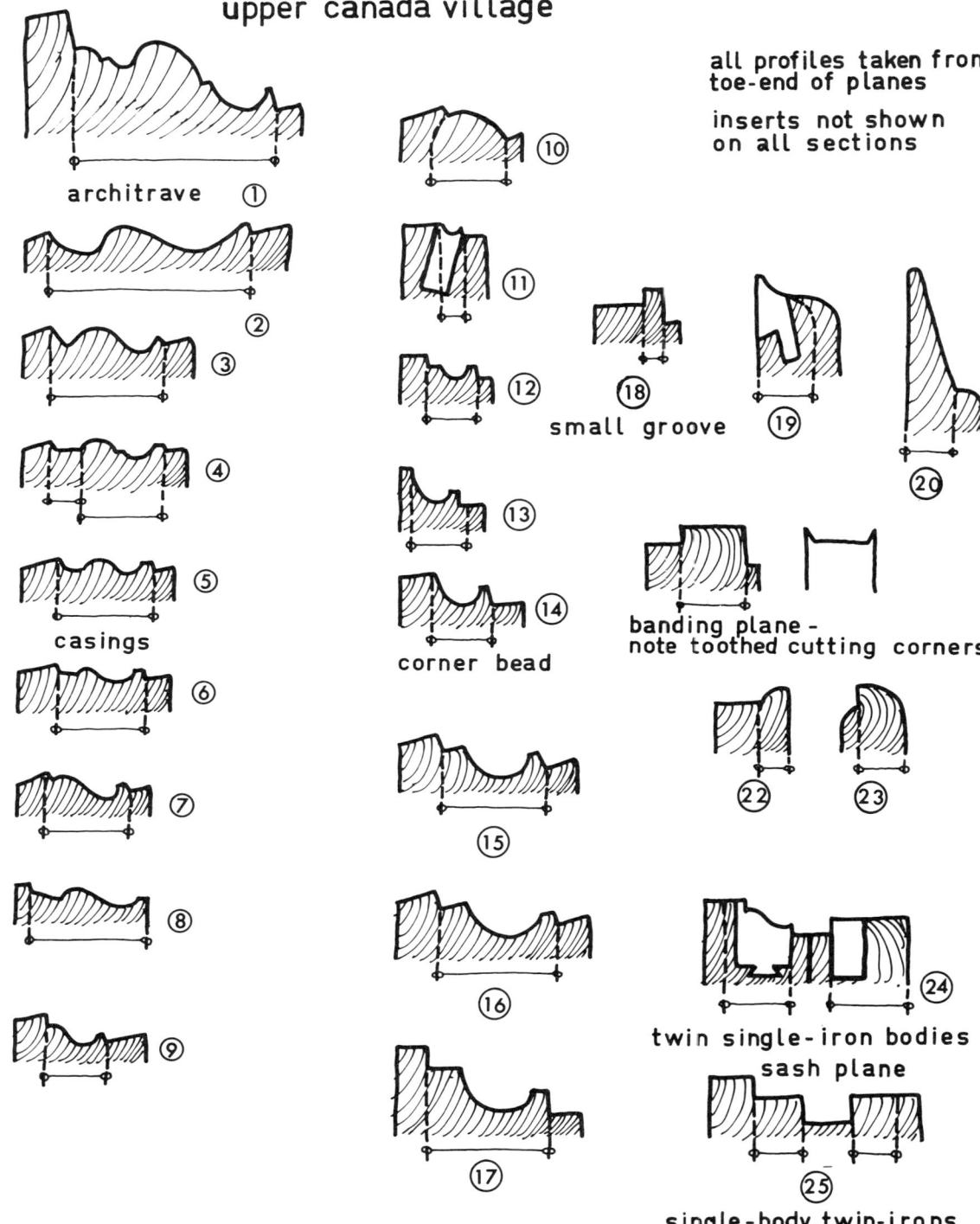

A regular plough, but of excellent quality.

After the jack, trying, and smoothing planes, perhaps the next most common kind were the plough and tongue planes. They were used in making a tongue-and-groove joint, the plough making the groove and the tongue making, of course, the tongue. Both planes generally had fixed stops or fences in order to ensure the accurate alignment and size of the two component parts, although some larger planes of this kind sometimes had movable fences. A plough generally had a side discharge and the tongue a regular throat. The plough plane could also be used in making a fairly common type of joint known as the spline. Grooves were cut in both the edges that were to be joined, and a spline or thin piece of wood of the same thickness as the groove was inserted into both grooves, thus aligning and fastening them at the same time.

Another group of planes that came in a pair were the 'hollows and rounds.' As their name indicates, these planes had simple concave or convex soles and irons of varied profiles. They were used for cutting larger flutes, beads, rounded corners, and surfaces of relatively large radius. They might, in fact, almost be considered large moulding planes. Their body width ranged from ½ inch (for a single flute ⅛ inch wide) to 2½ inches or more. If the iron was wide enough, they had a regular throat, and if not, a side discharge. The English carpenter named a plane by the shape of the surface it produced, and the American, for some reason, by the shape of its sole. Thus a convex sole producing a concave surface would be called a hollow in England and a round in America. These planes were manufactured, in England at least, in standard sets of eighteen pairs, with a width ranging from 3/16 to 1¾ inches and to even larger sizes if specially ordered. Carpenters would frequently own all sets from No 1 to No 10 and in even numbers from there up. Such a set of hollows and rounds was usually supplemented by a set of four-handed pairs – side rebates, side rounds, snipe bills, and side snipes.

# MOULDING PLANES – PROFILES

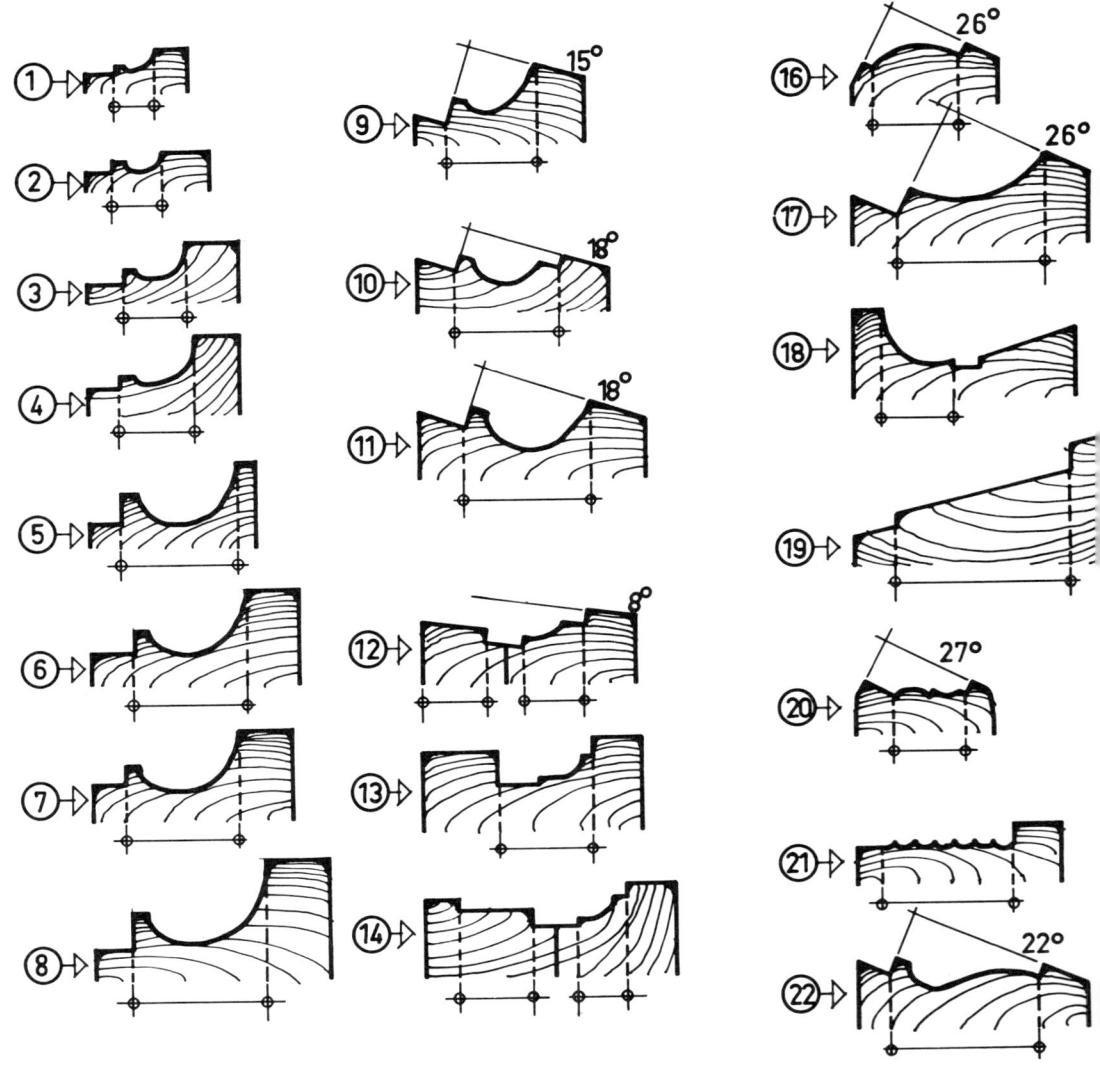

| 1-11 | EDGE MOULDING | 12-14 | SASH PLANES or SASH FILLISTER |
| 19 | BANDING PLANE for FIELDED DOOR PANELS etc. | 10 | PANEL BEAD for TONGUE-AND-GROOVE |
| 21 | BEADING PLANE | 17 | RABBETTED QUARTER-ROUND |
| 16 | CAVETTO | 22 | MODIFIED OGEE |
| 12&14 | 2-IRON DOUBLE PLANE | ←→ | WIDTH OF PLANE IRON |

all profiles from ft. george, niagara-on-the-lake, ontario

scale: 0" 1/2" 1" 2" 3"

# MOULDING PLANES – PROFILES

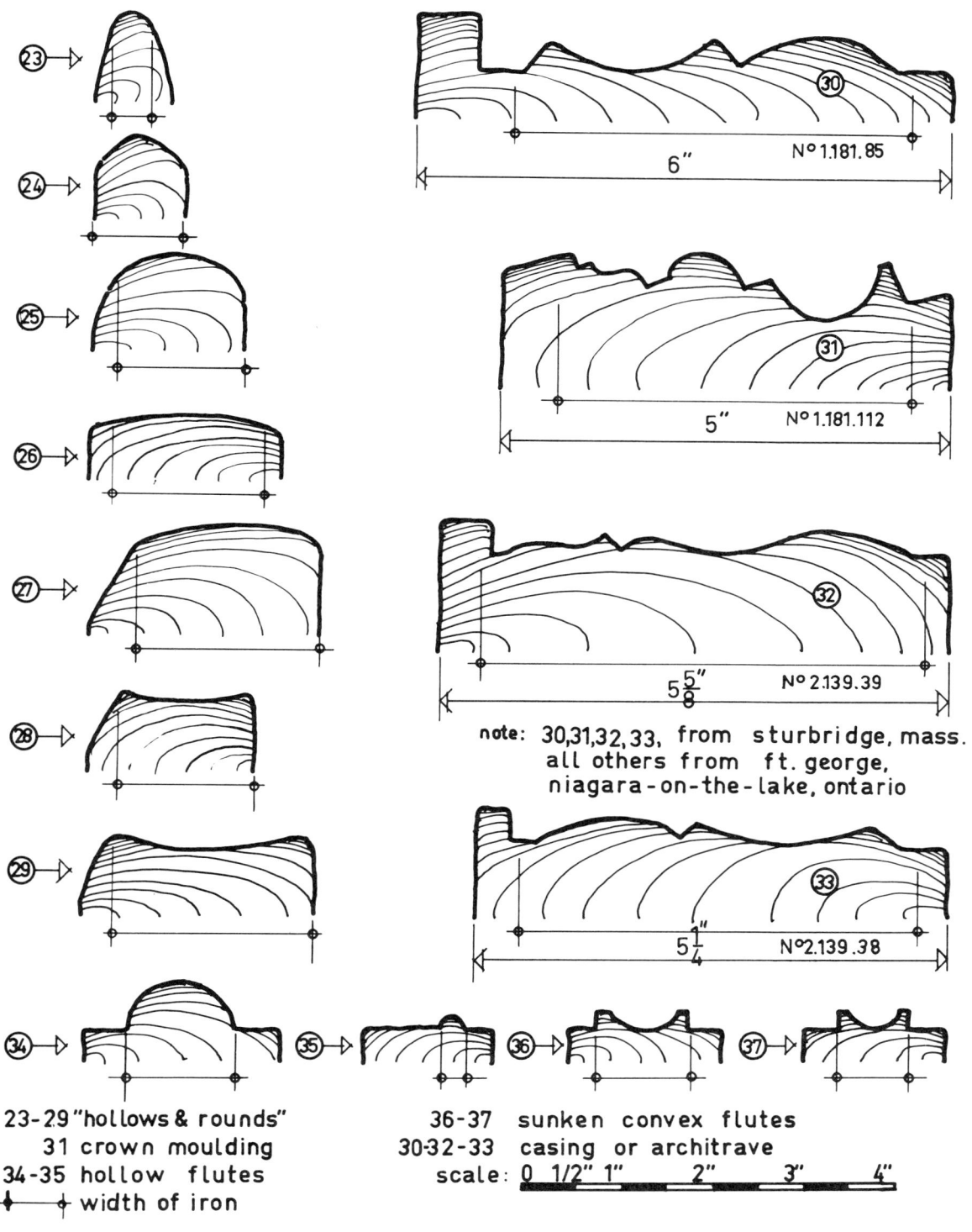

note: 30,31,32,33, from sturbridge, mass. all others from ft. george, niagara-on-the-lake, ontario

23-29 "hollows & rounds"
31 crown moulding
34-35 hollow flutes
●——● width of iron

36-37 sunken convex flutes
30-32-33 casing or architrave
scale: 0  1/2" 1"   2"   3"   4"

Even more varied in shape and size were the moulding planes proper. Mouldings were first used with any skill by the Greeks, and they serve three main purposes: to separate one surface from another; to crown or frame an area or opening; and to cover a joint between two adjacent surfaces. They are composed of flat and curved surfaces in an agreeable sequence. Although there are probably only about eight basic surfaces (each with its own variants), an infinite number of cross-sections is possible and since each plane cuts only one specific size and shape of curve, a great variety of moulding planes were manufactured and were to be found in the tool chests of Upper Canada's woodworkers. Such planes had blades to cut classical mouldings, derived via the Renaissance from the designs of Ancient Greece and Rome. Gothic mouldings were completely out of style in the Georgian and colonial eras, and when the Gothic revival brought a change of taste the industrial revolution also brought mould-cutting machines. Hence there are no moulding planes with Gothic profiles.

All moulding planes are designed to cut only along the grain, hence the iron is always at right angles to the travel. The narrowest plane may be only ½ inch wide in its body and the largest 6 inches. Up to about a width of 2 inches, the body is rectangular, but over that size it is generally L-shaped,

A lighter plough. The fence is adjustable with wooden adjusting and lock nuts.

Woodworking tools 385

'Rounds' were used to plane concave surfaces and they came in a great many sizes to fit the various radii. (In this example, the curator was unaware that he put the iron on the wrong side of the wedge. Using it in this position would clog the discharge after several cuts, and the user would soon discover his mistake.) The 'hollows' were used to plane convex surfaces and came in as many sizes as rounds.

Moulding planes varied in length from that of the standard one to the heavy plough. Below is a top view of the plough showing the cross handles both at the heel as well as at the toe end. The iron ring was used to fasten a rope for an additional hand to pull in case of very heavy cuts.

the horizontal part of the L being the sole. Moulding planes have no horn or handle, but the wider varieties have auxiliary grips attached to the toe in order that an apprentice can pull while his master guides and pushes the tool. The wedge always seems to have that peculiarly curved top; if one is found that lacks it, in all probability it is a replacement. The cutting edge of the blade is, of course, never straight and, except in the narrowest mouldings, the stem of the blade is narrower than the edge. The reason for this is obvious: since a great many irons had to cut right out to the very edge of the body, a throat of the same width as the edge would severely weaken the body, if not actually cut the plane in half. A throat serves two purposes: to provide a tapered groove in which the wedge can be jammed against the blade, and to provide a way of removing the shavings. If the throat is narrow there will not be enough room for all the shavings to come through it and therefore the plane must be built with the discharge on the side of the body. In very narrow planes the discharge may extend right through the body from one side to the other, and the wedge is then tapered to a point rather than an edge in order to facilitate discharge on both sides.

Some planes have two irons. The narrower blade is always placed ahead of the wider one, for the wider one needs more support and, being in the rear, can thus lean on the full width of the plane towards the heel. The discharge for the wide blade weakens the body of the plane to some extent and so the intermediate section of the plane between the two blades is subjected only to the strains from the narrower blade in front.

All shaping planes have one or two stops which may be fixed or movable. A stop, extending beyond the cutting edge, limits the cut in depth or width or both. Many moulding planes have stops incorporated in their body, one on the right of the body to limit the width of the cut and one on the left to limit the depth. The edges of these stops are at right angles to one another, but the vertical axis of the body and blade of the plane is inclined within this right angle at 10 to 15 degrees from the vertical. The plane is thus held at an angle to the stock when cutting a moulding. This ensures a better result, since the pressure exerted by the plane is now against two surfaces of the stock at the same time; if the plane were used simply either vertically or horizontally, with pressure on one surface only, the plane might drift, spoiling the moulding.

Rather similar to the moulding planes were the sash planes or fillisters. They had one purpose – to cut the characteristic bead and rabbet of a window sash. These planes may be either one-bodied, with one or two irons, or have two bodies fastened together. They have at least one fixed fence but more frequently two, since sashes were generally of two standard widths (1⅜ or 1¾ inches) and the second fence was fixed for one of these sizes.

For the most part, planes were factory-made. The few homemade ones were doubtless constructed for a specific job or just for the pleasure of making one's own tools. The majority of the planes to be found in Ontario are American products. There were over five hundred American plane

Woodworking tools 387

Reeding was a favourite form of ornamentation. Note the fixed fence on this reeding plane.

Most moulding planes have a side discharge and an L-shaped body.

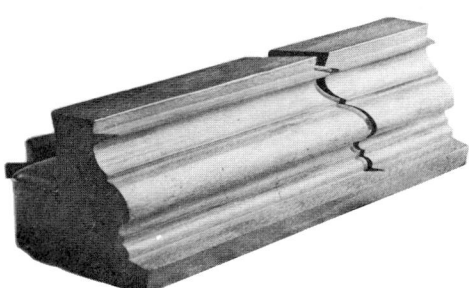

A wide moulding demanded a rather wide body and iron. This made cutting quite difficult. Single-body moulding planes hardly ever exceeded 6 inches in width. Note that the mouth extends practically across the whole sole.

For wide mouldings two irons were used at times, with the narrower placed ahead of the wider one.

manufacturers, according to Mr and Mrs K.D. Roberts of Farmington, Connecticut, who collect names of old plane manufacturers as a hobby. They have also found twelve Canadian makers. A similar hobbyist in England, Mr W.L. Goodman of Bristol, has the names of 350 English plane makers. The manufacturer usually stamped a cartouche, with his company's name and location as part of the stamp, on the heel or toe of the plane. It was also the practice for the owner to stamp his name in the heel, but his can easily be differentiated from the maker's stamp by the fact that the letters are stamped individually and irregularly.

Collecting tools can be an interesting and fairly inexpensive hobby. There are many still to be had and the prices are still much less than a Boston rocker or a dry sink. Collections are to be found in practically every museum in Ontario, and the most impressive are at Upper Canada Village, Fort York, Fort George, and Pioneer Village near Toronto.

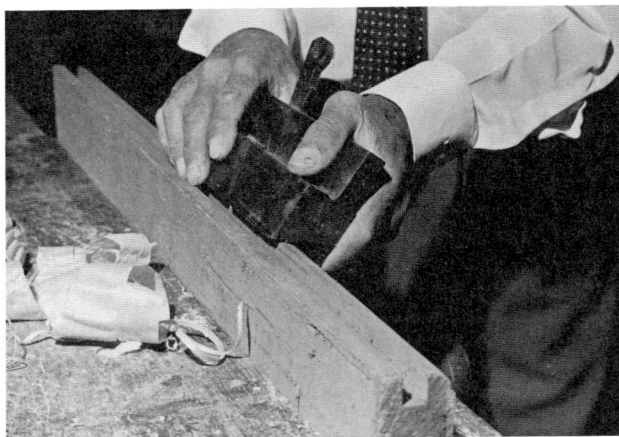

A 'moving fillister.' This model has a movable fence and a fixed stop. It is a type of banding plane designed to cut wider bands than the usual rabbet, for example, in a fielded panel. It must therefore cut both across and with the grain. For this reason the iron is set at a slight angle and is sharpened on one side as well as the bottom edge. The stop determines the depth of the cut and the fence is set to the required width.

RIGHT The angle of the body while in use varies slightly, but should be about 10 to 15 degrees from the vertical.

A carpenter usually impressed his name at least at the heel end of the body.

# 11
# PRESERVATION AND RESTORATION

There has been a welcome increase in recent years in the concern shown by both public bodies and private individuals in the survival of old buildings. Young couples are moving and converting log cabins into weekend skiing cottages or saunas, and historical societies in many parts of the province are striving to create and maintain a living record of the past. Preserved buildings are a form of visual and concrete history, valuable not only in terms of general education and tourism but also as a demonstration of our respect for the founders and makers of our society.

All of this is good, but there are dangers and difficulties. The main danger, in my experience, is that people can be carried away by an enthusiasm that is both ill-informed and undirected. It is not enough simply to entrust the restoration of a building to an 'old country carpenter.' It would be naïve to presume that because he is old and from the country he is knowledgeable about, far less an authority on, the methods of construction used in the building. In fact, given the changes that occurred during the nineteenth century in the methods of building with wood, it is most unlikely that he is acquainted with the methods contemporary with the building, or even that he has somehow acquired such an appreciation of wood that he knows, as it were instinctively, what should be done. In a word, restoration must be authentic and so must be based on sound knowledge and research. And that, despite the fact that this book is only a tentative beginning, is its only practical message.

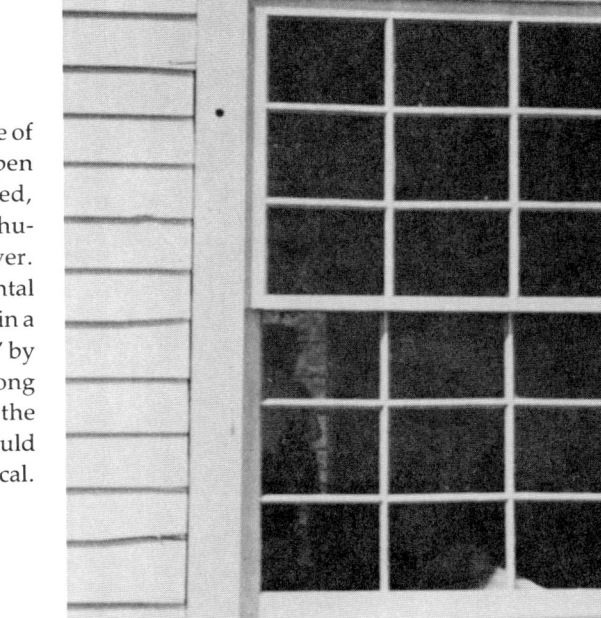

An example of what can happen when untrained, unbounded enthusiasm takes over. This fundamental error occurs in a house 'restored' by a layman; the long dimension of the glass pane should be vertical.

Main entrance to the old city hall, Toronto. E.J. Lennox, architect, 1890–99

Again, interest or enthusiasm in restoration must be shaped by a policy. Among voluntary groups concerned with preserving old buildings, agreement on a policy may indeed be the most important factor in the continuing existence and strength of the group. Problems and solutions will always be different, but there are some basic considerations that should underlie a group's thinking. First, perhaps, every effort should be made to preserve the ambience and general historical associations of a building: its siting, both in relation to terrain and to other buildings, and its orientation should be as similar to the original as possible. Second, personal preferences must never override factual evidence: if a builder put a door in a place that offends our modern eye, for example, we should not move the door. Third, there is a possibility that museums, indoor and outdoor, organized by local societies may tend to duplicate one another, and it could be argued, from a provincial point of view, that they should try to avoid this and concentrate, if possible, on one individual and differentiable local project. Fourth, a full record of all discussions and decisions should be kept for posterity.

The main difficulty facing any scheme of building conservation is always the shortage of money. There may be differences between historians and architects on what is worth preserving, but such a difficulty is inevitable and somehow a balance can be struck. But money is almost always the key problem. There are few people or few societies that can afford the thousands of dollars that would be required to reconstruct Captain Steele's house at Fairvalley or the Langton cottage at Fenelon Falls. The costs of research and of authentic restoration are high, but they ought to be paid; and these costs force us to select and plan projects with the greatest care. It is important, too, not to forget the costs of the continual repair and maintenance required by a restored building just as by any other.

## Basic principles

The preservation of historic buildings is a discipline in its own right which demands specialized knowledge and skills. The work has two obvious and different sides: historical and archeological research, on the one hand, and the actual physical preservation of the fabric on the other. The professional historian and researcher must be called upon to supply all possible documentary evidence. Then, armed with this information, the trained architect and craftsman determine what needs to be done.

Success in an enterprise of preservation thus requires the combined efforts of research and craftsmanship. In this field there is no need for complicated jargon, but attention should be paid to the fact that three terms are frequently used in a loose fashion for the same task, even though they are not interchangeable. These terms are 'preservation,' 'restoration,' and 'reconstruction.' The proverbial little credo of the preservationist puts these words in their proper order of significance and makes them self-explanatory:

It is better to preserve than to repair,
Better to repair than to restore,
Better to restore than to reconstruct.

The first step in any preservation attempt must be an exhaustive search for documentary evidence of the historical, personal, and environmental associations of the building. If the building is of historical significance only, architectural considerations of an aesthetic or stylistic nature will have no bearing on restoration decisions. If, on the other hand, the building is of architectural significance, then relevant features must be preserved, irrespective of any historical associations or lack of them. Where there are such clear-cut issues, no problem will arise; if, however, a combination of these or other factors come into play, a balance between them must be struck, and the end result will be a structure demonstrating the aspects that are important.

The search for documentary evidence, though generally a time-consuming effort, may be carried on in a more or less leisurely fashion. But the physical preservation of the structure is a quite different matter. No building can be left open to the weather for long. If the work has to be halted for the winter, this must be done at a stage early enough to prevent the risk of damage by frost. Otherwise it will be necessary to provide heat, and costs will rise sharply.

Thus, there should be a complete photographic and architectural documentation of the building before any physical work upon it begins. As the work of preservation goes forward, it is important to maintain detailed records of its progress. Minutes of meetings must be kept so that the thinking and discussion that led to final decisions are preserved. A complete file of all the historical documents employed must be made and this file should also hold drawings, specifications, bills, and accounts dealing with the operation.

A thorough physical analysis of the existing structure is of the first importance in restoration. This work should begin from the inside out, since the roof and walls will protect the building if the interior has to be disturbed. It may be that the plaster will need to be removed from all walls and ceilings (or parts thereof), to determine the age of the building or structural alterations. The frame must be examined for two things: deterioration of the fabric and mutilations resulting from alterations or additions by later builders. An experienced architect would be able to detect, upon exposing the frame, any mutilations, and a scrutiny of them may help to reconcile documentary evidence which otherwise may seem to conflict with the existing state of the building. Deterioration is due to bad maintenance, or none at all, and, together with mutilations, they are the chief problems encountered in restoration work.

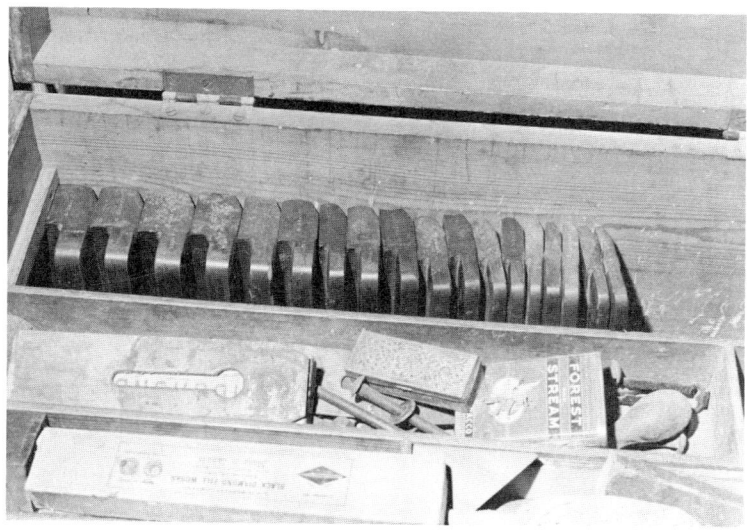

The tool chest of a modern carpenter engaged in restoration work. Fort George

Where deterioration has set in, the affected members must be removed and replaced by sound timber, preferably of the same vintage as that of the original structure. The area near the deterioration must be thoroughly sterilized by means of liberal quantities of industrial preservatives. The joints between new and old timbers must also be coated with a preservative as a precautionary measure. It is good practice to record the date of installation on each new piece. Needless to say, wherever a member is replaced, the fashion in which it is done must be consistent with the methods used in the original structure. *No structural liberties must ever be taken.* To break this commandment is to generate false information. Consistency in method of construction may be expensive but necessary.

A successful job of physical preservation can be of immense educational value to others, and we should do our best to make it so. Timber framing, for example, is a most difficult area of research, since the frame disappears from view when a building is completed. The most essential architectural feature thus becomes inaccessible for study, and can be viewed only when a building is being demolished or undergoing extensive alterations. For this reason, in a restored structure all significant architectural elements should be made available for study by means of glass panels or removable shutters in walls. Such devices need not be prominent, to the horror of those in charge of interior decoration. In special cases, an entire wall might even be stripped to expose permanently a structural detail of particular value.

Generally speaking, a preservation project will concern a single building without thought of any change of site. When the structure does have to be moved to a new location, a quite different set of problems arises. The building must now be examined for vulnerable areas that could be damaged during transport. At these strategic points temporary bracing is required. The entire operation must be cleared with all authorities concerned, such as the Department of Highways, Hydro-Electric Corporations, telephone and railway companies, and the municipalities affected. All this entails great expense, and, if the building is of considerable height, transfer to a new site may be impossible. In some instances the removal of the roof makes the operation much easier. Frame structures are usually sufficiently rigid as to make it unnecessary to dismantle them; dismantling greatly simplifies the work of transportation to a new location, but reassembly is an enormously complicated and expensive undertaking.

More complicated still is the task of assembling a number of buildings, as in the case of a village to commemorate pioneer life. This sort of enterprise lies outside the scope of this study, but one necessary feature of it may be mentioned, namely, the siting of the buildings in the new location. The relationship of the various buildings to one another in the same complex must always be maintained. And it would be a grave mistake for a building that was designed to face south to be relocated facing north.

As for the tools, and the method of employing them to replace defective pieces, these should always approximate those used by the early builders.

As a rule, a true expert in restoration would never tolerate modern power tools, except in areas where it makes no difference. However, the type of work to be done must be taken into consideration. For example, a modern electric reciprocating saw closely follows the motion of the old keyhole saw and therefore could be used in some instances. On the other hand, a device like an electric router has no place whatever on a restoration site.

The close analysis of a structure in order to recover its original form can be a piece of investigation exceeding in thrills and challenge that of the detective in a first-rate crime novel. The preservationist must develop a similar intuitive power of observation, logic, and deduction from circumstantial evidence. An example of this kind of deductive analysis is provided later in this chapter.

## Practical hints

Although it remains true that only experts, and indeed a team of them, should be entrusted with the preservation of large and important historical structures, there nevertheless remains a considerable field of activity for the amateur. A great many of us harbour a natural desire to restore and refurnish an old house for our own use, because any sensitive and intelligent person is bound to feel the charm of the past, to admire the honest skill of long-dead craftsmen, and to wish to live under a roof so obviously made by man for man out of good natural materials. Our modern, industrialized, machine-dominated society has only intensified this deep human desire.

In this section, then, I shall try to answer the most frequent requests for advice and assistance addressed to me by laymen contemplating the purchase of an old residence in order to transform it into a satisfying home or by small local museums with restricted budgets.

The first piece of advice is to be cautious in one's choice. When a likely building has been found, it is prudent to pay for a thorough inspection in order to make certain that the fabric is sound. Such an inspection should not be concerned with style, planning, or design, but rather to establish the feasibility of restoration. Anyone familiar with construction – an architect, engineer, or competent tradesman – can be charged with this task. If the structure has so deteriorated as to require substantial repair, the next step is to obtain an approximate estimate of the cost. The information thus secured may lead one to proceed confidently or to abandon the project entirely.

Once the decision to go ahead has been made, and the building acquired, the next question – and it can be a disconcerting one – is where and how to begin.

Buildings fall into three types: log, frame, or masonry in stone or brick. Each of these will be given separate consideration. Since a number of features are common to all three, the discussion of them will not be repeated unless a new problem arises by reason of change of material or some other circumstance. Readers should refer to the main text of this book for further information concerning details.

The log building is made entirely of wood except for chimneys, fireplaces, and perhaps a masonry foundation. Only later houses will have a regular basement or cellar; earlier housekeepers managed with a trap door in the kitchen floor that led to an underground storage pit for vegetables and certain fruits.

The first requirement is of course a solid foundation. It is to be expected that this will be composed of rubble stone in mortar. If the building, after many years, remains quite plumb and true, it is likely that the foundation is perfectly sound. Where a cellar exists and its walls show evidence of dampness, it is advisable to excavate outside down to their base and lay weeping tile to drain into some convenient ditch or dry well. If the mortar shows signs of disintegration, a mason must be employed to repoint the joints. Where a foundation has settled excessively, one of two courses may be followed. If it appears that no more settling will occur, the building must be raised, the sills levelled, and the gaps filled with masonry. If there is the slightest possibility that the settling process is not yet complete, new footings will have to be placed under the old ones. In the trade this is called 'underpinning.' It is expensive, and, unless the final result warrants the high cost, the project had better be dropped.

A very poorly laid rubble foundation wall; the miller's house near German Mills, now demolished

Over the years the foundation of the shed has sunk so drastically that two full brick courses have been exposed over the doorway. A manifest case of inadequate footings. This was a plank shed attached to an existing brick residence with full basement. Bolton

The condition of the logs is, of course, the supreme determining factor. No matter how secure the foundation, if the logs are decayed beyond remedy there is no saving the building. The most common cause of deterioration is rot. Many people are unaware that wood rots, not by nature, but as the result of a fungus growth. A National Research Council bulletin explains this: 'The reproductive power of fungi is fantastic when it is considered that one square foot of dry-rot fungus fruit-body can produce five million spores per minute over a period of several days. These microscopic dust-like particles are shed in clouds from the mature fruit-body, and being very light, can drift for long distances. There is therefore every likelihood that spores of wood-rotting fungi will be present wherever wood is used.'[1] Rot, then is an ever-present danger. Mere dampness is never, by itself, the cause. Deterioration begins when special conditions of moisture and temperature are present which are favourable to the growth of the fungus. So it is never enough simply to replace the affected parts with sound ones, since these in turn may again soon fall victim; it is the cause that must be eliminated if we are to rid ourselves of the trouble.

The effect of wet rot – a portion of the wall plate in the Sharon study built about 1828.

Decay will generally affect the bottom logs first, but not necessarily. If the building is to remain on the original foundation, the affected portions, or even entire logs, should be removed well beyond the last evidence of decay. All adjacent areas must be thoroughly treated with a commercial fungicide before the new part is set into place. It is good practice even to treat the new part with preservative wherever possible as a precaution. In the total reconstruction in 1971 of the Park River Post, a fur trading post south of Thunder Bay, every single piece of timber was so treated.

If the building is solid and is to be moved to a new location, the quickest and best method is to engage a professional house-mover. He will see to all necessary arrangements and will spare the owner a sea of troubles. Should dismantling be necessary, certain procedures are advisable. All timbers must be identified so that they can be re-erected in their original order. A simple method is to identify each log by its position in a wall and by its orientation. For example, N.1.W. will indicate that this is the north end of the first log in the west wall; the south end of this log would therefore be marked S.1.W. There is perhaps no need to point out that dismantling is construction in reverse, and therefore the logs must be numbered from the bottom up, since the last log to be handled in the dismantling will be the first log to be handled in the reassembly. Since the rafters also must be replaced in their proper order, the rafter end and its corresponding seat in the plate must also be identified.

Door and window frames will likely be pegged to the logs. Considerable care is needed not to damage them when removing the walls. Each frame must be identified as to its position and, here again, it is good policy to treat the frames with preservative before reinstalling them.

In many instances exterior trim will have to be replaced. The purist will insist on trim planed by hand in the same profile as the original. A compromise that would save money is to get this trim pre-cut on a machine, slightly oversized, so that it can then be easily finished by hand. Whatever the procedure, no sawmarks must ever show on exposed surfaces.

The head of openings is the most difficult to waterproof. For this reason a drip cap is generally set directly over the trim. This piece of construction is always a potential danger spot because the cap never fits tight enough to prevent moisture from getting in behind. In order to prevent this, the best method is to install proper flashing. Where flashing is not possible, the alternative is to treat adjoining surfaces with preservative and then set the cap in place with non-hardening caulking before it is nailed. On the subject of waterproofing, it should be pointed out that when a building is moved to a new foundation it is wise to lay a modern waterproofing material between the top of the foundation and the bottom of the first log, in order to prevent ground dampness from entering the wood. Polyethylene film is excellent for the purpose.

Obviously, all roofing must be removed when a building is dismantled. For the new roof on an average building in Ontario, only one sort of material

# Preservation and restoration 399

Moving a building is a complicated business and would better be left to professionals.

is acceptable – cedar shingles. If the building remains on its original site, or can be moved intact, the existing shingles may perhaps be good enough to last many years. But under no circumstances must asphalt shingles be allowed to remain on the roof or be used as the replacement.

A word about the type of cedar shingle may be helpful. The prevalent notion is that the most authentic is the thick-butt, handsplit, cedar shingle manufactured in British Columbia. But even in earlier days much more refined shingles than these were being used. Most pioneer museums exhibit a tool known as a 'shingle horse.' This device held the handsplit shingle firmly so that the end of it might be thinned with a draw knife in order to impart a slight taper and secure a better fit. The process, of course, had the effect of smoothing out the irregular surface so dearly loved by romantics. It follows that to lay thick-butt shingles with an irregular alignment of the butts is a modern affectation, since such material was employed only on the very earliest shacks and shanties. Most of our early buildings, especially those still in existence, would have been covered with the tapered shingle laid in regular alignment, since any good carpenter in those days would disdain the crude workmanship good enough for a mere shack. Pioneer craftsmanship and crudeness are by no means synonymous.

Leaky roofs were common in early days, but only the ultra-purist would demand such a nuisance for the sake of authenticity. Hence, when a roof is being done over it is advisable to place a waterproof membrane between shingles and sheathing in order to prevent this unpleasant condition of pioneer times. Modern flashing is also appropriate around dormers, chimneys, and roof ridges except that, when applied to masonry, it should be of the 'stepped' type. Since this work must be executed by a professional roofer or tinsmith, it will be sufficient to instruct him as to what is wanted. Flashing may be of galvanized iron or copper, which is more expensive.

Early chimneys have no flue lining. If a new brick chimney has to be built, it is advisable to install this lining unless the inside surface is kept quite smooth without any projecting mortar at the joints. This advice holds good for stone chimneys as well.

An exposed joint is always vulnerable unless constructed properly. The New England pioneers discovered this very early. At first they followed tradition in the use of half-timber, but they soon found it necessary to protect the frame by means of weather-boarding. The same holds for log construction, wherein each joint between the logs is exposed for its entire length. According to many early accounts, these had to be re-chinked frequently. If the logs are to remain exposed in a restored building, re-chinking will have to be accepted as normal and frequent maintenance work. A good method is first to pack the joint with oakum or other modern sealer. Over this a strip of expanded metal lath should be nailed and a cement mortar used as chinking. If the logs are hewn 'quite true' and if they are closely laid, ordinary caulking with a gun before chinking may be satisfactory.

The interior can be treated in several ways, depending on the use to which the building will be put: if it is for summer occupancy only, the logs can be left exposed. All loose slivers should be removed and the whole wall given several coats of white shellac mixed with beeswax. This will seal the wall sufficiently and, in time, will yield a quite satisfactory patina of age. If the building is to be used year-round, the walls may be lined either with lath and plaster or panelling. In either case, the logs should be packed with oakum as much as possible at their joints, then covered with sheets of building paper, after which vertical 1¾ inch strapping should be applied. Two inch insulating bats should then be placed between the strapping, a vapour barrier laid upon the whole wall, and the final finish applied. This method will thicken the wall by several inches and may necessitate adjusting the interior trim around the openings. If the walls are to be lined with boards, they should be placed vertically and should be as wide as the owner can afford. Knotty pine should not be used in true restoration because the pioneer carpenter looked upon a knot as a blemish and would not have tolerated the use of such defective wood. If plank partitions are required, they should be about 1½ inches thick and should extend the full height from floor to ceiling. Such boards should be tongue-and-groove with a bead. Once again they should be as wide as the owner can afford.

Note the complete erosion of the mortar caused by a leak in the roof. Eversley church

Ceiling beams were generally exposed in old log houses. The floor of the attic formed the ceiling of the room below. If the dwelling in the process of restoration is to be used all year round, this attic floor should be covered with insulation.

All wood used in the interior should be thoroughly seasoned in order to avoid the opening up of joints after the first few seasons. This is always unsightly. It is therefore advisable to buy lumber a full year before it is to be used, which should then be stored with cleats between each layer to permit free circulation or air. The weight of the pile will prevent warping.

Flooring should be tongue-and-groove, although butt joints can also be satisfactory if the boards are properly seasoned. Floor boards are held down either by nails or pegs. If the flooring is tongue-and-groove, modern flooring nails can be used for toe-nailing. If common nails are used, however, the nailheads will show even if driven flush with the upper face. Hence either true cut nails must be used or a rose head will be needed in each case (this is a lengthy procedure but would impart the desirable tone to the floor). Should pegs be used, a little cheating becomes inevitable. As already explained, pegs are intended to take a shear stress. Pegs holding down a floor, however, are doing their work only by means of friction between them and the material into which they are inserted. Consequently a slight shrinkage in either peg or board will cause the floor to come loose. In order to prevent this disaster, we allow ourselves a trifling piece of make-believe. The hole for the peg will be drilled only half way through the board. Then a nail or, better still, a screw will be sunk in each peg-hole to become the true means of holding the floor in place. The half-peg is then inserted to mask the screw. It should be glued into place and its exposed end sandpapered level with the floor.

The frame house is more difficult to analyse and inspect since most of its structural members are covered from view. Little need be added to what has already been suggested regarding foundations. Pronounced cracks in the plaster of interior walls may indicate subsidence. Cracks in the cellar wall have the same significance. If these appear to be old, the chances are that the footings have reached a stable condition and that further damage will not occur.

The frame will usually have been fairly well protected from the weather, but warping of old siding can permit water to enter behind it and cause trouble. Such moisture will naturally run down the studs and collect on the sills. Sills, therefore, are the first members to be thoroughly inspected, even if this means removing some exterior siding; if deterioration is excessive, they must be replaced. This is a major and expensive operation, demanding the attention of experienced workers; since it is no job for amateurs, it would be pointless here to go into details of method. Rafters should also be inspected for water stains. A leak in a roof will send water down a rafter and, if the leak is considerable, moisture will accumulate on the plate, causing damage at the rafter seat. I have seen plates completely disintegrated at such places. If water stains are followed up along the rafter, they will usually lead to the source of leaks, which may be caused either by badly weathered shingles or by poor flashing around chimneys and dormers.

In many cases window sashes will have been replaced at some point with fashionable large panes, perhaps even with a single pane in each opening, in both upper and lower sashes. These large panes will have to be removed in order to restore the original appearance. Sashes should therefore be carefully inspected to determine whether they are original. If traces of earlier muntin bars survive, the sash may be presumed to be original. If there is no trace of muntin bars, this means that the entire sash is a later 'improvement.' The scars of the vanished muntin will also indicate the size of the original glass panes.

One must always be on the alert for later additions or alterations, such as the 'removal' of a door or window. Inside the house these can frequently be difficult to detect since they will have been covered over, appearing to be part of the original wall. If there are grounds for suspecting such a change, one of two alternatives must be taken: either some of the outside covering must be removed at suspected areas or interior lath and plaster must be cleared away. The latter course is perhaps preferable since inside repairs are more easily made. (This procedure may be likened to that of an archeologist digging an exploratory trench across a promising area.) The strip of lath and plaster to be removed need not be wide – four to six inches will do. This must be carried out, however, at a height such that a hidden door or window will not be missed. If this 'test' is done too low or too high, it may not reveal such openings and one will be led to wrong conclusions.

The existence of an earlier stairway, which has been removed, can frequently be traced by joints in the floorboards where the stairwell has been

Very clear evidence of later alteration; here the plate has been raised several feet in order to gain headroom in the attic.

covered over. Stains against the wall, or repairs in the lath and plaster, may also be valuable guides. Similarly, joints in the floorboards may establish the earlier presence of a hearth. If the entire fireplace has disappeared and cannot be detected from construction visible in the basement, there will always be a definite break in the lath which now covers this space.

Baseboards may reveal the relative age of a house. If both types A and B (as illustrated) occur in the same room or building, type A will be the older and probably original one; type B is of a later date.

Decorative woodwork that has deteriorated or lost some of its pieces should not present too great a problem in restoration since enough evidence will remain in place to make it posssible to rebuild the blank places correctly. A problem may arise if entire units have been removed, such as porches, bay windows, or balconies. In such cases reconstruction becomes necessary. If early photographs are available they may be of some assistance, but often they will not be clear or sharp enough to provide the necessary details of design. To give such reconstruction at least a semblance of historic validity, one should study the prevailing patterns of the area and choose the one that occurs most frequently. This will at least place the reconstructed building more in keeping with local characteristics and give it a sense of authenticity.

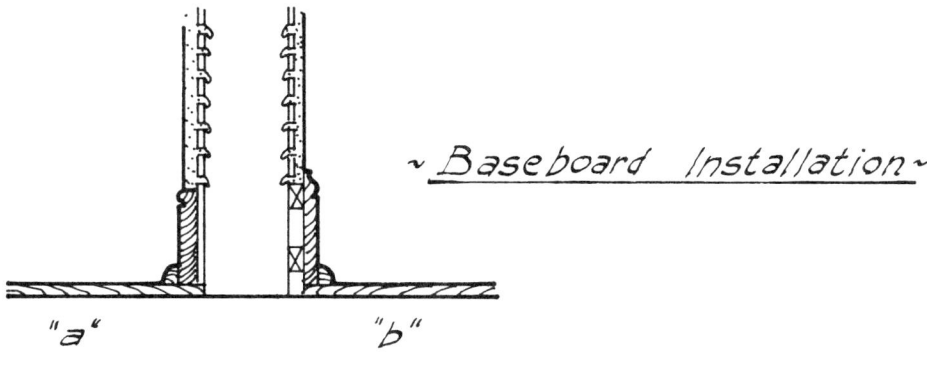

Some fretwork patterns on frame houses can easily be traced by either placing heavy wrapping paper over the pattern and rubbing the outlines with crayon or by placing cardboard behind it and tracing through it. It would also be advisable to visit nearby museums on the chance of finding a few actual full-size carpenter's patterns which were used to create such fretwork. (A good collection of patterns can be seen, for instance, in Westfield Village near Rockton.)

Stone and brick masonry, as already pointed out, are essentially the same except for the aggregate used. Stone itself will not deteriorate, and so the only item to be checked when considering restoration of this sort of masonry is the mortar; if it is sound, with good solid joints, nothing need be done. If excessive weathering has occurred, or if the mortar itself has deteriorated badly, it must be scraped out and replaced. A good formula is cement, lime, and sand mixed in the proportions of approximately one part cement, three parts lime, and seven parts sand. Mortar can easily be coloured to match existing tints. The best season for repointing is late summer or early fall, depending on the weather. A badly deteriorated joint permits moisture to enter the wall and such moisture must be allowed to evaporate during the dry months before the joints are sealed. If the deterioration has not gone too far, it may be enough to apply a coat of commerical, silicone, weather-proofing. Expert advice is necessary, however, since the kind of weather-proofing intended for stone is different from that used for brick, and damage may result if the wrong type is applied. This material is not a waterproofing, but only a water-repellent, and will thus need to be repeated about every four of five years.

Example of a type 'a' baseboard installation. McFall house, Bolton

To move a masonry structure intact, or to dismantle and rebuild it, is an undertaking for experts. The amateur would scarcely be able to meet the cost anyway, so the matter will not be dealt with here.

Where plans call for a restoration process extending over a period of several years, priority of course goes to the roof, which must be inspected for leaks, bad weathering, and deteriorated flashing. Roof-framing members must also be examined.

Alterations made in stonework at a later date are most easily detected either by relative weathering or by the existence of joints. If the changes came long after the construction of the original building, weathering will provide the most definite clue. If they followed quite early, weathering may have covered over all signs, in which case only the joints indicate what was done. No amount of weathering can obliterate a joint.

Restoring or repairing brick may present problems. The variations in hardness and consistency of early bricks are explained by the fact that bricks were frequently made on the premises, in individual kilns, and perhaps even by amateurs. If bricks were too soft or insufficiently fired, they may have weathered so badly as to force the abandonment of restoring a building. Replacing bricks in a wall is a most difficult task since, to begin with, weathering cannot be imitated and, secondly, it is practically impossible to match the colour. However, if such work is undertaken, a word of caution is in order. Even someone with skills and experience may have no appreciation of the problems involved, and if the expense can be met, it is best to call a specialist in brick restoration. If this is out of the question, then the next best solution is to ask a mason to lay up a test panel; only if it matches the original brick satisfactorily should he be allowed to proceed.

Silicone treatment is a good idea if deterioration is not severe. The same precaution applies here as in stonework and an expert should be consulted as to the best formula.

If the house is decorated with typical Victorian spools, fretwork, cast-iron grills and railings, these details also need to be examined carefully. So many coats of paint will have been laid on as to obscure completely some finer mouldings or fill smaller cavettos or scotias. It is best to strip all paint and begin afresh. There is no need to warn the reader that this will be a most laborious, boring, and time-consuming operation, although one which pays great dividends in the end. This is especially true when it is a labour of love undertaken by a dedicated and tenacious lover of history and old buildings.

In a wooden railing, each baluster must be checked individually for sound seating, since most nails will have rusted out over the years. Dampness may also have caused damage at the lower extremity. For cast-iron work not much can be done except to clean off the loose rust and apply new paint. The main problem with rust will lie at the points of fastening, where it may have completely destroyed the screws or bolts that hold the railing in place. It may be necessary to drill out the bolts and retap the holes for a new set of galvanized fasteners.

406 Building with Wood

With a few exceptions, the interior of a masonry building does not differ from that of a frame construction. One major difference is the seating of the joists in the wall. In a frame wall there will generally be sufficient air space around the seat to permit circulation and thus keep the ends dry. In masonry, such ends sit in a pocket. If this pocket is sufficiently large and if the wall is in good condition, no trouble should be anticipated. On the other hand, if the joists rest in a tight pocket and the wall has weathered badly, especially at the joints, moisture may have reached these ends. If there is doubt, several ends should be inspected to make sure of their soundness. This inspection will require the removal of plaster on the inside.

Anyone who has read this far will realize that only the basic conditions that should be investigated have been covered. Each case has its own problems for which general rules possess only limited value. Let us conclude with a final rule that will soon be verified by experience. In restoration work one should never set oneself a timetable, since the unexpected can always be counted upon. *Carpe diem* is the best attitude, and one should literally let each day be sufficient unto itself. In the end, when the project is complete and the handiwork is contemplated with justifiable pride, in spite of sore muscles, an aching back, and an empty pocketbook, you will probably declare that it was the experience of a lifetime, fun while it lasted, but that you will never attempt the like again.

In order to illustrate how some of the above rules are applied to actual cases, and how structural detective work is carried out, several case histories are here included. These may be of interest only to those intent on restoration work.

If brickwork has spalled as badly as in this example, and if this condition is extensive, restoration had better not be attempted, unless one is prepared to replace all face-brick.

## CAPTAIN E. STEELE'S HOUSE, FAIRVALLEY

There is now only a slight depression in the ground where this house known as 'Purbrook,' once stood. The conjectural reconstruction is based on two sketches done while it was standing, one in watercolour and the other in pencil, and on two descriptions of it, one by Mr J.R. Hale of Orillia and the other by Mrs M.E. Wilson, the only surviving member of the Steele family, who was born in the house. I also had a photograph of the church that Captain Steele built just across the road, which is now also destroyed. The size and shape of the Steele house were easily worked out, as were also exterior details of doors and windows. Indeed, the photograph of the old church (which had the same kind of windows), Mrs Wilson's recollections, and the existence of similar windows in the Officers' Mess at Penetanguishene (which Captain Steele surely knew well), all combined to make the windows no problem at all. More problematic were the fireplaces: both sketches showed three chimneys; Mrs Wilson stoutly maintained, however, that there were four fireplaces, but she could remember the exact location of only three of them. Since she recalled that there were no fireplaces in any bedroom except the guest room, I concluded that the fourth fireplace must have been in the servant's room backing on to the kitchen fireplace. I had to make what, I suppose, is an informed guess about the stair to the loft. Mrs Wilson remembered that there was a loft and that there was no stair to it in the main part of the building. Hence, since it was usual in the old houses of New England to build the stair beside a fireplace, I decided that it was legitimate to surmise that this had been done in Captain Steele's house as well.

## DAVID WILLSON'S STUDY, SHARON

The second project was of a more practical nature. After a time every building demands more than casual maintenance if it is to survive; deterioration is slow but continuous and, if not attended to, there comes a time when repair is impossible or prohibitively expensive and the building has to be abandoned. Such was the fate of the Steele house, as well as of the Langton house, whose timbers are now hopefully stored in a barn. Such too was almost the fate of David Willson's study at Sharon, but the York Pioneer and Historical Society diagnosed its condition in the nick of time and was fortunately able at that time to afford the necessary prescription and treatment.

The study had been painted and reroofed as required over the years. But about thirty years ago it was moved some 300 feet to the north to a site directly over an underground watercourse, on the lower portion of a sloping grade, and shaded by trees all day long except in the early morning. Several corners had opened up, providing shelter for birds and a family of squirrels. The ground around the study was perceptibly damp much of the time, and the study took several days to dry out after a rainfall.

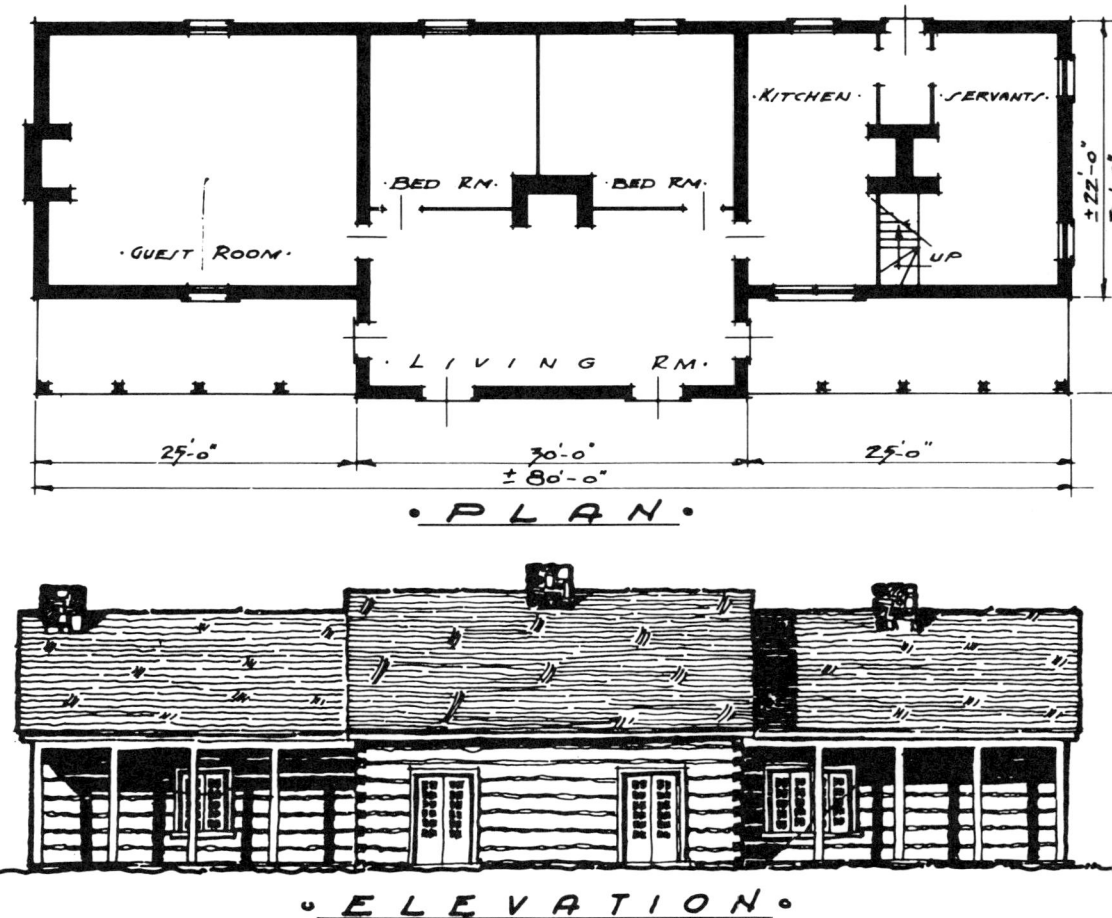

Captain Steele's log house, formerly near Fairvalley

The restored study at Sharon

A detailed examination revealed that portions of several timbers had completely disintegrated, some rafters rested on air, and several posts were completely hollow at the base. The oil in the paint at the foot of the posts had preserved an outer skin of wood to a depth of about $1/8$ inch, but there was nothing inside. Some said that it was the paint that was keeping the building up, but when one considered all the other rotted parts, it seems more probable that the study kept standing out of sheer habit. It had to be repaired and moved at once, and the society decided to restore it to its original design at the same time. Old photographs showed twelve lanterns, similar to those at the corners of the temple itself, spread along the eaves and the gable ends. (Photographs are especially valuable for calculating proportions and size since they are always in true perspective.) Records showed that the chimney, long since gone, had had an arched, brick, flue covering. It was easy enough therefore to design and build new lanterns, and the chimney was given an arched cover with bricks specially cut to size. New bricks had to be used because the old ones were too soft to last for any further length of time. All flashing is copper, and the roof sheathing is covered with waterproof paper over which handsplit cedar shingles of medium butt thickness were applied.

The difficult part lay in moving the study to a healthier environment about sixty feet to the south, on higher ground and away from trees. It was feared that the joints were so far gone that the building would collapse while being moved. All the rafters were therefore propped so as to take the strain off the plates and posts, and the main body of the study, as well as its outer columns, was supported on heavy timbers. The whole framework was carefully slid along the ground to a new concrete foundation; several columns dropped off, but the main framework was kind enough to remain standing. Once in its new site, all the diseased timbers were cut well back and replaced with sound timbers from a barn of about the same vintage as the study. All joints were dipped in preservative before assembly and the date 1961 painted on every new 'old' piece. The greatest difficulty now was in finding sufficient cut nails, but the Canada Wire and Cable Company of Leaside kindly donated several pounds of these nails from their meagre stock. The society practically counted each nail, using them only where the head would show. When the job was finished, only a handful were left over. This problem has been eased to a great extent since then because a number of craftsmen have begun to supply copies of old nails and other hardware.

The study is now in first-class physical shape and should require only the usual maintenance for many years to come. All the details of the restoration have been filed away, so that if the study should need further restoration, say in 2061, the restorers will have more accurate information at their disposal than the society did.

### THE CHURCH IN EVERSLEY

This simple fieldstone country church, built in 1848, was endowed by Lady Eaton and later signed over to the York Pioneer and Historical Society. A first cursory examination of the structure revealed nothing out of the ordinary. The stonework seemed to be in good condition except for certain places where the mortar had weathered rather badly because of a leak in the roof. There was also evidence of the foundation settling in the southwest corner. The stonework along the top of the north wall betrayed a peculiar change of character, and there were other fairly obvious indications of past alterations.

The pews of the interior were originally boxed, the doors having been removed later; the hinges of these little doors have left unmistakable marks on all pew ends. Several benches had been moved to a new location, as revealed by the markings on the floor and on the wainscotting.

No pulpit was to be seen; however, the raised platform upon which it had once rested was still in place, and when the floor-covering on this platform was removed, markings showed the size and site of the old pulpit. In shape it was a rectangle with splayed corners, which meant that it would have had a semi-octagonal front. It had at least one door similar in size to those of the pews. After rummaging about, a single panel with one long side, bevelled at an angle of 22½ degrees, was discovered. This matched the front panel bearing the Bible rest, which was found at the same time. The investigators also turned up a semi-elliptical, upholstered seat, which was soon identified as having been attached to the wall behind the pulpit. That this was the case was verified by marks on the wall and several matching nail holes.

Lying in a cupboard were two quarter-round, cove moulds, identical in paint and grain with the panels of the pulpit. When set on either side of the bottom rail of the main panel, they occupied the same space as the markings on the floor. In itself, this would not be proof of their original location but, since the original pews had this moulding at their base, it was a safe assumption that this was where they belonged. The steps to the pulpit, as well as the raised platform for the choir, were of a later date.

The ashlar walls were of good quality generally, except for several areas along the top of the north wall where the workmanship and choice of stone were strangely inferior. The walls were laid in the early English fashion, that is, built up in 'lifts' of a convenient height, each topped with smaller, fairly flat stones. This treatment gives the wall a slightly striated or coursed appearance, which is not too pronounced, but is easily detected by an experienced eye. Certain obvious markings along the roof slope at the west gable wall were at first interpreted as signs that the original, wide corniceboard had later been replaced with a narrower one.

Careful inspection of the attic space brought the realization that something quite drastic had happened. The plaster, on board lath, of the west wall, revealed a positive outline indicating that an earlier ceiling used to run up the slope of the rafters to the underside of the collar ties. The evidence was quite unmistakable. However, the east gable showed no corresponding outline, nor was there any sign of plaster ever having been applied.

The present ceiling is flat with its joists resting on the original plate. Instead of an interior cornice there is a curved transition from the vertical to the ceiling without any break of moulding.

The second major sign of an alteration was that the wall-plate showed rafter seat-cuts, which are not used today. These old cuts indicate a closer spacing of joists than is the case at present. The more recent rafters rest with a shoulder-cut directly on the top of the joists. This is unorthodox and unsound construction, the kind of thing only amateurs would do. As does all apparently new wood in the roof, these rafters show the marks of a circular saw. At one end, several original rafters had been re-used in a still more unorthodox fashion: their shoulders had proved too short by at least 6 inches or more, most likely owing to a slight change of pitch, and to provide them with support a short length had been nailed to the underside of the rafters to form new shoulders.

From all this evidence, it became clear that the whole roof structure had been replaced from the plate upwards. We can only guess why. It could not have been because of damage by fire, since there was no sign of burning anywhere. The best conjecture is that a high wind so badly damaged the roof that it was necessary to remove it entirely. If the blast was from the south, it would have pushed the roof to the north, dislodging the plate. The consequent damage to the top of the stonework of the north wall would have required repair and so account for the difference in the stonework, noted above. The roofless church would have had to be repaired in great haste, probably by volunteer labour, and to this the poor stonework and amateur carpentry are probably due. It was likely considered a good idea to re-use the old rafters but this must have turned out to be too much trouble after the first few were replaced, for the idea was then abandoned and new rafters installed. At the same time, the ceiling was lowered.

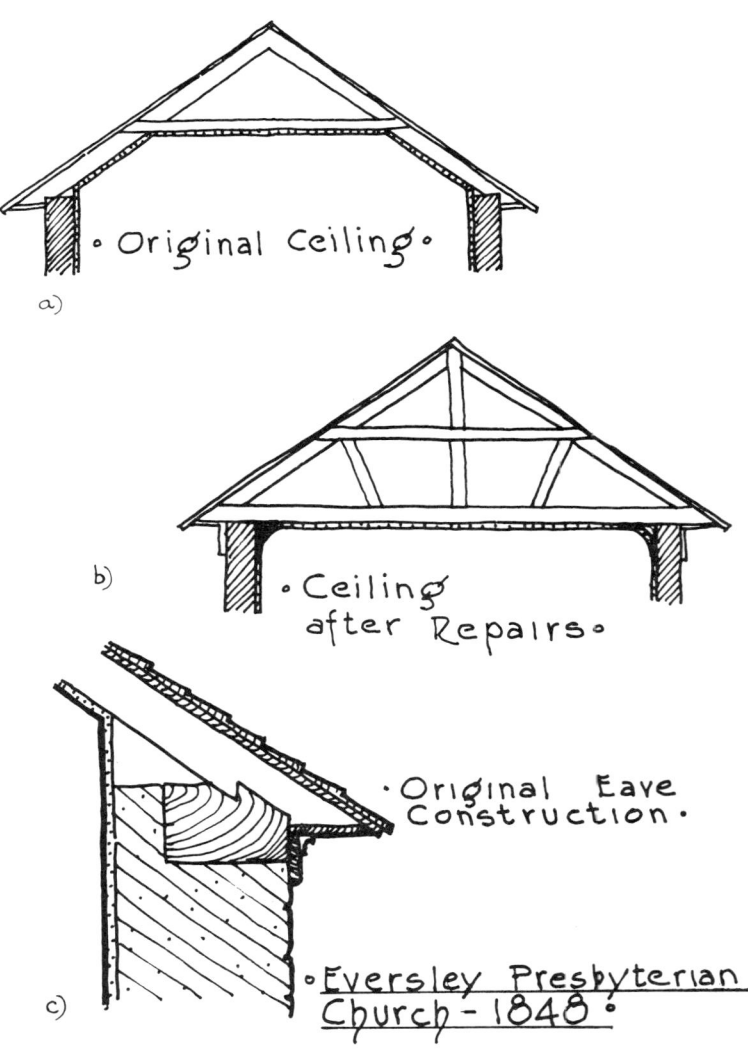

a) Original Ceiling

b) Ceiling after Repairs

c) Original Eave Construction

Eversley Presbyterian Church - 1848

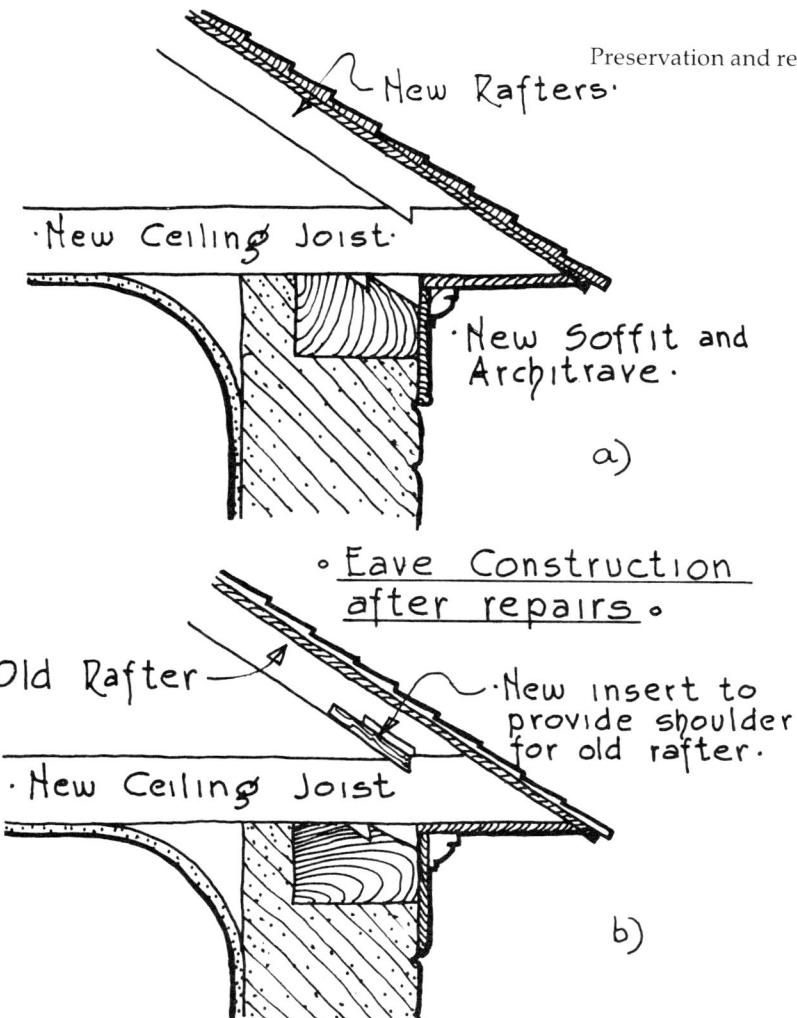

But what possible explanation can there be for the total absence of plaster on that east wall? Again I can only hazard a guess. Let us suppose that the men who dealt with the emergency began removing lath and plaster at the east gable, and that they cleared the surface, down to the springing of the new curved ceiling corner, not only of plaster but of all strapping as well. By the time they had worked along the sides up to the west gable, they realized that what they were doing was not really necessary since the new ceiling would not rise higher than the plate level and everything above this would be concealed. So they decided to save themselves much tedious labour by clearing only a strip sufficiently wide to permit the springing of the curve, leaving all the rest in place – to the delight of later restorers.

The small stone porch came under study next. At first it seemed a later addition. But some chipping at the joints at the junction of the two walls made it plain that the stones were properly keyed – almost certain proof that the porch was erected with the rest of the church.

The Gothic window openings were filled with three sashes: the tympanum above, and two rectangular ones below; the upper being fixed and the lower sashes sliding. Several must have so deteriorated as to necessitate replacement. Again, this seems to have been undertaken by inexperienced workmen because the sashes were replaced with the putty facing in – a structural crime no professional would commit.

According to older residents in the area, the church once boasted a small steeple. Of this there is no structural evidence; it probably disappeared with the rebuilding of the roof. When sufficient funds become available, it should now be possible to restore this building accurately enough in all respects except for the steeple. Of that, no physical traces are left and no documentary evidence has yet been unearthed.

In conclusion, it should be noted that the first hint of drastic alterations was a slight change in the character of the stonework along the top of the north wall.

THE ANDREW MCFALL HOUSE

This house at 99 King Street, Bolton, is situated on town lot 40 as shown on the Gardhouse Plan of 1881. The following information is a brief documentary history of the land on part of which this house stands. This lot is part of township lot 9, concession VII, Albion, a 200-acre area which was patented to J.G. Chewett on 24 August 1820. In 1821, Chewett sold this whole township lot to George Bolton, and shortly afterwards he and his uncle, James, built a mill on what is now called Mill Street. James Bolton bought out his nephew and later moved the mill to a new site in 1847, where

Two views of the Andrew McFall house in Bolton after completion of phase 5

it stood until demolished in 1969. At about this time 'he also built a large cottage and stables on the rising ground on King Street.' In 1845 he bought the west half of township lot 9 from his nephew. In 1855 this parcel of land was sold to an Edward Lawson, who in turn sold it to John Gardhouse in 1860. By 1932 a Mrs Harry Sheardown was owner of the property.

In 1881 Andrew McFall purchased the mill, as well as the property on 99 King Street, that is, the eastern part of the original plot. The bill of sale is of considerable interest:

In Chancery in Re Gardhouse
Valuable Grist Mill and other property, Gardhouse vs. Gardhouse. Pursuant to the Decree made in this cause and bearing date the 21st day of January 1881.
Parcel 7: A lot on Mill Street – lot 38 on said plan of the estate containing 25¾ perches, more or less, and used hitherto as vegetable garden. There is a frame and board-built 5-roomed cottage-roof house, 40 × 26 upon it.
Parcel 9: A lot on King Street alongside the last described lot being No. 40 on the said plan of the estate containing 53½ perches, more or less. There is a 5-roomed cottage-roofed dwelling house 29 × 26 feet, with a good stone cellar underneath and a new kitchen at the back, 20 × 21 feet; also a good well and pump. [This is the dwelling that is now part of the present building at 99 King Street.]

The original cottage seems to have undergone several minor changes even before 20 February 1882, when McFall bought half of a quite different house on Mill Street from the then owner, Mrs Gardhouse. This half was moved and joined to the original cottage and, from then on, the combined house has undergone many drastic alterations and additions until both halves have come to differ beyond recognition from the originals.

*Excerpts from the diary of Andrew McFall*

| | |
|---|---|
| Feb. 20, 1882 | Spoke to Mrs. Gardhouse about the old house. She wants $60 for ½ of it. Hardwick wants $30 to move it. |
| Mar. 13 | Hardwick moving house along M… Street. |
| Mar. 14 | Hardwick took house and put it down most of the day. |
| Mar. 17 | Paid Mrs. Gardhouse $60 last night for old house – charged to real estate. |
| Mar. 29 | Hardwick and man levelling house and putting in posts. |
| Apr. 4 | Hardwick and man started at the house. |
| Apr. 5 | Hardwick and man at house. |
| 6 | |
| 7 | |
| Apr. 8 | Settled with Mrs. Gardhouse for everything except nails. |
| 10 | Hardwick & man at house |
| 11 | " |
| 12 | " |
| 13 | " |
| Apr. 19 | Gave Strength a contract to lath and plaster all required in the house & furnish labour for $9.00. |
| Apr. 20 | Settled with Hardwick for moving & carpenter work with house, $60.00 in all. |
| Apr. 25 | Booth hauling stone for house. |
| Apr. 26 | Booth hauling stone & brick. |
| May 13 | String & man here part … |
| May 15 | Booth at house from A.M. |
| May 17 | Booth often digging cistern drain. |
| May 18 | Booth & Morrison at drain, whitewashing & planting potatoes. |
| May 20 | Got some carpet & furniture & paper. |
| May 21 | J. Stork down for lumber, bought 1000 feet inc. 4 bus. shgs. M. Smith a good portion of the day. |
| May 24 | Furniture came by train. |
| Aug. 31 | Settled with M. Hardwick for work done on house in the spring. |

Historically and structurally, this house is of no particular significance, except as personal family history. But the documents are quoted in detail simply because so much happened to the house in the course of its existence that it seems worthwhile to take the reader through each step in detail as an example of structural detective work. Additions and alterations to this house can be divided into five distinct phases.

*Phase 1*
It began as a single-storey, frameless, plank cottage, about 17 by 26 feet. The sills rested on posts and both the quality of materials and the workmanship strongly suggests that it was meant to lodge only summer help, perhaps

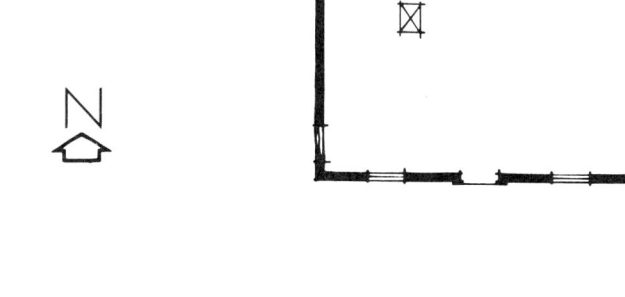

Phase 1

from the mill. There is no evidence concerning the interior plan at this time, nor are we sure when it was built. But it is definitely pre-1860 because it is shown on Tremaine's map of that year. The post foundation has been verified: several of them were found during the most recent alterations.

## Phase 2

Sometime prior to 1881, according to the bill of sale, several changes had been made. For year-round living the original size was too limited, and so a lean-to was added on the north side which, of course, required a new door in this wall. Since a basement is a necessity for a proper home, a partial one was excavated under the east portion of the house. The west wall of the basement stopped about 6 feet short of the west end of the building which retained the supporting posts. Entrance to the basement was from outdoors by an outside stairway, probably with the usual double-leafed cover, and from inside by a trap door in the floor. Actually there were two trap doors.

Phase 2
After adding lean-to between phase 1 and phase 2

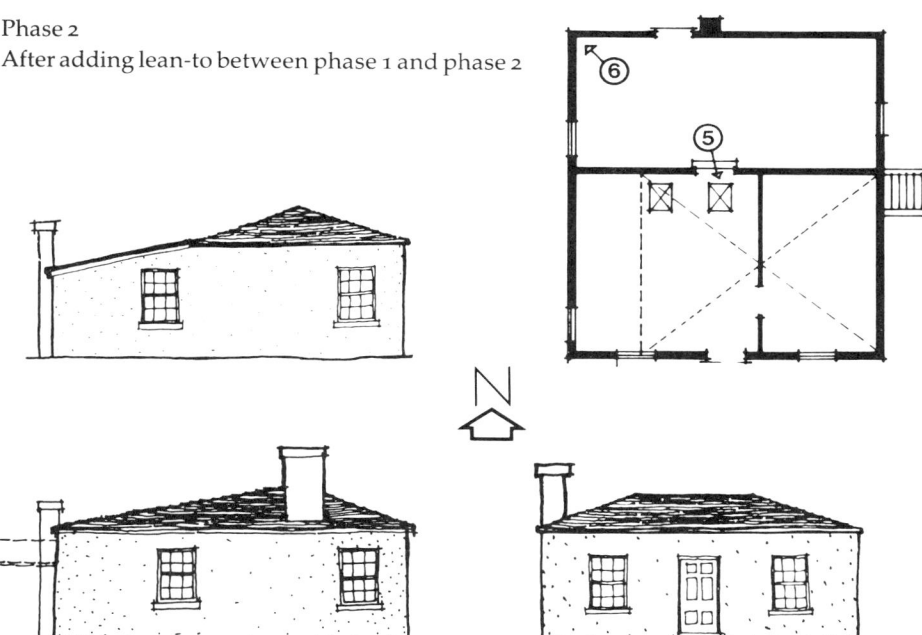

The reason for two remains obscure. A possible explanation is that the west one, which permitted access to a hole in the ground for storing vegetables and fruit, was there from the outset. When it was decided to dig a partial basement under the house, it was found that the original trap door was now useless since it occurred too close to the basement wall. A second trap (5) was therefore cut several feet to the east of the first. The arrangement of interior partitions is unknown except for a single one of plank. This was obviously installed before the floor boards were put down because, when later removed, a gap in the floor had to be filled with a strip of wood (4).

The lean-to, also of vertical plank construction, had the usual sloping ceiling. The floor was at grade level and thus about 16 inches below the house floor; this necessitated a step down from the south room into the lean-to. The latter was given two windows, one at the west end and a larger one at the east. A door in the north wall gave access to the backyard. At this time also, the well, mentioned in the bill of sale, was dug to the north. During this time the house was probably roughcast outside and plastered on the inside, except for the plank partition.

The bill of sale states that there was 'a good stone cellar underneath.' This is not correct. All walls are of brick masonry with one layer of rather large boulders as a foundation. The cellar floor was of earth. No provision for ventilation was made, with the inevitable result that the floor joists soon began to deteriorate severely.

A brick fireplace (3) was almost certainly built at some time between phases 2 and 3 and was located at the west end. The bricks were laid four courses to every 12 inches, directly against the bare plank wall. The mortar joints left an unmistakable pattern, after its removal in phase 5. That it was constructed after the basement was dug is a reasonable deduction; otherwise, why dig a three-quarter basement, and then build an extra foundation for a fireplace just 6 feet away?

The bill of sale describes this cottage as containing five rooms. But in the diagram no partition is shown except the plank one, since this is the only one for which we have unmistakable evidence.

*Phase 3*
In 1882, after Andrew acquired one-half of Mrs Gardhouse's dwelling, major changes were in store for the old cottage. The half-house, after having been moved along Mill Street, was not attached to the old structure but set down 6 feet away to the east. The space between was intended to become the hallway of the combined house. Several problems had to be solved at once. The floors had to be even with each other and ceiling heights allowed to vary without causing embarrassment. Since both houses were to stand under a common roof, the eave lines had to match. Since the east portion was not touched by the work going on in 1970, it was not possible to tell whether any structural changes were necessary to bring this about. It is an interesting coincidence, though, that the pitch of the roof in both houses was almost identical.

Phase 3

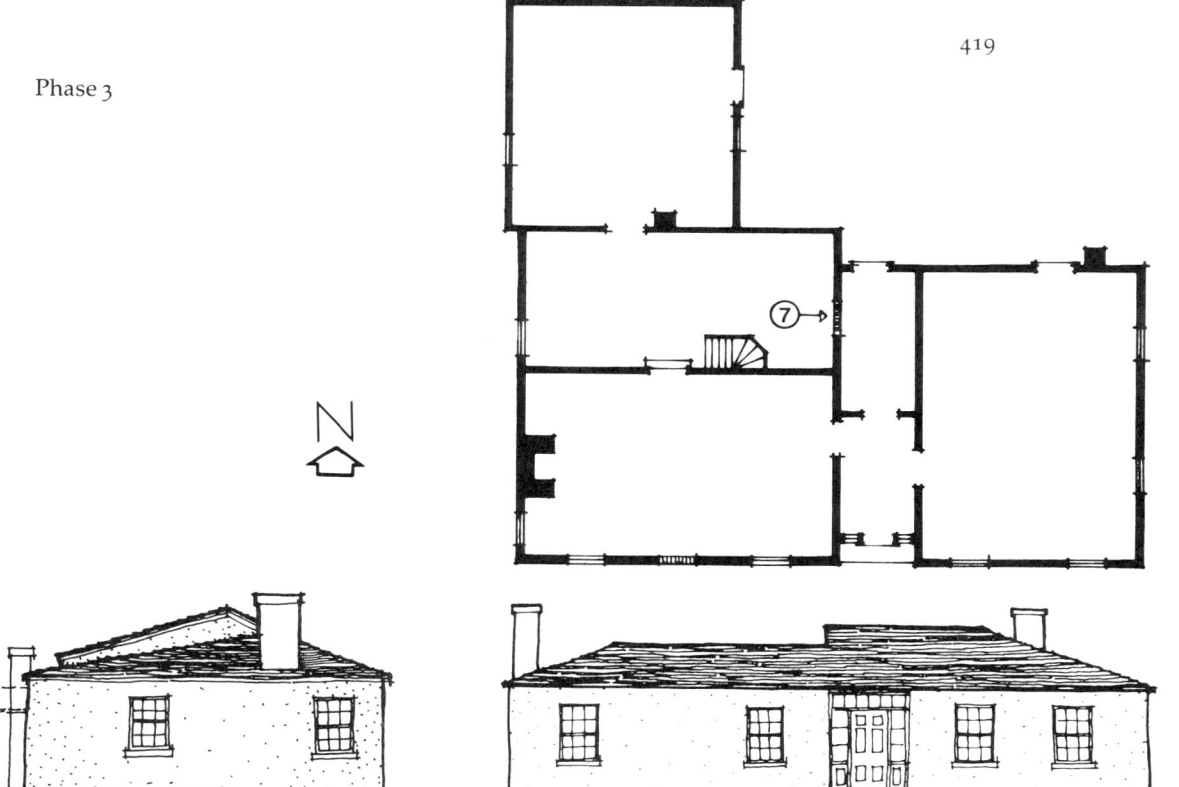

The second house also had a cottage roof, but cutting the house in half resulted in the east end retaining the original hip while the west end became a gable which was closed in and roughcast. No interior partitions are marked in the east half either, since there survives no hint of their arrangement. The plank partition in the west house was removed at this time. The fireplace had been installed and, since the east house had no fireplace, it is reasonable to assume that the west room with the promised comfort of the new hearth became the parlour. The lean-to now became a kitchen and the new addition would be given over to bedrooms. The change in function of the lean-to called for the ceiling to be raised to the level of the front part of the house as well as a chimney, which was built against the north wall (this chimney was removed during the alterations in 1970). Since the east portion had no basement and no heat, still another chimney was built against its north wall.

The south door in the west house was now closed up and a new one provided to give entrance to the new hallway. The east window in the lean-to was covered over because the new house extended beyond it; the material used was the boards that had formed the partition in phase 2. These were nailed against the outside of the east wall of the original house. Wallpaper surviving on these old boards was left intact, and its five layers provided modern investigators with five interesting samples (7).

At some time between phases 2 and 3 another addition was made to the west house. This was later described in the bill of sale as a 'new kitchen at the back, 20 × 21 feet.'

A new entrance to the basement was now needed since the hallway ran over the old exterior entrance. The lean-to provided the needed access, and it is likely that the opening in the floor was closed with a large, hinged trap door.

*Phase 3a*

Now that the house was to become a first-class residence, something had to be done about the lean-to. During phase 2 this structure was probably no better than a woodshed, very likely without so much as plaster on the walls. Now it had to be made respectable. Since its height at the north plate was barely 7 feet, the ceiling needed to rise considerably in order to make the interior into a decent room. So the north and west walls were built up and a new plate put in place (10). A second effect was simultaneously achieved, namely, that of making the line of the eave at the north wall level with that in the south wall at the front of the combined building. The new roof over the total area was achieved in the following manner: since the pitch of each was practically identical, the west roof was simply extended up until it reached the ridge of the east half. The north slope was now carried over to the new plate at the north wall of the lean-to. The slope of this portion of the roof was now broken, but this did not seem to disturb the owner. The original roof was never removed. At this point the lean-to was probably plastered on the inside.

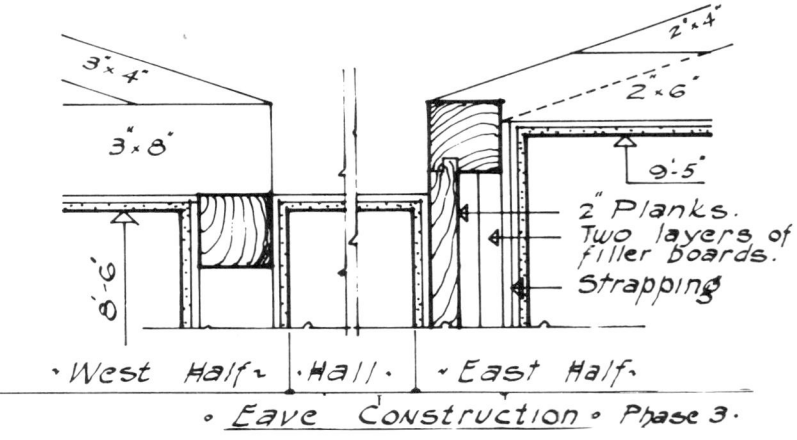

Section at the junction of the original building, the 'west half,' and the half-house moved from Mill Street, the 'east half.' Note that the ceiling heights vary, but the eaves-line has been made similar in both halves to allow for a unified roof appearance.

*Phase 4*

Later still there arose the need for an extra bedroom. A relatively minor alteration made this possible. The door in the middle of the hallway was closed up and the central partition in the hall extended into the east room and closed in with a new partition and a door. A new door was also cut into this room from the living room. At this time one of the several ill-judged structural alterations occurred. The east wall of the central hall contained the original tie beam of the half-house. The new north bedroom required a window, but instead of using the space taken up by the outside door for this purpose, the door was completely closed up and a new opening cut in a place directly central to this beam. This meant removal of the supporting post as well as one of the lateral corner braces. Structurally this was the most unsound of all the alterations. It could only have been done by a man who did not understand how a house was built. There is also evidence of an outside chimney having been erected against the north wall of the east house. This chimney may have been constructed during phase 2 since, without its own stove, this half of the dwelling would be hard to keep warm.

Phase 5

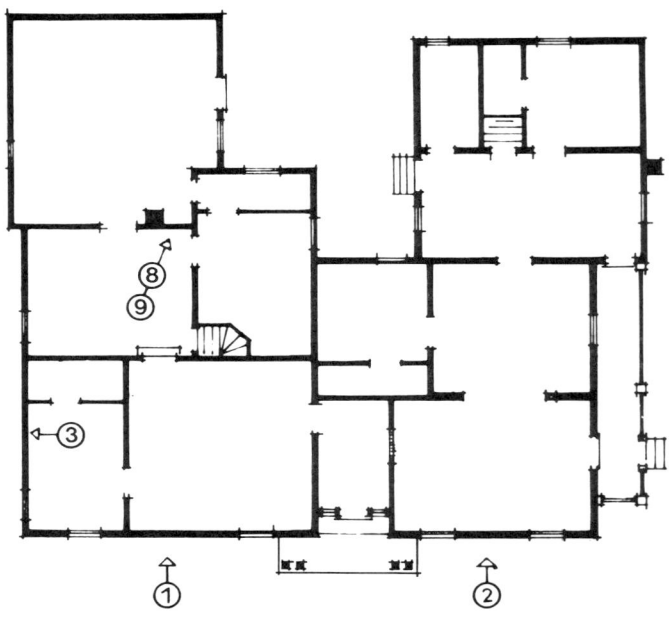

*Phase 5*

The most extensive alterations and additions were made in 1912. About this time period it was decided to turn the house into a two-family home requiring duplicate basements, living rooms, bedrooms, kitchens, bathrooms, and heating arrangements. These changes were so extensive that development can be considered separately.

The hallway was retained as the main entrance to the west apartment. The fireplace was removed because its full depth projected into the room, occupying too much space. The chimney was retained but set on a bracket just below the ceiling to receive a stovepipe. A new stud partition was installed towards the west end, forming a new bedroom with a rather large closet. An additional bedroom and bathroom were provided in a lean-to by drastic means. Almost one half of the north wall was cut out, and a new stud wall erected in line with the entrance to the cellar. This wall was extended about 4 feet past the original north wall. The space thus obtained became a bedroom with a new bathroom at the north end. The new projection required a new roof, so the slope of the north roof was extended to reach over it. Since the roof slope was retained in this portion, the new north plate had to be slightly lower than the existing one, so the ceiling over this new portion was lowered about 6 inches to make it even with the new north plate. The old window in the east wall had been closed during phase 3, so a new one had to be cut.

Since the hallway now belonged to the west apartment, the door to the east was closed, as well as the door leading from the previous living room into the bedroom of phase 4. A new archway was built in the east apartment half way between the north and south walls, to form new living and dining rooms. The window in the new living room was enlarged to become the main entrance door. The additional bedroom, kitchen, and bathroom had to be newly built at the north end. This addition had a complete basement under it. The chimney against the old north wall was removed and a new one built. To protect the new main entrance door, a porch was added.

This dual arrangement lasted until 1970, when A.D. McFall, a lawyer and grandson of Andrew, converted the west half into an office and living quarters for his own use. The building now passed through yet another convulsion. This one will present even greater problems to a future researcher, since much of the original evidence had to be destroyed either because of extreme deterioration or because of the latest planning requirements.

Perhaps it will be of interest to recapitulate some of the steps taken in the initial investigation, together with the deductions, hypotheses, and conclusions whereby it became possible to unravel the complicated story that has been set down above. The numbers in the plans refer to the corresponding numbers beside the photographs; the arrows point in the direction from which the picture was taken.

From the diary and the bills of sale, it was clear that the present building consisted of a single entire cottage and part of a second one. In the written records there was no hint of its ever having been turned into a duplex. However, mention was made of work being carried on in 1912 and, since several doors had been covered up on one side but not on the other, it was assumed that this year saw the last substantial alterations.

The west or original house was clearly built earlier than 1860. Its long side faced a street and, since all front doors at that time opened onto the street, it could be assumed that a front door must have once existed in this wall, especially since the window-spacing suggested its presence. A narrow strip of lath and plaster, removed from the inside between these two windows, was enough to confirm the suspicions.

At the west end there was evidence of a foundation for a fireplace. Again the removal of plaster proved its existence (3). The bricks had been laid directly against the planks and so left stains at all mortar joints. By removing more lath and plaster the size of the fireplace was exactly determined. Joints in the floor boards also revealed the extent of the hearth, and joints in the lath, where it had been filled in, showed the exact width.

The floor-covering was now taken up and the trap doors were located as well as the original plank partition.

The very fact that the floors in the north rooms were lower than that in the south immediately suggested a lean-to. They were a common feature of

LEFT The fireplace was removed during phase 5. Note the two different types of lath, as well as the traces of brickwork mortar joints against the boards that form the west wall of the original cottage.

RIGHT On a hunch we stripped a portion of the east wall in the original lean-to and discovered yet another window which had been completely concealed by later alterations. This window was also closed in from the other side by boards which, very obviously, had been removed from some plank partition, since they were still covered with wallpaper, much to our delight (see photo 7, page 426). On removing some of the later flooring in the original portion of the house, the location of this plank partition was quite obvious (above).

BELOW This is the second trap door in the original cottage floor.

After removing some lath and plaster, the original end plate of the lean-to was revealed.

early houses, and the existence of one here was quickly confirmed by removal of plaster in the northwest corner (6). As soon as the height and slope of the end plate were discovered, the east window attracted our curiosity because its head was much higher than that in the west end. It was therefore decided to follow the north plate eastward. Before long it became clear that very drastic alterations had taken place. The entire plate had been cut away and the plank wall from this point on had been replaced with a stud wall (8 and 9). The abnormal height of the east window prompted us to remove more plaster, revealing the original east window (7). The wallpaper on the boards used to cover this window was of interest: the original living room had been papered several times and it is reasonably certain that these boards were taken from the original partition.

After all lath and plaster had been removed from the north wall, a most interesting group of structural changes was revealed (note the original plank partition and plate at the lower left of 9). At some time between phases 2 and 3 the new north plate, which extended the full length of the building, was raised about two feet. At another period the north kitchen was added (the roof slope is quite evident at the top of 9). During phase 4, when the extra bedroom was needed, this wall was again pierced. The plate for this partition was just high enough so as not to pass under the second or 'new' plate; this, therefore, had to be cut into to permit the partition to extend north and provide space for the north bedroom.

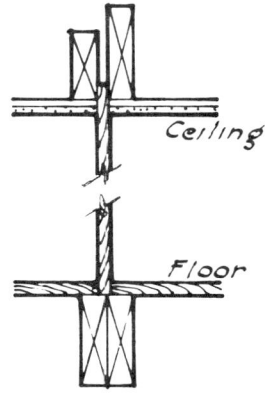

· Original Plank Partition ·
· Phase 2 ·

426 Building with Wood

The attic space over the original lean-to revealed the most interesting structural expediency. At the bottom of picture 11 is the roof of the original cottage. When the half-house was added during phase 3, the result was a gable facing west. This was roughcast and properly flashed where it joined the old roof. The work can be seen in the middle of the picture. When it was decided to roof over the entire west portion, the old roof was extended to meet the ridge of the half-house whence it sloped towards the 'new' north plate in the lean-to. The original roof was never removed and is still in place.

Since the 1970 alterations did not touch the east part of the house, I was not able to study it for possible changes. In any case, the west, original house is by far the more interesting and complex object of investigation and it is for this reason that it has received most of our attention.

Thus ends the long and adventuresome history of two halves of a single house at 99 King Street in Bolton, and the 'detective story' that unravelled its tortured past.

The original east window

Tracing the north plate eastward, another structural alteration was revealed. When the lath and plaster was stripped away from this wall, the alteration was clearly exposed.

The change from plank wall to stud partition

When the lath and plaster was stripped from the walls of the original lean-to, the construction providing for a level ceiling was visible.

**11** After phase 3, McFall decided to have the ridge of the original cottage raised to meet that of the new addition. To do this he left the original roof in place and simply built the new one over it. Here we can see the space between the original and the new roof.

## A last word

The strength of a culture seems to me to be directly proportional to the effort put forth to preserve its past for the benefit of future generations. The corollary of this is that a nation that feels there is little in its past worth preserving will not in the future have much left to preserve.

A remarkable illustration of these sentiments occurred in Poland after the Second World War, when 80 to 100 per cent of the historic inner core of Warsaw had been destroyed. Immediately after the war, plans were drawn up for the restoration of the city: the whole country was united in one of the most prodigious reconstruction efforts in Europe, simply because the spirit of the Polish nation would not permit a blank to exist in its visual history.

The magnitude of the Polish effort can be gauged by comparison with another well-know restoration. The rebuilding of Warsaw was begun immediately after the cessation of hostilities in 1945 and was completed in 1953 at a cost of $300 million; the reconstruction of Williamsburg in Virginia lasted about fifty years and cost about $88 million. In all fairness, one must recognize the tremendous pressure and necessity to rebuild quickly in Europe, and Williamsburg had experienced a gradual decline by ageing over centuries whereas Warsaw went through one brief, cataclysmic eruption of ruthlessness. Nevertheless, such reconstruction was an almost superhuman effort on the part of the Polish people, especially so since the cost of the restoration at that time was an astronomical figure even for a wealthy nation. To quote Dr S. Lorentz, director of the National Museum in Warsaw: 'The enemy had intended to raze Warsaw, and nearly did it. Therefore it was our duty to resuscitate it. The reconstruction of Warsaw is the last victorious act in the fight with the enemy, which lasted five years, both openly and underground. It is the finishing touch of our unbending resistance against enemy violence.'

At present Canadians are slowly beginning to realize that they have an architectural history worth preserving and that its preservation will greatly strengthen and give substance to their culture. This development, according to the time-clock of history, is a fairly new one, and we must be prepared, in our attempts at preservation, to learn as we go along, to run into the occasional blind alley, and to be patient with technical errors. Our sense of historic values is growing slowly and we have a long road ahead of us to catch up with older lands. It is a sad commentary on the slowness of this development, when as late as May 1976, the Ontario Teachers' Federation found it necessary to make a strong recommendation to the Ontario government that the study of Canadian history be made a compulsory subject in our secondary schools!

A sense of history must be developed not only in the average citizen but, even more importantly, also in our political leaders. They are the people, after all, who make our laws. There have been distinguished exceptions among our past political leaders. Governor Simcoe, for example, fully appreciated the importance of architecture in establishing the character of a city by insisting that in the first two streets in the new town of York the owner had to build a house of a definite minimum size, 'according to the prevailing mode of building.' This, of course, was Georgian architecture; it was only in the back streets that every resident was permitted to 'follow his fancy.' Unfortunately, esteem for architectural values has deteriorated considerably since then, and too many of our elected representatives continue to live in a culturally rarified atmosphere. Great strides have been made in the last decade or so, however. Both federal and provincial governments have taken important steps to assist in architectural preservation. One of the more positive steps has been the establishment of Heritage Canada. The philosophy behind this organization, however, is to place a greater emphasis on area or district planning and conservation rather than on single units; there is inherent danger in this line of thinking, for after the planning is completed we may find some of the pieces missing. It should be noted, too, that Heritage Canada was set up only as recently as 1973, and then only because of public pressure (the public is always ahead of the politicians).

This is, nevertheless, a most welcome development; but there must be established as well an intensive training program for architects in the principles and techniques of architectural preservation. In this area, we are still woefully weak. Such training programs are not now available in Canada, and any student interested in this area must go abroad. In order to be successful in Canada, such programs must receive the full support of all levels of government as well as the various schools of architecture, if planning and function are to be continuous.

The Ontario government now makes several experts in museum work available to the public for the asking, a most important first step. This assistance should be broadened to include experts in technical matters and restoration procedures.

Attempts to save something of our past are being made at the local level by many well-meaning enthusiasts who, because of lack of knowledge and training, may confuse rather than enlighten. Such efforts may be misguided, but without them not much would be achieved; persons who are willing to work but lack knowledge and experience should be educated and guided. What is urgently needed now, even at the risk of being overwhelmed by an unwieldy bureaucracy and strangling red tape, is an information centre specializing in every facet of historical preservation. Such an institution should be readily available to the public and should therefore be located in one of our larger cities; its main features would be a reference library, a museum of examples and specimens, exhibits of construction methods and materials, workshops where actual demonstrations could be conducted, and, most important of all, facilities to provide leads to experts who would give advice either voluntarily or for a nominal fee.

An indication of how important historical architectural preservation is in the eyes of the Western world is the fact that, at a meeting in Venice in May 1964, the machinery for international cooperation in this endeavour was set up in the shape of ICOMOS, the International Council on Monuments and Sites, with headquarters in Paris; one of the main purposes of this institution is the training of architects and engineers in the philosophy and techniques of architectural conservation.

To sum up, a threefold program is needed in Canada to train experts in architectural restoration. Firstly, university courses at the undergraduate level should be set up to expose students to the philosophy and problems of restoration. If a student subsequently desires to specialize, he or she should be able to take a two-year course at the post-graduate level; only graduates from an architectural school should be admitted to this phase of study. Secondly, an information centre and museum as outlined above should be established. Finally, opportunities should be provided for laymen to meet specialists locally in order to solve the problems in a particular area.

In the meantime, we must not overlook the needs of today. If we are not alive to the urgency of immediate problems, we may find ourselves someday splendidly equipped with the knowledge to preserve and restore old buildings with little left to preserve.

# Notes

CHAPTER 1: INTRODUCTION

1 Isham and Brown, *Early Connecticut Houses*, chap. 9
2 McGregor, *British America*, 443
3 Preston, ed., *Kingston before the War of 1812*, 32, 393
4 Roy, *Kingston: The King's Town*, 45
5 Mathews, *Oakville and the Sixteen*, 36
6 Robertson, *Landmarks of Toronto*, VI, 265
7 *Ibid.*, 120
8 Séguin, *La maison en Nouvelle-France*

CHAPTER 2: LOG CONSTRUCTION

1 Traquair, *The Old Architecture of Quebec*, 15, 16; Jefferys, *Picture Gallery of Canadian History*, I, 82
2 Shurtleff, *The Log Cabin Myth*
3 Addy, *Evolution of the English House*
4 Garvan, *Architecture and Town Planning in Colonial Connecticut*, 82, and Crossley, *Timber Building in England*, 112–13
5 Earle, *Home Life in Colonial Days*, 5
6 Innocent, *Development of English Building Construction*, 269
7 Harris, *Journal of a Tour into the Territories Northwest of the Alleghany Mountains*
8 Traquair, *The Old Architecture of Quebec*, 7
9 Campbell, *A History of Nova Scotia*, 88, 153
10 Cruikshank, ed., *Simcoe Papers*, II, 108
11 McCubbin, 'The Haunted Honeymoon House,' *Chatelaine*, Feb. 1953
12 Miller, *A Century of Western Ontario*, 26
13 *Canadian Journal of Corrections*, Oct. 1964, pp. 408 ff.
14 Radcliff, ed., *Authentic Letters from Upper Canada*, 16

15 McGregor, *British America*
16 *Ibid.*, 557
17 Cruikshank, *Simcoe Papers*, V, 203
18 Jarvis Papers, Metropolitan Toronto Library
19 For example, Canniff, *History and Settlement of Upper Canada*
20 Shirreff, *A Tour through North America*, 178
21 McGregor, *British America*, 557 f.
22 Langton, *A Gentlewoman in Upper Canada*
23 McGregor, *British America*, chap. 15, VIII
24 Robertson, *Landmarks of Toronto*, III, 40
25 *Ibid.*, II, 738
26 *A Gentlewoman in Upper Canada* and *Early Days in Upper Canada: Letters of John Langton*

CHAPTER 3: TIMBER FRAMING

1 Bell, *Carpentry Made Easy, etc.*, 55
2 Innocent, *Development of English Building Construction*, 119
3 Innis, *Select Documents in Canadian Economic History*; Oliver, *History of American Technology*
4 Bell, *Carpentry Made Easy*, 50
5 Isham and Brown, *Early Connecticut Houses*
6 Traquair, *The Old Architecture of Quebec*, 14
7 Innis, *Select Documents*, 377
8 Donald, *The Canadian Iron and Steel Industry*
9 Lambert, *Travels through Canada and the United States in the years 1806, 1807, 1808* (London 1814); both Lambert and Baddeley quoted in *Association of Preservation Technologists*, V, 3 (1973), 17
10 *Harper Encyclopedia of Science*, II, 274, and *Oxford History of Technology*, V, 467
11 Bell, *Carpentry Made Easy*
12 Séguin, *La maison en Nouvelle-France*, 26; reproduced by permission of the National Museum of Man, National Museums of Canada
13 P.-L. Lapointe, in *Association of Preservation Technologists*, VIII, 1 (1976)

CHAPTER 4: PLANK CONSTRUCTION

1 From an unpublished manuscript by T. Ritchie, Building Division, National Research Council, Ottawa 1969
2 Massachusetts Historical Society, *Collections*, 4th series, VII (1865), 118–20
3 J.B. Felt, *Annals of Salem* (1827), 119, as quoted in Kimball, *Domestic Architecture of the American Colonies*
5 A photograph of this house appears in Isham, *Early American Houses*, plate 12, and in Garvan, *Architecture and Town Planning in Colonial Connecticut*.
6 Isham and Brown, *Early Connecticut Houses*, 258

CHAPTER 5: BARNS

1 Under the sponsorship of the University of California, a study of medieval barn framing in England is being carried out by Professor Walter W. Horn, an historian, and Mr Ernest Born, FAIA, an architect in San Francisco; their complete findings should be published soon.
2 Report of the Commissioner of Agriculture, Washington 1864, by the Hon. Frederic Watts of Carlisle, Pennsylvania; also Schoemaker et al., *The Pennsylvania Barn*, 29
3 Séguin, *Les granges du Québec*, 28–9. The entire section on the Quebec barn owes a great deal to this book. Séguin's list of sizes is as follows:

| Dimensions | | | Nombre de granges | Dimensions | | | Nombre de granges |
|---|---|---|---|---|---|---|---|
| 80 | pieds sur | 24 | 1 | 40 | " | 24 | 16 |
| 80 | " " | 20 | 1 | 40 | " " | 20 | 1 |
| 70 | " " | 30 | 1 | 35 | " " | 26 | 1 |
| 60 | " " | 30 | 8 | 35 | " " | 25 | 1 |
| 60 | " " | 26 | 1 | 35 | " " | 24 | 4 |
| 60 | " " | 25 | 1 | 34 | " " | 20 | 1 |
| 60 | " " | 24 | 4 | 30 | " " | 30 | 1 |
| 56 | " " | 30 | 1 | 30 | " " | 27 | 1 |
| 55 | " " | 30 | 1 | 30 | " " | 26 | 1 |
| 55 | " " | 26 | 1 | 30 | " " | 25 | 2 |
| 50 | " " | 30 | 3 | 30 | " " | 24 | 38 |
| 50 | " " | 28 | 2 | 30 | " " | 20 | 28 |
| 50 | " " | 26 | 2 | 25 | " " | 30 | 1 |
| 50 | " " | 24 | 9 | 25 | " " | 24 | 1 |
| 45 | " " | 30 | 2 | 25 | " " | 20 | 1 |
| 45 | " " | 28 | 2 | 24 | " " | 24 | 1 |
| 45 | " " | 24 | 1 | 20 | " " | 25 | 1 |
| 40 | " " | 30 | 8 | 20 | " " | 24 | 1 |
| 40 | " " | 28 | 1 | 20 | " " | 20 | 19 |
| 40 | " " | 26 | 1 | 20 | " " | 18 | 2 |
| 40 | " " | 25 | 2 | 20 | " " | 15 | 2 |
| | | | | | | | 177 |

CHAPTER 6: CHURCH, MILL, AND BRIDGE

1 Price, *The British Carpenter*; Tredgold, *Elements of Carpentry*
2 Fitzgerald, *Thornhill – An Ontario Town*, and a manuscript in the North York Public Library
3 Button, *I Married an Artist*
4 Morrison, *Early American Architecture*, 31

## 434 Notes

5 McGregor, *British America*
6 Craig, *Early Travellers in the Canadas*, 139

### CHAPTER 7: NON-WOOD CONSTRUCTION

1 Morrison, *Early American Architecture*, 248, 135
2 *British American Cultivator*, II, Feb. and March 1843
3 *Ibid.*
4 Innocent, *Development of English Building Construction*, 159
5 Fitzgerald, *Thornhill – An Ontario Town*, 23
6 Bolton, *Bolton: Some History and Events*
7 *Centennial of Bogarttown School*

### CHAPTER 8: POLYGONAL BUILDINGS

1 Fletcher, *A History of Architecture on the Comparative Method*, 927
2 Pugin, *Contrasts*
3 *Jersey Journal*, 1960
4 Winfield, *History of the County of Hudson*, 381
5 *Antiques*, April 1957, p. 342
6 Ross, *The Book of Boston*, 153
7 Séguin, *Les granges du Québec*, and Société Historique du Québec
8 *Journal of the Society of Architectural Historians*, May 1964, pp. 101 ff.
9 Turcotte, 'Wonderful Days at Grimsby Park,' *Hamilton Spectator*, 11 May 1963
10 *Newmarket Era*, 1951 and 1952; a series of articles entitled 'The Story of Sharon'
11 Trewhella, 'The History of Newmarket,' unpublished ms.

### CHAPTER 10: WOODWORKING TOOLS

1 Innis, *An Economic History of Canada*, 76
2 Cruikshank, ed., *Simcoe Papers*, II, 66, 69; 21 and 28 Sept. 1793
3 McGregor, *British America*, 532
4 A.B. Dove, an article on nails in *Wire and Wire Products*, xxx, no 6 (June 1955); and Oliver, *History of American Technology*
5 Lajeunesse, *The Windsor Border Region*, 47, 260
6 Preston, ed., *Kingston before the War of 1812*, 55
7 *Ibid.*, 65, 112
8 Earle, *Home Life in Colonial Days*
9 Radcliff, ed., *Authentic Letters from Upper Canada*, 6

### CHAPTER 11: PRESERVATION AND RESTORATION

1 *Canadian Building Digest*, National Research Council Bulletin, 111

# Bibliography

Addy, S.O. *Evolution of the English House.* London: Macmillan 1898
*American Heritage Book of Great Historic Places,* Bruce Calton, ed. New York: Simon & Shuster 1957
*Antiques.* New York: Straight Enterprises, April 1957

Barnard, Henry. *School Architecture.* New York 1849
Bell, William. *Carpentry Made Easy, etc.* Philadelphia 1857, 1875, 1883
Blake, V.B., *et al.* Historical sections of the *Conservation Reports* of the province of Ontario
Bolton, James H. *Bolton: Some History and Events.* Bolton Enterprise 1931
Briggs, Martin S. *The Homes of the Pilgrim Fathers in England and America.* Oxford 1932
*British American Cultivator* (Toronto), II, Feb. and March 1843
Brown, James B. *View of Canada and the Colonists.* Edinburgh 1851
Bulfinch, Thomas. *Bulfinch's Mythology (The Age of Fable).* New York: Random House
Bullock, Jr, O.M. *The Restoration Manual.* Toronto: Burns and MacEachern, 1966
Burrows, C.A. *The Annals of the Town of Guelph, 1827–1877.* Guelph Herald 1877
Button, Billy. *I Married an Artist.* Toronto: Ryerson Press 1951

Campbell, G.G. *A History of Nova Scotia.* Toronto: Ryerson Press 1948
*Canadian Journal of Corrections,* Oct. 1964, pp. 408 ff
Canniff, William. *History and Settlement of Upper Canada.* Toronto 1869
Card, Raymond. *The Ontario Association of Architects.* Toronto: University of Toronto Press 1950
*Centennial of Bogarttown School* (pamphlet published by the school)
Champdor, Albert. *Babylon.* Toronto: Ryerson Press 1958
Craick, W. Arnot. *Port Hope: Historical Sketches.* Port Hope: Williamson Press 1901
Craig, Gerald. *Early Travellers in the Canadas.* Toronto: Macmillan 1955
Crossley, Fred H. *Timber Building in England.* London: Batsford 1961
Cruikshank, E.A., ed. *Simcoe Papers,* 4 vols. Toronto: Ontario Historical Society 1923

Diderot, D., ed. *Encyclopédie*. Paris 1751–72
Donald, W.J.A. *The Canadian Iron and Steel Industry*. Boston: Houghton Mifflin 1915
Dove, A.B. In *Wire and Wire Products*, xxx, no 6 (June 1955) (article on nails)
Duhamel, Roger, FRSC. *City on the Ottawa*. Ottawa: Queen's Printer 1961

Earle, Alice Morse. *Home Life in Colonial Days*. New York: Macmillan 1898

Firth, Edith. *The Town of York*. I, *1793–1815*. Toronto: University of Toronto Press 1962
Fitch, J.M. *American Building*. Boston: Houghton Mifflin 1947
Fitchen, John. *The New World Dutch Barn*. Syracuse University Press 1968
Fitzgerald, Doris M. *Thornhill – An Ontario Town*. Thornhill 1964
Fletcher, Sir Banister. *A History of Architecture on the Comparative Method*, 17th ed. London: Athlone Press 1961
Fowler, O.S., and L. *A Home for all ... and the Octagon Mode of Building*. New York: Samuel R. Wells 1853
Freese, S. *Windmills and Millwrighting*. London: Cambridge University Press 1957

Garvan, Anthony N.B. *Architecture and Town Planning in Colonial Connecticut*. New Haven: Yale University Press 1951
Gloag, John. *Victorian Taste, 1820–1890*. London: Black 1962
Gotch, J.A. *The Growth of the English House*. London: Batsford 1928
Guillet, E.C. *Early Life in Upper Canada*. Toronto: Ontario Publishing Company 1938; *The Lives and Times of the Patriots*. Toronto: Nelson 1938; *Pioneer Settlements*. Toronto: Ontario Publishing Company 1933; *The Valley of the Trent*. Toronto: Champlain Society 1957; *The Pioneer Farmer and Backwoodsman*. Toronto: Ontario Publishing Company 1963
Guldbeck, P. *The Care of Historical Collections*. Nashville: American Association for State and Local History 1972

Hall, Basil. *Travels in North America, 1827–1828* (1829)
*Harper Encyclopedia of Science*. New York: Harper and Row 1963
Harris, Kenneth D. 'Restoration of Port Royal, Nova Scotia,' *Journal of the Royal Architectural Institute of Canada*, July 1940
Harris, Thaddeus M. *Journal of a Tour into the Territories Northwest of the Alleghany Mountains*. London 1803
Harris, and Lever, *Illustrated Glossary of Architecture*. London: Faber and Faber 1966
Harvey, John. *Conservation of Buildings*. Toronto: University of Toronto Press 1972
Henry, L.J., and Paterson, G. *Pioneer Days in Ontario*. Toronto: Ryerson Press 1938
Hewett, Cecil Alec. *The Development of Carpentry, 1200–1700*. Newton Abbot: David & Charles 1969
Heyes, Esther. *The Story of Albion*. Bolton, Ont.: Bolton Enterprises 1961
Hodgins, J.G. *Documentary History of Education in Upper Canada*, 28 vols. Toronto: King's Printer 1894–1910
Holbrook, Stewart H. *Dreamers of the American Dream*. New York: Doubleday 1957

Honigman, J. *Foodways in a Muskeg Community*, NCRC-62-1. Ottawa: Department of Northern Affairs and Natural Resources 1961

Horn, Walter W., and Born, Ernest. *The Barns of the Abbey of Beaulieu, etc.* University of California Press 1965

Hunter, A.F. *A History of Simcoe County.* Toronto, 1909; reprinted 1948

Hussey, Dr John A. *The History of Fort Vancouver.* Portland, Oregon: Abbot, Kerns & Bell Company 1957

Innis, Harold A. *The Fur Trade in Canada.* Toronto: University of Toronto Press 1956

Innis, H.A. *Select Documents in Canadian Economic History, 1497–1783.* Toronto: University of Toronto Press 1929

Innis, Mary Q. *An Economic History of Canada.* Toronto: Ryerson Press 1935

Innocent, C.F. *Development of English Building Construction.* London: Cambridge University Press 1916

Isham, Norman M. *Early American Houses and Glossary of Colonial Architectural Terms.* New York: DaCapo Press 1967

Isham, Norman M., and Brown, Albert F. *Early Connecticut Houses.* Preston and Rounds, 1900; reprinted Dover Publications, New York 1966

Jarvis, William. Papers, in the Metropolitan Toronto Library.

Jefferys, C.W. *Picture Gallery of Canadian History.* Toronto: Ryerson Press 1950

Jennings, John. *Boston – Cradle of Liberty.* New York: Doubleday 1947

*Jersey Journal.* Jersey City Public Library, NJ, 1960

Johnson, Allen, and Malone, Dumas, eds. *Dictionary of American Biography* (article on Orson Squire Fowler), VI, 565–6

Johonnot, James. *Country School Houses.* New York 1859

*Journal of the Arizona Archeological and Historical Society*, XXVIII, Oct. – Dec. 1962

*Journal of the Society of Architectural Historians*, May 1964 (article on jails), 101 ff

Jury, W. *Sainte-Marie among the Hurons.* Montreal: Palm Publishing Press 1949

Kelly, J. Frederick. *Early Domestic Architecture of Connecticut* (1924). New York: Dover reprint 1963

Kimball, Fiske. *Domestic Architecture of the American Colonies* (1922). Dover reprint 1966

Lafever, Minard. *The Modern Builder's Guide.* New York, 1946

Lajeunesse, Ernest J. *The Windsor Border Region.* Toronto: University of Toronto Press 1960

Langley, B. and T. *The Builder's Jewel.* London 1754

Langton, Anne. *A Gentlewoman in Upper Canada.* Toronto: Clarke Irwin 1950

Langton, John. *Early Days in Upper Canada: Letters of John Langton.* Toronto: Macmillan 1926

Lessard, M., and Marquis, H. *Encyclopédie de la Maison Québécoise.* Montreal: Les Editions de L'Homme 1972

*Life* editors. *America's Arts and Skills.* New York: Dutton 1957

Lukomskij, G. *Russische Baukunst.* Munich 1923

McCubbin, Doris. 'The Haunted Honeymoon House,' *Chatelaine* (Toronto), Feb. 1953
McGregor, John. *British America*, 2nd ed. London 1833
McKay, Wm. A. *The Pickering Story*. Pickering Historical Society 1961
McKee, H.J. *Recording Historic Buildings*. Washington, DC: Department of the Interior, National Park Service 1970
McLean, Alexander. *History of Jersey City, N.J.* (1895)
McRae, Marion, and Adamson, T. *The Ancestral Roof*. Toronto: Clarke Irwin 1963
Mathews, Hazel C. *Oakville and the Sixteen*. Toronto: University of Toronto Press 1953
Mayne, Captain. Commandant, Detroit River, 20 Nov. 1796. 'Estimate of Materials for Building a log House 25 feet long and 20 feet wide with a Double Chimney ...' (total cost £61-4-9). Public Archives of Canada, British Military Records, 'C' Series, RG 8, vol 723
Meer, F. van der, and Mohrman, Christine. *Atlas of the Early Christian World*. Edinburgh: Nelson 1958
Mercer, Henry C. *The Origin of Log Houses in the United States*. Bucks County Historical Society, Doylestown, Pa. 1924, and *Ancient Carpenters' Tools*. Doylestown 1951
Miller, Audrey Saunders, ed. *The Journals of Mary O'Brien, 1828–1838*. Toronto: Macmillan 1968
Miller, Orlo. *A Century of Western Ontario*. Toronto: Ryerson Press 1949
Moogk, Peter. *Building a House in New France*. Toronto: McClelland & Stewart 1977
Mongait, Alexander. *Archeology in the U.S.S.R.* Moscow: Foreign Language Publishing House 1959
Morrison, Hugh. *Early American Architecture*. Oxford University Press 1952
Moxon, Joseph. *Mechanick Exercises*. London 1703

Needler, G.H. *Otonabee Pioneers*. Toronto: Burns and MacEachern 1953
*Newmarket Era*, 1951 and 1952. A series of articles entitled 'The Story of Sharon'
Nicholson, P. *Builder's and Workman's Director*. London 1848

Oliver, J.W. *History of American Technology*. New York: Ronald Press 1956
Ontario Historical Society. *Ontario History*
*Oxford History of Technology*. Oxford: At the Clarendon Press 1958

Palmer, F.H.E. *Russian Life in Town and Country*. New York: Putnam 1901
Potter, Alonzo, and Emerson, George. *The School and the Schoolmaster*. New York 1842
*Preservation and Conservation: Principles and Practices*. Proceedings of the First North American International Regional Conference held Sept. 1972 in Williamsburg and Philadelphia. Washington, DC: Smithsonian Institution Press 1976
Preston, Richard A., ed. *Kingston before the War of 1812*. Toronto: University of Toronto Press 1959
Price, Francis. *The British Carpenter*. London 1733
Pugin, Augustus W.N. *Contrasts*. London: Dolman 1932

Radcliff, Thomas, ed. *Authentic Letters from Upper Canada*. Toronto: Macmillan 1953
Radford, W. *Up-to-date Barn Plans*. Chicago: Farm Press Publications 1909
Radford, W.A. *Framing*. Chicago 1908
Reaman, G. Elmore. *The Trail of the Black Walnut*. Toronto: McClelland & Stewart 1957
*Report of the Commissioner of Agriculture for the Year 1864*. Washington, DC
Reynolds, Helen W. *Dutch Houses in the Hudson Valley before 1776* (1928). Dover reprint 1965
Richards, Godfrey, trans. 'The First Book of A. Palladio's Architecture,' in the *Journal of the Society of Architectural Historians*, Oct. 1961
Ritchie, T., et al. *Canada Builds, 1867–1967*. Toronto: University of Toronto Press 1967
Robertson, J. Ross. *Landmarks of Toronto*, 6 vols. Toronto: Evening Telegram 1894–1914
Robertson, J. Ross, ed. *Mrs. J.G. Simcoe's Diary*. Toronto 1915; reprinted Macmillan 1965
Roskoshny, Herman. *Russland: Land und Leute*. Greszner Verlag
Ross, Marjorie D. *The Book of Boston: The Federal Period, 1775–1837*. New York: Hasting 1961
Roy, J.A. *Kingston: The King's Town*. Toronto: McClelland & Stewart 1952
Russell, Peter. Papers, in the Metropolitan Toronto Library

Saltsman, L.F. *Building in England down to 1540*. Oxford University Press 1952
Schmidt, Carl F. *The Octagon Fad*. Privately printed, Scottsville, NY 1958
Schoemaker, Alfred, et al. *The Pennsylvania Barn*. Lancaster, Pa. The Pennsylvania Dutch Folklore Center Inc. 1955
Séguin, R.-L. *Les granges du Québec du XVIIe au XIXe siècle*. Ottawa: Musée Nationale du Canada, Bulletin no 192, 1963
Séguin, R.-L. *La maison en Nouvelle-France* Ottawa: Musée Nationale du Canada, Bulletin no 226, 1968
Shaw, William H. *History of Essex and Hudson Counties* [NJ], II
Shelburne, Vt., Museum Catalogue of Woodworking Tools (1957)
Shirreff, Patrick. *A Tour through North America*. Edinburgh: Farmer 1835
Shurtleff, Harold R. *The Log Cabin Myth*. Cambridge, Mass.: Harvard University Press 1939
Smith, Donald M. *At the Forks of the Grand*. Paris, Ont.: Walker Press 1952
Smith, James K. *Alexander Mackenzie*. Toronto: McGraw-Hill 1973
Smith, W.L. *The Pioneers of Old Ontario*. Toronto: Morang 1923

Traquair, Ramsay. *The Old Architecture of Quebec*. Toronto: Macmillan 1947
Tredgold, Thomas. *Elements of Carpentry*. London 1870
Trewhella, Ethel Willson. 'The History of Newmarket' (unpublished ms.)
Tunis, Edwin. *Colonial Living*. Cleveland: World Publishers 1957
Turcotte, Dorothy, R. 'Wonderful Days at Grimsby Park,' *Hamilton Spectator*, 11 May 1963

Unesco. *The Conservation of Cultural Property*, XI. Paris 1968
Upper Canada Village, Research library

Waterman, T.T. *The Dwellings of Colonial America*. Raleigh: University of North Carolina Press 1950
*Weekly Mercury* (Guelph), 12 Jan. 1911
Welsh, Peter C. *United States Patents, 1790 to 1870: New Uses for Old Ideas*. Washington, DC: Smithsonian Institution, Paper 48, 1965
West, Trudy. *The Timber-frame House in England*. Newton Abbot: David & Charles 1969
Winfield, C.H. *History of the County of Hudson* [NJ] (1874)
Winkle, Daniel van. *History of the Municipalities of Hudson County, New Jersey, 1830–1923*, I.
Winkle, Daniel van. *Old Bergen History and Reminiscence* (1902)
Wish, Harvey. *Society and Thought in Early America*. New York: Longmans 1950
Wood-Jones, R.B. *Traditional Domestic Architecture in the Banbury Region*. Manchester University Press 1963

The sources listed here come from my own library or they have been checked by me personally.

# Picture credits

DIAND Department of Indian Affairs and Northern Development, Ottawa
GSC Geological Survey of Canada, Ottawa
PAC Public archives of Canada, Ottawa

*pages*

15    Fort Chimo and McDermot's store: GSC
16    Heartman's store and Fort McLeod: GSC
17    Fort Langley: Public Archives of British Columbia, Victoria; Fort Rupert: PAC
18    Fort Nascopie: GSC; Fort St James: Hudson's Bay Company Archives, Winnipeg
19    Red River settlement: PAC; Red River cottage: Professor J. Russell, University of Manitoba, Winnipeg
20    Fort Pelly: GSC
21    Church of England, Winnipeg: watercolour in the PAC
22    Church, Fort Simpson: PAC
38    The Woods: Mary O'Brien's letter is in the Public Archives of Ontario; the sketch of the house is from Miller, ed., *The Journals of Mary O'Brien*
53    Blockhouse, Jones' Falls: photograph by F.C. Curry, Brockville
73    Hull: PAC
75    White Otter Castle: DIAND
134   Gleason House: Isham and Brown, *Early Connecticut Houses*
141   Cahokia: Illinois Division of Parks and Memorials, Chicago
142-3 Pichet house: DIAND
144   Lartigue apartments: National Museums of Canada, Ottawa
145   Paradis house: School of Architecture, McGill University, Montreal

Picture credits

146-7, 149-51 Fafard house: DIAND
154-7  French construction details: DIAND
161    Johnson house: DIAND; Dolphis Pitre house: *Star*, Windsor
163    Fort William: DIAND
187-8  Construction details: DIAND
208-9 (bottom), 211 (top) Stratford barn: *Beacon Herald*, Stratford
223    Heidelberg barn: *Free Press*, London
224, 227, 228 Quebec barns: Inventaire des Oeuvres d'artde la province de Québec, Université Laval, Quebec City
225    Cap à l'Aigle: McCord Museum, McGill University, Montreal

# Index

adobe 274
adze 55, 372, 373
Ameliasburg 319, 321
Ancaster 340
anchorbeam 205
arches 92-3, 212-13
ashlar 269-71
Atikokan 75
Auburn 160-1
augers 364, 365, 374
Aurora 118, 308, 311, 313, 354
axes 28, 34, 360, 362
Aylmer 334

Baddeley, Lieut. 120
Baillargeon, Hermidas 164, 168
Balderson 8
Baldwin 282, 286, 288
balloon framing 20, 24, 105, 108, 121-3, 126, 131; first used 122; joists in 131; second floor 132; transition to 124; *see also* Carmichael house
bank barn 8, 199
bannisters 88
Banwell, Henry 167, 170-2; house 11, 109, 162, 164-72
bargeboard 342
barns 190-228; doors 8, 191, 213; Langton's 84; log 191-7; Ontario 190-221; polygonal 217, 228, 294, 330-5; Quebec 222-8, 294; stone 212-16, 225, 227; twelve-sided 216-17; barn raising 217-23
Barnum house, Grafton 355
barracks 36
Barrett, William 302; house, Port Hope 302-4
Barrie 297, 337
base moulding 167
baseboards 403
basements 126; full 129; half 182; in log barn 195; wall thickness 299
Baysville 266, 355, 358
beam framing 9
beams: in barn 154, 194; cedar 182; ceiling 39, 238, 401; church floor 235; extra beam-support 154; in deadhouse 309; needle beams, bridge 253; round 111, 126
Bear, John 233, 251
bearing surfaces 104
Beaverton 58-9
Beehive, near Fenelon Falls 70-1, 72
Beetle (or Commander) mallet 372, 374
Belfountain 214, 271
Belleville 344
bents 107, 130
Berrisford, Col. W.H. 279

Bewdley 306
binding, logs 44
Bird, Henry James 299
Bird house, Bracebridge 293, 299–302
Blair 213
Bloomfield 323
board and batten 123, 124, 132, 164
Boggarttown 98, 279
Bolton: deadhouse 308, 313; houses 176, 178, 397; McFall house 404, 414–28; mill 232–3, 245; mud brick 279; polygonal house 325
Bond Head 10, 343
bond timbers 275
bonds, standard brick 262–7
books on building 6, 11, 103, 105, 107, 291
Boughton, Levi 282, 285–7; house, Paris 284, 285
Boulton, D'Arcy 51
Bowmanville 316, 340, 346
boxwood, in planes 377
Bracebridge 293, 299–302, 319
bracing (props) 92, 105, 107, 125, 175, 232, 245, 394; barn 205, 211; church 231, 235; corner 126, 135, 186, 235; diagonal 109, 152; double, in heavy framing 109; double, in mill 232, 245; in French log construction 109; horizontal 109, 132; lateral 107, 152; longitudinal 152; roof in Quebec 152; single diagonal, in mill 231; tenoned 128; transverse, *see* cross-bracing
Brampton 316, 328
Brantford 179
Brass, Lieut. David 8
bricks: fill 128; masonry construction 14, 262–8, 355; veneer: on log buildings 36, 264, 268, on frame house 265, on log-butt house 265; cornices on octagonal house 299; restoration 404–6; 'wooden' 355, 358
bridges: covered 233, 251; rural Ontario 232; short-span 232; West Montrose 251–60

British: building technology 4, 5, 8, 26, 27–8, 34, 116; barns 199; stone 270; tools 362, 365
British Columbia 13, 15, 16, 20, 399
broad axe 372, 373
Brockville 35, 213
Brougham 47, 67, 104, 277, 279
Brown, James 10
bugs (bedbugs) 41
building: contracts and specifications, Quebec/Ontario compared 158; construction in Canada, compared to Russia and England 84; dating construction 51; materials 11; techniques, culture and 8; technology: history and 4, most significant development in nineteenth-century 121, problems of weather and geography 5; regulations (codes, by-laws) 11, 12–13; skills, French 14, 19
Burnside, Brockville 213, 215–16
Butler house, Niagara-on-the-Lake 180–1
Butler's Rangers 8

cabin barn 199
Cahokia, Ill. 141, 144
Calabogie 338–9
Caledon 335
Cambridge 272
Campbell, Chief Justice 51
Campbellford 83
Canadian Frame 15, 148
Cap à l'Aigle 225
Cap Santé 146–51
Cape Breton 144
carapace 177
Carleton, Sir Guy 360
Carmichael house, Toronto 123, 131–2
Carp 339
carpenter shop, Upper Canada Village 362
Carrying Place 266
Cartwright, Richard 12
casement windows 55, 59, 61

cast-iron 405
Castle Frank 27, 70
Castle Grange 214, 271
Cataraqui 370–1
cavity construction, brick 264
cedar 34, 43; joists and beams of 182; shingles 399
ceilings: beams 39, 238, 401; construction, Continental (or Dutch) and English Colonial 39; framing 9; height 39; joints, English 39; joists: method of securing 59, mortise and tenon 168, restoration 412–13, size of and spacing 58, uneven spacing of 60
cellars 39, 104, 418
cemetery records 312
central heating 121, 293
centre-chimney floor plan, Pennsylvania-German 30
Chapleau 70
chapter houses 290
Charlesbourg 144
Chaussegros de Léry, Joseph Gaspard 370
Cherry Valley 336
chimneys 13, 16, 32, 35, 66, 89; catted clay 32; construction in US 32; octagonal houses 299; outside 32, 66; support for central 167; in restoration 400, 419
chinking 14, 29, 30, 35, 41, 44, 56–7, 140, 141, 400; with daubing 174; moss as, when no pitch available 86; plaster 56; Quebec/Ontario compared 160; rare type in Ontario 56
chisels 372, 374
churches 230–1; Dalhousie Mills 295, 335; Evangelical United Brethren, Wallenstein 40; Eversley 401, 410–14; Fort Simpson Anglican (log) 21, 22; Grace, Markham (Meyerhoffer) 97, 110, 130, 231, 234–41; Greenstead, Essex 26; Madill (log) 41; McNab, Welland 262; Paris Plains Methodist 288; polygonal 295, 296, 335; Red River Anglican 21; Richmond Hill Presbyterian 310; St Andrew's, Scarborough 266; St James Anglican, Paris 285, 287; St Mary's, Chicago 122; St Thomas Anglican, Shanty Bay (mud) 278–80; Salem, Mass. 174
clapboard 33, 129, 174; as roofing material 57
Claremont 35, 55
Clarke house, Prescott 212–13
clay block 121
cleft planks 55
Clendinning, John 44
climate shock 6
cloacinas 291
cob (mud) walls (murs de torchis) 225
cobblestone treatment 282–8
Cobden 316
Cobourg 51
Colborne 330
Coldwater 201, 204
collar-purlin 152
collar-tie 96, 116; double 152
colombage pierroté (half-timbering) 14, 27, 140
common bond 262, 264
compression 92; joints 92, 113, pinned 128
Connecticut 6, 110, 174, 388; *see also* Gleason house
construction, *see* building
Cooksville 110, 125
cooper's tools 377
corners: assembly 95; cornering 26, 28, 50–7, 72, French method of 70, log-butt 72–5, log barn 190, military type 50; pieces 72; plates, interlocking 135; posts 74, 130, 131, trunks as 26; typical construction 181; rot 14
cornices 40, 299, 353
Cornwall 120, 167
cottages: English 28; Langton's 83–90; modern 75; octagonal 317

courthouses: Cahokia, Ill. 141; Guelph 214; London 40; Virginia 33
Craigleith 115, 374
crawl space 131, 182
Cree council house 294
cribwork 72
cross-bracing 235, 249; central longitudinal 152; cross-ties 107; lateral 142; in mill 249; principle of 109
crosscut saw 47, 372
crown land: sale of 12; stipulations 12, 13
croze 377
cruck construction 26
Cruikshank, Col. G.W. 279
cupola vents 205
Cyclopean flat arch 213

Dalhousie Mills 294, 295, 335
daubing 174
Dawes Road house, Toronto 46, 48–9, 51
dead load (static) 230
deadhouses 298, 308–13
decorative woodwork 342–58, 403
Denis cottage, York Mills 8, 9, 110, 279
Dent, John Charles 336
De Puisaye house, Niagara-on-the-Lake 100, 101, 119
deterioration 393, 397, 402
Detroit 26, 148, 164, 170, 370
Dickson, William 51
Diderot 99, 361, 365–7
Dixie 112, 127
Dodge, Christopher 369
Doon 213, 251
doors 44, 59, 65; in barns 8, 191, 213; carriage 213; har-hung 8; in jails 72; in log houses 47; masonry openings 93; placement 40, 41
dovetail keying 14, 29, 55
dowels, continuous 186
dragon beam 8, 9
drawbores 92, 97
Dresden 66–7

drip cap 398
Duclos Point 319
Duff's Corner 353
dumb waiter 300, 302
Duncan house, York Mills Road 351
Dundurn Castle, Hamilton 121, 180, 338
Dunlop, Charles 159–60
Durham County 329
Dutch influence: church 290; house 29–31, 39, 55; Schoharie barn 142, 206–7

Early American building technology 5, 133
eaves 18, 21, 110, 420
Eckhardt house, Unionville 8
Edgeley 29, 37, 59; see also Stong house
Elliott, Col. 66
Elmira 40
encorbellement 225, 227
English: bond 262, 263; cottage 28; heavy timber barn 203; medieval roof 153
Enniskillen 371
Erin 217, 332–3
Eversley 401, 410–14
expansion 11
exteriors: decorative woodwork 341–58; inward tapered wall 142; roughcast 179

facing: brick 267; stone 285, 287
Fafard house, Cap Santé 146–51
Fairvalley 61, 392, 407–8
Farwell, Lloyd 200
fasteners 97–103, 375, 401, 405; see also nails, pegs, pins, spikes
Fenelon Falls 13, 70–1, 72, 83, 85, 88, 392; see also Langton, John
fenestration, see windows
fieldstone: barn 213; coursed 269–71; cut 273; random 269; restored church 410–14; split 269, 270
fill 14, 129; brick 26, 115; horizontal logs 164; pegged 159, 163; in Quebec 141, 159; timber 114, 144, 146; wattle-

and-daub 26, 115; wood 29; *see also* chinking
fillisters 378, 386, 388
finial 343
Finnish settlers 31, 193
fire regulations 13, 41
fireplaces 32, 65, 66–7, 89, 118, 418, 422; back-to-back 90; common fate of 122; replaced by stoves 67, by windows and doors 67; Pennsylvania type 31
fireproofing 118–19, 121
Fish, Benjamin 242; mill 97, 242–50
Fisher barn, Kitchener 212–13
Fisher house, Toronto 98, 102, 109, 120, 121, 133, 136–9, 186, 262
flashing 35, 398, 400, 402
Fleming, Sir Sandford 115, 374
Flemish bond 262, 266
floors: attic, in mill 247; beam connections 95; framing 135; joists 164; in log house 55; plank 39; in restoration 401; supports 111; tools used for flooring 55
footings 104
forbay 199
forced air heating 121
forts: Albany 102, 294–5, 340; Chimo 15; Chipewyan 215; Garry 15, 16; George 388, 393; Langley 17; McLeod 16; Nascopie 18; Pelly 20; Pontchartrain 26; Rupert 17; roof trusses in 152; St James 18, 20; William 163; York 36, 50, 388
foundations 5, 104, 126; logs, wood used 43; walls 131, in barn 72, 194; in the west 152
Fowler, Orson Squire 291–4, 296; folly 291–2
framing: types of buildings 24; meaning of 'frame' 107; types of frames 108; parts of frame wall 104; neatest example 128; comparison of framing details, historical development 133–9; joints 94–7; restoration 402–4
Franklin stove 118, 120

Franktown 69–70
Frazer, Samuel de Burgh 37–8; house, near Midland 37–8, 55
Freeman, William 213, 215
French construction: across the continent 4, 13–24, 26; in Ontario 8, 9, 64, 70, 159–72; *see also* Quebec
French doors 55, 61, 85, 303
fretwork 342, 343, 404
frogs, in bricks 263, 264, 266–7
frost heaving 88, 104
frow 375
full shoulders 94
Fullarton 333, 335
furnaces 121

gables 8, 19, 22, 57, 65, 108, 167, 345, 348
Galt 119, 213, 339
Galt, John: house and office, near Guelph 33, 48, 72
galvanized sheet iron 220
gambrel roof 116, 216–17, 332
Gananoque 334
Georgian style 32, 86, 89, 154, 204, 343, 429
German influence 8, 28, 29, 31, 57–8, 118, 190, 213
German Mills 396
gingerbread 342–3
girders 107, 194, 196
girts 135
glass 32, 59, 370, 371
Gleason house, Farmington, Conn. 109, 133–9
Goderich 213, 297–8, 336–7, 339
Gothic style 12, 40, 89 132, 283, 290, 293, 310, 347, 384
Grafton 355
Grand Pré 34
Granton 316–17
Grimsby Park Temple 305–6, 335
grooved post construction 14–24, 140–51, 159–63, 163, 225
Guelph 33, 72, 213, 214, 269, 297, 329, 336, 340

Halfpenny, William 6
half-timber 27, 140
Hall, Basil 34, 120
Hamilton 121, 180, 339, 353
Hamilton house, Paris 283, 285
Hargrave, William 214, 216
Harris, Thaddeus M. 33
har-tree 8
hatchets 369
Haviland, John 197
Hawkesbury 217, 326–7, 333–4
hay barn 202
hearth support 104, 113
heat 118, *see also* fireplaces, stoves
heavy timber barn 198
Heidelberg 223
Helliwell house, Toronto 278–9
Henry, Alexander 22
Henry, William: house, Sutton 176, 180, 182–4
hip roof 8, 18, 55, 116, 180
hold-downs 16, 225
hollows and rounds 381, 385
Honey, Dr R. 159–60; house 160–2
hookpins 130, 375
Hopetown 35, 65
horizontal: corner bracing 186; lath 303; timbering 26
Houghton 120
Howe, Joel 369
howel 377
Hudson's Bay (or Canadian) Frame 15, 20, 148
Hull 72, 73, 163
Huttonville 316

Ile d'Orléans 141
Ingersoll 328
Innocent, C.F. 174
insulation 119, 400
Irish (Scotch-Irish) 31, 32, 33
ironworks 118, 120, 123
Isham, Norman M., and Albert F. Brown 6, 110, 133, 174
Islington 340

jails 40, 42, 72, 297, 298, 336–7
jamb, post as 146
Jameson, Anna 69
Jarvis, William 46, 47, 57, 78–81
Jefferys, C.W. 279
Johnson, Sir John: house, Williamstown 161
Johnson, Pauline 179
joiners 7, 11, 107
joints 5, 7, 11–12, 92–7; in compression 11, 97; in tension 92, 97; alternate butt 179; brick 263; corner 201; dovetail 97, 107; expansion 11; exposed 400; floorboard 403; half-dovetail 137, 164, 197; open half-dovetail 111; half-mortise 111; half-lap dovetail 96, 97; lapped dovetail 155; lap(ped) nailed 122, 185; in mill 232, 250; pinned and scarfed 96–7, 107, 164, 196, 197; ridge boards 94, 110; roof 106; *see also* mortise and tenon
joists: first-floor 131; mill floor 250; round 164; sawn 126; sill and floor detached 111
Jones' Falls 53
Jordan 113

Kapuskasing 193
Kelly, J.F. 174
Keswick 325
Kettleby 117, 308
keying 14, 28, 29, 50–7, 179, 268; dovetailed 45; interior walls and 63; in log barn 197; methods of 52; military 52; Pennsylvania 29, 42; Swedish 28; unsound 62; with wedge-shaped round logs 62
King City 308, 313
king posts 22, 94, 116, 132, 152, 240–1
King's Mill 8
Kingston 53, 81, 269
Kingsville 294, 322, 324–5
Kitchener 130, 200, 212–13
Kleinburg 267
knee wall 48

Labrador 15, 18
Lachute 185–7
Lafontaine 38, 39
Lambeth 323
L'Ange Gardien 227
Langton, Anne 36, 83
Langton, John 13, 28, 36, 52, 59, 83; house 7, 37, 46, 57, 58, 61, 83–90, 104, 392
lanterns: in deadhouses 310, 311, 313
lap-keying 51
Lartigue, Sieur 144
lath 116–18, 369; handsplit 100, 115, 117, 129, 239; sawn 100, 117–18
lather's hatchet 118, 369
lean-to 217, 417–18, 420; roofs 116
Leaside 319, 321
Lefaives Corners 38, 39, 333
Lennox, E.J. 391
Leskard 326
Lévis 294
libraries 290
lights 37, 39, 44, 59, 61, 89, *see also* windows
Lindsay 329
lintels 26, 92–3, 184; stone 213
Little Current 329
live load 230
load bearing 92, 135, 230
log-butt construction 72–5, 226
log cabin myth 31
log construction 14, 16, 26–90; restoration 396–401
log houses: compared to English Georgian and New England colonial 32; average cost 47; fate of first 200; frequency 68–9; general procedure of building 44; largest 55; structural specifications for 76–82; types and comparative sizes, in southern Ontario 46; typical dimensions 12, 47, 51; typical structural features 65
London 12, 40, 51, 66, 323, 335, 340
Longford Mills 74
lookouts 129

Lowville 328, 345
Lucknow 330–1
lumber: sawn 131; seasoned 11
Lynden 348–9
Lyndhurst 120

maison-cour 225
Maitland 167
mallets 372, 374
Malton 325–6
Manitoba 15, 16; Frame 15
mansard roof 116, 327
Maple 274, 316, 318
Markham 44, 56, 97, 98, 119, 230, 242, 279, 349; *see also* churches, Grace; Fish, Benjamin
Marmora 120
Martin, Simeon 200
masonry construction 93, 262–88
Massachusetts 121, 174, 296
McArthur, Peter 64
Macdonald, Angus 242–3
McDonell, Alexander 40
McFall, Andrew 416; house, Bolton 404, 414–28
McGillivray, William 163
McGregor, John 7, 41, 44, 66, 68, 365
McIlraith house, Hopeton 35
McKellar 330
McQuat, James 75
Meaford 335
Mennonites 217
Merrick, Solyman 369
Meyerhoffer, Rev. Philip V. 235
Midland 37–8, 55
Miles, Abner 57, 78–80
military construction 51; keying 52
milk cooling house 205
Millbrook 328
mills 8, 55–6, 123, 230–3; Benjamin Fish 97, 242–50; Oakland 231; Toronto 175; Woodbridge 230
Milton 328, 332
Mitchell, Charles 285
Modified American technology 5, 133

monkey wrench 369
Monteith house, Paris 285
Montreal 14, 26, 158–9, 226, 323, 369
Moogk, Brig. W. 180
Moosonee 295
Morrisburg 350, 352–3
mortar 14, 29, 226, 267, 404; *see* chinking
mortier blanchi 225
mortise and tenon joints 12, 14, 97, 106, 107, 131, 184; open 94, 110; pinned 111, 137; replaced by nailed lap 122; simple 94; two-pin, in church 241
mortising: chisel 363, 374; machine 363, 375
Morton 336
Mosport 273, 347
mouldings 89, 380, 382–7; mould-cutting machine 375; plane 378
Moulinette 108, 124–5
Mount Pleasant 322–4, 334, 339
mud-brick construction 8, 274–82
mullion 61
muntin bars 39, 246, 402

nails 97, 99, 100–2, 123, 180, 234, 4 366–9, 371
newel post 301
Newmarket 279, 308, 310–11, 312, 313
Niagara 47, 51, 82, 329, 340
Niagara-on-the-Lake 100, 119, 180–1, 186
Noble, Col. Arthur 34
Nobleton 346
Normandale 120
Normandy 141, 154, 190, 225
Norval 316
Nova Scotia 34

Oakland 231
Oakville 12–13
Oakwood 329
O'Brien, Edward and Mary 38, 280
octagonal buildings: first in North America 290; smallest in Ontario 328; *see* polygonal buildings

Orillia 53
Osgoode Station 334
Oshawa 326
Ottawa 335, 340
Ouse Lodge, Paris 286
outbuildings, log 69, 70
overhangs 58, 343
overshot barn 199
Oxford Mills 59

Palatine German settlers 148
Palermo 344
Palladio 104–5, 201, 204
Paradis house, Charlesbourg 144–5, 152
Paris 282–8, 306, 347, 352–3
Park River post 22–4, 398
Patten house, Paris 283
pegs 92, 97, 375, 401
Penetanguishene 38, 58, 61, 407
Pennsylvania-German construction: bank barn 8, 69, 199–200, 227; heavy timber barn 198; influence on Ontario 5, 8–9, 29–31; keying 29; saddle-notching 29–51; stonemasons 213, 270; *see also* Schneider house; Schmidt barn
Penryhn house, Port Hope 315
pent roof 8
Peterborough 35, 41, 55, 83, 159, 319–20
Philadelphia 31, 297, 365, 371
Pichet house, Ste-Famille 141–3, 159, 160
Pickering 177, 271, 374
Picton 319–20, 326, 352–3
pièce sur pièce 14
pierced wood 342–3
Pierson, J. 101
pilasters 299
Pinkney house, Cooksville 110, 125–7
pins 97–9, 250, 375; pin-cutter 99
Pitre house, Tecumseh 159, 161–2
planes 369, 374, 375–88
plank construction 14, 28, 45, 141, 174–88, 416, 418, 423–7
planks 14, 55; as load-bearing members

177; horizontal 179; as roof-boarding 106; tongue-and-groove 57; vertical 57, 176
plaster 129, 275; chinking 56
plates 104; position of 110; raising 110, 403; secondary 130
plumbing, indoor 293, 302
pointing 404
polygonal buildings 228, 290–340
Pontypool 345
porches 5, 58, 135, 302, 344; overhang at roof 64
Port Carling 308, 313
Port Hope 292, 302–4, 315, 326–7, 336, 340, 354
Port Sandfield 314–15, 329, 340
Poste-du-lac-des-Allumettes 163
poteaux construction 140; poteaux et pièce coulissante 140, 193
prefabrication 34, 205
Prescott 212
preservation and restoration 4, 10, 390–430; basic principles 392–5; brick 404–6; frame 394, 402–4, 407, 409; log 396–401, 407–8; plank 416, 418, 423–7; stone 404–6, 410–14
principals 104–5, 108
privies 314–15, 340
props 16
pugging 118
Pugin 290
purlins 26, 152, 197

quarters (or prick-posts), *see* studs
quatrefoil windows 303
Quebec: barns 190, 224–8; building regulations 118; plank construction 14, 174, 185–8; stoves 118; timber framing 140–59; *see also* French construction
Quebec City 226
Queen's Rangers 47, 82
Queensville 308, 312–13
quoins 72–3, 89, 213, 287, 310, 354, 358

rabbet 174, 378
Radcliff, Thomas 41, 51, 371–2
rafters 96, 106, 167, 220; in barn 205; deadhouse 309; placement of 110, 116, 154
raising bees 107, 217–23
Rama Indian Reserve: barn 44, 45, 201; log house 45
random fieldstone 269
Red River 21; Frame 15, 19, 148
Rednersville 346
Renfrew 335
restoration, *see* preservation
Richards, Godfrey 103–4, 105
Richmond 371
Richmond Hill 108, 110, 115, 308, 310
ridge: boards 106, 110, 197, 205; joints 94; poles 16, 22, 152
Ridgeville 352–3
Ridout, George 120
Rigaud 224
Roblin Mills 340
Rockton 404
Rockwood Academy 213, 214
Rocky Mountain Frame 148
roofs 5, 8, 12, 106, 116, 130, 152; boarding 106, 335; French/English compared 152; at gable end 130; joints 106; Langton's 84; in octagonal buildings 299; paired rafters 167; pitch 132, 152, 154; porch 58; in restoration 398, 400; shingled 21; thatched 16, 225; trusses 116, in church 231, 239, 240, in fort 152; typical Quebec frame 19, 152–7; weatherproofing 57
Rosemont 36
rot 43, 397
round: barns 217, 333; houses 48, 318; logs 44, 51, 201
rubble 269, 272
running (stretcher) bond 262, 264
Russell, Peter 40, 46, 47, 76–8
Russian: influence 28; 'izbah' 84; stove 86

saddle-notching 29, 51–2, 54
St-Hermas 185–6, 188
St Jacobs 200, 219
St Mary's 347
St Maurice forge 118, 120, 360
St-Michel 228
Ste-Famille 141
Ste-Monique 155
Ste-Scholastique 154, 156–7
Salter, Eric 69–70
sandstone imitation 89
Sandwich 109, 162, 164
sashes, *see* windows
Saskatchewan 20
sawmills 57, 123
saws 363, 365, 372, 375
saw-tooth ornament 18, 21
Scadding, John 48, 50, 51, 71
Scandinavians 28, 193
scantling 11, 76
Scarborough 266, 345, 348
Schmidt, Johannes: barn 194–5
Schneider house, Kitchener 130
Schoharie: barn 142, 206–7; parsonage 148
schools 29, 40, 42, 57, 59, 272, 296, 304
Schweitzerscheuer barn 200
Scott, John 10
Scottish: barn 213; stonework 213–14, 270
screws 97, 102–3
Séguin, R.-L. 224
Selkirk, Lord 19, 37
settling 43, 109, 181, 250
shanty 33–5, 70; Langton's 83
Shanty Bay 35, 38, 54–5, 57, 61, 278–9
Sharon 101, 110, 263, 311, 314, 340, 347, 397, 407, 409–10
Shaw, Capt. 70
shear pins 184–5, 186
shear stress 92
sheathing 129, 164, 176
shed (or pent) roof 57
sheer-pole (or gin-pole) 107
Sherk, David 223

shingle house 399
shingles 12, 18, 21, 33, 34, 226, 260, 399
Shirreff, Patrick 66
Shurtleff, Harold R. 27, 28
siding 39, 114, 176, 179
sills (sole plates) 104, 107, 112, 131
Silver Islet 42, 72
Simcoe 323, 328, 330, 334
Simcoe, Col. John Graves 12, 36, 51, 70, 362, 429
skyscraper, log 75
slats 106, 220
slave cabins 32
slick 374
slit barn 212, 213
Smith house, Edgeley 37
Smith house, Toronto 33
soffit 130, 413
Sorel 370
Southampton 329
Sowden house, Paris 286
Spark, Capt. James 58, 71
speaking tube 302
specifications: bridge 258–60; French style, Park River post 23–4; French style in Ontario 160–1; log houses 12, 76–82; in Quebec 158–9
Speedside 335
spikes 72, 97, 102, 368
split: fieldstone 270; logs 72
spoolwork 342, 343
squared logs 29, 48; dovetailing of 51; squaring 104
stairways 301, 402; bannisters 88; curved 303
steam heating 121
Steele, Capt. E. 61, 407; house, Fairvalley 37, 46, 55, 61, 72, 86, 392, 407, 408
Stewart, George A. 160–1
stockenchurch 26
Stokes, John 311
stone: alterations 405; barns 212–16, 225, 227; block 121; chimney 66; facing 285, 287; fireplace 32;

fireproofing 118–19; imitation joints 89; masonry 14, 269–73; quoins 287; wall 270
stonemasons 12, 269
Stong house, Edgeley 29–30, 53, 59, 67, 110; pighouse 63
stoves 118–21
stovewood (log-butt) 72
Stratford 209
stress 11, 28, 92–3
stretcher bond 262, 264
Strickland, Samuel 35
Stroud 335
stucco 225, 274–5
studs 105, 110–11, 122, 130, 164, 174
Sullivan, John 72
Summerville 273
summers 39, 135
supports 26, 104
Sutton 176, 180, 182–4, 186, 263, 308, 313, 340
Swedish log construction 14, 28, 51
Swiss influence 28, 29, 58, 199–200

Talbot, Col.: house 70
tapered: half-shoulder 94; mortise and tenon 239
taverns 40
Tecumseh 159, 161
tenons 10, 14, 27; mortised 131; recessed 176; tusk 10, 205, 207; *see also* mortise and tenon joints
tension, *see* stress
Terry, Parshall 115
thatched roofs 16, 225
Thessalon 216–17, 294, 334
Thomson, William 245
Thornbury 333
Thornhill 230
Thornton, Dr William 290
Thunder Bay 42, 72, 398
tie-beams 16, 95, 107, 135, 152, 154, 162, 166, 196
tie-logs 35, 52, 55
tie-rods, bridge 253

Timmins 193
tithe barns 154, 270
Todd, Isaac 12
Tollendale 326
tongue-and-groove boards 88, 125
tools 360–88; *see also* individual tools
Toronto: Bank of Upper Canada 51; Capt. Spark's cottage 58, 71; Carmichael house 123, 131–2; Castle Frank 27, 70; city hall 391; Dawes Road house 46, 48–9, 51, 52, 58–9, 60, 98; deadhouses 308; Drury house 279; Grange 51; Helliwell house 278–9; jail 72, 297, 337; Lambeth Palace 70; log houses 70; mill in Mississauga 175; Normal School 51; octagonal barn 217, 332; Parshall Terry house 115; polygonal buildings 319, 335, 339; Smith house 33; synagogue 335; Tecumseh Wigwam 71; *see also* Fisher house, York
Totten house, Paris 287
Tower Farm, Bewdley 306–7
tower framing, church 235, 237
Traill, Catharine Parr 35
trap doors 39, 417–18
treenails (trunnels) 59, 61, 65, 92, 375
Trenton 114, 356
Trois-Rivières 118, 226
trunnels, *see* treenails
trusses 92; barns 211; bridges 232, 251; and domestic construction 116; king-post 152; roof 152
tusk tenon 10, 205, 207

unburnt brick (mud) construction 274–82
Unionville 8, 350
United Empire Loyalists 6, 7, 34, 46, 159, 190, 360, 370–1

Vancouver 17, 20, 294; island 15, 17
Vaudreuil 224
vaults, *see* deadhouses
ventilation: in barns 205, 208; shafts 302

vergeboard 342
vertical: expansion 11; lath 303; log construction 26; posts 175; post-and-fill construction 193; timbering 26, 28
Virginia 27, 32, 33, 290, 371, 428
Vitruvius 26
Vivian mill, Oakland 231
voussoirs 213

Walker barn, Coldwater 201, 204, 213
Wallenstein 40
walls: ducts 121; French style 142; interiors 71, 182, 183; in log houses 47–9; mow 194; in octagonal house 299; in plank-on-plank construction 180; Quebec/Ontario compared 159; squared timber 71; stone 270
warping 11, 43–4, 104
Waterford 336
Waterloo County 29, 42, 107, 213, 217, 258, 270; *see also* West Montrose
Watford 334
weatherboarding 5, 174, 342
Webb, Joseph P. 117, 118
Weber, Abram 223
Weber, John C. 252
wedges 29, 30, 54, 56, 178, 205; wedge-shaped notching 51
Welcome 314–15, 340
Welland 262
West Montrose 230, 233, 251–2, 258, 272
western (or platform) framing 123

Whitby 213
Whitehorse 11, 34, 75
Williamstown 161
Willson, David 314, 407; study 407, 409–10
wind pressure, church framing 230
winding 104
windows 32, 37, 39, 44, 59–61, 89, 250, 390, 402; casement 55, 59, 61; double-hung 39, 59; in French construction 143; in jail 72; in log walls 47; masonry openings 93; in mud house 277; muntin bars 39, 402; quatrefoil 303; in restoration 390, 402; sash planes 378, 386
Windsor 8, 66, 109, 159, 164, 186
Winnipeg 19, 21
withes 44
Woodbridge 51, 61, 108, 110, 115, 128–30, 230
Woodchester, Bracebridge 299–302
'wooden' bricks and stones 354, 355, 358
Woodstock 333
woodworking tools 360–88

York (Toronto) 12, 13, 36, 40, 41, 68–9, 120, 371, 429
York County 213, 274–5
York Mills 8, 110, 279, 351
Yorkville 275
Yukon 34

This book

was designed by

ANTJE LINGNER

and was printed by

University of

Toronto

Press